D0933238

OPERATION
BARBAROSSA

OPERATION BARBAROSSA

HITLER'S INVASION OF RUSSIA 1941

DAVID M. GLANTZ

First published in 2001
Previously published under the title *Before Stalingrad* in 2003 by
Tempus Publishing
This new edition published in 2011

Reprinted 2012

The History Press
The Mill, Brimscombe Port
Stroud, Gloucestershire, GL5 2QG
www.thehistorypress.co.uk

British Library Cataloguing in Publication Data.
A catalogue record for this book is available from the British Library.

ISBN 978 0 7524 6070 3

Typesetting and origination by The History Press
Printed in Great Britain

CONTENTS

PREFACE

The sudden, deep and relentless advance of German forces during Operation Barbarossa has long fascinated military historians and general readers alike. Spearheaded by four powerful panzer groups and protected by an impenetrable curtain of effective air support, the seemingly invincible Wehrmacht advanced from the Soviet Union's western borders to the immediate outskirts of Leningrad, Moscow, and Rostov in the shockingly brief period of less than six months. Historians have described the German advance as a veritable juggernaut; a series of successive offensives culminating in November 1941 with the dramatic but ill-fated attempt to capture Moscow.

As described by Western military historians, the Barbarossa juggernaut began in June and July when the German Army smashed Soviet border defenses and advanced decisively and rapidly along the northwestern, western, and southwestern strategic axes. By early July German forces had shattered Soviet forward defenses, encircled the bulk of three Soviet armies (the 3rd, 4th, and 10th) west of Minsk, and thrust across the Western Dvina and Dnepr rivers, the Soviet's second strategic defense line. Once across the two key rivers, the panzer spearheads of German Army Groups North and Centre lunged deep into the Baltic region along the Leningrad axis and toward the key city of Smolensk on the Moscow axis. To the south, Army Group South drove inexorably eastward toward Kiev against heavier Soviet resistance, while German and Rumanian forces soon invaded Moldavia and threatened the Soviet Black Sea port of Odessa.

During Operation Barbarossa's second stage in late July and early August, German Army Group North raced through Latvia into Estonia and Soviet territory south of Leningrad, captured the cities of Riga and Pskov, and subsequently pushed northward toward Luga and Novgorod. Simultaneously, Army Group Centre began a month-long struggle for possession of the vital communication centre of Smolensk on the direct road to Moscow. In heavy fighting, the army group partially encircled three Soviet armies (the 16th, 19th, and 20th) in the Smolensk region proper and fended off increasingly strong and desperate Soviet counterattacks to relieve their forces beleaguered near the city. All the while, Army Group South drove eastward toward Kiev, destroyed two Soviet armies (the 6th and 12th) in the Uman' region southwest of Kiev, and blockaded Soviet forces in Odessa. This stage ended in late August, when Hitler decided to halt his direct thrusts on Leningrad and Moscow temporarily and, instead, attack and eliminate Soviet forces stubbornly defending Kiev and the central Ukraine.

In Operation Barbarossa's third stage, from late August through September, Army Groups Centre and South jointly struck Soviet forces defending in the Kiev region, while other Army Group South forces attacked eastward deeper into the Ukraine. Within a period of two weeks, German forces encircled four of the Soviet Southwestern Front's armies (the 5th, 21st, 26th and 37th) east and southeast of Kiev. The elimination of the Kiev bulge and its over 600,000 defenders paved the way for the Germans' final triumphant drive on Moscow.

The German High Command commenced Operation Typhoon – its final assault on Moscow – in early October. While Army Groups North and South continued their advance on Leningrad in the north and toward Khar'kov and across the

Dnepr into the Donbas in the south with reduced forces, the reinforced Army Group Centre mounted a concerted offensive to capture Moscow. Attacking across a broad front from north of Smolensk to south of Briansk, three German panzer groups tore gaping holes through Soviet defenses and quickly encircled five Soviet armies (the 16th 19th, 20th, 24th and 32nd) around Viaz'ma and three Soviet armies (the 50th, 3rd and 13th) north and south of Briansk. Having destroyed the bulk of the Soviet Western, Reserve and Briansk Fronts, by the end of October German forces had captured Rzhev, Kalinin, Viaz'ma, Briansk, Orel, Kaluga and Volokolamsk, Mozhaisk, and Maloiaroslavets on the distant approaches to Moscow. Further south, General Heinz Guderian's Second Panzer Army drove eastward through Orel toward Tula, the key to Moscow's southern defenses. All the while, an increasingly frantic *Stavka* threw hastily formed reserves into battle to protect its threatened capital.

After a brief respite prompted by November rains and mud, Operation Typhoon culminated in mid-November when the German High Command attempted to envelop Soviet forces defending Moscow with dramatic armoured thrusts from the north and south. However, in early December 1941, the cumulative effects of time and fate combined to deny the German Army a triumphant end to its six months of near constant victories. Weakened by months of heavy combat in a theatre of war they never really understood, the vaunted Wehrmacht and Luftwaffe finally succumbed to the multiple foes of harsh weather, alien terrain and a fiercely resistant enemy. Amassing its reserve armies, in early December the *Stavka* halted the German drive within sight of the Moscow Kremlin's spires and unleashed a counteroffensive of its own that inflicted unprecedented defeat on Hitler's Wehrmacht.

Western historians have described Operation Barbarossa in panorama, focusing primarily on the notable and the dramatic while ignoring the seemingly mundane incidents that formed the backdrop and context for the more famous and infamous actions.

Although they have argued among themselves over the motives, sequencing, timing and objectives associated with each stage of the operation, they have, nevertheless, tended to emphasize the offensive's apparently seamless and inexorable nature. This is quite natural, since they lacked Soviet sources. Precious few of these historians have been able to discern Soviet military intent or the full scale of Soviet actions during this period. Lacking Soviet sources and perspectives, these historians have agonized over the paradox that the Wehrmacht's string of brilliant offensive successes ended in abject defeat in December 1941.

Today, over fifty years after the war's end, newly available Soviet sources together with more detailed analysis of existing German sources permit us to address and answer many of these and other questions that have frustrated historians for more than half a century.

David M. Glantz
Carlisle, Pennsylvania
January 2001

PLANS AND OPPOSING FORCES

Plan 'Barbarossa'

In the year of our Lord 1189, Frederick I Barbarossa (Red Beard), Emperor of Germany and self-styled Holy Roman Emperor, took up the cross and led the Third Crusade against Saladin's Muslim armies that had just captured Jerusalem. Led by ironclad knights, the armies of Frederick's First Reich swept eastward through Hungary, the Balkans and Asia Minor, intent on liberating Christianity's holy places from infidel control. Over 700 years later, Adolf Hitler, Führer of his self-styled German Third Reich, embarked on a fresh crusade, this time against the Soviet Union, the heartland of hated Bolshevism. Inspired by historical precedent, he named his crusade Operation Barbarossa. In place of Frederick's ironclad knights, Hitler spearheaded his crusade with masses of menacing panzers conducting what the world already termed Blitzkrieg ('lightning war').

When Hitler began planning Operation Barbarossa in the summer of 1940, Germany had been at war for almost a full year. As had been the case throughout the late 1930s, Hitler's diplomatic and military audacity had exploited his foes' weaknesses and timidity, producing victories that belied the real strength of the Wehrmacht (Armed Forces) and Luftwaffe (Air Force). Before the

Second World War began on 1 September 1939, Hitler's fledgling armies had reoccupied the Rhineland (1936), annexed Austria (1938), dismembered Czechoslovakia (1938) and annexed Memel' (1939), all bloodlessly and with tacit Western approval. Once the war began, Hitler's armies conquered Poland (September 1939), seized Denmark and Norway (April 1940) and vanquished the West's finest armies to occupy the Netherlands, Belgium and France (May-June 1940), driving the British Army from the continent at Dunkirk in utter defeat. Protected by its formidable moat, the English Channel, and its vaunted High Fleet, Britain survived Hitler's vicious and sustained air attacks during the ensuing Battle of Britain, but only barely.

It was indeed ironic, yet entirely characteristic of Hitler, that military failure in the Battle of Britain would inspire him to embark on his crusade against Soviet Bolshevism. Even though defeat in the skies during the Battle of Britain frustrated his plans to invade the British Isles in Operation Sea Lion, Hitler reverted to his characteristic audacity. Inspired by his army's unprecedented string of military successes, he set out to achieve the ambitious goal he had articulated years before in his personal testament *Mein Kampf*, the acquisition of 'living space' (*lebensraum*) to which he believed the German people were historically and racially entitled. Conquest of the Soviet Union would yield that essential living space and, at the same time, would rid the world of the scourge of Bolshevism.

Militarily, however, the ground invasion and conquest of the Soviet Union was a formidable task. The German Wehrmacht had achieved its previous military victories in Western Europe, a theatre of operations that was well developed and distinctly limited in terms of size. It had done so by employing minimal forces against poorly prepared armies that were utterly unsuited to counter or endure Blitzkrieg and whose parent nations often lacked the will to fight and prevail. The conquest of the Soviet Union was an entirely different matter. Plan Barbarossa required the Wehrmacht to vanquish the largest military force in the world and ultimately advance to a depth of 1,750 kilometres (1,050 miles)★ along a front of over 1,800 kilometres (1,080 miles) in an underdeveloped theatre of military operations whose size approximated all of Western Europe. Hitler and his military planners assumed that Blitzkrieg would produce a quick victory and planned accordingly.

To achieve this victory, the Germans planned to annihilate the bulk of the Soviet Union's peacetime Red Army before it could mobilize its reserves, by conducting a series of dramatic encirclements near the Soviet Union's new western frontier. Although German military planners began contingency planning for an invasion of the Soviet Union in the summer of 1940, Hitler did not issue his Directive 21 for *Fall* ['case' or 'operation'] *Barbarossa* until 18 December (see Appendix I). When he finally did so his clear intention was to destroy the Red Army rather than achieve any specific terrain or political objective:

> The mass of the [Red] army stationed in Western Russia is to be destroyed in bold operations involving deep penetrations by armoured spearheads, and the withdrawal of elements capable of combat into the extensive Russian land spaces is to be prevented. By means of rapid pursuit a line is then to be reached from beyond which the Russian air force will no longer be capable of attacking the German home territories.[1]

Two weeks before, in one of many planning conferences for Barbarossa, Hitler had noted that, in comparison with the goal of destroying the Soviet armed forces, 'Moscow [is] of no great importance.'[2] Both he and his military advisers were confident that, if his forces did destroy the Red Army, Stalin's communist regime in Russia would collapse, replicating the chaos of 1918. This assumption, however, woefully underestimated the Soviet dictator's control over the population and the Red Army's capacity

---

★ In converting from kilometres to miles the ratio has been rounded off to 1km = 0.6 miles. The exact ratio is 1km = 0.62137 miles.

for mobilizing strategic reserves to replace those forces the Germans destroyed in its initial vital encirclements. Only later in 1941, after the Red Army and Soviet government displayed resilience in the face of unmitigated catastrophes, did the Germans began believing that the capture of Moscow was the key to early victory.

To destroy the Red Army, Hitler massed 151 German divisions (including 19 panzer and 15 motorized infantry divisions) in the east, equipped with an estimated 3,350 tanks, 7,200 artillery pieces and 2,770 aircraft.[3] The Finns supported Barbarossa with 14 divisions and the Rumanians contributed 4 divisions and 6 brigades to the effort, backed up by another 9 divisions and 2 brigades.[4] The German Army High Command [Oberkommando des Heeres – OKH] controlled all Axis forces in the Eastern Theatre. The OKH, in turn, subdivided these forces into an Army of Norway operating in the far north and Army Groups North, Centre, and South, with four panzer groups deployed from the Baltic Sea southward to the Black Sea. A German air fleet supported each of these four commands. Plan Barbarossa tasked Field Marshal Fedor von Bock's Army Group Centre, which included two of the four panzer groups (the Second and Third), with conducting the main offensive thrust. Advancing precipitously along the flanks of the Belostok salient, Bock's two panzer groups were to link up at Minsk to create the campaign's first major encirclement. Thus, the mass of German offensive power was located north of the Pripiat' Marshes, the almost-impassible ground that effectively divided the theatre into northern and southern regions.

German military planners sought to exploit Russia's lack of decent roads and railroads laterally across the front and into the depths to prevent the mass of Soviet troops from regrouping from one sector to another or withdrawing eastward before they were surrounded. However, German intelligence overestimated the degree of Red Army forward concentration and was totally unaware of the groups of reserve armies that the Soviets were already deploying east of the Dnepr river. Once the border battles had ended, Plan Barbarossa required the three German army groups to advance along diverging axes, Army Group North towards Leningrad, Army Group Centre toward Moscow and Army Group South toward Kiev. Thus, from its inception, Plan Barbarossa anticipated dangerously dissipating the Wehrmacht's military strength in an attempt to seize all of Hitler's objectives simultaneously.

Soviet War Planning: The Answering Strike

Ironically, the Ribbentrop-Molotov Non-Aggression Pact, which Stalin and Hitler negotiated in August 1939, actually contributed to the catastrophic defeat the Red Army suffered during the initial stages of Operation Barbarossa. By signing the infamous agreement, Stalin hoped to forestall possible German aggression against the Soviet Union and, while doing so, create a buffer zone by seizing eastern Poland and the Baltic States. However, the Soviets' subsequent occupation of eastern Poland in September 1939 and the Baltic States a year later brought the Soviet Union into direct contact with Germany and forced the Red Army General Staff to alter its war plans fundamentally. Beginning in July 1940, the Red Army General Staff developed new war plans identifying Germany as the most dangerous threat and the region north of the Pripiat' River as the most likely German attack axis.[5] Stalin, however, disagreed with these assumptions and in October 1940 insisted his General Staff prepare a new plan based on the assumption that, if it attacked, Germany would likely strike south of the Pripiat' River into the economically vital region of the Ukraine.[6] With minor modifications, this plan became the basis for Mobilization Plan (MP) 41 and associated Red Army operational war plans.

Ordered by Stalin and prepared in early 1941 by G.K. Zhukov, the new Chief of the General Staff, State Defense Plan 1941 (DP 41) reflected the assumption 'that the Red Army would begin military operations in response to an aggressive attack.'[7] Therefore, while defensive in a strategic sense, the plan and the military thought that it echoed was inherently offensive in nature. DP 41 and its associated mobilization plan required the Red Army to deploy 237 of its 303 divisions in the Baltic Special, Western Special and Kiev Special Military Districts and the 9th Separate Army, which, when war began, would form the Northwestern, Western, Southwestern and, ultimately, Southern Fronts.[8] As a whole, Red Army forces in the western Soviet Union were to deploy in two strategic echelons. The first was to consist of 186 divisions assigned to four operating *fronts*, and the second was to include 51 divisions organized into five armies under High Command (*Stavka*) control. In turn, the four operating *fronts* were to deploy their forces in three successive belts, or operational echelons, arrayed along and behind the new frontier. The first operational echelon formed a light covering force along the border, and the second and third echelons, each of roughly equal size, were to add depth to the defense and conduct counterattacks and counterstrokes.

Mobilization difficulties in early 1941, however, precluded full implementation of DP 41. Consequently, on 22 June 1941 the first strategic echelon's three operational belts consisted of 57, 52 and 62 divisions, respectively, along with most of the Red Army's 20 mechanized corps deployed in European Russia.[9] The five armies deployed in the second strategic echelon under *Stavka* control, which ultimately consisted of 57 divisions assembling along the Dnepr and Dvina rivers, was virtually invisible to German intelligence. Its mission was to orchestrate a counteroffensive in conjunction with the counterattacks conducted by the forward *fronts*. However, by 22 June 1941 neither the forward military districts nor the five reserve armies had completed deploying in accordance with the official mobilization and deployment plans.[10] As in so many other respects, the German attack on 22 June caught the Soviets in transition. Worse still, Soviet war planners had fundamentally misjudged the situation, not only by concentrating their forces so far forward, but also by expecting the main enemy thrust to occur south of the Pripiat' Marshes. Thus the Red Army was off-balance and concentrated in the southwest when the main German mechanized force advanced further north.[11]

The German Army and Luftwaffe

Even though the German Army seemed at the height of its power in June 1941 by virtue of its stunning victories in 1939 and 1940, it was by no means invincible. The German officer corps had traditionally prided itself on its doctrine, a unity of training and thought that allowed junior officers to exercise initiative because they understood their commander's intentions and knew how their peers in adjacent units would react to the same situation. Although disagreements about the correct employment of armour had disrupted doctrinal unity in the mid-1930s, subsequent victories vindicated the minority of younger German theorists' faith in mechanized warfare. The Wehrmacht's panzer forces clearly demonstrated that massed mobile offensive power could penetrate enemy defenses in narrow front sectors, exploit to the rear, disrupt enemy logistics and command and control, and encircle large enemy forces. While follow-on infantry then destroyed the encircled forces, the panzers could continue to exploit success deep into the enemy rear area.

In practice, however, earlier campaigns also demonstrated that the enemy could often escape from these encirclements if the infantry failed to advance quickly enough to seal the encirclement. This occurred because Germany never had enough motor vehicles to equip more than a small portion of its infantry troops. The vast majority of the German Army throughout the Second World War consisted of foot-mobile infantry and horse-drawn artillery and supplies, sometimes forcing the mechanized and motorized spearheads to pause while their supporting units caught up by forced marches.

Since panzer forces were vital to the implementation of German offensive doctrine, Hitler created more of them prior to Barbarossa by reducing the number of tanks in existing and new panzer divisions. The 1941 panzer divisions consisted of two to three tank battalions each with an authorized strength of 150 to 202 tanks per division (in practice, an average of 125 operational tanks). In addition, the panzer division included five infantry battalions, four truck-mounted and one on motorcycles. Few of these motorized infantry units were equipped with armoured personnel carriers; hence the infantry suffered higher casualties. The panzer division, which also included armoured reconnaissance and engineer battalions, three artillery battalions equipped with guns towed behind trucks or tractors, and communications, antitank and anti-aircraft units, totalled roughly 17,000 men. The slightly smaller motorized infantry divisions consisted of one tank battalion, seven motorized infantry battalions and three or four artillery battalions.[12] The organization of the first four *Waffen* (combat) SS divisions was identical to that of regular army motorized infantry divisions, although they later evolved into lavishly equipped panzer divisions. The 1941 motorized (panzer) corps consisted of two panzer and one motorized infantry division, while two to four of these motorized corps formed a panzer group. During Barbarossa, several panzer groups, augmented by the addition of army (infantry) corps, were renamed panzer armies.

Since German operations in 1939 and 1940 were predominantly offensive, defensive doctrine was based largely on 1918 practices. Defending infantry relied on deep and elaborate prepared defenses, kept the bulk of forces in reserve and relied on elastic defense and rapid counterattacks to defeat the attacker. Defensive doctrine rested on three assumptions, all of which proved invalid in Russia. The assumptions were that sufficient infantry would exist to establish defenses in depth, that the enemy would make his main attack with dismounted infantry, and that German commanders would be allowed to chose where to defend and be permitted to defend flexibly as the situation required. The typical German infantry division consisted of three regiments each of three infantry battalions, plus four horse-drawn artillery regiments, with a strength of 15,000 men. Since the division's principal infantry antitank weapon, the 37mm antitank gun, had already proven inadequate against French and British heavy armour, infantry divisions had to employ their 100mm or 105mm medium artillery battalion and the famous 88mm anti-aircraft guns against enemy tanks.[13]

The German Luftwaffe (Air Force) shared in the German Army's lofty reputation. The 2,770 Luftwaffe aircraft deployed to support Barbarossa represented 65% of Germany's first-line strength.[14] Although the Messerschmitt Bf-109f fighter was a superb aircraft, other German models were rapidly approaching obsolescence. The famous Ju-87 *Stuka* dive-bomber could survive only when the enemy air force was helpless while the Dornier-17 and Ju-88, Germany's primary bombers, as well as the versatile Ju-52 transport, were inadequate both in range and load capacity. Since German industry had not made up for losses during the Battle of Britain, Germany actually had 200 fewer bombers in 1941 than it had possessed the previous spring.[15] Given these shortages and the requirement to operate from improvised forward airfields, it was exceedingly difficult for German pilots to provide effective air superiority or offensive air strikes over the vast expanse of European Russia. In short, the Luftwaffe was primarily a tactical air force, capable of supporting short-term ground offensive operations, but not a deep and effective air campaign.

Germany's greatest weaknesses lay in the logistical realm. Only 40,000 miles of hard-surfaced, all-weather roads and 51,000 miles of railroads spanned the vast Soviet Union, and the railroads were of a wider gauge than those found in Germany. Even though they frantically converted captured rail-lines to western gauge as they advanced, German logistical organs had to transfer most of their supplies forward employing whatever Soviet-gauge rolling stock they could capture. Nor did the panzer and motorized divisions possess adequate maintenance capacity for a long campaign. The mechanical complexity of the tanks and armoured personnel carriers coupled with numerous models with mutually incompatible parts confounded the German supply and maintenance system. Worse still, earlier campaigns had depleted stocks of repair parts, and trained maintenance personnel were also in short supply. Therefore, it was no wonder that the German Blitzkrieg had lost much of its sharp armoured tip by late 1941.

Perhaps Germany's most fundamental logistical vulnerability was the fact that it had not mobilized its economy for war. Severe shortages of petroleum and other raw materials limited German production and transportation throughout the war. The German industrial economy was already dependent on three million foreign workers by June 1941, and the labor shortage became more acute with each new draft of conscripts for the army. As in the previous campaigns, Hitler was banking on a quick victory rather than preparing for a prolonged struggle. In fact, he was already looking beyond the 1941 campaign, planning to create new mechanized and air formations for follow-on operations in North Africa and Asia Minor. Hitler dedicated virtually all new weapons production to such future plans, leaving the forces in the east chronically short of materiel. The Wehrmacht had to win a quick victory or none at all.[16]

The Red Army

Despite its imposing size, the Red Army was in serious disarray in June 1941. It was attempting to implement a defensive strategy with operational concepts based on the offensive deep battles [glubokii boi] and deep operations [glubokaia operatsiia] theory developed in the 1930s, to the detriment of effective defense at the operational level. In addition, it was attempting to expand, reorganize, and re-equip its forces, simultaneously, in the wake of the Red Army's abysmally poor performance in Poland (1939) and the 1939-1940 Finnish War. Worse still, the military purges, which began in 1937 and were continuing, produced a severe shortage of trained and experienced commanders and staff officers capable of implementing any concepts, offensive or defensive. In contrast to the German belief in subordinate initiative, the purges and other ideological and systemic constraints convinced Red Army officers that any show of independent judgement was hazardous to their personal health.[17]

Red Army troops also suffered from the political requirement to defend every inch of the existing frontier while avoiding any provocation of the Germans. The Red Army had already largely abandoned and cannibalized their pre-1939 defenses along the former Polish-Soviet frontier and were erecting new 'fortified regions' in the western portions of the so-called 'Special Military Districts.' Despite prodigious efforts, however, the new defenses were incomplete when the Germans attacked. The bulk of forward rifle forces were garrisoned as far as 80 kilometres (48 miles) east of the frontier, and NKVD border troops and scattered rifle elements manned frontier defenses.

While the Red Army's logistical system was in disarray, its soldiers were at least fighting on their own terrain. Even before the harsh Russian winter arrived, Red Army soldiers demonstrated their ability to fight and survive with far fewer supplies than a typical Western soldier required. As German forces lunged ever deeper into European Russia, Soviet supply lines shortened, while German forces struggled with ever-lengthening lines of communication and having to deal with millions of prisoners and captured civilians. At the same time, however, the rapid German advance overran many of the Red Army's logistical depots in the Western Soviet Union. In addition, since much of the Soviet Union's vital defense industry was located west of Moscow, Soviet authorities had to evacuate 1,500 factories eastward to the Urals before German forces arrived, often in near-combat conditions. Although the evacuation effort was ultimately judged successful, the Soviets abandoned vital mineral resources and suffered enormous disruption of their wartime production in the process.

Organizationally, the Red Army's structure reflected its doctrinal and leadership deficiencies. First, it lacked any equivalent to the panzer group or panzer army that were capable of conducting sustained deep operations into the enemy rear area. Its largest armoured formation was the mechanized corps, a rigid structure that contrasted unfavorably with the more flexible German motorized corps. Formed hastily in late 1940 and still forming when war began, each mechanized corps contained two tank divisions and one motorized division. Since the former, which had a strength of 10,940 men and 375 tanks, was tank-heavy and lacked sufficient support, the mechanized corps also included a motorized division and various support units. At least on paper, each of the unwieldy mechanized corps totalled 36,080 men and 1,031 tanks.[18] Worse still, most mechanized corps were badly deployed, occupying scattered garrisons with the corps' divisions often up to 100 kilometres (60 miles) apart. Some corps were subordinated to army headquarters with the mission of conducting local counterattacks in support of the army's rifle corps, while others were to conduct major counterstrokes under *front* control. This made it impossible for the corps to perform the decisive offensive operations required of them by the State Defense Plan.[19]

At least superficially, the Soviet rifle division, which had an authorized 14,483 men organized into three rifle regiments of three battalions each plus two artillery regiments, a light tank battalion and supporting services, was similar to the German infantry division.[20] On paper, a Soviet rifle corps contained two to three rifle divisions; a field army consisted of three rifle corps (with three divisions each), one mechanized corps, several artillery regiments and an antitank brigade. In practice, however, the Red Army was woefully under-strength, with most divisions numbering 8,000-10,000 men or less even before the German onslaught.[21] In late May 1941, the Soviet government attempted to remedy this problem by calling up 800,000 additional reservists and accelerating the graduation of various military schools. These additional personnel were just joining their units when the attack came. In practice, most field armies mustered only six to ten divisions organized in two rifle corps, with an incomplete mechanized corps and little maintenance support.

Thus, although Germany possessed clear qualitative and even quantitative advantages over the Soviet Union in a short struggle, if its first onslaught failed to knock out the Red Army, the Soviet Union was capable of overwhelming Germany in the long term. In the first place, but unrecognized by the over-confident Germans, the Soviets had sizeable forces available in the internal military districts and Far East and an immense mobilization potential. In addition, the Red Army was beginning to field a new generation of weaponry, including multiple rocket launchers (the famous 'katiushas') and new tanks (T-34 mediums and KV heavies) that were markedly superior to all current and projected German vehicles.[22]

The Red Air Force (*Voenno-vozdushnikh sil* – VVS) posed little immediate threat to the Luftwaffe even though its approximate 19,533 aircraft, 7,133 of which were stationed in the western military districts, made it the largest air force in the world. Its equipment, like that of the Red Army, was obsolescent and suffering from prolonged use. The Great Purge had struck aircraft manufacturers and designers as well as military commanders, ending the previous Soviet lead in aeronautics.[23] Newer types of aircraft, such as the swift MiG-3 fighter and the excellent Il-2 *Sturmovik* ground attack airplane, which were, in some ways, superior to their German counterparts, were just entering service in spring 1941, leaving the Air Force with a mixture of old and new equipment. Transition training to qualify pilots to fly these new aircraft lagged since Air Force commanders feared that any training accidents would lead to their arrest for 'sabotage.'[24] Thus when Barbarossa began, many Soviet fighter pilots in the forward area had as few as four hours' experience in their aircraft. The changeover to new equipment was so confused that numerous Soviet pilots had not become familiar with the appearance of new Soviet bombers and erroneously fired on their own aircraft on 22 June.

Doctrinal concepts for the employment of massed air power expressed by A.N. Lapchinsky, the 'Russian Douhet,' the occupation of eastern Poland in 1939 and Soviet successes in the air during combat against Japan and Finland in 1939 and 1940 generated a false sense of superiority among many senior aviation officers. In the event of war, they expected to launch a massive air offensive from the new territories. However, relatively few airfields in the forward area were operational, with many being torn up for expansion in the spring of 1941, and the few that existed lacked revetments and anti-aircraft defenses to protect the crowded parking aprons. The VVS was also plagued by disunity of command and severe command turbulence. Some air divisions supported specific ground armies or *fronts*, others were directly subordinate to the general staff, and still others were dedicated to the regional air defense of the homeland. In the context of the chaotic opening campaign, where tenuous communications and chains of command evaporated, such divisions made it difficult to bring coordinated air power to bear at key points. Nor did most Soviet aircraft have radios in 1941. Worse still, the purges liquidated three successive Air Force commanders and many other senior officers, and the rippling effect of promotions left inexperienced officers in command at all levels. Few of these officers were capable of correcting the VVS's overly rigid and essentially outdated tactics.[25]

Warning of War

The most vexing question associated with Operation Barbarossa is how the Wehrmacht was able to achieve such overwhelming political and military surprise. We now know that Stalin received ample warning of the impending attack from a wide variety of sources, including diplomatic, NKVD, intelligence and many other seemingly credible sources.[26] Nor did the Germans take any special precautions to conceal their massive force build-up in eastern Poland. In fact, German high-altitude reconnaissance aircraft flew over Soviet territory on more than 300 occasions, prompting repeated diplomatic protests but little defensive action, while German espionage agents and German-backed Ukrainian guerrillas infested the western Soviet Union in the spring of 1941. The German Embassy in Moscow evacuated all non-essential personnel as early as 16 June 1941, and by 21 June no German merchant ship remained in Soviet-controlled ports.

At first glance, therefore, it is easy to accept the standard interpretation that Joseph Stalin's obstinate blindness was responsible for the debacle. June 1941 is often cited as a classic example of a leader ignoring evidence of an opponent's *capability* to attack because he doubted the *intention* to attack. Undoubtedly, Stalin was guilty of wishful thinking, of hoping to delay war for at least another year in order to complete the reorganization of his armed forces. He worked at a fever pitch throughout the spring of 1941, trying desperately to improve the Soviet Union's defensive posture while seeking to delay the inevitable confrontation. In addition, however, there were numerous other reasons for Stalin's reluctance to believe in an immediate German offensive. First, the Soviets feared that Germany's other enemies, especially Great Britain and the Polish resistance, would provide misleading information in order to involve Moscow in the war. Similarly, the Soviet leaders were concerned that excessive troop concentrations or preparedness in the forward area might provoke Hitler, either by accident or as a pretext for some limited German action such as seizure of border lands and demands for more economic aid. Stalin was not, after all, the first European leader to misunderstand Hitler, to believe him to be 'too rational' to provoke a new conflict in the east before he had defeated Britain in the west. Certainly Hitler's own logic for the attack, that he had to knock the Soviet Union out of the war to eliminate Britain's last hope of assistance, was incredibly convoluted.

This Soviet fear of provoking, or being provoked by, a 'rational' German opponent goes far to explain the repeated orders forbidding Soviet troops to fire even at obvious border violators and reconnaissance aircraft. It also helps explain the scrupulous Soviet compliance with existing economic agreements with Germany.

Stalin apparently thought, or hoped, that by providing Hitler with the scarce materials so vital to the German economy, he would remove one incentive for immediate hostilities. Thus in the eighteen months prior to the German invasion, the Soviet Union shipped two million tons of petroleum products, 140,000 tons of manganese, 26,000 tons of chromium and a host of other supplies to Germany. The last freight trains rumbled across the border only hours before the German attack.[27]

In addition to this belief in a rational Hitler, there were institutional reasons for the Soviet intelligence failure of 1941. The purges had decimated Soviet intelligence operations as well as the military command structure. Only the military intelligence service, the Main Intelligence Directorate [*Glavnoe razvedyvatel'noe upravlenie* – GRU], remained essentially intact, and the GRU chief, Lieutenant General F.I. Golikov, had apparently succumbed to German deception efforts. Golikov duly reported indications of German preparations, but he labeled all such reports as doubtful, while emphasizing indications of continued German restraint. Other intelligence officials were so afraid of provoking Stalin or Hitler that their reports were slanted against war.

German deception operations also contributed to Soviet hesitation. First, the planned invasion of Britain, Operation Sea Lion, was continued as a cover story for Barbarossa. The German High Command (*Oberkommando der Wehrmacht* – OKW) confidentially informed their Soviet counterparts that the troop build-up in the east was actually a deception aimed at *British* intelligence, and that Germany needed to practice for Sea Lion in a region beyond the range of British bombers and reconnaissance aircraft.[28] Meanwhile, Hitler directed that the German troop concentration be portrayed as defensive precautions against a possible Soviet attack, again encouraging the Soviets to avoid any threatening troop movements. A host of other German deceptions suggested impending operations from Sweden to Gibraltar. Then, in May 1941, the German Foreign Ministry and OKW encouraged rumors that Berlin might demand changes in

Soviet policy or economic aid. This led many Soviet commanders to believe that a German ultimatum or some other diplomatic warning would precede any attack.

The German invasion of Yugoslavia and Greece during April–May 1941 also helped conceal Barbarossa. This invasion not only provided a plausible explanation for much of the German build-up in the East but also caused a series of delays in the attack on Russia itself. Thus, intelligence agents who correctly reported the original target date of 15 May 1941 were discredited when that day passed without incident. By late June, so many warnings had proved false that they no longer had a strong impact on Stalin and his advisors.

Viewed in this context, the Soviet strategic surprise is much more comprehensible. Among a myriad of conflicting signals, identifying an imminent threat was difficult at best. Late on the evening of 21 June, Stalin did approve a confused warning message to his commanders (see Appendix I). Unfortunately, the archaic communications system failed to notify many headquarters prior to the first German attacks. Only the naval bases and the Odessa Military District were sufficiently remote to react in time. Some commanders risked Stalin's displeasure by taking their own precautions, although such initiative was the exception rather than the rule.[29]

In retrospect, the most serious Soviet failure was neither strategic surprise nor tactical surprise, but *institutional* surprise. In June 1941 the Red Army and Air Force were in transition, changing their organization, leadership, equipment, training, troop dispositions, and defensive plans. Had Hitler attacked four years earlier or even one year later, the Soviet Armed Forces would have been more than a match for the Wehrmacht. Whether by coincidence or instinct, however, the German dictator invaded at a time when his own armed forces were still close to their peak while his arch-enemy was most vulnerable. It was this institutional surprise that was most responsible for the catastrophic Soviet defeats of 1941.

Reflections

For the Soviets, the 1930s was a decade of alternating hope and frustration. Faced with growing political and military threats from Germany in the west and Japan in the east and with equally disturbing western apathy in the face of these threats, the Soviet Union felt increasingly isolated on the international stage. Diplomatically, Moscow promoted global disarmament, while internally it reformed, modernized and expanded its military establishment. Soviet formulation of advanced strategic, operational and tactical war-fighting concepts in the early 1930s was accompanied, after 1935, by a steady expansion of its armed forces, an expansion that continued unabated until June 1941. This peacetime 'mobilization' made the Soviet armed forces the largest in the world.

Size, however, did not equate to capability. What the Soviets would call 'internal contradictions' negated the progress of Soviet arms and undermined the Soviet state's ability to counter external threats. Foremost among these contradictions was Stalin's paranoia, which impelled him to stifle original thought within the military institutions and inexorably bend the armed forces to his will. The bloodletting that ensued tore the brain from the Red Army, smashed its morale, stifled any spark of original thought and left a magnificent hollow military establishment, ripe for catastrophic defeat.

Less apparent was the political contradiction inherent in the nature of the Soviet state. Communist absolutism placed a premium on the role of force in international politics, and encouraged its military leaders to study war in scientific fashion to formulate advanced military concepts in service of the all-powerful state. Yet the abject obedience required of the officer corps to the Party, and hence to the state, conditioned passive acceptance by them of the bloodletting that ensued. Just as political leaders like Bukharin admitted to false crimes against the state for the 'greater good', so military leaders also served or perished at the whim of Stalin.

These contradictions undermined the Red Army's ability to serve the state effectively and condemned to failure any attempts to reform. In the end only unprecedented crisis and abject defeat in war would impel successful reform. It is to the credit of the emasculated officer corps that, when this defeat came, the surviving officers had a sufficient legacy from the enlightened days of the early 1930s to allow them to overcome institutional constraints and lead the Red Army to victory.

THE BORDER BATTLES
22 JUNE–9 JULY

The Initial Strikes

At precisely 0315 hours on the morning of 22 June 1941, as the last minutes of the shortest night of the year ticked away, a storm of shellfire from thousands of German artillery pieces shattered the calm along a 1,800-kilometre (1,080-mile) front. As the red blaze of explosives reinforced the feeble light of a new dawn, thirty Luftwaffe bombers manned by handpicked crews and flying in groups of threes delivered terror and destruction to Soviet airfields and cities. Minutes later, from Memel' on the Baltic Sea southward to the Prut River, the first wave of 3½ million German soldiers deployed along the border lunged forward, beginning the greatest military offensive the German Army had ever undertaken. Barbarossa had begun. Achieving total tactical surprise, the invaders utterly shattered Soviet border defenses within hours. Amid the chaos, thousands of stunned Red Army officers and soldiers muttered grimly, '*Eto nachalo*' (It has begun).[1]

As soon as the sun rose, the Luftwaffe followed up its initial attack with a force of 500 bombers, 270 dive-bombers and 480 fighters that struck sixty-six Soviet airfields in the forward areas. These strikes succeeded in destroying over 1,200 Red Army Air Force aircraft on the first day of the war, most of them before they could take off. Within only days, the Luftwaffe secured undisputed air supremacy over the battlefield and paralysed all Soviet troop and rail movements.[2]

In most regions the initial Wehrmacht ground advance encountered weak and patchy resistance. German assault troops overran many border posts before the NKVD border guards could assemble, although in some regions troops assigned to local fortified regions fought to the last man, delaying the Germans for a few hours while Red Army divisions struggled frantically to man their assigned forward defensive positions. Like a defiant shoal in a hostile sea, the citadel at Brest defiantly held out against the invading forces until 12 July.[3]

Understanding that effective organization and crisp command and control differentiate armies from mobs, the Germans did all in their power to disrupt both in the Red Army. Even before the initial air strikes, Brandenburger special operations troops in Red Army uniforms parachuted or infiltrated into the Soviet rear areas, cutting telephone lines, seizing key bridges and spreading alarm and confusion. Within only hours, these measures and the paralyzing effect of the German air and ground onslaught utterly destroyed the Red Army's organizational cohesion and command and control. Worse still, it was soon apparent that this destruction extended throug every level of Red Army command from infantry platoon to the High Command in Moscow.

Operations in Belorussia

Nowhere was this destruction more apparent and total than in the sector north of the Pripiat' Marshes, where the Wehrmacht was making its main attack with Field-Marshal Fedor von Bock's Army Group Centre.[4] The army group's initial mission was to penetrate Soviet defenses on both flanks of the Belostok salient, advance along the Minsk-Smolensk axis, and envelop, encircle and destroy Red Army forces west of the Dnepr river. Subsequently, it was to 'achieve the prerequisites for cooperating with Army Group North... with the objective of destroying enemy forces in the Baltic region and proceeding to Moscow.'[5] Bock's army group consisted of Colonel-General Adolf Strauss's Ninth and Field-Marshal Gunther von Kluge's Fourth Armies, and Colonel-General Herman Hoth's Third and Colonel-General Heinz Guderian's Second Panzer Groups.[6] The Third Panzer Group, consisting of General-of-Panzer-Troops Rudolf Schmidt's XXXIX and General-of-Panzer-Troops Adolf Kuntzen's LVII Motorized Corps, was to advance north of the Belostok salient through Vilnius to Minsk. The Second Panzer Group, with General-of-Panzer-Troops Heinrich-Gottfried von Vietinghoff's XXXXVI, General-of-Panzer-Troops Joachim Lemelsen's XXXXVII, and General Freiherr von Geyr's XXIV Motorized Corps, was to attack eastward across the Bug river from south of Brest to link up with Hoth's panzer group at Minsk. Field-Marshal Albert Kesselring's Second Air Fleet, with 1,500 aircraft (more than half of the total 2,770 planes committed to Barbarossa), provided Bock with air support.

Opposing Army Group Centre, Army-General D.G. Pavlov's Western Special Military District, which became the Western Front the moment war began, was deployed in single echelon with three armies forward and the field headquarters of Lieutenant-General P.M. Filatov's 13th Army far to the rear.[7] Lieutenant-General K.D. Golubev's 10th Army, supported by Major-Generals M.G. Khatskilevich's and P.N. Akhliustin's powerful 6th and the virtually tank-less 13th Mechanized Corps defended the apex of the Belostok salient. Lieutenant-General A.A. Korobkov's 4th Army with Major-General S.I. Oborin's 14th Mechanized Corps deployed on Golubev's left flank, and Lieutenant-General V.I. Kuznetsov's 3rd Army supported by Major-General D.K. Mostovenko's 11th Mechanized Corps was on Golubev's right. Pavlov's reserve consisted of Major-General M.P. Petrov's 17th Mechanized Corps located near Slonim and Major-General A.G. Nikitin's 20th Mechanized and Major-General A.S. Zhadov's 4th Airborne Corps stationed near Minsk.

Faced with Bock's onslaught, Pavlov's front suffered immediate paralysis of its command and control. The headquarters of Korobkov's 4th Army was never able to establish reliable communications with headquarters above and below it. Even though Kuznetsov's 3rd and Golubev's 10th Army were in tenuous radio communications with Pavlov's headquarters, they were hardly more functional as command elements. On the first day of the war, on Pavlov's order, his deputy Lieutenant-General I.V. Boldin flew through a swarm of hostile German aircraft to the 10th Army's headquarters outside Belostok to organize a counter-attack. Golubev's headquarters consisted of two tents in a small wood alongside an airstrip, where the Army commander attempted to counter the Germans despite shattered telephones, constant radio jamming, and total confusion. Golubev tried in vain to launch a counterstroke on 23 June with his few available forces in accordance with prewar plans, but within days the 10th Army ceased to exist except as fugitives seeking to break out of the German encirclements.[8]

Besides the sheer force and speed of the vastly superior German forces' advance, the greatest difficulty the Soviet defenders experienced was lack of virtually any information about the current situation at the front. The reality was far worse than anyone in Moscow believed, resulting in a series of impossible orders to counterattack with units that had ceased to exist. At 2115 hours on the evening of 22 June, Stalin and Timoshenko issued NKO Directive No. 3, which ordered a general counteroffensive against the Germans, and, during the next several days, they stubbornly insisted the forward *fronts* implement this directive (see Appendix I).[9] In many cases subordinate commanders passed on these orders even though they knew the real situation, simply because they feared retribution for refusing to obey. After several days the enormity of the initial defeat became obvious to all. Even then, however, the General Staff in Moscow was hard pressed to get accurate, timely reports from the front. Staff officers were sent out to patrol the forward area and report back each evening.

On numerous occasions the staff called Communist Party chiefs in various villages and collectives to determine the extent of the German advance.

On Army Group Centre's left flank, Hoth's Third Panzer Group struck eastward along the vulnerable boundary line between the Northwestern and Western Fronts, easily outflanking the latter's 3rd Army, and reached Vilnius by the evening of 23 June.[10] Although badly rattled, on 24 June Pavlov once again attempted to organize a counteroffensive under his deputy, Boldin. Assigning Boldin nominal control of the 6th and 11th Mechanized and 6th Cavalry Corps, he ordered the force to attack northward towards Grodno to prevent the exposed Soviet units around and north of Belostok from being encircled. Lacking effective communications, air cover, logistical support and sufficient modern tanks, Boldin's effort was doomed from the start.[11] The few tanks, cavalry and infantry that survived the gauntlet of intimidating air strikes arrived in the Grodno region long after Hoth's panzers had raced eastward toward Vilnius and fell victim to devastating infantry ambush and antitank fire. By the end of 25 June, the 6th Cavalry Corps had suffered over 50% casualties (mostly from air attack) and one tank division was out of ammunition. Another division could muster only three tanks, twelve armoured carriers and forty trucks.

Although Boldin's futile effort did permit many Red Army units to escape from the Belostok area eastward toward Minsk, the relief was only temporary. Hoth's panzer group raced past Vilnius toward Minsk on the Western Front's northern flank and, at the same time, Guderian's Second Panzer Group penetrated Soviet defenses south of Brest and advanced precipitously toward Minsk on Pavlov's southern flank.[12] Pavlov had no choice but to pull back, but was in no position to do so in orderly fashion. He attempted a general disengagement to new defenses behind the Shchara River at Slonim on the night of 25-26 June. However, the few units that actually received the orders to withdraw were not able to break contact. Having already lost much of their fuel, motor transport and air support, Pavlov's distraught forces withdrew eastward in disarray, on foot and under constant German air attack.[13] To the east, advancing German armoured spearheads ambushed the headquarters of Filatov's 13th Army, Pavlov's second-echelon force, which was in the process of deploying its scattered divisions forward, and captured classified reports describing Soviet defense plans.[14]

Since German aircraft had destroyed most of the bridges across the Shchara River, most of Golubev's 10th Army was not able to cross the river. In a virtual state of panic, on 26 June Pavlov reported to Moscow that 'up to 1,000 tanks [of the Third Panzer Group] are enveloping Minsk from the northwest; ...there is no way to oppose them.'[15] In desperation, he then ordered his reserve 20th Mechanized and 4th Airborne Corps to conduct a joint air-assault and ground operation to halt advancing German forces at Slutsk, but this effort too failed.[16] By 30 June, despite Pavlov's frenetic measures, Hoth's and Guderian's panzer groups had closed their pincers around a huge pocket west of Minsk containing much of Pavlov's totally disorganized 10th, 3rd, 4th, and 13th Armies. The Western Front virtually ceased to exist as an organized force. Within a month, Stalin tried and executed Pavlov, his chief of staff, Lieutenant-General V.E. Klimovskikh, and several others on charges of 'criminal behavior in the face of the enemy.'[17] Pavlov's immediate successor, Marshal-of-the-Soviet-Union S.K. Timoshenko, had no time to organize defenses along the Berezina River east of Minsk, and the German armoured juggernaut pushed rapidly forward across the Berezina River toward the Dnepr in early July.

In 18 days of combat, German Army Group Centre advanced 600km (360 miles), occupied all of Belorussia and inflicted 417,790 casualties on the Western Front, including 341,073 soldiers killed, captured or missing. In addition, the Western Front lost 4,799 tanks, 9,427 guns and mortars and 1,777 combat aircraft.[18] However, despite the dramatic German success in this first fantastic encirclement, there were flaws in the German victory.

Because the advancing Germans were not able to assemble the forces necessary to seal off the encircled Red Army forces hermetically, large numbers of Red Army soldiers escaped, leaving their heavy equipment behind. Afraid that his panzer groups would advance too far too fast, Hitler ordered them to pause while his infantry eliminated the encircled enemy. This hesitation, in turn, prompted the first of many debates that would ensue in German command channels regarding how the campaign should be conducted. Fearing that conservative hesitation would permit Red Army to regroup, Colonel-General Franz Halder, the OKH chief, hoped that Guderian would continue the advance with his Second Panzer Group on his own initiative! The prescient Halder also noted that many Red Army troops were fighting to the death, and that German intelligence was incorrectly identifying many large Red Army formations.[19] All of this boded ill for the future.

Operations in the Baltic Region

While Bock's army group was savaging Pavlov's Western Front, Field-Marshal Ritter von Leeb's Army Group North replicated Bock's feats on the approaches through the Soviet Union's Baltic republics. Leeb's mission was to advance along the Leningrad axis, destroy Soviet forces in the Baltic region, capture Lenin's namesake city and link up with Finnish forces near Lake Ladoga. His army group consisted of the Eighteenth and Sixteenth Armies and the Fourth Panzer Group with a total of six army and two motorized corps, backed up by three security divisions and an army corps in reserve.[20] Colonel-General Erich Hoepner's Fourth Panzer Group, consisting of Colonel-Generals Hans Reinhardt's and Erich von Manstein's XXXXI and LVI Motorized Corps, was to spearhead the army group's advance.[21] Colonel-Generals Georg von Kuechler's and Ernst Busch's Eighteenth and Sixteenth Armies, each with three army corps, were to advance on the flanks and in the wake of the advancing panzers.[22] Leeb retained the

XXIII Army Corps in army group reserve and could, if need be, call on the L Army Corps, deployed in his sector as Army High Command (OKH) reserve. This cast of players would initiate the Battle for Leningrad.

Leeb's strong and experienced force faced Colonel-General F.I. Kuznetsov's Baltic Special Military District, which became the Northwestern Front at the outbreak of war, with responsibility for defending the northwestern strategic axis and the approaches to Leningrad. Kuznetsov's *front*, the weakest of the three deployed along the western border, consisted of three armies and two mechanized corps. Lieutenant-Generals P.P. Sobennikov's 8th Army and V.I. Morozov's 11th Army, supported by Major-Generals A.V. Kurkin's and N.M. Shestopalov's 3rd and 12th Mechanized Corps, formed Kuznetsov's first echelon, and Major-General M.E. Berzarin's 27th Army was in the *front*'s second echelon.[23] Powerful on paper, Kuznetsov's forces suffered from the same debilitating deficiencies that plagued the entire Red Army on the eve of war and were only partially reorganized, trained and re-equipped. Since Stalin's orders prevented him from mobilizing and defending properly, within weeks Army Group North crushed his defenses and quickly turned the approaches to Leningrad into a war zone.

Leeb's forces advanced on 22 June, ripped apart partially-manned Soviet defenses and plunged deep into Soviet territory, pre-empting Soviet defense plans and generating chaos in the Red Army's ranks. Kuznetsov tried to implement his defense plan but, given the precipitous and violent German attack, did so in wooden and haphazard fashion. After counterattacking in vain with his 3rd and 12th Mechanized Corps, on 25 June his two shattered armies withdrew in disorder northward toward the Western Dvina river.[24] The newly formed Soviet *Stavka* [High Command] hastily tried to establish new defenses, ordering Kuznetsov to defend along the Western Dvina with his shattered 8th and 11th Armies and the fresh 27th and 22nd Armies and 21st Mechanized Corps.[25] However, when the 27th Army failed to occupy its defense in time, on 26 June Manstein's LVI Panzer Corps captured a bridgehead over the river. Deprived of his last defensive barrier along the northwestern axis, Kuznetsov withdrew his 8th Army northward toward Estonia and the 11th and 27th Armies eastward, leaving the approaches from Pskov and Ostrov to Leningrad unprotected.[26] Faced with the imminent loss of the Western Dvina river line, on 29 June the *Stavka* ordered Kuznetsov to defend along the former Stalin Line (from Pskov to Ostrov), but Kuznetsov failed to do so in time.[27] Reinhardt's XXXXI Panzer Corps seized crossings over the western Dvina from the 8th Army on 30 June, while von Manstein's LVI Panzer Corps expanded its bridgehead at Daugavpils.

Faced with looming disaster, on 30 June the *Stavka* shuffled the *front's* senior command cadre, replacing Kuznetsov with Lieutenant-General P.P. Sobennikov, the former 8th Army commander, and appointing Lieutenant-General F.S. Ivanov in Sobennikov's stead. At the same time, it sent Lieutenant-General N.F. Vatutin, the Deputy Chief of the General Staff, who had played a vital role in preparing pre-war Soviet defense plans, to serve as Sobennikov's chief of staff, effective 4 July. Vatutin's instructions were to restore order to the *front* at all costs and actively resist the German advance. Meanwhile, the OKH ordered Leeb to advance through Pskov to Leningrad and Lake Ladoga to invest Leningrad. Hoepner's Fourth Panzer Group was to advance northerly or northeastwardly from Pskov, while Kuechler's and Busch's infantry cleared Soviet forces from Estonia and the Baltic coast and protected his right flank against attack from Nevel'. Hours later, the OKH added the area between Velikie Luki and Lake Il'men' to Hoepner's objectives, but ordered him not to advance further without special authorization.

Hoepner's panzer group advanced from the Dvina river on 2 July. Reinhardt's XXXXI Panzer Corps captured Ostrov on 4 July and Pskov on 8 July, crushing Soviet defenses along the Stalin Line and entering Leningrad region (*oblast'*). To the south, Manstein's LVI Panzer Corps seized Rezekne on 3 July, but was then bogged down for days trying to traverse the nearby swamps, prompting Hoepner to transfer Manstein's 3rd Motorized Division to Reinhardt's corps. At the same time, Kuechler's Eighteenth Army spread into Latvia, pushing back Ivanov's severely weakened 8th Army, and supported Reinhardt's panzers to the south, while Busch's Sixteenth Army supported Manstein's armour and protected the army group's right flank. By 6 July the border battles were over. Leeb's army group and Hoepner's panzers had pre-empted *Stavka* mobilization and defense plans, utterly defeated Kuznetsov's Northwestern Front and advanced northeastward through the Stalin Line.

The first three weeks of dramatic combat along the north-western axis proved costly to Kuznetsov's *front*. Leeb's army group had advanced 450km (270 miles) and captured much of the Soviet Union's Baltic republics. During this period, Kuznetsov's *front* lost 90,000 soldiers, more than 1,000 tanks, 4,000 guns and mortars and over 1,000 combat aircraft. Worse still, his forces had not been able to establish credible defenses anywhere, and Leeb's forces now posed a deadly threat to Lieutenant-General M.M. Popov's Northern Front (the former Leningrad Military District), the bulk of whose forces were defending against a Finnish attack from the north. Popov and his military council were acutely aware of the new threat, so much so that on 25 June they decided to erect new defenses along the Luga River south of the city, but they could man the Luga defenses only with scratch forces transferred from other *fronts*.[28]

Operations in the Ukraine, 22 June-10 July

German Army Group South, commanded by Field-Marshal Gerd von Rundstedt, experienced less initial success south of the Pripiat' Marshes than its neighbors to the north. This was because the Western Bug river, which ran along much of the common border in this area, impeded the initial German assault and provided the NKVD and Red Army troops with precious minutes to react. More importantly, Colonel-General M.P. Kirponos, the Southwestern Front commander, had maintained closer contact with the border guards in the days prior to the invasion, moving his forces smoothly through the various stages of alert. Because of the pre-war Soviet belief that any German attack would focus on the Ukraine, Kirponos was blessed with a relative wealth of mechanized formations to counter First Panzer Group. Even though none of his mechanized corps were fully equipped or trained, they gave a much better account of themselves than their counterparts in the Western Front.[29]

Rundstedt's mission was to advance deep into the Ukraine from both southern Poland and Rumania, destroy Soviet forces in the western Ukraine and Galicia, capture Dnepr river bridgeheads at and south of Kiev and prepare for subsequent operations to the east (Rostov and Stalingrad) or northeast (Khar'kov and Voronezh). His army group consisted of two distinct groups separated by a 330km (198-mile) gap. The main group, attacking from southern Poland, included Field-Marshal Walter von Reichenau's Sixth and Lieutenant-General Karl Heinrich von Stuelpnagel's Seventeenth Armies, and Colonel-General Ewald von Kleist's First Panzer Group. Spearheaded by Kleist's armour, this group of seven army and three motorized corps was to attack due east, north and south of L'vov to seize Kiev. Rundstedt also hoped to encircle sizeable Soviet forces southwest of Kiev between Kleist's advancing armour and the Seventeenth Army's formations. Kleist's First Panzer Group, Rundstedt's vital armoured spearhead, consisted of Lieutenant-Generals von Manteuffel's III, von Wietersheim's XIV and Werner Kempf's XXXXVIII Motorized Corps, which fielded a total of five panzer and four motorized divisions.

Rundstedt's second shock group, designated to conduct a delayed supporting attack from Rumania, consisted of Colonel-General Franz Ritter von Schobert's Eleventh Army and the Rumanian Third and Fourth Armies, with a total of three German and five Rumanian army corps. This force was to attack from

Rumania to clear Soviet forces from southern Ukraine and the Black Sea coast and, if possible, encircle Red Army forces in the Kamenets-Podol'skii and Vinnitsa regions in cooperation with the Seventeenth and Sixth Armies. Initially, Rundstedt's force was backed up by a reserve of one infantry and three security divisions. Colonel-General Alexander Lohr's Fourth Air Fleet totalling 750 aircraft was to support Rundstedt's assault.[30]

Kirponos's *front*, the strongest on the western borders, consisted of four armies, eight mechanized and seven rifle corps and one airborne corps.[31] Lieutenant-Generals M.I. Potapov's 5th, N.I. Muzychenko's 6th, F.Ia. Kostenko's 26th and P.G. Ponedelin's 12th Armies were arrayed in a single echelon from along the Bug river in the north, southward to the Carpathian Mountains. Kirponos's mechanized contingent was the strongest in the west, permitting him to assign six mechanized corps to his four forward armies, two of which he allocated to each army defending along the projected German main axes north and south of L'vov. Major-Generals K.K. Rokossovsky's and S.I. Kondrusev's 9th and 22nd Mechanized Corps supported Potapov's 5th Army, while Major-Generals A.A. Vlasov's and I.I. Karpezo's 4th and 15th Mechanized Corps did the same for Muzychenko's 6th Army. In addition, *Komdiv* [Division-commander] A.D. Sokolov's 16th Mechanized Corps supported Kostenko's 26th Army and Lieutenant-General D.I. Riabyshev's 8th Mechanized Corps backed up Ponedelin's 12th Army. The General Staff assigned Kirponos's forward forces significant reserves, including Major-Generals N.V. Feklenko's and V.I. Chistiakov's 19th and 24th Mechanized Corps and Lieutenant-Generals M.F. Lukin's and I.S. Konev's 16th and 19th Armies. Lukin's and Konev's armies, however, were still deploying forward to the Dnepr river line on 22 June as part of the *Stavka* Reserve.

Early on 22 June, the leading divisions of Kleist's First Panzer Group lunged eastward across the Western Bug river into and through the forward positions of Potapov's 5th Army, followed closely by the infantry of Reichenau's Sixth Army. When General

Kirponos received Directive No. 3 on the night of 22-23 June, his units were still assembling from garrisons as much as 400km (240 miles) away and had to move forward under near-constant German air attacks. Nevertheless, on 22 June and for four days thereafter, Kirponos steadfastly resolved to implement the major counterstroke mandated by the directive. To strengthen his resolve, Stalin dispatched Zhukov to direct Kirponos's operations on the spot.[32] However, circumstances forced Kirponos to commit his forces piecemeal, often in hasty attacks from the march which struck the flanks of the German penetration in less than coordinated fashion.

Initially, Kirponos ordered his 22nd and 15th Mechanized Corps to strike the northern and southern flanks of the penetrating German force and restore the border defenses. However, by late on 23 June Karpezo, the 15th Mechanized Corps commander, was only able to commit a weak forward detachment from his 10th Tank Division into battle. The feeble response permitted the German 11th Panzer Division to reach Berestechko, 60km (24 miles) deep into the Soviet defenses. The following day, the 215th Motorized and 19th Tank Divisions of Kondrusev's 22nd Mechanized Corps finally struck the III Motorized Corps' 13th and 14th Panzer Divisions east of Vladimir-Volynskii. After heavy fighting, during which Soviet divisions suffered severe losses, including Kondrusev and every regimental commander in the 19th Tank Division, German forces reached the outskirts of Lutsk on the Styr' River. Nor did Karpezo's 15th Mechanized Corps achieve any success. His 10th and 37th Tank Divisions failed to halt the 11th Panzer Division, which advanced another 30km (18 miles), leaving the 297th Infantry Division to protect its flank and rear.[33] Despite the 22nd Mechanized Corps best efforts, the German 13th and 14th Panzer Divisions captured Lutsk late on 26 June. To the south, the 299th, 11th, and 75th Infantry Divisions raced forward to filled in the gap between the two panzer divisions and, ignoring the 15th Mechanized Corps' pesky but ineffective attacks, the 11th Panzer occupied Dubno.[34]

By late on 26 June, Kleist's panzer group was ideally positioned to conduct a pursuit through Rovno to Kiev, the industrial and political centre of the Ukraine. By this time, however, Kirponos had finally been able to assemble sufficient forces to conduct a concerted counterstroke, even though the three rifle corps slated to participate in the operation had not yet arrived. At Zhukov's direction, he ordered Rokossovsky's 9th and Feklenko's 19th Mechanized Corps, which were still deploying westward from Rovno without their motorized divisions, to attack forward German positions between Lutsk and Dubno. Potapov, the 5th Army commander, personally controlled the two corps. To the south, Kirponos ordered Major-General R.N. Morgunov, his chief of Armoured Forces, to coordinate the assault by Karpezo's 15th and Riabyshev's 8th Mechanized Corps toward Dubno on the German's right flank. Although Kirponos provided for adequate air support, Potapov's staff proved too inexperienced to coordinate the support effectively. Worse still, Zhukov's and Kirponos's confusing orders dispersed the divisions of Vlasov's powerful 4th Mechanized Corps, preventing them from supporting the 8th Mechanized Corps' assault.[35]

Despite all of the problems, the counterstroke north and south of Dubno began on 26 June, producing a tank battle of unprecedented proportions (over 2,000 tanks fought along a 70km (42-mile) front). Initially, the 8th and 15th Mechanized Corps struck the German 57th Infantry Division in the flank and forced it to withdraw 10km (6 miles). That night, however, Zhukov ordered Riabyshev's 8th Corps to press on to Dubno, directly into positions occupied by the 16th Panzer Division, which was following in the 11th Panzer's wake. A mobile group formed around Colonel I.V. Vasil'ev's 34th Tank Division attempted to do so on 27 June, but German air, artillery and armour surrounded and severely mauled the divided corps. Not until 1 July were the remnants of the 8th Mechanized Corps able to break out and escape eastward. Karpezo's 15th Mechanized Corps was again stymied by air attacks and swamps, and accomplished little.

To the north, the 40th and 43rd Tank Divisions of Feklenko's 19th Mechanized Corps also tried to advance on 26 June, but ran directly into the attacking 13th and 11th Panzer Divisions, which knocked them back to Rovno. Farther south, even though his view of the battlefield was limited, it was obvious to Rokossovsky, the 9th Mechanized Corps' commander, that the counteroffensive order was unrealistic.[36] Nonetheless, he dutifully complied with Zhukov's order and also attacked on 27 June, but lost contact with Feklenko's corps and suffered heavy losses among his obsolete light tanks. When ordered to renew the attack the next day, he chose instead to take up defensive positions and ambush the leading task force of 13th Panzer Division as it approached Rovno. For perhaps the first time in the war, German forces ran into massed Soviet artillery fire, and suffered severe losses. After two days of escalating German air and ground attacks, Rokossovsky received orders to fall back.

This fierce if costly and unsuccessful Soviet counteroffensive delayed Army Group South for at least a week, helping to create the situation that later tempted Hitler to redirect part of Army Group Centre away from Moscow in order to secure the Ukraine. The German victories at Brody and Dubno rendered untenable Kirponos's defenses south of L'vov. Thus, Muzychenko's 6th Army abandoned its defenses in the Rava-Russkaia region on 27 June and fell back to L'vov. Three days later, after Kleist's panzers had occupied Rovno and Ostrog, the 6th Army abandoned L'vov to avoid encirclement from the north. The same day, the *Stavka* ordered Kirponos to withdraw his forces by 9 July to new defenses anchored on the Korosten', Novgorod-Volynskii and Letichev Fortified Regions along the 1939 Soviet-Polish border. The order applied also to his 26th and 12th Armies to the south, which then began an arduous 200km (120-mile) withdrawal.[37]

During their withdrawal, the 6th, 26th, and 12th Armies were constantly threatened with envelopment by First Panzer Group's motorized corps and by the Seventeenth Army from the north and, later, the Eleventh Army from the south. In early July General

Mackensen's III Motorized Corps drove inexorably eastward from Rovno toward Novgorod-Volynskii and the Dnepr river beyond and, to the south, General Kempf's XXXXVIII Motorized Corps advanced toward Shepetovka. Both thrusts threatened to seize a portion of Kirponos's new fortified line and encircle his armies withdrawing in the south. Kirponos reacted by ordering Potapov's 5th Army to attack the German armoured spearhead from the north with the 27th Rifle and 22nd Mechanized Corps. Although the attack by the two already enfeebled corps failed, it did delay Mackensen's advance for two days, providing more time for Kirponos to withdraw his beleaguered forces to their new defenses.[38]

During this stage of the fighting, panic often gripped Soviet forces. To forestall this panic, Kirponos began forming 'blocking detachments,' with orders to shoot any soldier who withdrew from combat without proper orders.[39] As the withdrawal proceeded, between 6 and 9 July, Mackensen's and Kempf's armour captured Berdichev, Novgorod-Volynskii and Zhitomir, precipitating a new round of struggle as Kirponos tried to maintain the integrity of his defenses. The XXXXVIII Motorized Corps' occupation of Berdichev was most dangerous because it threatened to encircle the Southwestern Front's left wing. To forestall that eventuality, Kirponos ordered Muzychenko's 6th Army, reinforced with Sokolov's 16th Mechanized Corps and the remnants of Karpezo's 15th Mechanized Corps to hold firmly south of Berdichev. At the same time, Kirponos raised Peoples' Militia formations in Kiev and Khar'kov to man defenses in the Kiev Fortified Region.

On 2 July Kirponos's problems were compounded when Rundstedt's southern shock group struck Soviet defenses in Moldavia.[40] A week before, on 25 June, the *Stavka* had formed the Southern Front, commanded by Colonel-General I.V. Tiulenev. It ordered the new *front*, which consisted of Colonel-General Ia.T. Cherevichenko's 9th Army, already stationed in the Odessa Military District, and Lieutenant-General A.K. Smirnov's 18th Army, formed on the base of the Moscow Military District, to defend the border with Rumania. Rundstedt intended to use the German Eleventh Army to encircle Soviet forces in southern Ukraine in cooperation with the Seventeenth Army, while the Rumanian Third and Fourth Armies cleared the Black Sea coast and captured Odessa.

Schobert's Eleventh Army penetrated Soviet defenses, captured Iassy and reached the Prut River on the first day of action, while foiling counterattacks by Cherevichenko's 9th Army and Lieutenant-General Iu.V. Novosel'sky's 2nd Mechanized Corps. Overestimating the strength of the German attack, Tiulenev asked for and received *Stavka* permission to withdraw to new defenses along the Dnestr River. Days later, after learning of the real situation, the *Stavka* countermanded its decision, ordering Tiulenev to recapture the line of the Prut river. Despite the resulting confusion, the line stabilized temporarily between the Dnestr river and Prut and Smirnov's 18th Army dug in to defend the Mogilev-Podol'skii Fortified Region, protecting the Southwestern Front's left flank.[41]

The border battles in the Ukraine clearly demonstrated that German armour was not invincible and gave future commanders like Rokossovsky their first expensive but useful lessons in mechanized warfare. Despite its relative success, the Southwestern Front suffered mightily, losing (with the Southern Front's 18th Army) 241,594 soldiers including 172,323 killed, captured or missing, 4,381 tanks, 5,806 guns and mortars, and 1,218 combat aircraft.[42] Worse still, German Army Group South was now ideally positioned to strike southward from west of Kiev into the Southwestern and Southern Fronts' rear area.

The War Within the War

Hitler's faith in quick victory was based in part on his belief that large portions of the Soviet population would welcome liberation from Stalinism. Initially at least, this assumption seemed justified when many Latvians, Lithuanians, Ukrainians and other subject nationalities proved cooperative if not enthusiastic about the arrival of German forces.[43] A prudent Stalin, aware of this eventuality and recalling the resistance to his harsh inter-war collectivization program, ordered half a million ethnic Germans and other nationalities to be shipped east.

From the very start, however, German occupation policy belied Hitler's hopes by deliberately alienating local populations. Harsh OKW orders, based on the flimsy excuse that Moscow had not signed the Geneva and Hague accords on the law of war, set this new tone. The 'Commissar Order' declared that Soviet political officers were not prisoners of war and should be shot out of hand, and a second order specified that, in the event that a German soldier committed offenses against civilians or prisoners, disciplinary action was optional, at the discretion of the unit commander. Although some senior German commanders refused to publish these orders and protested them to their superiors, many others simply carried them out.[44] No doubt Nazi ideology, which was pervasive in the Wehrmacht, contributed to this attitude.[45]

Like soldiers in many armies, who feel it necessary to dehumanize or demonize their opponents in order to overcome the natural reluctance to kill, many Wehrmacht soldiers regarded the Soviet people as bumbling and potentially treacherous sub-humans. The horror of war on the Eastern Front reinforced these attitudes and, quite naturally, atrocities resulted. This unofficial German attitude produced widespread instances of brutality and murder against Soviet prisoners-of-war and civilians, which, in turn, served to alienate potential allies, generate widespread resistance and contribute to the rise of equally brutal partisan resistance.

While German genocidal policies towards the Jews, a Europe-wide phenomenon, exacerbated the horrors in the East, it tended to mask the incidence of related German brutality toward the non-Jewish, Slavic population, which Hitler also considered as *Untermenschen*. Although the sheer numbers of victims defy precise definition, almost three million Russians, Belorussians and Ukrainians suffered enslavement and, frequently, death or permanent injury in Germany. Another 3.3 million Soviet prisoners of war died of starvation, disease, and exposure in German prisoners-of-war camps, fully 58% of the total number of captured Red Army soldiers.[46]

The German official policies for systematically expropriating food and raw materials often condemned the inhabitants who remained in the occupied territories to slow death. Given these policies, even Soviet collaborators felt little loyalty to the occupiers. Therefore, while guerrilla resitance in 1941 was limited primarily to by-passed Red Army soldiers, as the war progressed the partisan threat rose to catastrophic proportions. In turn, the bitter partisan struggle increased the brutality on both sides. When asked to compare combat in the East with that elsewhere, a German panzer officer noted, 'War in Africa and the West was sport; in the East, it was not.'[47]

Reflections

Hitler's Barbarossa crusade began in spectacular fashion. Employing Blitzkrieg tactics, his panzers thrust up to 600km (360 miles) into the Soviet heartland in the first three weeks of war, gobbling up most of Belorussia and large segments of the Baltic region and the Ukraine. The Wehrmacht demolished the Red Army's first strategic echelon, encircled and swallowed up the bulk of the Western Front west of Minsk and reached the Dnepr river along the Moscow axis. In the process, it tore the heart out of the Red Army, inflicting at least 747,870 casualties, including 588,598 killed, wounded, or missing, roughly one sixth of the Red Army's June 1941 strength, and eliminating 10,180 Red Army tanks and 3,995 aircraft.[48] By any measure, this victory was indeed both unprecedented and astounding.

However, the successful beginning belied several unpleasant realities that would increasingly plague the German military leadership and, later, Hitler as well. Firstly, although perishing or surrendering in great numbers, Red Army soldiers were also fighting, often with a ferocity that astonished German soldiers. Secondly, after three weeks of fighting, the Wehrmacht was already behind its offensive timetable, particularly in the Ukraine. Nor had it bagged as large a percentage of the Red Army as anticipated in the border regions. The more perceptive German commanders also began noting the inability of German intelligence to accurately predict which large Soviet formation would next appear and when and where.

Thirdly, while German armoured spearheads were lodged deep into the Baltic region, Belorussia and Ukraine, the German advance was beginning to lose its symmetry. Specifically, the advance by Army Groups North and Centre was outstripping that of Army Group South. The problem of the Pripiat' Marshes was just beginning to raise its ugly head and, in light of Kirponos's stout resistance south of the Pripiat', it was already questionable whether or not German Army Groups Centre and South would emerge from the region marching abreast. If they failed to do so, Hitler's strategy of marching directly on Leningrad and Moscow would have to be revised.

Finally, German commanders were becoming aware that the 'Russian kilometre' meant far more than a kilometre in the West. The crude transportation network in the east coupled with the immense distances that had to be traversed challenged carefully articulated plans and made both combat advances and logistical support a nightmare. The Germans were slowly learning that fighting the Red Army also meant overcoming the impediments of its largely peasant rear.

While the enthusiasm and optimism engendered by the Wehrmacht's dramatic victories in late June and early July 1941 masked these unpleasant realities in mid-summer, the nagging question remained, 'For how long would they do so?'

THE SOVIET RESPONSE

Command and Control

The staggering defeats the Red Army suffered during the initial three weeks of war exacerbated the consternation that had seized Stalin and his satraps when Hitler began Operation Barbarossa. Even though the Soviet leadership reacted in wooden fashion, it did what was prudent and necessary under the circumstances. Mobilization continued at a frantic pace, Stalin organized central command and control organizations and organs and, in a steady stream of orders, Commissar of Defense Timoshenko and Chief of the General Staff Zhukov demanded Red Army forces implement the State Defense plan. Within only days of the German invasion, this command *troika* ordered the Red Army's forward *fronts*, already savaged by the brutally efficient German war machine, to strike back at their tormentors and drive them from Russian soil. To see to it that they carried out the orders, both Timoshenko and Zhukov personally visited the operating *fronts*.

Despite their bravado, however, these orders rang hollow, particularly to those who were responsible for carrying them out since it was clear that they were simply incapable of doing so. In vain, and at immense human and material cost, *front* after *front*, army after army, corps after corps of the Red Army's first strategic echelon attempted to do what the State Defense Plan required of them and quickly and dramatically perished. Nevertheless, in late June and early July, Stalin, Timoshenko and Zhukov hastily and stoically formed and deployed forward the first of many groups of *Stavka* reserve armies. In succession throughout July and August, these armies occupied row after row of reserve defensive positions stretching eastward from the Dnepr river to the approaches to Moscow proper.[1]

While the Soviet regime responded rationally to the German invasion, it soon recognized that the Wehrmacht and its Blitzkrieg tactics clearly outclassed the Red Army. In fact, the attacking German forces destroyed the Soviet command and control system, dismembered the cumbersome Red Army, disrupted Soviet mobilization and threatened to smash the Soviet Union's military–industrial base. Given the resulting devastation and havoc, the Soviet leadership realized that survival required doing far more than issuing strident attack orders and raising and fielding new armies. Therefore, Moscow began fundamentally altering its command and control system and procedures, its military force structure and organization and its military–industrial base, all during the first three weeks of the war. While doing so, the Red Army temporarily abandoned many of its prewar doctrinal concepts, making the first of many painful but effective adjustments to the reality of modern war.

The first order of business was to establish a wartime national command structure from the existing Peoples' Commissariat of Defense [*Narodnyi komissariat oborony* – NKO] and Red Army General Staff [*General'nyi shtab Krasnoi Armii* – GshKA], which could effectively control mobilization and direct the war effort.[2] Even though this structure's nomenclature and organization changed frequently during the first six weeks, the changes had little practical impact on the day-to-day conduct of the war. Stalin began the organization effort on 23 June, when he activated the *Stavka* [headquarters] of the Main Command [*Stavka Glavnogo Komandovaniia* – SGK], a war council that was the 'highest organ of strategic leadership of the Armed Forces of the USSR.' Chaired by Defense Commissar Timoshenko, the *Stavka* included a political component consisting of Stalin and V.K. Molotov and a military component made up of G.K. Zhukov, K.E. Voroshilov, S.M. Budenny, and N.G. Kuznetsov. After a bewildering series of changes in name and membership, the council ultimately emerged on 8 August as the *Stavka* of the Supreme High Command (*Stavka Verkhnogo Glavnokomandovaniia* – SVGK), with Stalin as titular Supreme High Commander.[3]

Stalin exercised his full wartime powers as chairman of the State Defense Committee [*Gosudarstvennyi Komitet Oborony* – GKO], a virtual war cabinet. Formed on 30 June 1941 by a joint order of the Presidium of the USSR's Supreme Soviet, the Communist Party Central Committee and the Council of People's Commissars (CNK), 'all power was concentrated' in this 'extraordinary highest state organ in the wartime Soviet Union.'[4] The committee's initial members were Stalin, V.M. Molotov (deputy chairman), K.E. Voroshilov, L.P. Beriia, and G.M. Malenkov.[5] The GKO directed the activities of all government departments and institutions as a whole, including the *Stavka* and the General Staff, and directed and supported all aspects of the war effort. In addition, each member specialized on matters within the sphere of his own competency.[6] GKO resolutions had the full strength of law in wartime, and all state, party, economic, all-union and military organs were responsible 'absolutely' for fulfilling its decisions and instructions.[7]

The *Stavka* worked under the specific direction of the Politburo of the Communist Party Central Committee and the GKO. Its responsibilities included evaluating political-military and strategic conditions, reaching strategic and operational-strategic decisions, creating force groupings and coordinating the operations of groups of *fronts*, *fronts*, field armies and partisan forces. The *Stavka* directed the formation and training of strategic reserves and material and technical support of the armed forces, and resolved all questions related to military operations.

Subordinate to the *Stavka* was the Red Army General Staff, which the *Stavka* relied upon to provide strategic direction for the war.[8] The *Stavka* reached all decisions regarding the preparation and conduct of military campaigns and strategic operations after thorough discussions of proposals made by the General Staff and appropriate *front* commanders. While doing so, it discussed the proposals with leading military, state and Communist Party leaders and with the heads of involved People's Commissariats. Throughout this process, the *Stavka* directly supervised *fronts*, fleets, and long-range aviation, assigned missions to them, approved operational plans and supported them with necessary forces and weaponry. It also directed the partisan movement through the Central Headquarters of the Partisan Movement. In practice, however, the term *Stavka* came to be used loosely to describe Stalin, the Supreme High Command, and the General Staff that served both. A separate Red Army Air Force Command (*Kommanduiushii VVS Krasnoi Armii*) was also established to sort out the wreckage of the Red Air Force.

Despite this frenetic establishment of command structure, neither Stalin nor his chief military advisers exercised strong centralized control during the first days of the war, primarily since the command communications system did not function. Stalin himself appeared to withdraw from public view and even from the day-to-day conduct of the war, perhaps in shock.[9] Late on 22 June, the day of invasion, Premier and Minister of Foreign Affairs Molotov made a halting, plaintive radio address, announcing the German attack but apparently still unwilling to believe that total war had begun. Not until 3 July did Stalin himself address the nation, when he delivered a strong radio address calling for guerrilla resistance and the destruction or evacuation of anything useful to the invader. Already in this speech, Stalin began to stress Russian nationalism instead of loyalty to the Soviet state, an emphasis that the regime continued throughout the war.

Meanwhile, Stalin dispatched his principal military advisors, including Timoshenko, Zhukov, Vasilevsky and Budenny, from the capital as soon as the war began in a desperate attempt to learn what was happening and restore some degree of control over the deteriorating situation. On 10 August Stalin restored some semblance of stability to command and control by appointing Shaposhnikov to replace Zhukov as Chief of the Red Army General Staff, while senior commanders who enjoyed Stalin's trust acted as theatre commanders or trouble-shooters, changing location frequently to provide government-level emphasis to crisis areas.[10]

The cornerstone of Stalin's new rationalized command and control system for the Red Army were three theatre-level, multi-*front* strategic commands termed High Commands of Directions [*Glavnye komandovaniia napravlenii*], which Stalin formed on 10 July.[11] These commands were designed to provide unity of control over all *fronts* and other forces operating along a single strategic axis. Originally, K.E. Voroshilov headed the Northwestern Direction, including the Northern and Northwestern Fronts and the Baltic and Northern Fleets, Timoshenko the Western Direction, including the Western Front, and Budenny the Southwestern Direction, including the Southwestern and Southern Fronts and Black Sea Fleet. When Timoshenko assumed direct control of the Western Front in late July, Lieutenant-General V.D. Sokolovsky nominally became head of the Western Direction. The commissars or 'Members of the Military Council' for the three direction commands were three future leaders of the Communist Party, A.A. Zhdanov, N.A. Bulganin and N.S. Khrushchev respectively. In practice, however, Stalin and the *Stavka* frequently bypassed the three Direction Commands by issuing orders directly to subordinate headquarters. This layer of command proved to be superfluous and ineffective and was eliminated during 1942.

In the best Stalinist tradition, the initial defeats brought renewed authority to the political commissars, who assumed co-equal status with force commanders and chiefs of staff. While many career soldiers were released from prison to help fight the invaders, others took their places in a general atmosphere of suspicion.[12] Pavlov was not the only commander to face summary execution. Many soldiers who escaped from German encirclements returned to Soviet lines only to find themselves disarmed, arrested and interrogated by NKVD 'rear security' units looking for cowardice and sabotage. In addition, 95,000 civilian members of the Communist Party and Communist Youth organization (KOMSOMOL) were mobilized at the end of June; some of these went into specially formed shock units, while others were expected to reinforce the dedication of the surviving Red Army units.

The renewed Communist Party influence and terror in the army was unnecessary, since virtually all soldiers were doing their utmost without such threats. The moving force behind this Party involvement was the sinister L.Z. Mekhlis, whom Stalin appointed as Chief of the Red Army's Main Political Directorate on 23 June 1941. In addition, Mekhlis served as a deputy People's Commissar of Defense, a position in which he continued his job as political watchdog over the Soviet officer's corps.[13] Voroshilov, Zhukov and most career military officers despised Mekhlis for his role in the Great Purges and resisted his efforts to meddle in the conduct of the war. Ultimately, Mekhlis himself fell victim to his own system.

The Great Purges, which were still continuing when war began, had a lasting impact on the Red Army's performance in the initial period of war, since many of the initial Soviet defeats resulted directly from the surviving Soviet officer corps' inexperience. Field commanders at every level occupied positions for which they were unqualified, lacked the practical experience and confidence necessary to adjust to changing tactical situations and tended to apply stereotypical solutions, distributing their subordinate units according to textbook diagrams without regard for the actual terrain. The results were predictable. Forces that operated without regard to such principles of war as unity of command and concentration and attacked and defended in stylized and predictable fashion quickly fell victim to the more experienced Germans.[14]

Headquarters at every level lacked trained staff officers necessary to coordinate maneuver, fire support and logistics. The border battles in the Ukraine were typical, with field army headquarters proving incapable of coordinating simultaneous attacks by more than one mechanized corps and unable to direct the few available aircraft to provide effective support to the ground units. There were exceptions, of course, but the overall performance of the Red Army hierarchy was so poor that it contributed to the confusion caused by the surprise attack. Small wonder that both German and Western military observers concluded that the Red Army was on the verge of final disintegration.

Soviet staffs also lacked effective communications to control their subordinates and report the situation to their superiors. Once German infiltrators and air strikes hamstrung the fixed telephone network, many headquarters were unable to communicate at all. Even the military district headquarters, which upon mobilization became *front* commands, were short of long-range radio equipment and skilled radio operators. Existing Soviet codes were so cumbersome that commanders often transmitted their messages 'in the clear,' providing ample tactical intelligence for the German radio intercept units.

In other words, the Red Army had too many headquarters for the available trained staff officers and communications. Moreover, the initial defeats caused the average strength of divisions, corps, and field armies to decline so precipitously that the remnants no longer justified the elaborate hierarchy of headquarters left in command. This, plus a general shortage of specialized weapons such as tanks and antitank weapons, suggested that the organizational structure of the Red Army required a drastic simplification.

Reorganization

The ensuing wholesale reorganization of the Red Army that took place through the summer of 1941 was nothing more than a series of stopgap measures forced on the *Stavka* by necessity: the unpleasant fact was that the Wehrmacht had either smashed or was in the process of smashing the Red Army's prewar structure, leaving the *Stavka* no choice but to reorganize the Red Army if it was to survive at all. Despite this sad reality, the fact that the *Stavka* was able to conceive of and execute so extensive a reorganization at a time when the German advance placed them in a state of perpetual crisis-management was a tribute to the wisdom of the senior Red Army leadership. As it surveyed the wreckage that was its army, the *Stavka* decided to replace the complex army structure with simpler and smaller organizations at every level of command: a force that its inexperienced officers could command and control, and a force that could survive. Hence, *Stavka* consciously formed obviously more fragile and, hence, more vulnerable forces, all for the sake of officer education. In short, the *Stavka* saved the Red Army by reorganizing it, all the while abandoning temporarily any hopes of implementing its sophisticated prewar operational and tactical concepts. At the same time, the *Stavka* also tacitly accepted the immense casualties their new 'light' army suffered in the ensuing year. The fact that the *Stavka* gradually rebuilt a 'heavier' Red Army in spring 1942 was indicative of the temporary nature of the 1941 reorganization.

Stavka Directive No. 01 (dated 15 July 1941) and associated instructions began the reorganization and truncation process.[15] The directive ordered Direction, *front* and army commanders to eliminate the rifle corps link from armies because they were 'too cumbersome, insufficiently mobile, awkward and unsuited for maneuver.'[16] It created new, smaller field armies which the few experienced army commanders and staffs could more effectively control. These consisted of five or six rifle divisions, two or three tank brigades, one or two light cavalry divisions and several attached *Stavka* reserve artillery regiments. The rifle divisions were also simplified, giving up many of the specialized antitank, anti-aircraft, armour and field artillery units included in peacetime division establishments. Such equipment was in desperately short supply, and the new system centralized all specialized assets so that the army commanders could allocate them to support the most threatened subordinate units. In the process, the authorized strength of a rifle division decreased from 14,500 to just under 11,000 men, and the number of artillery pieces and trucks decreased by 24% and 64% respectively.[17] The actual strength of most divisions was much lower and, as time passed, many of these weakened units were re-designated as separate rifle brigades. During the fall of 1941 and early 1942, the *Stavka* formed about 170 rifle brigades in lieu of new rifle divisions. These demi-divisions of 4,400 men each consisted of three rifle and various support battalions subordinate directly to brigade headquarters and were significantly easier for inexperienced Soviet commanders to control.

Directive No. 01 also abolished mechanized corps, which seemed particularly superfluous given the current shortage of skilled commanders and modern tanks. Most motorized rifle divisions in these corps were re-designated as the normal rifle divisions that they in fact were. The surviving tank divisions were retained on the books at a reduced authorization of 217 tanks each. Some of the original, higher-numbered reserve tank divisions that had not yet seen combat were split to produce more armoured units of this new pattern.[18] Virtually all such tank units were subordinated to rifle army commanders. In fact, tanks were so scarce in the summer and fall of 1941 that tank brigades were the largest new armoured organizations formed during this period. Some of these brigades had as few as 50 newly produced tanks, with minimal maintenance and other support.[19] For the moment, therefore, the Red Army had abandoned its previous concept of large mechanized units, placing all the surviving tanks in an infantry-support role.

Associated directives also mandated expansion of cavalry units, creating 30 new light cavalry divisions of 3,447 horsemen each.[20] Later in the year, this total rose to 82 such divisions but, because of high losses, by late December the divisions were integrated into the cavalry corps. Apparently Civil War-era commanders like Budenny were attempting to recover the mobility of that era without regard to the battlefield vulnerability of such horses. German accounts tended to ridicule such units as hopeless anachronisms. Still, given the shortage of transportation of all types, the Soviet commanders felt they had no choice. During the winter of 1941-42, when all mechanized units were immobilized by cold and snow, the horse cavalry divisions (and newly created ski battalions and brigades) proved effective in the long-range, guerrilla warfare role that Stalin and Budenny had envisaged.

At the same time as independent operations for mechanized forces were sacrificed, so the Red Air Force abolished its Strategic Long-range Aviation command temporarily. Tactical air units were reorganized into regiments of only 30, rather than 60, aircraft.

Organization was easier to change than tactical judgement, however. Soviet commanders from Stalin down displayed a strange mixture of astuteness and clumsiness well into 1942. Most of the great changes in Soviet operational and tactical concepts and practice did not occur until 1942-43, but, during the crisis of 1941, the *Stavka* began the first steps in this process. Many of the instructions issued at the time seem absurdly simple, underlining the inexperience of the commanders to whom they were addressed. For example, on 28 July 1941, the *Stavka* issued Directive No. 00549, entitled 'Concerning Measures to Regulate the Employment of Artillery in the Defense.'[21] The directive ordered commanders to form integrated antitank regions along the most likely avenues of German mechanized advance and forbade them from distributing their available artillery evenly across their defensive front. In August the *Stavka* formally criticized commanders who had established thinly spread defenses lacking depth or antitank defenses. While creating such depth was easier said than done when so many units were short of troops and guns, the basic emphasis on countering known German tactics was a sound approach.

Whether attacking or defending, many Soviet officers tended to maneuver their units like rigid blocks, making direct frontal assaults against the strongest German concentrations. This was poor tactics at any time, but it was especially foolhardy when the Red Army was so short-handed and under-equipped. The December 1941 Soviet counteroffensive at Moscow suffered from such frontal attacks, exasperating Zhukov. Thus, on 9 December he issued a directive that forbade frontal assaults and ordered commanders to seek open flanks in order to penetrate into the German rear areas.[22] Such tactics were entirely appropriate under the conditions of December but would not necessarily have worked against the Germans during their triumphant advance of June through October.

Force Generation

The abolition of mechanized corps retroactively corrected a glaring error in German intelligence estimates about the Red Army. Prior to the invasion, the Germans had a fairly accurate assessment of the total strength of the active Red Army, but they had almost no knowledge of the new mechanized corps and antitank brigades. German intelligence analysts apparently believed that the Red Army was still at the 1939 stage, when large mechanized units had been abandoned in favor of an infantry support role. Prior to 22 June, the Germans had identified only three of the sixteen mechanized corps in the forward military districts.[23] The massed appearance of these mechanized units in the field against First Panzer Group at the end of June was almost as great a surprise as the first encounters with KV-1 and T-34 tanks.

Yet the greatest German intelligence error lay in under-estimating the Soviet ability to reconstitute shattered units and form new forces from scratch. Given the German expectation of a swift victory, their neglect of this Soviet capability is perhaps understandable. In practice, however, the Red Army's ability to create new divisions as fast as the Germans smashed existing ones was a principal cause of the German failure in 1941.

For much of the 1920s and 1930s, the Red Army had emphasized the idea of cadre and mobilization forces, formations that had very few active duty soldiers in peacetime but would gain reservists and volunteers to become fully-fledged combat elements in wartime. As war approached in the late 1930s, the Red Army tended to neglect this concept, gradually mobilizing most of its existing units to full-time, active duty status. Still, prewar Soviet theory estimated that the army would have to be completely replaced every four to eight months during heavy combat. To satisfy this need, the 1938 Universal Military Service Law extended the reserve service obligation to age 50 and created a network of schools to train those reservists. By the time of the German invasion, the Soviet Union had a pool of 14 million men with at least basic military training. The existence of this pool of trained reservists gave the Red Army a depth and resiliency that was largely invisible to German and other observers.

From the moment the war began, the Peoples' Commissariat of Defense began a process that produced new groups or 'waves' of rifle armies over a period of several months.[24] At the outset of war, the General Staff's Organizational and Mobilization Directorate was responsible for mobilization and force generation. However, the wartime General Staff was too busy dealing with current operations to deal effectively with the matter. Therefore, on 29 July the *Stavka* removed the directorate from the General Staff and assigned it to the NKO, renaming it the Main Directorate for the Formation and Manning of the Red Army [*Glavnoe upravlenie formirovaniia i ukomplektovaniia Krasnoi Armii* – GUFUKA].[25] Under NKO supervision, the military districts outside the actual war zone then established a system for cloning existing active duty units to provide the cadres that were filled up with reservists. The NKO summoned 5,300,000 reservists to the colors by the end of June, with successive mobilizations later.[26] In addition to the 8 armies the NKO mobilized and deployed in late June, it raised 13 new field armies in July, 14 in August, 3 in September, 5 in October, 9 in November and 2 in December (see Table 1).[27]

This mobilization system, in conjunction with active duty units that moved from the eastern military districts to the west, retained enough strength to generate the armies that defended Moscow from October through early December 1941. The *Stavka* replicated its mobilization efforts the following year when it formed 10 additional reserve armies in the spring of 1942

The Soviet mobilization system generated a total of approximately 285 rifle divisions, 12 re-formed tank divisions, 88 cavalry divisions, 174 rifle brigades and 93 tank brigades by 31 December 1941. Despite heavy losses, these additions brought the Red Army's line strength to 401 division equivalents on 1 August, 450 division equivalents on 1 September and 592 division equivalents on 31 December. At the same time, the army's personnel strength rose from 5,373,000 on 22 June to 6,889,000 on 31 August and an estimated 8 million on 31 December. These totals included 97 divisions transferred from the east to the west and 25 'People's Militia' divisions raised in Moscow and Leningrad.[28] (The latter were made up primarily of militant urban workers who, in some cases, lacked the physical stamina and military training necessary to be effective soldiers.) Whereas prewar German estimates had postulated an enemy of approximately 300 divisions, by December the Soviets had fielded more than twice that number. This allowed the Red Army to lose more than 4 million soldiers and 200 divisions in battle by 31 December, roughly equivalent to its entire peacetime army, yet still survive to continue the struggle.[29]

Of course, the prewar and mobilization divisions were by no means equivalent. For all their shortcomings, the divisions lost in the first weeks of battle were far better trained and equipped than their successors. The newly mobilized divisions and brigades lacked almost everything except rifles and political officers. Perhaps more importantly, they had little time to train as units, to practice procedures so that soldiers and subordinate units knew their roles in combat. The continued poor performance of Soviet divisions in the fall and winter of 1941 must be viewed in light of the speed with which they were created and the total inexperience of their commanders and troops. This performance, however, contributed to the German impression of an inferior enemy who did not realize that he had already been defeated.

Saving Soviet Industry

The Red Army's equipment and ammunition shortages of 1941 were exacerbated by the massive redeployment of Soviet heavy industry to avoid capture. Prior to the German invasion, the vast majority of Soviet manufacturing capacity was located in the western portion of the country, particularly major industrial areas such as Leningrad and the eastern Ukraine. As early as 24 June, the GKO created a Council for Evacuation to relocate these plants eastward to the Urals and Siberia. The task of coordinating this massive undertaking fell to N.A. Voznesensky, head of the Soviet industrial planning agency GOSPLAN. Voznesensky was one of the few senior civilians who dared to speak bluntly to Stalin; on 4 July he won approval for the first war economic plan. The Council's deputy chairman, the future premier A.N. Kosygin, controlled the actual evacuation. Voznesensky and Kosygin had to do more than simply move factories and workers, however. In the centrally directed Soviet economy, nothing would happen without careful advance planning to ensure that these factories would mesh with existing plants and raw material supplies in the new locations. Workers had to be housed and fed in remote towns whose size tripled overnight. Electric plants had to keep operating until the last possible moment to facilitate dismantling in the old locations, then be moved and re-assembled at the new sites. All this had to be done at a point when the industrial sector was shifting gears to accommodate wartime demand and the periodic loss of skilled laborers to the Army.[30]

The most pressing problem was the evacuation of the factories, especially in the lower Dnepr river and Donbas regions of the Ukraine. Here the stubborn delaying tactics of the Southwestern

Front paid dividends, not only by diverting German troop strength away from Moscow but also by giving the Council for Evacuation precious time to disassemble machinery. The long lines of railroad cars massed in the region puzzled German reconnaissance aircraft. Eight thousand freight cars were used to move just one major metallurgy complex from Zaporozh'e in the Donbas to Magnitogorsk in the Urals. The movement had to be accomplished at great speed and despite periodic German air raids on the factories and rail lines. In the Leningrad area, the German advance was so rapid that only 92 plants were relocated before the city was surrounded. Plant relocations did not begin in this region until 5 October, but by the end of the year a former Leningrad tank factory was producing KV-1s at a new site in the Urals. More than 500 firms and 210,000 workers left the Moscow area in October and November alone.

All this machinery arrived in remote locations on a confused, staggered schedule with only a portion of the skilled workforce.[31] By the time the trains arrived, bitter winter weather and permafrost made it almost impossible to build foundations for any type of structure. Somehow the machinery was unloaded and reassembled inside hastily constructed, unheated wooden buildings. Work continued even in the sub-zero night, using electric lights strung in trees and supplemented by bonfires. In total, 1,523 factories including 1,360 related to armaments were transferred to the Volga, Siberia, and Central Asia between July and November 1941. Almost 1.5 million freight cars were involved.[32] Even allowing for the hyperbole so common to Soviet accounts, this massive relocation and reorganization of heavy industry was an incredible accomplishment of endurance and organization.

Because of the relocation, Soviet production took almost a year of war to reach its full potential. The desperate battles of 1941 had to be fought largely with existing stocks of weapons and ammunition, supplemented by new tanks and guns that often went into battle before they had even been painted.

Scorched Earth

Despite their best efforts, the Council for Evacuation was unable to relocate everything of value. In the case of the Donbas mines, where 60 per cent of the USSR's coal supplies were produced, evacuation was impossible. In such cases, the Soviet regime not only had to survive without facilities and resources, but it had to ensure that the invaders could not convert those facilities and resources to their own use. The painfully harvested fruits of Stalin's Five Year Plans had to be destroyed or disabled in place.

Much of the Soviet self-destruction focused on transportation and electrical power. Railroad locomotives and locomotive repair shops that could not be moved were frequently sabotaged, a fact which proved important in the winter weather, when German-build locomotives lacked sufficient insulation to maintain steam pressure. The Dnepr river hydroelectric dam was partially breached by Soviet troops as they withdrew, and workers removed or destroyed key components of hydro-turbines and steam generators throughout the region. In the countryside the extent of destruction of buildings and crops varied considerably from region to region. On the whole, Russia proper had more time to prepare for such destruction than did the western portions of Belorussia and the Ukraine.

Moscow's success in evacuating or destroying so much of its hard-won industrial development shocked German economic planners, who had counted on using Soviet resources to meet both Hitler's production goals and their own domestic consumer demands. Soviet raw materials such as chromium, nickel and petroleum were vital to continued German war production, and captured Soviet factories had promised an easy solution to overcrowding and labour shortages in Germany proper. Moreover, the successful evacuation of the Soviet railroads forced the Germans to commit 2,500 locomotives and 200,000 railcars to support the troops in the east. This, in turn, meant that the Germans had to convert large portions of the captured rail network to their own, narrower gauge, instead of using the existing, broader Russian gauge.[33] Thus, the Soviet evacuation effort not only preserved industrial potential for future campaigns but also posed a continuing and unexpected drain on the German economy.

Still, despite all efforts a considerable portion of the industrial plant and the harvest fell into German hands. Hitler increasingly defined his objectives for 1941 in terms of seizing additional economic resources, and the German advance sought to satisfy those objectives.

Reflections

The postwar Soviet leadership often boasted that, during the initial days of its Great Patriotic War, the Soviet Union and Red Army experienced the equivalent of a nuclear first strike, yet survived. While overstated a bit, this claim is not far from the truth. Hitler's naked aggression dismembered and destroyed a vast chunk of the peacetime Red Army and caught the Soviet defense establishment in the middle of already disruptive wholesale institutional reforms. In additional to the physical destruction it wrought on the Red Army and the political and economic infrastructure in the western Soviet Union, it thwarted orderly mobilization of military forces and the economy for war and produced chaos in force deployments.

To Hitler's surprise, however, once set in motion, despite the disruption, the mobilization proceeded apace, generating forces at a speed that first escaped and then staggered the Germans' imagination. Even though the mobilized armies, divisions and brigades were shadow and threadbare versions of what they were supposed to be, the mobilization process ultimately proved that, in many respects, quantity is an adequate substitute for quality. In addition, amid the chaos and destruction, the GKO, *Stavka* and General Staff were able to reorganize their forces so that they could continue the fight, survive, and even turn the tide of battle by early December.

However, all that Soviet command organs were able to accomplish in the military and economic realms in the summer of 1941 were temporary expedients designed only to prolong the fight and halt the German juggernaut somehow and somewhere. In early July it was by no means a certainty that the Red Army could do so.

THE BATTLE FOR SMOLENSK
10 JULY—10 SEPTEMBER

The Situation on 9 July

On 3 July Halder, the head of OKH, noted in his diary:

> The objective to shatter the bulk of the Russian Army this [western]
> side of the Dvina and Dnepr has been accomplished… east of [these
> rivers] we would encounter nothing more than partial forces… It is
> thus probably no overstatement to say that the Russian Campaign
> has been won in the space of two weeks.[1]

German forces had destroyed the Western Front's forward
elements and severely mauled those of the Southwestern and
Northwestern Fronts. They stood on the Dvina and Dnepr rivers,
ready to resume their exploitation once supplies, infantry support
and Hitler's nerve caught up with the victorious panzer groups.
Many German commanders must have felt, like Halder, that the
war was won, whereas in fact the struggle had only just begun.

The Red Army defended the approaches to the Dnepr river
and the river line itself with the remnants of the Western Front's
shattered 13th and 4th Armies, backed up by five armies from
Marshal-of-the-Soviet-Union S.M. Budenny's Group of Reserve
Armies.[2] Budenny's forces had begun moving into the region as

early as late May, but on 1 July were not yet fully assembled. Stalin had placed Timoshenko in command of the Western Front on 1 July, transferring four of Budenny's reserve armies, the 19th, 20th, 21st and 22nd, to his command. The fifth reserve army, Lieutenant-General M.F. Lukin's weak 16th, defended Smolensk, the next major city on the road from Minsk to Moscow. This desperate move sacrificed the original plan of using these armies as a strategic counteroffensive force. To restore the lost strategic depth, while other armies were mobilizing, two of the first wave of armies mobilized in wartime, the 24th and 28th, concentrated around Viaz'ma and Spas-Demensk east of Smolensk to protect the approaches to Moscow.[3]

All of these armies suffered severe shortages of tanks, communications, antitank weapons and anti-aircraft guns, and senior commanders were changed on almost a daily basis. These formations had received little opportunity to prepare for battle, resulting in an uneven performance. Still, the Germans had no knowledge of the existence of these forces until they bumped into them. The result was a series of poorly coordinated but intense struggles around Smolensk from early July through September 1941, struggles that stopped the German forces in their tracks for the first time in the war.

The Red Army's July Counteroffensive

In early July, while Army Group North's Fourth Panzer Group was crossing the Western Dvina river and advancing rapidly into Latvia and Army Group South's First Panzer Group was struggling to reach Kiev, Army Group Centre's Third and Second Panzer Groups approached the Dnepr river east of Minsk. Realizing that the German advance might split the entire Soviet strategic defense in the west asunder, the *Stavka* ordered its three forward *fronts* to strike back and halt or repel the advancing German juggernaut. Commencing one after another in early July, the *Stavka* ordered counterstroke after counterstroke, indicating its continuing faith in 'offensiveness' and the viability of its State Defense Plan. Soon, however, the *Stavka's* dreams evaporated, as its attempt to orchestrate a fully-fledged counteroffensive instead degenerated into a series of poorly coordinated and futile counterstrokes and counterattacks.

The first of the *Stavka's* counterstrokes began on 6 July, when Lieutenant-General P.A. Kurochkin's 20th Army, spearheaded by the newly arrived 5th and 7th Mechanized Corps, went into action against Hoth's Third Panzer Group, whose divisions were advancing on Polotsk, Vitebsk and Orsha. Days before, on 4 July, the *Stavka* had ordered Timoshenko's Western Front to

> organize a reliable defense along the Western Dvina and Dnepr river lines, and, after concentrating reserves arriving from the depths of the country, deliver a series of counterstrokes along the Lepel', Borisov and Bobruisk axes.'[4]

Timoshenko decided first to attack the flanks and rear of the advancing German forces from the Orsha and Polotsk regions with Major-General-of-Tank-Forces I.P. Alekseenko's and Major-General V.I. Vinogradov's full-strength 5th and 7th Mechanized Corps along with seven rifle divisions.[5]

Kurochkin's 6 July attack precipitated an intense engagement near Senno and Lepel' between the two mechanized corps and the lead elements of the XXXIX and XXXXVII Panzer Corps' 7th, 12th, 17th and 18th Panzer Divisions. In five days of confused fighting, the Germans defeated and decimated both Soviet mechanized corps and their supporting rifle forces and continued their rapid advance toward Polotsk, Vitebsk and Orsha.[6] Beset also by a host of command and control and logistical problems, the 5th and 7th Mechanized Corps lost 832 tanks (out of over 2,000 engaged) and many personnel in the struggle. Subsequently, on 11 July the two corps withdrew in disorder eastward across the Dnepr toward Smolensk.[7]

The battle for Smolensk proper began on 10 July, when Guderian's Second Panzer Group crossed the Dnepr, dismembered the 13th Army, whose remnants had just escaped from the Minsk pocket, and began penetrating eastward toward Smolensk. Fielding only four under-strength rifle divisions and no armour, and now under a new commander, Lieutenant-General F.N. Remezov, the 13th Army offered little resistance.[8] By 13 July Guderian's XXXXVI Panzer Corps had passed north of Mogilev and his XXIV Panzer Corps south of the city, encircling the 13th Army's 61st Rifle and 20th Mechanized Corps in Mogilev on the river's western bank.[9] Although the two beleaguered corps resisted fiercely for another two weeks (until 26 July), their efforts failed to halt Guderian's advance. Similarly, Lieutenant-General I.S. Konev's 19th Army literally counterattacked as it dismounted from railroad trains on 11-13 July, in a futile effort to recapture the Vitebsk region from Reinhardt's XXXIX Motorized Corps. By the evening of 13 July, Guderian's 29th Motorized Infantry Division was only 11 miles from Smolensk, and Konev's 19th Army had almost disintegrated.[10]

After the 20th Army's mechanized counterstroke failed, on 12 July the *Stavka* ordered the Western Front to launch counterstrokes all along its entire front in a desperate attempt to restore its positions along the Dnepr. It directed Timoshenko's Western Direction Command to:

Immediately organize a powerful and coordinated counterstroke by all available forces from the Smolensk, Rudnia, Orsha, Polotsk, and Nevel' regions to liquidate the enemy penetration at Vitebsk. Do not weaken the Orsha and Mogilev front....Support the counterstroke with all *front* air forces and the long-range bomber aviation corps....Conduct active operations along the Gomel' and Bobruisk axis to exert pressure on the rear of the enemy's Bobruisk grouping.

[signed] Zhukov[11]

Zhukov's directive required the 22nd, 19th, 20th, 13th, 4th, and 21st Armies, arrayed from north of Vitebsk to south of Gomel', to attack in coordinated fashion and preempt any German advance on Smolensk. Even though none of these counterstrokes attained its intended end, several achieved notoriety, if not fleeting success.[12] Korobkov's 4th and Remezov's 13th Armies mounted their counterstrokes along the Sozh river against the advancing 4th Panzer Division's right flank. The feeble but fierce attack, which sought to liberate 13th Army forces encircled in Mogilev, left quite an impression on the Germans. Years later, German participants still referred to the battle as 'The Timoshenko Offensive.' Heinz Guderian wrote:

> Since July 13th the Russians had been launching heavy counter-attacks. Some twenty enemy divisions moved from the direction of Gomel against the right flank of my Panzer Group, while the Russians encircled in Mogilev and Orsha attempted simultaneously to break out, the former garrison in a south and southeasterly direction, the latter toward the south. All of these operations were controlled by Marshal Timoshenko, with the obvious objective of belatedly frustrating our successful crossing of the Dnepr.[13]

Despite the attack's imposing name, in reality, Timoshenko conducted his 'Offensive' with the 4th and 13th Armies' miserable remnants, divisions which numbered less than 3,000 men each. Even so, the action did produce enough confusion in German ranks for small elements of the 13th Army to escape the Mogilev encirclement.

While Timoshenko was conducting his 'Offensive,' Lieutenant-General M.G. Efremov's 21st Army unleashed heavy attacks against the German Second Army's XXXXIII and LIII Army Corps, whose forward elements had reached the Dnepr river at Rogachev and Zhlobin. He also orchestrated an attack northward toward Bykov on the Dnepr jointly with Korobkov's 4th Army. Attacking on 13 July, *Komkor* [Corps commander] L.G. Petrovky's

63rd Rifle Corps drove German forces westward from Rogachev and Zhlobin, while Colonel F.F. Zhmachenko's 67th Rifle Corps, reinforced by Major-General S.M. Krivoshein's 25th Mechanized Corps, launched futile attacks against Guderian's southern flank.[14] Although it was unique, the 63rd Rifle Corps' success was also fleeting, since German forces recaptured Rogachev and Zhlobin within a week.

During this frenzy of offensive activity, Efremov's three-division cavalry group, commanded by Colonel-General O.I. Gorodnikov, raided deep into the German rear area southwest of Bobruisk from Rechitsa in conjunction with the 66th Rifle Corps's 232nd Rifle Division.[15] Although this attempt to disrupt German command, control, communications, and logistics along Guderian's lines of communications was partially successful, the subsequent German advance to the gates of Smolensk rendered it, as well as the Rogachev and Zhlobin successes, utterly superfluous.

Guderian steadfastly refused to be distracted by the Soviet counterattacks. After regrouping his panzer group, his divisions resumed their advance on 13 July, in tandem with Hoth's Third Panzer Group, attacking further north. Lemelsen's XXXXVII Motorized Corps marched eastward from Orsha toward Smolensk with the 29th Motorized Division in the lead, followed closely by the 18th and 17th Panzer Divisions. Twenty-five kilometres (15 miles) to the south, Vietinghoff's XXXXVI Motorized Corps, with the 10th Panzer Divisions in the lead followed by the 'Grossdeutschland' Infantry Regiment and SS 'Reich' Motorized Division, lunged eastward across the Dnepr toward the Sozh and Desna rivers. Hoth launched his attack simultaneously from the Vitebsk region. Reinhardt's XXXIX Motorized Corps advanced from Vitebsk with its 20th and 7th Panzer Divisions fanning out to the northeast to envelop Smolensk from the north. In haste, the *Stavka* ordered Lukin's 16th Army to defend Smolensk together with the remnants of Kurochkin's 20th and Konev's 19th Armies.

However, by themselves, Guderian's 29th Motorized and 18th Panzer Divisions were too weak to envelop Smolensk and link up with Hoth's exploiting armour. Even before the advance, the 18th Panzer Division's commander noted that the heavy casualties must stop 'if we do not intend to win ourselves to death.'[16] Furthermore, Hoth's advance swung too far north, parallel to Guderian's but toward Polotsk and Velikie Luki. By permitting his forces to join the Ninth Army's advance toward Velikie Luki, Hoth's spearheads reached the area east of Smolensk on 16 July, too late to assist Guderian's assault on the city. Thereafter, the 29th Motorized Division spent three days in vicious house-to-house fighting to pry the forces of Lukin's 16th Army out of the city. The fact that 18th Panzer Division had only twelve operational tanks bore mute witness to the ferocity of the fighting and the debilitating effect of it on German panzer forces when unsupported by infantry divisions.

At this point Hitler, Kluge, Hoth and Guderian were preoccupied with sealing off the Russian force almost encircled in the Smolensk region, which now consisted of the bulk of the 16th, 19th, and 20th Armies. Wishing to continue the advance on Moscow, Guderian dispatched his 10th Panzer Division eastward to secure a bridgehead over the Desna river at El'nia. By contrast, Kluge at Army Group Centre and Hitler's own staff wanted to destroy as many of the newly located Soviet units as possible. The violent Soviet attacks on the two panzer groups' flanks convinced Guderian that he had enough force available to hold El'nia or bottle up the 16th Army east of Smolensk, but not both.

While the Germans hesitated, Zhukov acted decisively to prevent Timoshenko's three armies from being encircled and to halt any further German exploitation to the east. Representing the *Stavka*, on 20 July Zhukov ordered the Western Front, reinforced by four armies from the *Stavka's* Front of Reserve Armies, to orchestrate a major counteroffensive, the largest to date, designed to defeat German forces at Smolensk and rescue the beleaguered 16th, 19th and 20th Armies.[17] Zhukov directed Timoshenko to form four operational groups (each named after its commander) from the reinforcing 29th (Group Maslennikov), 30th (Group

Khomenko), 24th (Group Kalinin) and 28th (Group Kachalov) Armies. He then ordered the four groups, plus a fifth under the command of Rokossovsky, which was already defending the Iartsevo region, to launch concentric attacks toward Smolensk.[18]

Beginning on 21 July, Timoshenko's five operational groups fiercely assaulted German positions from Belyi in the north southward through Iartsevo to Roslavl' in an attempt to relieve Soviet forces partially encircled north of Smolensk. Despite strenuous *Stavka* efforts to coordinate these counterstrokes according to time and aim, the offensive developed unevenly but achieved some notable successes. Withstanding constant heavy Luftwaffe air strikes, Rokossovsky's scratch force managed to halt the 7th Panzer Division in heavy fighting around Iartsevo from 18-23 July and then counterattacked on 24 July, all the while maintaining communications with the three armies defending north of Smolensk.[19]

While Timoshenko's groups pounded German forces around Smolensk, the surviving 16th, 19th and 20th Armies' forces, now unified under Kurochkin's command, fought hard to maintain their positions and keep an exit open to the east. Despite their efforts, by 26 July the XXXIX Panzer Corps' 20th Motorized Division (Third Panzer Group) and the XXXXVII Panzer Corps' 17th Panzer Division (Second Panzer Group) finally linked up east of Smolensk, surrounding large portions of Kurochkin's force. Assisted by strenuous Soviet counterstrokes north, east, and south of Smolensk, the remnants of the force occupying this shrinking encirclement finally broke out eastward through the narrow Iartsevo corridor by 4 August. Third Panzer Group once again attempted to break through Rokossovsky's positions at Iartsevo at the end of the month, but Soviet artillery and a few KV-1 tanks stopped the 7th and 20th Panzer Divisions almost immediately.[20]

This hastily conducted series of Red Army counterstrokes placed immense pressure on overextended German panzer units and caused frightful casualties on both sides but, in the end, failed due to bad coordination, weak fire support and an almost total lack of logistical support. On 31 July Guderian's XXIV Motorized Corps struck back at the most successful of the attacking Soviet groups (Group Kachalov) south of Smolensk and within days destroyed it, paving the way for future German operations either eastward or to the south against the northern flank of Soviet forces defending Kiev. Army Group Centre and its two panzer groups had successfully repelled each separate Soviet counterstroke. However, the cumulative effect of these poorly coordinated Soviet actions was to deprive the Germans of operational flexibility, erode their offensive strength, and convince the German leadership of the wisdom of halting direct offensive action along the Moscow axis in favor of a thrust into the seemingly more vulnerable Ukraine.

Largely due to the fierce Soviet resistance around Smolensk, during the second half of July, Hitler and the OKH altered their strategy for the conduct of the campaign. Führer Directive No. 33, dated 19 July, ordered German forces to 'prevent the escape of large enemy forces into the depths of the Russian territory and to annihilate them' (see Appendix 1).[21] A supplementary directive issued on 23 July reiterated Hitler's intention to capture Leningrad before marching on Moscow and assigned the Third Panzer Group to Army Group North for the duration of the operation against Leningrad.[22] Later still, on 30 July Hitler issued Directive No. 34, which began by stating:

> The course of events in recent days, the appearance of large enemy forces before the front, the supply situation, and the necessity of giving the Second and Third Panzer Groups 10 days to restore and refill their formations has forced a temporary postponement of the fulfillment of aims and missions set forth in Directive Nr. 33 of 19 July and the addendum to it of 23 July....
>
> Army Group Centre will go on the defense, while employing the most favorable terrain in its sector. You should occupy favorable jumping-off positions for conducting subsequent offensive operations against the Soviet 21st Army and you can

carry out limited objective offensive operations to this end. A soon as the situation permits, the Second and Third Panzer Groups are to be withdrawn from battle and quickly refilled and re-equipped.[23]

In effect, Hitler's decisions meant that, because of the growing Soviet resistance on the Moscow axis, henceforth the Wehrmacht would make its main effort against Leningrad in the north and Kiev and the Ukraine in the south. Consequently, German forces abandoned their attacks east from Smolensk for two months. At this stage, the magnitude of the Soviet defensive success at Smolensk was not immediately apparent to senior German commanders and received little coverage in their memoirs. However, the reality was that the momentum of the Blitzkrieg was slipping away, not only because of the hesitation of the German High Command but also because of the stubborn resistance of Soviet troops. By contrast, the limited victories around Smolensk raised Red Army morale and provided precious time for Timoshenko and the *Stavka* to reorganize for the defense of Moscow. Sadly, neither took advantage of the opportunity. Instead, inspired by its partial successes in July, August and September, and urged on by Zhukov, the *Stavka* mounted a series of even more ambitious counterstrokes on a broad front east of Smolensk.

The Red Army's August and September Counteroffensive

The Red Army's July counterstrokes around Smolensk and on the approaches to Leningrad and Kiev blunted and slowed, but failed to halt, the German advance along all three strategic axes. Undeterred, in August the *Stavka* ordered all of its operating *fronts* to organize fresh counterstrokes. While the fighting east of Smolensk achieved considerable notoriety, the full scope and coordinated nature of the Soviet offensive along all three strategic axes remains largely unappreciated. In fact, in mid- and late August the *Stavka* mounted offensive operations virtually simultaneously at Staraia Russa, on the approaches to Kiev and, in the largest effort of all, on a broad front east of Smolensk.

By the end of July, the German invaders were becoming aware of the true scope of their enterprise. The enormous success of their initial advance had caused them to outrun their fragile logistical structure, and this prompted the OKH's 30 July decision to declare a virtual standstill so that Army Group Centre could rest and refit. Second Panzer Group's embattled bridgehead over the Desna river at El'nia was 720km (432 miles) from the nearest German railhead. Poor roads made it difficult for wheeled vehicles, let alone foot infantry, to keep pace with the dwindling number of tanks in the spearheads. The infantry was running short on boots, and staff officers began to plan for large quantities of winter clothing. Through 31 July, the three army groups had suffered 213,301 casualties in six weeks, but had received only 47,000 replacements.[24]

At the same time, Adolf Hitler resisted requests to issue newly produced tanks and major repair assemblies, trying to reserve them for both new and reconstituted panzer units after the campaign season ended. On 14 July, for example, he ordered increased production of submarines and new tanks, reducing the production priority of the army in the field. The extent of Hitler's micro-management was illustrated by a conference at Army Group Centre headquarters on 4 August, when a group of senior commanders had to plead with the dictator to release a mere 350 replacement engines for Mark III tanks.[25]

The one thing the Wehrmacht was not short of was targets. Halder, who had thought the war won in early July, realized his mistake by 11 August:

> The whole situation makes it increasingly plain that we have underestimated the Russian colossus... [Soviet] divisions are not armed and equipped according to our standards, and their tactical leadership is often poor. But there they are, and if we smash a dozen

of them, the Russians simply put up another dozen... They are near their own resources, while we are moving farther and farther away from ours. And so our troops, sprawled over an immense front line, without any depth, are subjected to the incessant attacks of the enemy.[26]

Not all German leaders saw the situation so clearly and pessimistically, but many of them sought clearer guidance as to how to bring the war to a quick conclusion. Even Hitler grumbled that, if he had known Guderian's prewar figures for Soviet tank strength were so accurate, he might not have started the war.[27] The solution that the dictator and many of his senior commanders chose was to emphasize surrounding and destroying Soviet units that had been previously bypassed, apparently to prevent cadres from escaping to fight another day. Younger commanders like Guderian and von Manstein opposed this policy because it slowed their exploitation and allowed the enemy to reconstruct defenses after each breakthrough. All of this had provided the context for Hitler's decision to issue Directive 34.

Army Group Centre began implementing Directive 34 on 6 August, immediately after Guderian's Second Panzer Group had completed liquidating encircled Group Kachalov. That day, the infantry divisions of Strauss's Second Army and the XXIV Motorized Corps' 3rd and 4th Panzer Divisions of Guderian's Second Panzer Group struck southward across the Sozh river toward Gomel'. Anticipating such a move, on 23 July the *Stavka* had formed a new Central Front, under Colonel-General F.I. Kuznetsov's command, consisting of Lieutenant-General M.G. Efremov's 21st and Lieutenant-General V.F. Gerasimov's 13th Armies. They ordered this new *front* to protect Gomel' and the Sozh river sector.[28] Guderian's attack sent Efremov's 21st Army reeling back to the south and threatened to form a breach between the Soviet Southwestern Front's forces defending Kiev and the Western and Reserve Fronts' forces defending east of Smolensk.[29] By 18 August Guderian's panzers and the Second

Army's infantry had captured Pochep and reached the outskirts of Gomel' and Starodub, threatening to separate the 21st and 13th Armies from one another and driving a wedge between the Central and Reserve Fronts.

Only days before, late on 14 August, the *Stavka* tried to thwart German intentions by forming the new Briansk Front under Lieutenant-General A.I. Eremenko.[30] Eremenko's mission was to plug the gap between the Western and Reserve Fronts defending east of Smolensk and the weak Central Front, defending south of the Sozh river, and to protect Kiev against an attack from the north. The *Stavka* assigned Major-General Ia.G. Kreizer's 3rd Army, Major-General M.P. Petrov's new 50th Army and the Central Front's 13th Army to Eremenko's new *front*.

On 21 August Hitler validated the *Stavka's* worries by accelerating Guderian's southward advance. He issued new orders (over the objections of many of his generals) which diverted the entire Second Army and Second Panzer Group southward deeper into the Ukraine. Guderian's Second Panzer Group began its southward advance on 25 August, striking the Central Front and driving it in disarray through Gomel' and Starodub toward the Desna river. The same day the *Stavka* responded by ordered Timoshenko's Western Front, the Reserve Front (now personally commanded by Zhukov) and Eremenko's new Briansk Front to mount concerted counterstrokes along the Smolensk, El'nia and Novozybkov axes in order to thwart Guderian's thrust and, in fact, defeat all of Army Group Centre.

Timoshenko's forces were to 'energetically continue their ongoing offensive, destroy the opposing enemy and, in cooperation with forces of the Reserve Front's left wing, reach the Velizh, Demidov, and Smolensk front by 8 September.'[31] To do so, the 16th, 19th, 20th and 30th Armies were to launch the first counterstroke toward Dukhovshchina, north of Smolensk, and its 22nd and 29th Armies were to support this assault with an attack towards Belyi and Velizh. The Western Front's mission was to sever German communications lines west of Smolensk and capture the city. In essence, this offensive was a continuation of earlier offensive action that had begun on 8 August with only limited results.

Analogous orders to Zhukov required him:

> To launch an offensive with [your] left-flank 24th and 43rd Armies... finish off the enemy El'nia grouping, capture El'nia, and subsequently reach the Dolgie Nivy, Khislavich and Petrovichi front by 8 September by attacking in the direction of Pochinok and Roslavl'.[32]

Major-General K.I. Rakutin's 24th Army was to conduct Zhukov's main attack against the German bridgehead across the Desna at El'nia.

In the third and most ambitious segment of the Smolensk counter-offensive, Eremenko's Briansk Front was to attack the very teeth of Guderian's advance, crush the Second Panzer Group and restore coherent defenses north of Kiev. Eremenko was to do so by attacking Guderian's advancing Second Panzer Group along a broad front extending from Zhukovka in the north to Iampol' in the south.[34]

At the same time, the *Stavka* abolished the Central Front, whose situation was already precarious, reinforced Eremenko's Briansk Front and assigned it responsibility for much of the Central Front's former sector, and designated Efremov, the former Central Front commander, as Eremenko's deputy. Thus, Eremenko's *front*, which now consisted of the 50th, 3rd, 13th and 21st Armies, unified control of all forces operating along the Briansk, Gomel' and Mozyr' axes. The *Stavka* hoped that the cumulative effect of its new offensives would forestall or utterly negate the effects of Guderian's offensive toward Kiev.

By 25 August, Timoshenko's Western Front had been conducting active offensive operations for over a week in response to a 15 August *Stavka* order. Subsequently, by the end of the month, its offensive encompassed the entire *front* sector from

Toropets to Iartsevo. Despite careful planning, however, combat conditions forced Timoshenko to initiate his counterstroke in piecemeal fashion. Initially, 19th Army, reinforced by the 101st Tank and 64th Rifle Divisions, the 43rd Mixed Aviation Division and considerable artillery support, forced the Vop river and, on 18 August, penetrated 10km (6 miles) deep into the defenses of the German 161st Infantry Division. Lieutenant-General I.I. Maslennikov's 29th Army supported the effort in the Velizh sector by seizing crossings over the Western Dvina river before being halted by German reserves.[34]

Zhukov expanded the Western Front's mission on 21 August and again on 25 August by ordering it to capture Velizh, Demidov and Smolensk. In the meantime, Hoth's Third Panzer Group attacked the Soviet 22nd and 29th Armies, forcing them to withdraw across the Western Dvina river until engineer reinforcements halted the German thrust. In the process, the Germans encircled the 22nd Army in the Velikie Luki region, ultimately decimating the army. Khomenko's 30th Army came to its neighbor's assistance on 29 August by attacking and penetrating German defenses east of Velizh. Major-General L.M. Dovator's Cavalry Group (the 50th and 53rd Cavalry Divisions) then exploited the gap to begin a deep raid into the German rear area which lasted over a week, tying down three German divisions dispatched to contain Dovator's group and protect German rear area installations.

After several preliminary attacks on 28 and 29 August, on 1 September the Western Front's 16th, 19th and 20th Armies launched a combined assault on German defenses east of Smolensk along the entire front from Dukhovshchina to Iartsevo. These assaults began a nearly constant nine-day battle that placed immense pressure on the defending Germans but resulted in only limited Soviet gains at a heavy cost in casualties. Finally, on 8 September Shaposhnikov, the Chief of the General Staff, reluctantly ordered the Western Front to go over to the defensive, ending the three weeks of fighting east and northeast of Smolensk and the so-called 'Dukhovshchina Offensive'.[35] Although no official tally has been released, the Western Front suffered heavy casualties in the failed operation. This bloody toll undoubtedly contributed to the *front*'s rapid collapse in October, when German forces began Operation Typhoon.

Acting on orders received from Zhukov on 15 August, Rakutin's 24th Army began assaulting German positions in the El'nia bridgehead on 17 August. Five divisions of the German Fourth Army defended the exposed bridgehead on the east bank of the Desna river. After achieving only limited gains at a cost of heavy losses, on 21 August Rakutin requested and received Zhukov's permission to halt the attack. A stubborn Zhukov then asked the *Stavka* to approve a fresh assault on the seemingly vulnerable German bridgehead. Meanwhile, Rakutin's army regrouped and was reinforced by three additional divisions, bringing its total strength on 23 August to 10 divisions, including the 102nd and 105th Tank and 103rd Motorized Divisions.[36] The *Stavka* issued its directive for the renewed assault on El'nia on 25 August. This time it closely coordinated the assault with offensives by the Western Front against German forces at Dukhovshchina and by the Briansk Front against Roslavl' and Novozybkov. Armed with fresh *Stavka* guidance, Zhukov ordered Rakutin's 24th Army to capture the El'nia bridgehead and Lieutenant-General P.A. Kuznetsov's 43rd Army to capture Roslavl'. The Briansk Front's 50th Army was to support the 43rd Army's assault by attacking northwestward from Zhukovka. Subsequently, the two Reserve Front armies were to advance to the Dolgie Nivy and Petrovichi line by 15 September.

Rakutin's 24th Army attacked on 30 August and succeeded in penetrating German forward defenses in extremely heavy and difficult fighting. Despite strong and repeated German counterattacks, by 4 September Rakutin's northern and southern shock groups had deeply enveloped the defending Germans, threatening their El'nia force with encirclement. Worse still for the Germans, the heavy fighting raging elsewhere along the front prevented them from reinforcing their beleaguered bridgehead defenses. Army Group Centre had no choice but to order its forces in the bridgehead to conduct a fighting withdrawal from their forward positions.

During the heavy fighting, Zhukov spoke by telephone with his masters in Moscow. The ensuing conversation included an interesting exchange:

> *Zhukov:* Today a German soldier deserted to our side, who indicated that this evening the 267th Infantry Division will relieve the beaten 23rd Infantry Division, and that he also observed SS units. The attack to the north is still advantageous because it will occur against the junction of two divisions. Over

> *Stalin:* You should not place too much faith in prisoners of war. Interrogate him under torture and then shoot him.[37]

After several more days of heavy fighting, on 5 September the 19th Rifle Division penetrated into El'nia and, assisted by the 100th, 103rd, 309th and 120th Rifle Divisions, captured the city on the morning of 6 August. Pursuing the Germans, Rakutin's forces crossed the Desna river, advanced 25km (15 miles), and by 8 September reached German prepared defenses along the Ustrom and Striana rivers, where the advance ground to a halt in the face of heavy German resistance. Two days later, at Zhukov's request, the *Stavka* permitted the Western and Reserve Fronts to halt their offensives at Dukhovshchina and El'nia, largely because of the *fronts'* heavy losses and the deteriorating situation in the Briansk Front's sector to the south, where Guderian's armour was now wrecking havoc on Eremenko's attacking forces. The *Stavka* directive noted:

> The prolonged offensive by Western Front forces on the well-dug-in enemy has led to heavy losses. The enemy has withdrawn to prepared defensive positions, and our units are being forced to gnaw their way through them.

> The *Stavka* orders that you cease further attacks on the enemy, go
> over to the defense, firmly dig in, and withdraw six-seven divisions
> into reserve at the expense of secondary axes and the firm defense
> in order to create a powerful maneuver group for a future offensive.
>
> B. Shaposhnikov[38]

Soviet assessments judged that the absence of requisite tanks and
air support prevented complete encirclement and destruction of the
defending German force. Nevertheless, the El'nia operation was the
first occasion when Soviet forces successfully penetrated prepared
German defenses and regained a sizeable chunk of occupied
territory. The cost of the victory, however, was excessive. Out of a
total of 103,200 men committed to combat, the Soviets lost 31,853
men (10,701 killed, captured, or missing and 21,152 wounded).[39] For
their outstanding role in the battle, four Red Army divisions (the
100th, 127th, 153rd and 161st) received the designation 'guards'.

The *Stavka* critiqued the Reserve Front's offensive and found it
wanting in several respects:

> The recent 24th and 43rd Armies' offensive did not provide
> completely positive results and led only to excessive losses both
> in personnel and in equipment. The main reasons for the lack
> of success were the absence of the required attack grouping in
> the armies, the attempt to attack along the entire front, and the
> insufficiently strong, overly short, and disgracefully organized
> aviation and artillery preparation for the infantry and tank attacks.
> Henceforth, it is necessary to cease and not tolerate disorganized
> and weakly prepared artillery and aviation support of infantry and
> tank attacks unsupported by required reserves.
>
> B. Shaposhnikov[40]

In utter defiance of *Stavka* measures to prevent it, Guderian's
Second Panzer Group continued its threatening advance
southward toward Starodub. The *Stavka* responded early on 26
August by informing Eremenko,

It seems possible to envelope the Starodub position, destroy the enemy in Starodub and close up the 13th and 21st Armies' flanks. The Supreme High Command considers the conduct of such an operation completely feasible and capable of yielding good results.[41]

In essence, this and subsequent *Stavka* directives ordered the Briansk Front to begin its attacks to thwart Guderian's advance even before the *front* had completed its formation. This precipitous action, coupled with Guderian's headlong southern advance, led inevitably to the piecemeal commitment and abject defeat of Eremenko's force. Nevertheless, the *Stavka* insisted that the futile assaults continue.

After Eremenko's first counterstroke failed, on 28 August the *Stavka* ordered him to conduct an air operation to halt Guderian's drive:

Employ the Briansk and Reserve Fronts' air forces, the 1st Reserve Aviation Group, and no fewer than 100 DB-3 aircraft for the operation to destroy the enemy tank group. In all, 450 combat aircraft must participate in the operation. The operation will begin at dawn on 29 August or 30 August and will be completed by day's end on 31 August 1941.[42]

Although the air attacks proceeded as planned, they had virtually no impact on Guderian's southward advance. Faced with this failure, two days later an increasingly desperate *Stavka* ordered Eremenko to launch a concerted offensive with his entire *front* against the already successful German force:

Launch an offensive and, while attacking in the direction of Roslavl' and Starodub, destroy the enemy grouping in the Pochep, Novgorod-Severskii, and Novozybkov region. Subsequently exploit the offensive in the general direction of Krichev and Propoisk and reach the Petrovichi, Klimovichi, Belaia Dubrava, Guta-Karetskaia, Novozybkov, and Shchors region by 15 September.[43]

Thus, Eremenko's mission was to encircle and destroy Guderian's panzer group in the Pochep, Trubchevsk,and Novozybkov region and, subsequently, reach the Petrovichi, Klimovichi and Shchors line. By doing so, the *Stavka* expected the Briansk Front to protect both the Moscow axis and the junction between the Briansk and Southwestern Fronts. This was clearly too much to ask of Eremenko, even if he was referred to by his Soviet peers as the 'Soviet Guderian.' The most serious problems were the gaps between his and the former Central Front's forces and a woeful shortage of experienced command and staff cadre.[44]

Despite these problems, Eremenko issued his attack order early on 2 September. His order required an advance along two axes, 'to destroy the opposing enemy (the 17th, 18th and 3rd Panzer Divisions and the 29th Motorized Division) and to reach the Petrovichi, Klimovichi, Belaia Dubrava, Guta-Karetskaia, Novozybkov and Shchors line by 15 September.'[45] The offensive plan was a complex and demanding one, especially for inexperienced forces. The *front*'s 50th and 3rd Armies were to attack along the Roslavl' axis in conjunction with the Reserve Front's 43rd Army. The *front*'s mobile group, which consisted of the 108th Tank Division, the 141st Tank Brigade and the 4th Cavalry Division, commanded by deputy *front* commander Ermakov, was assigned a key role in the operation. It was to attack through the 3rd Army's combat formation and spearhead the *front*'s advance through Pogar to Novgorod-Severskii. At the same time, the *front*'s 13th and 21st Armies were to converge on Semenovka to encircle and destroy the main force of Guderian's panzer group in the Pochep, Starodub and Novgorod-Severskii region. Thus, the planned attack axes of the *front*'s two shock groups were separated by 140km (84 miles). The offensive plan also ordered the *front* to fulfill its ambitious missions by 15 September. Given the confused operational situation, the complex regrouping required and massive supply problems, the Briansk Front could not meet its offensive timetable. Therefore, Eremenko asked for and received permission to delay his attack until 3 September.

Even after obtaining permission to delay the attack, the *Stavka* continued to bombard his headquarters within urgent and repeated messages to hasten his preparations. For example, on 31 August Shaposhnikov radioed:

> The offensive on Roslavl' by the Reserve Front's 43rd Army is developing successfully. However, the enemy is bringing forces up for an attack from the south. Consequently, it is necessary to speed up the preparations for the 50th Army's offensive and to begin it on 1 September or, in the last resort, on 2 September, in order to assist the 43rd Army's attack and prevent the enemy from concentrating forces against it. The 50th Army must continuously and energetically continue reconnaissance with reinforced battalions along its front.[46]

Heeding the *Stavka*'s entreaties, Eremenko commenced his offensive on 2 September, a day earlier than he intended. After a two-hour artillery preparation, both shock groups attacked into the teeth of Guderian's advancing forces. Inadequate air support, poorly organized attacks and a host of other negative factors combined to thwart the offensive from its very start. Indeed, even the day *before* his attack commenced, Stalin and Shaposhnikov berated Eremenko, caustically stating:

> The entire *Stavka* is dissatisfied with your work. Despite the work of aviation and ground units, Pochep and Starodub remain in enemy hands. This means that you nibbled away at the enemy a little but did not manage to budge him. The *Stavka* demands that the ground forces operate in cooperation with aviation, knock him out of the Starodub and Pochep region, and properly destroy him. Until this is done, all conversations will remain empty words.... Guderian and his entire group must be smashed to smithereens. Until this is done, all of your assurances of success will have no value. We await your reports about the destruction of Group Guderian.[47]

Despite the *Stavka*'s threats and entreaties, Guderian's panzers continued their advance relentlessly, easily brushing aside Eremenko's attacking forces. By late on 2 September the 3rd Army's 108th Tank Division was already half encircled and fighting desperately, and its accompanying 4th Cavalry Division had been decimated and withdrawn from combat to refit.[48] On 6 September the *front*'s mobile group remained encircled and was fighting for its very life. At this juncture, Stalin granted Eremenko permission to extract the encircled group, if he could, once again bitterly criticizing his performance:

> I know that the 108th Tank Division has fallen into encirclement and has lost many tanks and crews. This could have occurred only because of your bad management. It is not permissible to launch a division into the attack alone, neither covering its flanks nor protecting it with aviation. If aviation could not fly due to bad weather conditions, you should have postponed the tank division attack until the moment the weather improved and aviation was capable of supporting the tank division. Henceforth, I oblige you to not tolerate such rash actions. I also oblige you to find means to rescue the tankists and, in so far as possible, the tanks from encirclement. Also consider that the reference to pilots in bad weather is not always correct. *Shturmoviki* [assault aircraft] can fly even during bad weather, if the visibility is not less than 100-150 meters. Tell Comrade Petrov that I oblige him to refer to bad weather less and that it is a little better to employ *Shturmovki* for flights in bad weather.[49]

By this time the 108th Tank Division was a wreck. Its strength had fallen to 16 tanks and 5 armoured cars (2 KVs, 10 T-34s, 4 T-40s, 3 BA-10s, and 2 BA-20s), and the accompanying 141st Tank Brigade had only 38 tanks remaining (3 KVs, 14 T-34s, and 21 BTs).[50]

Eremenko did all in his power to forestall impending disaster but to no avail. For example, he requested *Stavka* approval to form blocking detachments to discourage any of his forces from retreating without orders. The *Stavka* approved his request on 5 September, stating,

> The *Stavka* has familiarized itself with your report and will permit you to create blocking detachments in those divisions that show themselves to be unreliable. The purpose of the blocking detachments is to prevent the unauthorized withdrawal of units and, in instances of flight, to halt them using all necessary weaponry.[51]

Guderian's panzers crossed the River Desna on 10 September and pushed on to Romny in the Soviet's deep rear. By this time the gap between the Briansk and Central Fronts had reached 60km (36 miles) and could not be repaired. In the meantime, the 50th Army's attack had also faltered. As a result of the operation's inauspicious beginning and Guderian's expanding offensive, on 12 September the *Stavka* altered the Briansk Front's offensive plan. The new plan, which represented sheer fantasy, required Eremenko to halt his offensive along the Roslavl' axis and regroup his forces to strike Guderian's left flank once again. This time the *Stavka* ordered him to:

> Finish with the enemy grouping in the Shostka, Glukhov, Putivl', and Konotop region in a firm and most decisive manner and link up with the Southwestern Front's forces. To do so you are authorized to halt your offensive along the Roslavl' axis and reinforce the 13th Army at the expense of the 50th Army by transferring tank units to the 13th Army. It is desirable that you complete the operation and fully liquidate the gap between the Briansk and Southwestern Fronts not later than 18 September.[52]

As further encouragement, the *Stavka* promoted Eremenko to Colonel-General and reinforced his shattered forces. These measures, however, were too late. By 15 September Guderian's forces linked up near Lokhvitsa with those of General von Kleist's

First Panzer Group, encircling 21st Army and the entire Soviet Southwestern Front.[53] In addition to ending in total disaster, Eremenko's ambitious offensive also spelled doom for the entire Soviet effort to recapture Smolensk. The human and material costs of the Roslavl'-Novozybkov operation were immense. Out of the 261,696 men and 259 tanks it committed to combat during the operation, the Briansk Front suffered about 100,000 casualties and lost 140 tanks.[54] More critical still was the parlous condition of the *front*'s forces after the offensive. Fewer than 200,000 men remained to oppose the concerted German attack that commenced less than three weeks later. More than half of these men would become victims to the new German onslaught.

The *Stavka*'s late-August and early-September Smolensk counteroffensive, which extended from Velikie Luki in the north to Shchors in the south, was a massive undertaking conducted by major elements of three *fronts*. It was the *Stavka*'s most ambitious offensive to date, and its scope and objectives far eclipsed the fragmented and hasty offensives of July and early August. Conversely, the *Stavka*'s late-August counteroffensive also became its most spectacular failure of summer 1941. However, the subsequent disasters of October and November, which, at least in part, emanated from the September disaster, permitted history to ignore all but fragments of the ill-fated counteroffensive.

Reflections

Combat along the critical Smolensk axis from July through early September 1941 clearly indicated that the *Stavka* well understood the nature of the catastrophe that was befalling its forces across the front, and acted forcefully to remedy the situation. The *Stavka* mandated virtually all of the counteroffensives, counterstrokes and major counterattacks cited above, and it strove to coordinate the timing and objectives of these counteractions. Despite this understanding, the *Stavka* thoroughly misunderstood the capabilities of its own forces and those of the Wehrmacht. Until late summer it congenitally overestimated the former and underestimated the latter. Consequently, the *Stavka* assigned its forces unrealistic missions; the results were predictably disastrous. Although its planning became more sophisticated as the campaign progressed and the missions it assigned its forces became more ambitious, *Stavka* misconceptions about what its forces could accomplish produced ever more spectacular Soviet defeats.

A significant factor in these defeats was the sad fact that Soviet command cadre, in particular its senior officers but also the Red Army's more junior officers, NCOs and enlisted soldiers, lacked the experience necessary to contend with the better-led and more tactically and operationally proficient Wehrmacht. The *Stavka* would not understand this reality until mid-1942. Finally, the Soviet military logistical and support infrastructure was totally inadequate to meet the requirements of modern, highly mobile war. In part at least, the *Stavka*'s ultimate realization of these shortcomings prompted the ensuing deafening silence in Soviet historical works that enveloped the very existence of these operations.[55]

In the German camp, the battles around Smolensk had immense significance, first and foremost because they impelled Hitler to alter his Barbarossa strategy. Although the Wehrmacht was sobered by the unprecedented and genuinely bitter Red Army resistance at Smolensk and suffered local reverses in the process, Hitler immediately perceived advantage in the situation. While the bulk of Army Group Centre held firm along the Moscow axis, Guderian's panzer army savaged Eremenko's *front* and threatened all Soviet forces in the Kiev region with utter destruction. All that remained to be seen in early September was whether Hitler and the Wehrmacht could take advantage of their unique opportunity.

THE BATTLE
FOR LENINGRAD
10 JULY–30 SEPTEMBER

Operations on the Distant Approaches, 10 July–7 August

On 9 July Leeb's Army Group North resumed its rapid thrust from the Pskov and Ostrov regions toward Leningrad. Having advanced roughly 450km (270 miles) during the first two weeks of Operation Barbarossa, he fully expected to cover the remaining 250km just as rapidly. As he advanced, Kuechler's Eighteenth Army drove into Estonia, Hoepner's Fourth Panzer Group fanned out toward Leningrad and Novgorod, and Busch's Sixteenth Army headed toward Staraia Russa.[1] Leeb's optimism seemed justified, since the opposing Soviet forces were indeed a shambles. Kuznetsov's Northwestern Front defended with Lieutenant-General F.S. Ivanov's 8th Army in southern Estonia while Lieutenant-General V.I. Morozov's 11th and Major-General N.E. Berzarin's 27th Armies withdrew from what remained of the Stalin Line. An immense gap existed in Kuznetsov's *front*, and most of his divisions numbered fewer than 2,000 men each.[2] Consequently, on 4 July Zhukov ordered Popov's Northern Front to occupy defenses along the River Luga south of Leningrad and assigned the Baltic Fleet and 8th Army to his control.[3]

Two days later, Popov ordered Lieutenant-General K.P. Piadyshev's newly formed Luga Operational Group (LOG) to man the Luga Defense Line.[4] When the group did so on 9 July, it consisted of two separate rifle divisions, one mountain rifle brigade, three militia divisions and several training school units.[5] In the week following Popov reinforced the LOG with the 41st Rifle Corps (four rifle divisions) and the 10th Mechanized Corps' 21st and 24th Tank Divisions.[6] The defense line itself extended from the Gulf of Narva to Lake Il'men' with a gap between Luga and Krasnogvardeisk through which the Northwestern Front's forces could withdraw. Behind it were three additional lightly fortified defense lines, the first roughly 20-30km (12-18 miles) from the city, the second an 'outer circle' anchored on the Krasnogvardeisk Fortified Region, and the third an 'inner defense' extending along the railroad line skirting the city's southern suburbs. In accordance with a 29 June *Stavka* order, Popov began forming fifteen people's militia divisions [*diviziia narodnogo opolchanii* – DNOs] to man the city's defenses.

Meanwhile, in accordance with his decision to form Main Direction Commands, on 10 July Stalin appointed Marshal-of-the-Soviet-Union K.E. Voroshilov to head the Northwestern Direction High Command with the mission of coordinating the Northern and Northwestern Fronts' and the Northern and Baltic Fleets' operations.[7] Beset by threats from north and south, on 13 July Voroshilov reorganized his forces southwest of Leningrad by transferring the battered 8th Army and 41st Rifle Corps from Northwestern to Northern Front control and by assigning the latter to the LOG. The LOG defended the southwestern approaches to Leningrad between Narva and Lake Il'men' while the Northwestern Front's 11th Army, newly formed 34th Army and 27th Army defended the Novgorod, Staraia Russa and Velikie Luki axes.[8] In his Order No. 3, issued the next day, Voroshilov demanded Red Army troops hold Leningrad 'at all costs'.

After advancing unimpeded for three days, Reinhardt's XXXXI Motorized Corps, with the XXXVIII Army Corps in its wake, reached the Luga south of Kingisepp on 13 July and captured several small bridgeheads across the river. There, only 110km (66 miles) from Leningrad, his advance stalled for six days in the face of fanatical Soviet resistance, resistance he could not overcome without assistance from Manstein's LVII Motorized Corps.[9] Unfortunately for Reinhardt, Manstein was unable to help because he too had encountered stiffer than anticipated resistance. His LVI Panzer Corps, supported by the I Army Corps, had advanced confidently toward Novgorod and Staraia Russa and his 8th Panzer Division had penetrated 40km (24 miles) to reach the town of Sol'tsy late on 13 July. Here, however, it faced a major counterstroke by the LOG's 177th Rifle Division and 10th Mechanized Corps, orchestrated by Lieutenant-General N.F. Vatutin, the Northwestern Front's new chief of staff. Skillfully exploiting the difficult terrain, the Soviet force struck back at the 8th Panzer, isolating it from the 3rd Motorized Division to its left and the SS 'Totenkopf' Division still lagging well to its rear.[10]

The surprise Soviet two-pronged assault forced the 8th Panzer Division to fight a costly battle in encirclement for four days. It also disrupted German offensive plans by forcing Hoepner to divert forces from the Kingisepp and Luga axes to rescue the 8th Panzer at Sol'tsy.[11] After weathering the crisis at Sol'tsy, the I Army Corps captured Shimsk on 30 July and forced Morozov's 11th and Berzarin's 27th Armies to withdraw to the Staraia Russa and Kholm line.[12] Busch's Sixteenth Army's pursued, capturing Kholm and Staraia Russa by 6 August and establishing a continuous front from Lake Il'men' to Velikie Luki. But Vatutin's counterstroke at Sol'tsy had delayed the German advance for about three weeks.[13] After advancing 450km (270 miles) in two weeks, Leeb's forces spent almost a month covering 120km and were still over 100km from Leningrad.

After the Sol'tsy counterstroke failed, Voroshilov strengthened his Luga defenses and assembled new reserves for the Luga Line. However, the Finnish Army's advance in Karelia and the Eighteenth Army's attack in Estonia complicated his task.[14] In addition, by 29 July Voroshilov and Popov simplified their force structure by splitting his LOG into the Kingisepp, Luga, and Eastern Sectors, each responsible for its own defense, and by ordering construction of the Krasnogvardeisk Fortified Region, subdivided into the Krasnoe Selo, Central, and Slutsk-Kolpino sectors.[15] Despite Voroshilov's efforts, on 30 July a dissatisfied Stalin summoned Voroshilov and Zhdanov to Moscow where he criticized them for 'lack of toughness' in conducting operations in the Northwestern Theatre. To stiffen their resolve, on 6 and 7 August the *Stavka* itself assigned *Kombrig* [Brigade commander] I.I. Pronin's new 34th Army and Lieutenant-General S.D. Akimov's new 48th Armies to the Northwestern Front. The former reinforced the Staraia Russa sector and the latter protected the region north of Lake Il'men.[16]

Operations on the Immediate Approaches, 7 August – 9 September

In late July Hitler planned his final assault on Leningrad. His Directive No. 33, issued on 19 July, and a supplement issued on the 23rd reiterated his intention to capture Leningrad before marching on Moscow and announced that Army Group Centre's Third Panzer Group would be assigned to Army Group North.[17] On 8 August an optimistic Hitler ordered Leeb to encircle the city and link up with the Finnish Army. Leeb was to make his main attack between the Narva river and Lake Il'men with three shock groups from Hoepner's panzer group and Kuechler's Eighteenth Army, and a secondary attack south of Lake Il'men with Busch's Sixteenth Army.[18] The Northern Group (the XXXXI Motorized and XXXVIII Army Corps and, later, the 8th Panzer Division) was to attack toward Kingisepp and Leningrad from its Luga river bridgeheads, and the Luga Group (the LVI Motorized Corps with the 8th Panzer Division in reserve) was to attack through Luga towards Leningrad. The Southern Group (the I and XXVIII Army Corps) was to attack the Soviet 48th Army along the

Shimsk-Novgorod-Chudovo axis, envelop Leningrad from the east and sever its communications with Moscow. On Leeb's left flank, the Eighteenth Army was to advance on Narva and seize the Estonian coast and Tallinn. On his right, the Sixteenth Army was to defeat the Soviet 11th, 34th, 27th and 22nd Armies south of Lake Il'men, capture Staraia Russa and Velikie Luki and sever the vital Moscow-Leningrad railroad line east of the Valdai Hills.[19]

Fully expecting the renewed German onslaught, the *Stavka* ordered Voroshilov and Vatutin to mount yet another counterstroke to destroy German forces in the Sol'tsy, Staraia Russa and Dno regions. Vatutin's plan required the Northwestern Front's 48th, 34th, 11th and 27th Armies to attack the Sixteenth Army's X Army Corps, which occupied an exposed position at Staraia Russa. The concentric attacks by Akimov's 48th Army toward Utorgosh, west of Lake Il'men', and by Morozov's 11th, Pronin's 34th and Berzarin's 27th Armies south of the lake were designed to cut off and destroy the German X Corps and capture Sol'tsy, Dno, and Kholm, thereby disrupting the German advance on Leningrad.[20]

However, Vatutin's 12 August offensive achieved only fleeting success because the Sixteenth Army and X Army Corps attacked toward Novgorod and east of Staraia Russa on 10 August, pre-empting and disrupting the 48th and 11th Armies' attacks. Nonetheless, the 34th, 11th, and 27th Armies attacked as planned early on 12 August. While the Germans halted the 27th Army's advance at Kholm, the 34th Army advanced 40km (24 miles) and reached the Dno-Staraia Russa railroad line early on 14 August. The determined assault enveloped the X Army Corps at Staraia Russa and threatened the rear of the German main panzer force advancing on Novgorod.[21] Despite its auspicious beginning, the Soviet counterstroke soon floundered because of the roadless terrain and command and control difficulties. In the midst of the counterstroke, on 14-15 August, Leeb diverted the SS 'T' Motorized and 3rd Motorized Divisions, the LVI Motorized Corps headquarters and the VIII Air Corps from Luga and Novgorod to Dno to assist the beleaguered X Army Corps. By 25 August the LVI Motorized Corps' counterattack had crushed the 34th and 11th Armies and driven them back to the Lovat' river.[22]

Vatutin's failed counterstroke forced the OKH to mount a major offensive against Soviet troop concentrations south of Lake Il'men, thus weakening and delaying the German advance on Leningrad and Moscow.[23] After several rain delays, Army Group North's LVI Motorized, II and X Army Corps and Army Group Centre's LVII Motorized Corps advanced through Demiansk toward Valdai against the Soviet 11th, 34th and 27th Armies. The 19th Panzer Division captured Demiansk on 31 August, and the 20th Panzer Division and the II Army Corps encircled and destroyed a large Soviet force, reached Ostashkov and closed the gap between Army Groups North and Centre.[24]

Undeterred by Vatutin's counterstroke, on 8 August Leeb's forces resumed their advance on Leningrad. Reinhardt's XXXXI Motorized and XXXVIII Army Corps advanced along the Kingisepp–Krasnogvardeisk axis in heavy rain, trying to reach the open country south of the Narva–Leningrad railroad, from which they could wheel eastward towards Leningrad. Two days later, Manstein's LVI Motorized and I and XXVIII Army Corps attacked toward Luga and Novgorod. The XXXXI Motorized and XXXVIII Army Corps' penetrated Soviet defenses and captured bridgeheads over the Luga river at Ivanovskoe and Bol'shoi Sabsk after three days of heavy fighting, and, after the 8th Panzer Division joined them, severed the Kingisepp–Krasnogvardeisk rail line on 11 August.[25] The XXXXI Motorized Corps then wheeled its forces eastward toward Krasnogvardeisk, while the accompanying infantry attacked westward toward Kingisepp.[26] Although Reinhardt's motorized corps failed to overcome Red Army resistance at Krasnogvardeisk for six days, German infantry occupied Kingisepp, forcing the 8th Army to withdraw its forces from Narva to the Luga.[27] Leeb's failure to destroy Soviet forces at Narva and Kingisepp forced him to postpone the XXXXI Motorized Corps' assault on Krasnogvardeisk while his infantry eliminated the threat to his right flank.[28] The XXVI and XXVIII Army Corps did so from 22 August to 1 September, ultimately forcing Ivanov's 8th Army to withdraw into a bridgehead south of Oranienbaum.[29]

While Leeb's forces were smashing the Northern Front's defenses at Kingisepp and assaulting Krasnogvardeisk, Manstein's LVI Motorized Corps and the L Army Corps attacked along the Luga axis on 10 August, and the XXVIII and I Army Corps attacked along the Novgorod axis on Manstein's right flank.[30] The three corps smashed the LOG's and 48th Army's partially prepared defenses protecting Luga and Novgorod and broke through the Luga Line, capturing Shimsk on 12 August, Novgorod on 16 August, Chudovo on 20 August and Luga on 24 August.[31] The assault reached the banks of the River Volkhov, severing the Moscow-Leningrad railroad line and communications between Akimov's 48th Army and the remainder of the Northwestern Front. The LOG was almost encircled and the 48th Army was a shambles, with only 6,235 men, 5,043 rifles, and 31 artillery pieces remaining with which to defend the southeastern approaches to Leningrad.[32]

Faced with these disasters, on 23 August Voroshilov assigned the 48th Army to the Northern Front and ordered it to defend the approaches into Leningrad from the southeast. Meanwhile, the *Stavka* divided Popov's Northern Front into the Leningrad Front under Popov and the Karelian Front under Lieutenant-General V.A. Frolov.[33] On 27 August, the GKO assumed direct control over the Karelian, Leningrad and Northwestern Fronts by abolishing the Northwestern Direction High Command, merging its staff into the Leningrad Front. This ended Voroshilov's satrapy over military affairs at Leningrad even though Voroshilov replaced Popov briefly as *front* commander on 5 September.[34] With German forces only 40km south and 100km southwest of Leningrad, on 27 August the *Stavka* began deploying its fresh 54th, 52nd and 4th Armies along and east of the Volkhov to prevent German and Finnish forces from linking up northeast of the city.[35]

Meanwhile, Leeb concentrated his forces for what he expected to be the final drive on Leningrad. He ordered General Rudolf Schmidt's XXXIX Motorized Corps, newly arrived from Army

Group Centre, and the Sixteenth Army's I and XXVIII Army Corps to penetrate into Leningrad from the southeast along the Leningrad-Moscow road.[36] At the same time, Hoepner's panzer group and Kuechler's Eighteenth Army were to attack Leningrad from the south and the west, while the remainder of Busch's Sixteenth Army defended his right flank along the Valdai hills and Volkhov river. Soviet defenses opposite the assembling German host were a shambles. The Leningrad Front's 8th Army manned defenses west of Leningrad while the LOG, minus the 41st Rifle Corps, which was half-encircled south of Krasnogvardeisk, defended the Krasnogvardeisk Fortified Region. To the east, the weakened 48th Army defended north of Chudovo, and the Northwestern Front's hastily assembled Novgorod Army Group (NAG) screened along the Volkhov river.[37]

Schmidt's XXXIX Motorized Corps easily penetrated the 48th Army's defenses, captured Liuban' on 25 August and sent the 18th Motorized Division northeastward toward Kirishi, the 12th Panzer westward toward Kolpino, and the 20th Motorized northwestward toward Volkhov. Popov tried to plug the yawning gap southeast of Leningrad by reinforcing his Slutsk-Kolpino Group with two divisions, and ordered the LOG and 48th Army 'to organize a strong defense and conduct counterattacks, but to no avail.'[38] Schmidt's 12th Panzer and 20th Motorized Divisions, followed by three infantry divisions, captured Tosno and Mga and reached the Neva river on 29 August. At the same time, the 18th Motorized Division captured Kirishi and Liuban', threatening to sever the last rail line east from Leningrad and splitting Soviet forces defending southeast of Leningrad. Following closely after the advancing panzers, the XXVIII Army Corps wheeled westward towards Leningrad proper, driving Soviet forces back to the Izhora and Neva rivers in heavy fighting between 30 August and 8 September. Thereafter, determined Soviet resistance at Iam-Izhora forced the Germans to halt their advance.

With his left flank torn apart, on 31 August the *Stavka* authorized Popov to reorganize his fortified regions south of the city into Major-General I.G. Lazarov's 55th Army, defending the western sector, and Lieutenant-General F.S. Ivanov's 42nd Army, defending its eastern sector.[39] Popov ordered Akimov's 48th Army to recapture Mga and reinforced the army with an NKVD Rifle Division formed from Karelian border guards.[40] Although the NKVD division managed to recapture Mga on 30 August, the town fell to the 20th Motorized Division the next day. After a week of heavy fighting, the 20th Motorized and reinforcing 12th Panzer Division cracked Akimov's defenses, captured Siniavino on 7 September and seized Shlissel'burg on the southern shore of Lake Ladoga the next day.[41] An OKW communiqué announced triumphantly that 'the iron ring around Leningrad has been closed,' signaling the beginning of the Leningrad blockade.

The loss of Shlissel'burg was a disaster for both Popov and Leningrad's now besieged population since it left the Germans in control of virtually all of Leningrad's ground communications with the remainder of the country. Henceforth, resupply of the city was possible only via Lake Ladoga or by air. Fortunately, the Neva Operational Group contained the German attack along the Neva river and, further east, Marshal-of-the-Soviet-Union G.I. Kulik's 54th Army halted the German advance east of Siniavino. Unfortunately, the German advance to Krasnogvardeisk and capture of Chudovo and Tosno encircled Piadyshev's LOG south of Krasnogvardeisk. Abandoning the region north of Luga on 20 August, the group tried to infiltrate through German lines to Krasnogvardeisk, but was cut to pieces and utterly destroyed by German forces.[42]

The loss of Shlissel'burg on 8 September convinced the *Stavka* and Leningrad Front that the fight for Leningrad was fast approaching its climax. However, most in the German camp felt the climax had already passed and Leningrad was German for the taking. On 5 September Halder wrote in his diary, 'Leningrad: Our objective has been achieved. Will now become a subsidiary theatre of operations.'[43] Accordingly, Hitler decided to avoid the prospect of unnecessary casualties in assaulting a city that was already doomed. Enticed by new opportunities in Army Group Centre's sector, on 6 September he ordered Leeb to encircle and starve Leningrad rather than seize it by frontal assault and issued his Directive No. 35, which ordered Army Group Centre to embark on its Moscow adventure, Operation Typhoon. At the same time, Hitler ordered Leeb

> To encircle enemy forces operating in the Leningrad region…
> in cooperation with Finnish forces so that a considerable number
> of the mobile and First Air Fleet formations, particularly the VIII
> Air Corps, can be transferred to Army Group Centre no later
> than 15 September.'[44]

On 4 September German forces began shelling Leningrad daily with 240mm guns from the region north of Tosno, and, four days later, German aircraft began pounding the city with daylight air raids.

Finnish Army operations in Karelia further complicated the defense of Leningrad. Although the Finns were supposed to help capture Leningrad, from 22 June through 10 July they conducted only limited-objective operations, and after 10 July they limited their operations to the sector west of Lakes Onega and Ladoga against the Soviet 7th Army. Beginning on 31 July, however, Finnish forces attacked the Leningrad Front's 23rd Army defending the Karelian Isthmus, forcing the army to withdraw to new defensive positions astride the isthmus only 30km (18 miles) from Leningrad's northern defenses. Although the Finns advanced no further, the mere threat of a Finnish attack adversely effected the Leningrad Front's defense in other sectors.[45]

At the end of the first week of September, the Wehrmacht began operations to isolate and destroy Leningrad. As anticlimactic as it seemed to the Germans, no Russians doubted the battle was at its climax.

The Defense of Leningrad, 9-30 September

On 29 August Leeb ordered his forces to encircle Leningrad by capturing bridgeheads over the Neva and the towns of Uritsk, Pulkovo, Pushkin (Detskoe Selo), Kolpino and Izhora, and establish a tight ring around the city before Hoepner's Fourth Panzer Group departed for Army Group Centre.[46] He organized his force into the Krasnogvardeisk and Slutsk-Kolpino Groups. The former deployed with the XXXVIII Army Corps on the left, the XXXXI Motorized Corps (the 1st and 6th Panzer and 36th Motorized Divisions) in the centre and the L Army Corps on the right, with the 8th Panzer Division in reserve.[47] Its mission was to capture Krasnogvardeisk and reach the Gulf of Finland coast, thereby isolating Soviet forces west of Leningrad. The latter, under Hoepner's command, consisted of the XXVIII Army Corps and elements of the 12th Panzer Division. Its task was to penetrate Soviet defenses along the Izhora river and capture Slutsk and Kolpino.[48] Further east, Schmidt's XXXIX Motorized Corps (the 20th Motorized and 12th Panzer Divisions) was to widen the corridor to Lake Ladoga, screen the River Neva and drive Soviet forces eastward from Siniavino.

Voroshilov defended the southern approaches to Leningrad with his 8th, 42nd and 55th Armies. Ivanov's 42nd Army manned the Krasnogvardeisk Fortified Region from Krasnoe Selo to Pustoshka, Lazarov's 55th Army defended the Slutsk-Kolpino Fortified Region from Pustoshka to the Neva, and the 8th Army, now commanded by Major-General V.I. Shcherbakov, defended the coastal sector west of the city.[49] Voroshilov retained four divisions, two brigades and a tank battalion in reserve.[50] On 11 September the Leningrad Front's strength was 452,000 men, about two-thirds of which were deployed south of Leningrad facing an equal number of Germans. East of the Shlissel'burg corridor, Kulik's 85,000-man 54th Army was assembling at Volkhov, in the rear of the decimated 48th Army, now commanded by Major-General M.M. Antoniuk.[51]

Reinhardt's XXXXI Motorized and the XXXVIII Army Corps attacked toward Krasnogvardeisk and the coast on 9 September, a day after the Luftwaffe began three days of heavy aerial bombardment of the city and eight days after the fierce artillery bombardment began.[52] In the face of heavy counterattacks, the XXXXI Motorized Corps' 36th Motorized and 1st Panzer Divisions penetrated the 3rd DNO's defense, advanced 10km (6 miles) and cut the Krasnogvardeisk-Krasnoe Selo road. With the 6th Panzer Division engaged in heavy fighting for Krasnoe Selo, Leeb reinforced the 1st Panzer Division with the only forces at hand, a single tank battalion, while an increasingly desperate Voroshilov committed his last reserves to battle.[53] The 1st Panzer Division captured Dudergov on 11 September and Krasnoe Selo on 12 September, but was halted at Pulkovo in Leningrad's southwestern suburbs.[54] By this time, the 1st Panzer and 36th Motorized Divisions had outflanked the 42nd Army's defenses at Krasnogvardeisk and were threatening the rear of 55th Army's forces defending Slutsk and Kolpino. The way was now open for Reinhardt's XXXXI and the L Corps to seize Krasnogvardeisk, advance toward Slutsk and Pushkin and link up with XXVIII Army Corps, which was attacking Pushkin from the east. However, reinforcements were necessary in order to do so.

Once again, however, reinforcements were unavailable, since the 8th Panzer Division was still reorganizing and was unable to exploit the motorized corps' success. Worse still for Leeb, the 55th Army halted the XXVIII Army Corps' advance on Slutsk after only minimal gains.[55] Voroshilov then transferred the Krasnogvardeisk sector to 55th Army's control and ordered Lazarov's army to defend Pushkin, Krasnogvardeisk and Kolpino at all costs. Leeb faced a serious command and control problem since Hoepner could control neither Kuechler's corps on the left nor Schmidt's group on the right nor, as it turned out, his only reserve, the 8th Panzer Division. Nor was the attack synchronized, since the L Corps, still struggling north of Luga, was not ready in time.[56] The only saving grace was that Voroshilov too was at the end of his tether.

To make matters worse, the OKH's 10 September order requiring Leeb to transfer Reinhardt's XXXXI Motorized Corps to Army Group Centre 'in good condition' finally arrived, and Schmidt reported that the Soviet 54th Army and a cavalry division threatened his right flank.[57] Leeb responded by sending the 8th Panzer Division to assist Schmidt and the new 254th Infantry Division to Eighteenth Army to fill the gap once Reinhardt's corps departed.[58] He then persisted in his plans to take Leningrad, ordering the XXVIII Army Corps to advance westward toward Pushkin, Slutsk and Marino and the 6th Panzer Division to attack Pushkin from the west. After a day of regrouping, the rest of Reinhardt's corps was to spearhead one final attempt to breech Leningrad's defenses south of the Pushkin-Petergof road with the XXXVIII Army Corps on its left and the L Army Corps on its right.

With the German noose around Leningrad tightening, on 11 September an angry Stalin appointed Zhukov to command the Leningrad Front in place of the hapless Voroshilov.[59] Stalin also disbanded the 48th Army, already demolished by the Germans, and, on 12 September, assigned its forces to Kulik's 54th Army, which was still assembling at Volkhov. Stalin ordered Kulik to restore the broken front south of Lake Ladoga and sent Lieutenant-Generals V.F. Iakovlev's 4th and N.K. Klykov's 52nd Armies to defend the Volkhov river line north of Lake Il'men'. Zhukov arrived in Leningrad on 13 September with Major-Generals I.I. Fediuninsky and M.S. Khozin, his trusted lieutenants from Khalkhin-Gol days, and assumed command.[60] Immediately, he appointed Khozin as his chief of staff, suspended Voroshilov's plans to demolish Leningrad and ordered his forces 'not a step back' under penalty of being shot.[61]

The situation he faced was indeed grave. Krasnoe Selo and Uritsk had fallen, the Krasnogvardeisk Fortified Region was threatened, German forces were less than 10km from the coast and 12-18km south of the city and, to the east, were threatening to capture Volkhov and link up with the Finns. Identifying the

Uritsk and Pulkovo sectors as the most dangerous, Zhukov reinforced them and ordered relentless counterattacks to blunt the German advance.

Leeb resumed his advance on 13 September, just as Zhukov was arriving. Reinhardt's XXXXI Motorized and the XXXVIII Army Corps (the 1st and 58th Infantry, 1st Panzer and 36th Motorized Divisions) penetrated the 42nd Army's defenses north of Krasnoe Selo and approached Uritsk, and Zhukov reinforced the army with two rifle divisions, which launched desperate counterattacks.[62] In an attempt to regain the initiative, the next day Zhukov ordered Lazarov's 55th Army to defend Pushkin, Krasnogvardeisk and Kolpino stubbornly, while the *front* 'smothered the enemy with artillery and mortar fire and air attacks to prevent any penetration of the defenses.'[63] While Zhukov assembled fresh reserves, he ordered Shcherbakov's 8th Army 'to strike the enemy in the flank and rear' and Kulik's 54th Army 'to liberate the Mga and Shlissel'burg regions.'[64]

By this time, the XXXXI Motorized and XXXVIII Army Corps had driven 42nd Army's forces to the outskirts of Uritsk, only 4km from the coast.[65] In desperation, Zhukov backed up Ivanov's army with two more divisions and two brigades, which, on 16 September, occupied a second-echelon defense line south of Leningrad from the Gulf of Finland to the Neva river.[66] Soon after, Zhukov sent Fediuninsky to investigate the situation in 42nd Army. When Fediuninsky returned to report that morale in the 42nd as well as the 8th and 55th Armies was cracking, Zhukov ordered Fediuninsky to 'Take over the 42nd Army – and quick.'[67]

Zhukov's decision to attack was based on his perception that the Germans' precipitous advance to Uritsk had exposed the left flank of the German force assaulting 42nd Army. He therefore planned to pound the German force attacking Uritsk between the 8th Army's 'hammer' and the 42nd Army's 'anvil.' Shcherbakov's 8th Army was ordered to attack the German left flank with five rifle divisions, and when Shcherbakov demurred, claiming that his force was too weak to launch the counterattack, Zhukov relieved him on the spot and appointed Lieutenant General T.I. Shevaldin to command the army.[68]

However, the Germans foiled Zhukov's plan by preempting the 8th Army's counterattack. On 16 September the XXXXI Motorized and XXXVIII Army Corps attacked and defeated the 8th Army before it completed its counterattack preparations. The German force then captured Uritsk by nightfall, reaching the Gulf of Finland and isolating the 8th Army from Leningrad in the so-called Oranienbaum bridgehead. The diversion did, however, provide Fediuninsky enough time to solidify the 42nd Army's defenses south of Leningrad and withstand the heavy fighting that raged until month's end. Whipped on by an insistent Zhukov, the 8th Army's four divisions attacked toward Krasnoe Selo on 20 September, only to be driven back the next day by strong XXXVIII Army Corps counterattacks. There the front stabilized once and for all.[69]

While heavy fighting raged along the Uritsk axis, Leeb began a two-pronged assault to destroy the 55th Army's main force in the Krasnogvardeisk, Slutsk and Pushkin region by concentric attacks from east and west and smash the 42nd Army's left flank, thereby opening the door to Leningrad. On 12 September the XXXXI Motorized Corps' 6th Panzer Division and the L Army Corps' SS Police and 169th Infantry Divisions attacked eastward toward Krasnogvardeisk and Pushkin, and the XXVIII Army Corps' 96th and 121st Infantry Divisions attacked westward from the Izhora river toward Slutsk and Pushkin.[70] After capturing Krasnogvardeisk on 13 September, the two forces became bogged down in a fierce struggle for the Slutsk-Kolpino Fortified Region.

By 18 September, the 1st Panzer and SS Police Divisions finally captured Pushkin and the XXVIII Army Corps captured Slutsk, forcing the 55th Army to withdraw to new defenses at Pulkovo, Bol'shoe Kuz'mino, Novaia and Putrolovo. A final desperate assault by the 1st Panzer Division captured Pulkovo and Aleksandrovka, the terminus of the Leningrad southwest tram line, only 12km (7.2 miles) from the city's centre. However, there, on the southern slopes of Pulkovo Heights, the 1st Panzer's assault faltered when it encountered Soviet tanks that had just rolled off the Kolpino tank factory's assembly line. Although fighting lasted until 30 September, the tenacious Soviet defense at Pulkovo Heights convinced Leeb to halt his attacks, although the scheduled departure of the XXXXI Motorized Corps, which he dreaded so much, was also an important factor.[71]

By 30 September Zhukov's forces were indeed hemmed into Leningrad, but not as tightly as Hitler, the OKH and Leeb wished. Zhukov's defenses in the city's southern suburbs and along the Neva river were intact, and the Finns had yet to attack. Zhukov's iron will had produced a 'Miracle on the Neva,' and Leeb clearly understood he had lost his best opportunity to seize Leningrad. Worse still, from Leeb's perspective, rather than resting on his defensive laurels Zhukov set about exacting an even greater toll on Leningrad's tormentors by attacking once again. On Zhukov's recommendation, the *Stavka* ordered Kulik's 54th Army, still operating under its direct control, and Zhukov's Neva Operational Group (NOG) to launch converging attacks toward Siniavino and Mga to raise the Leningrad blockade.[72]

Kulik's army attacked on 10 September but advanced only 6-10km in 16 days of off-and-on heavy fighting, while Zhukov and the *Stavka* castigated him repeatedly for his army's dismal performance. Ultimately, Schmidt's XXXIX Motorized Corps forced Kulik's forces to withdraw to defensive positions eastward along the Nasiia river. Angrily, Zhukov insisted Stalin replace Kulik with his protégé Khozin.[73] Meanwhile, the NOG's forces crossed the Neva river on 20 September, seizing a small bridgehead at Moskovskaia Dubrovka but accomplishing little more.[74] While Zhukov's Siniavino offensive failed, it did force Leeb to transfer forces to the threatened sector and delayed the transfer of XXXIX Motorized Corps to Army Group Centre.[75]

Fighting in the Leningrad region died out in late September and the front stabilized temporarily. Despite the spectacular gains it had recorded since crossing the Western Dvina river in early July, Army

Group North had suffered 60,000 losses.[76] However, Leningrad's badly organized, trained and equipped defenders lost far more. The Northern Front reported 55,535 casualties between 10 July and 23 August out of 153,000 men engaged and the Leningrad Front 116,316 casualties from 23 August to 30 September out of 300,000 engaged. Finally, the Northwestern Front casualty toll from 10 July through 30 September added another 144,788 men out of 272,000 engaged.[77] By any count, the opposing forces were exhausted. As both sides licked their wounds and counted their casualties, they prepared to resume operations, knowing full well that, since Army Group North had failed to achieve its Barbarossa missions, struggle would inevitably continue.

Unfortunately for Leeb, the resources available to do so also dwindled. On 15 September, Hoepner's Fourth Panzer Group began departing for Army Group Centre.[78] Only Schmidt's XXXIX Motorized Corps (the 12th Panzer and 18th and 20th Motorized Divisions) and, as a later concession, the 8th Panzer Division, remained to provide Leeb with armour support.[79] On 24 September, he reported candidly to OKH that the situation had 'worsened considerably', he could no longer continue offensive operations toward Leningrad and his forces had no other choice but to go on the defense, a declaration that Hitler would not accept.[80]

Reflections

The Red Army's defense along the Leningrad axis lasted from 10 July to 30 September, after which the front south of Leningrad stabilized and remained stable until January 1943.[81] During the 50 days of often desperate and costly defense, Red Army forces disrupted Hitler's plan to seize Leningrad by concentric blows from the south and north. Combat intensified steadily as the Red Army increased its resistance and began conducting counterstrokes of its own. As a result, the tempo of the German advance decreased from a rate of advance of 5km (3 miles) per day in July, to 2.2km

(1.3 miles) per day in August and 1.4km (less than a mile) per day in September. The Red Army improved its defensive forces and techniques throughout this period by adopting extraordinary and sometimes draconian mobilization measures and by committing virtually all of its available manpower to combat. During July and August, it raised and fielded seven militia rifle divisions and an NKVD Rifle Division and was reinforced by four rifle divisions dispatched by the *Stavka*.

The strength and complexity of the German offensive also increased as the action developed. In July Army Group North and its Finnish Allies attacked simultaneously along the Petrozavodsk, Olonets and Leningrad axes. In mid-August the Germans penetrated Soviet defenses along the Novgorod axis, cut off and isolated much of the 8th Army in Estonia and attacked simultaneously along the Krasnogvardeisk and Karelian Isthmus axes. In late August and early September, German forces advanced simultaneously along the Mga, Krasnogvardeisk and Karelian axes. The Red Army tried to mount effective large-scale counterstrokes at Sol'tsy, Staraia Russa, Krasnoe Selo and Siniavino, but achieved little more than delaying the German advance. Even after the Red Army halted the German juggernaut on Leningrad's doorstep and frustrated their attempts to capture the city by direct attack, there was no doubt in either camp that the city remained in mortal danger of being encircled and destroyed.

A German directive issued on 22 September read:

> The Führer has decided to erase the city of Petersburg from the face of the earth. I have no interest in the further existence of this large city after the defeat of Soviet Russia… We propose to blockade the city tightly and erase it from the earth by means of artillery fire and continuous bombardment from the air.[82]

Driven by ambition, frustration and sheer hatred of the Russians, Hitler would force Leeb's army group to make one last exertion to encircle the city before the onset of winter.

THE BATTLE FOR KIEV
10 JULY–30 SEPTEMBER

The Situation on 9 July

Hitler began to seek targets which were still within reach before winter came and which would convince him and the world that Germany was in fact victorious. He was particularly anxious to seize Soviet industry and croplands, as well as to push the defenders beyond bomber range of the precious Rumanian oil fields. He therefore continued to insist that taking Moscow was far less important than securing the industry of Leningrad and the industrial and agricultural heartland of the Ukraine.

The Southwestern and Southern Fronts' unexpectedly stubborn resistance had slowed Army Group South's offensive. At a time when Army Group North's forces had crossed the Dvina and captured Pskov and Army Group Centre had crossed the Dnepr and was preparing to march on Smolensk, only the forward elements of the 13th Panzer Division had reached the approaches to Kiev. The main body of Kleist's First Panzer Group was still 100-200km (60-120 miles) west of the Dnepr while the Sixth and Seventeenth Armies' infantry lagged several days behind. To the south, German and Rumanian forces in Moldavia had made even less progress. In a week of fighting, they had advanced insignificantly toward Bel'tsy and Soroki and reached the outskirts of Mogilev–Podol'skii, but on 9 July their advance ground to a halt between the Prut' and Dnestr rivers.[1]

The Uman' Encirclement

On 3 and 4 July Rundstedt, the Army Group South commander, decided that, after seizing Zhitomir and Berdichev, Kleist, the commander of First Panzer Group, should turn two of his motorized corps southward toward Kirovograd. Using the Odessa road, the two corps could deeply envelop the Soviet main force in the Ukraine and Moldavia, preventing it from withdrawing to the Dnepr river, while his third corps captured bridgeheads over the Dnepr at Kiev. Reichenau's Sixth Army was to form two groups, the northern group to advance directly on Kiev and a southern group to accompany Kleist's armour and link up with Schobert's Eleventh Army to encircle and destroy the Southwestern Front. All the while, Stuelpnagel's Seventeenth Army would press defending Soviet forces from the West.[2]

While Army Group South focused on encircling Soviet forces in the Vinnitsa region, Kirponos, the Southwestern Front commander, and the *Stavka* remained convinced that the Germans' priority target was Kiev. Therefore, both did all in their power to halt the Germans at Kiev by attempting to cut off and destroy the sharp panzer tip of the advancing German infantry columns. On 7 July the *Stavka* ordered Kirponos to conduct the first in a series of planned counterstrokes aimed at blocking the German advance on Kiev and maintaining the already tenuous communications between his 5th and 6th Armies.[3] Potapov's 5th Army, which was withdrawing from the Korosten' Fortified Region, was to attack German forces advancing toward Kiev from the north, and Muzychenko's 6th Army was to strike the penetrating Germans from the south.[4]

However, Potapov's and Muzychenko's first attempt to do so failed. From 10–14 July, Potapov's 31st Rifle Corps, supported by the 9th, 19th and 22nd Mechanized Corps, struck Sixth Army's northern group at and east of Novgorod-Volynskii in an attempt to fulfill Kirponos's mission and rescue its 7th Rifle Corps, which the Germans had already encircled along the Sluch' river. Potapov's forces barely dented the German defenses in three days of heavy fighting.[5] This failure placed Muzychenko's 6th Army in a difficult situation, with its right flank deeply enveloped from the north and its centre under heavy assault by the Sixth and Seventeenth Armies. Worse still, the 16th and 18th Mechanized Corps arrived too late to participate in the action, and when the 16th Mechanized Corps finally did arrive, Muzychenko was forced to commit it along the Berdichev axis to protect his rear area.

On 12 July Kirponos withdrew the headquarters of Kostenko's 26th Army into *front* reserve, assigning it control of all forces concentrated east and northeast of Belaia Tserkov and ordering it to attack to the northwest to link up with Potapov's 5th Army.[6] However, Rundstedt then turned his entire northern group against the 5th Army and two corps from his southern group against the 26th Army, temporarily abandoning any attempt to storm Kiev. Only on 15 July, when the Germans captured Kazatin and severed Kirponos's lateral communications, did Kirponos suddenly realize that the Germans were making their main attack to the south in an attempt to cut off Soviet forces withdrawing to the Dnepr. Consequently, Kirponos begin planning to withdraw his forces eastward. On 17 July, but without *Stavka* permission, he informed Muzychenko and Ponedelin where their 6th and 12th Armies were to cross the Dnepr river. The following day, after Schobert's Eleventh Army had crossed the Dnestr at Mogilev-Podol'skii and Soroki, the *Stavka* finally understood that the Southwestern and Southern Fronts were in real danger of being enveloped. Even then, however, it authorized the 6th, 12th and 18th Armies to withdraw to the Belaia Tserkov', Kitai-Gorod and Gaisin line, more than 100km (60 miles) west of the Dnepr, but not to the Dnepr river itself.[7] In addition, the *Stavka* ordered Tiulenev, the Southern Front commander, to dispatch Novosel'sky's 2nd Mechanized Corps to the Uman' region to halt the German advance into the Southern Front's rear. This measure, too, was half-hearted and too late, since Soviet forces abandoned Belaia Tserkov' on 18 July and most of the 6th, 12th and 18th Armies' new defensive line was already in German hands.[8]

Kleist's panzers approached Tarashche and Uman' on 21 July, deeply enveloping the 6th and 12th Armies' main forces.[9] Kirponos then ordered Kostenko to wheel his 26th Army to the southwest to protect Muzychenko's and Ponedelin's withdrawal. Kostenko's attack successfully tied down Kleist's III and XIV Motorized Corps until 25 July, but on 20 July the XXXXVIII Motorized Corps managed to break contact and advance toward Uman'. By day's end, it reached and captured Monastyrishche, severing the two armies' withdrawal routes. Only the approach of Novosel'sky's 2nd Mechanized Corps blocked the XXXXVII Motorized Corps' advance, preventing the motorized corps from linking up with Seventeenth Army and encircling all Soviet forces east of Vinnitsa.

However, by this time Muzychenko's and Ponedelin's already weakened armies were in mortal danger. On 21 July they numbered a total of 24 divisions and 1 airborne and 2 antitank brigades, and since 22 June they had suffered 46,844 casualties, including 27,667 men missing in action.[10] The armies' remaining 130,000 men were exhausted and almost out of all supplies. The two armies were equipped with over 1,000 guns and mortars and 384 tanks, but were running short of ammunition, fuel and transport. In short, given total German air superiority, they were no match for the 13 German divisions and 200 tanks that opposed them.[11]

Finally, the *Stavka* ordered the 6th and 12th Armies attacked eastward to link up with the 26th Army.[12] Concerned over the concerted breakout effort, Kleist himself travelled to XXXXVIII Motorized Corps and reinforced it with two additional infantry divisions and the SS 'Adolf Hitler' Motorized Regiment. The increased German resistance, severe personnel losses and critical ammunition shortages forced Muzychenko and Ponedelin to cease their breakout attempt. Ponedelin, who commanded the combined group, reported to the *Stavka* that he was 'in an extremely serious situation and on the verge of a complete loss of combat capability.'[13] His rifle divisions had only a fourth of their artillery and 1,000–4,000 men each. Pleading that the complex situation prevented resupply of the two armies, on 24 July Kirponos received *Stavka* permission to subordinate both to the Southern Front. The following day Tiulenev ordered the two armies to withdraw to the Zvenigorodka and Uman' line and then punch a hole though to the east, meaning that they had to penetrate the XXXXVIII Motorized Corps' armoured cordon.[14] At the time, a 100km (60-mile) gap still existed between the two armies and Smirnov's 18th Army to the southeast, which was undefended by German forces and could have been used as an escape route for the 6th and 12th Armies. However, neither Budenny (the commander of the Southwestern Direction Command) nor the *Stavka* understood the situation, and both insisted that the two armies break out to the east. A compliant Tiulenev issued the appropriate orders to armies that were clearly no longer capable of carrying out the mission.

The *Stavka*'s intransigence settled the 6th and 12th Armies' fate. Three days later Tiulenev reported to the *Stavka*, 'It is impossible to determine the situation in the 6th and 12th Armies precisely because of the absence of communications.'[15] Thereafter, it took 29 days for the *Stavka* to determine what actually happened to Group Ponedelin. In truth, Tiulenev was also preoccupied with the predicament faced by his 18th Army, whose flanks were also being enveloped. At the same time, the *Stavka* incorrectly judged that the German intended to sweep the 6th and 12th Armies aside so that its forces could reach and capture crossings over the Dnepr between Kiev and Cherkassy for a subsequent advance into the Donbas. Accordingly, on 28 July the *Stavka* once again ordered Kirponos and Tiulenev to prevent the German advance to the Dnepr.[16] However, refusing to conform to the *Stavka*'s expectations, Kleist's and Reichenau's forces proceeded to smash Ponedelin's two armies.

Group Ponedelin's stout resistance in the Uman' region halted Kleist's forces for almost eight days and prevented him from linking up with the Seventeenth Army. Fearing that the encircled force would escape to the southeast, on 29 July Kleist ordered Kempf's XXXXVIII Motorized Corps to advance toward Pervomaisk, bypassing Uman' from the east.[17] At the same time, the Stuelpnagel at Seventeenth Army turned his XXXXIX Mountain Corps to the southeast, giving Ponedelin's group the opportunity to escape. However, Tiulenev missed the opportunity as well and demanded that Ponedelin march east. On 1 August Muzychenko and Ponedelin radioed the *Stavka* and *front*:

> The situation has become critical. The encirclement of the 6th and 12th Armies is complete. The direct threat of the breakup of the 6th and 12th Armies' combat formation into two isolated segments centred at Babanka and Teklievka regions is at hand. There are no reserves. Please clear the way by committing new forces in the Ternovka and Novo-Arkhangel'sk sectors. There is no ammunition. Fuel is running out.[18]

By this time, Kostenko's 26th Army had withdrawn to the Dnepr, but was holding on to bridgeheads at Rzhishchev and Kanev, and Smirnov's 18th Army had begun to withdraw to the southeast away from Group Ponedelin. Ominously, Uman' fell into German hands.

The German trap snapped shut around Ponedelin's forces on 2 August when Kleist's 11th Panzer Division linked up with the Seventeenth Army's 101st Jager Division at Dobrianka southeast of Uman'. The same day, the 16th Panzer Division made contact with Hungarian forces at Pervomaisk, creating yet another smaller encirclement. Even then, Tiulenev did not realize that his forces were in two encirclements. Thinking only that mobile forces separated Ponedelin from safety, Tiulenev ordered him 'to destroy the penetrating enemy by active operations toward the east and occupy and firmly hold on to the Zvenigorodka, Brodetskoe,

Novo-Arkhangel'sk, Ternovka and Krasnopol'e line.'[19] In reality, two motorized corps of First Panzer Group (six divisions) and two infantry divisions were attacking Group Ponedelin from the east and part of the Sixth Army, the Seventeenth Army and the Hungarian mobile corps were attacking from the west and southwest.

Group Ponedelin was left to its own devices after 4 August, even though the Southern Front made a feeble attempt to supply it by air. On 6 August Kostenko's 6th Army tried to fight its way out to the east and Ponedelin's 12th Army to the south, but to no avail. After one last attempt to escape on 7 August, the forces suffered the fate of those who perished earlier at Minsk. Of the 129,500 men left in the two armies as of 20 July, according to Southern Front count, 11,000 survived the encirclement, although most of these were rear service units.[20] The Germans recorded capturing 107,000 officers and men, including Generals Ponedelin and Muzychenko, 4 corps commanders and 11 division commanders, 286 tanks and 953 guns.[21] Another two corps commanders and six division commanders perished in the fighting.[22] To cap the tragedy, a vengeful Stalin published *Stavka* Order No. 270, accusing several of the unfortunate captive generals of crimes against the Homeland (treason). Soon after, military tribunals sentenced them *in absentia* to be shot. The sentences against Ponedelin and N.K. Kirillov, the 13th Rifle Corps commander, were carried out after their return from German captivity.[23]

While Kleist's forces were lunging south and southeast in late July to clear the southern bank of the Dnepr and encircle the 6th and 12th Armies, Reichenau's Sixth Army pivoted northward to protect Army Group South's left flank. Reichenau's XXIX Army Corps faced Lieutenant-General A.A. Vlasov's newly raised 37th Army at Kiev and his LI and XVII Army Corps confronted Potapov's 5th Army in defenses ranging west of Kiev and south of the Pripiat' Marshes through the Korosten' Fortified Region to Olevsk. The *Stavka* repeatedly ordered Potapov to launch counterattacks against German forces threatening the Korosten' Fortified Region and, if possible, to assist the 6th and 12th Armies to the south. For example, on 28 July the *Stavka* ordered the Southwestern and Southern Fronts to mount a joint operation to 'disrupt the enemy offensive by active operations and prevent him from reaching the Dnepr River.' To do so, 'having halted the withdrawal of the 26th Army,' the Southwestern Front was to 'regroup its forces and prepare for an offensive in the general direction of Radomyshl' and Zhitomir' to link up with the Southern Front.[24]

However, the subsequent encirclement of the 6th and 12th Armies in the Uman' region, which was completed by 4 August, rendered the *Stavka*'s order superfluous. Instead, Potapov's 5th Army was forced to launch the attack on its own. It did so beginning on 4 August with Major-General M.A. Usenko's newly assigned 1st Airborne Corps supported by the 15th and 31st Rifle and 9th and 22nd Mechanized Corps.[25] By 8 August the counterstroke had ended with heavy Soviet losses and little to show for the effort. Worse still, the German XVII Army Corps seized Korosten. Within days, the 5th Army withdrew into the safety of the Kiev defenses. German forces followed closely behind and soon reached the banks of the Dnepr south of Kiev.

The failure of the Malin counterstroke and the destruction of the Soviet 6th and 12th Armies left a huge expanse of terrain on the central Ukraine virtually naked of Soviet defenders. While the *Stavka* hastened to deploy fresh armies (Vlasov's 37th and Lieutenant-General D.I. Riabyshev's 38th) to shore up its defenses along the Dnepr river from Kiev to Kremenchug, the Southern Front's weakened 9th and 18th Armies withdrew eastward toward the Dnepr with German forces in pursuit.[26]

As context to this immense struggle, on 19 July Hitler issued his Directive 33 and, four days later, an addendum that ordered the bulk of panzer forces removed from Army Group Centre during the next phase of the campaign to support successful attacks in the north and south. This decision produced a prolonged period of disagreement within the German command. Even those who were willing to delay a direct advance on Moscow were concerned that Hitler's plan would place still more strain on the armoured spearheads, denying them the rest and repairs they required to regain their combat effectiveness. Nevertheless, on 30 July Hitler issued Führer Directive No. 34, once again emphasizing the northern and southern axes at the expense of the Centre.

Based on his judgement that Army Group Centre had lost much of its 'offensive punch' in the Smolensk fighting, Zhukov advised the *Stavka* on 29 July that the Wehrmacht would likely resume its advance on Moscow, but 'only after liquidating the threat posed to its flank by the Central Front from the southwest.'[27] Zhukov recommended the *Stavka* reinforce the Central Front so that it could protect Kirponos's northern flank and Kirponos abandon Kiev and withdraw his forces back to the Dnepr. Stalin, however, objected since he did not appreciate the threat to Kiev and considered the proposal blasphemous given its likely negative impact on the alliance with and assistance from Great Britain and the United States. The proposal prompted Stalin to replace Zhukov as Chief of the General Staff with Shaposhnikov on 30 July and assign Zhukov to command the Reserve Front.[28]

Both Shaposhnikov and his deputy, A.M. Vasilevsky, appreciated the threat to the Southwestern Front and tried to convince Stalin of the necessity to withdraw across the Dnepr. However, Stalin was convinced the Germans would attack directly toward Moscow and, therefore, rejected their appeals.[29] It is now clear that the Soviet intelligence reports at least in part accorded with the OKH's intentions.

The Kiev Encirclement

The debate within the German camp over its Barbarossa strategy began in early August. On 7 August, Hitler, Rundstedt and Rumanian Head of State Antonescu met at Army Group South's headquarters in Berdichev. Convinced that Rundstedt's victory at Uman' meant that his army group had achieved its first strategic aim, and that Moscow and Leningrad would fall as planned in the autumn, an exuberant Hitler awarded Antonescu the Knight's Cross.[30] Hitler, however, was incorrect since Plan Barbarossa called for the destruction of all Soviet forces west of the Dnepr, a task the Wehrmacht had yet to achieve. This was why on 12 August the OKH ordered Rundstedt's army group to destroy all Soviet forces between Zaporozh'e and the mouth of the Dnepr to trap the Southern Front's 9th, 18th and Coastal Armies against the Black Sea.[31] In addition, northwest of Kiev, Potapov's 5th Army hung like a sword of Damocles over the flank of Reichenau's Sixth Army, on the one hand preventing it from seizing Kiev and on the other threatening Army Group Centre's right flank.

When Reichenau's forward elements reached the outskirts of Kiev on 6 August, they were halted by Vlasov's 37th Army, which consisted of all forces defending the Kiev Fortified Region. Two days later, Reichenau's army went on the defense, and on 12 August Vlasov's forces counterattacked and restored most the fortified region's forward defenses. That day, Hitler ordered Rundstedt to 'halt the offensive on Kiev. As soon as ammunition resupply permits, the city must be destroyed by air bombardment.' Reichenau then turned his forces against Potapov's 5th Army.

Arguments raged on within the OKW and OKH throughout August, while Army Group Centre improved its positions south of the Desna river and the Red Army launched heavy counterattacks against Army Group Centre near Smolensk and El'nia and against Army Group North at Staraia Russa. Hitler reacted to the Staraia Russa crisis on 15 August by ordering Army Group Centre to halt its advance on Moscow and dispatching the XXXIX Motorized Corps to the Leningrad region, which brought the weakened Third Panzer Group's advance to a screeching but temporary halt. On 18 August Halder presented Hitler with yet another plan to continue the advance on Moscow, but three days later Hitler rejected Halder's proposal, instead ordering the OKH to prepare a directive to Bock to turn part of his Army Group Centre to the south. The directive specified that the priority objective for the year was control of the Donets Basin, the Crimea and the area around Leningrad rather than Moscow. The next day Hitler berated the commander-in-chief, Field Marshal Walter von Brauchitsch, blaming him for the frequent changes in objective! Halder proposed that both he and von Brauchitsch resign, but the Field Marshal replied that Hitler would not accept the resignations. Hitler then dispatched Halder to Bock's headquarters in Borisov on 23 August to deliver the OKW directive personally.[32]

Hitler's directive caused a furore in Borisov. Guderian objected strenuously, and both he and Halder flew back to Hitler's headquarters at Rastenburg to argue their case with Hitler. The trip was in vain. Hitler rejected their appeals and on 24 August Guderian returned to his panzer group, ordered one of his corps to cover his flank against Eremenko's Briansk Front and turned the rest of Second Panzer Group toward the south.[33] Still convinced that his intelligence was correct, Stalin kept his attention focused on the Moscow axis.

Meanwhile, others tried to convince Stalin that the danger rested along the Kiev axis. Kirponos argued that this was the case on 18 August. Shortly thereafter, Zhukov, now Reserve Front commander, sent Stalin a telegram stating that the enemy was 'throwing all of his shock, mobile and tank units against the Central, Southwestern and Southern Fronts, while defending actively against the Western and Reserve Fronts.'[34] Zhukov proposed the *Stavka* deploy a large shock group into the Glukhov, Chernigov and Konotop regions to disrupt enemy plans. Stalin indeed heeded Kirponos and Zhukov's warnings. He did so by assigning Eremenko's new Briansk Front the mission of dealing with Guderian, but at the same time, he insisted that Kirponos defend Kiev. Stalin remained convinced that Eremenko could not only protect the Briansk axis but also destroy German forces threatening the Southwestern Front's flank and rear. Therefore, he ordered the Southwestern Direction High Command to defend the Dnepr river line stubbornly and 'hold on to Kiev at all costs.'[35]

Accordingly, on 19 August the *Stavka* altered its defenses in the Kiev region. First, it ordered Kirponos to withdraw Potapov's 5th

Army back across the Dnepr, where it was to construct defenses on its western bank, and to employ Vlasov's 37th Army to defend a tight bridgehead around Kiev on the river's western bank. It then formed and deployed Lieutenant-General K.P. Podlas's new 40th Army to man positions along the Desna river near Novgorod-Severskii between the 21st and 13th Armies and to defend against Guderian's threat from the north. By doing so, Stalin was requiring two rifle divisions and an airborne corps that had been severely weakened in earlier battles along the Dnepr to stand firm against two panzer divisions backed up by two motorized and one cavalry division. At the same time, farther south, Tiulenev was to complete withdrawing his forces eastward across the Dnepr. Despite the *Stavka's* prudent measures, none fully succeeded.

The withdrawal of Potapov's 5th Army to and across the Dnepr did not occur as smoothly as planned. Potapov planned to begin his withdrawal on 21 August, occupy a series of phase lines, and complete it on 25 August. However, during its course, the 37th Army's 27th Rifle Corps, deployed on Potapov's left flank, permitted the German LI Army Corps to gain a foothold over the ' Dnepr at Okuninovo, north of Kiev and east of Gornostaipol'. This compromised the defenses on Potapov's left flank the very moment his army occupied its new positions, and within days his forces had to withdraw to the River Desna. Worse still, by 26 August, the forward elements of Guderian's panzer group were approaching Shostka and Korop, threatening Podlas's 40th Army before it fully assembled and splitting apart the Briansk Front's 21st and 13th Armies.[36]

At the same time, Tiulenev's Southern Front also had difficulty in withdrawing its forces across the Dnepr river. On 18 August Red Army engineers blew up the dam and hydroelectric station at Dnepropetrovsk prematurely. The water level of the Dnepr south of Zaporozh'e rose precipitously and the river widened to as much as 1.5km, destroying the intended crossing sites of the 9th and 18th Armies. Tiulenev, however, overcame the challenge and moved most of his forces across the river by late on 22 August.

By the end of August, the Southwestern and Southern Front occupied contiguous defenses along the Dnepr from Kiev southward to the Black Sea. Tiulenev's Southern Front manned defenses from the mouth of the Dnepr northward past Zaporozh'e and Dnepropetrovsk to the Vorskla river. Cherevichenko's 9th and Smirnov's 18th Armies defended from the Black Sea to the Dnepr bend south of Zaporozh'e, and the newly formed 12th and 6th Armies, commanded by Major General I.V. Galanin and Lieutenant-General R.Ia. Malinovsky, respectively, defended the Zaporozh'e and Dnepropetrovsk sectors. Far to the west, the Lieutenant-General G.P. Sofronov's Coastal Army defended Odessa, which German Army Group South had bypassed and encircled during its race to the Dnepr. To the north, Kirponos's Southwestern Front defended with Potapov's 5th Army along the already penetrated Dnepr line, Vlasov's 37th Army protected Kiev, and Kostenko's 26th and Riabyshev's 38th Armies defended southward along the Dnepr from just south of Kiev to Perevolochnaia south of Kremenchug.

By this time, Army Group South's forces had also closed on the River Dnepr.[37] While Reichenau's Sixth Army covered the front north and south of Kiev, Stuelpnagel's Seventeenth Army deployed along the Dnepr from Cherkassy to south of Kremenchug. Kleist's First Panzer Group occupied the Dnepr bend opposite and south of Dnepropetrovsk, while the Rumanian Third and German Eleventh Army reached the Dnepr from opposite Nikopol' to the Black Sea. Rundstedt's army group now outnumbered the Southwestern and Southern Front two-fold in aircraft and more than four-fold in armour.

The most serious threat to the Southwestern Direction High Command, however, was Guderian's Second Panzer Group. Therefore, on 30 August Stalin assigned Eremenko the mission of destroying Guderian's panzer group, which by this time was approaching the Desna river.[38] In fact, by 3 September Guderian's forces had seized bridgeheads over the Desna near Korop and Novgorod–Severskii and were directly threatening Kirponos's rear area, despite Eremenko's best efforts.[39] Eremenko himself explained his lack of success by pointing out the 'unsteadiness' of his troops and received *Stavka* approval to deploy blocking detachments to increase his forces' resoluteness.[40] However, even these draconian measures did not improve the situation and on 7 September Guderian's panzer reached Konotop.

Faced with Guderian's seemingly unstoppable advance, late on 7 September, Shaposhnikov and Vasilevsky once again tried to convince Stalin of the necessity of withdrawing Kirponos's forces. By this time, they argued, Kirponos was likely to encounter major problems even if he began to withdraw. Vasilevsky later described Stalin's reaction, 'The conversation was tough and uncompromising. Stalin reproached us, saying that like Budenny we took the line of least resistance – retreating instead of beating the enemy.'[41] Although the two General Staff officers convinced Stalin to permit Kirponos to withdraw his 5th and 37th Armies to better defenses, Vasilevsky added:

> In other words, this was a half-way measure. The mere mention
> of the urgent need to abandon Kiev threw Stalin into a rage and
> he momentarily lost his self-control. We evidently did not have
> sufficient will-power to withstand these outbursts of uncontrollable
> rage or a proper appreciation of our responsibility for the
> impending catastrophe on the Southwestern direction.[42]

While fierce fighting raged along the Southwestern Front's right flank in early September, the situation Kirponos faced further south was also deteriorating. The difficult terrain east of the Dnepr and north of Kiev, the strong resistance by Potapov's 5th Army and German logistical difficulties slowed the German Sixth and Second Armies' advance, prompting fears on Rundstedt's part that the Red Army forces would escape eastward. Therefore, on 28 and 29 August he ordered Kleist's First Panzer Group and the Sixth and Seventeenth Armies to cross the Dnepr in as many sectors as possible without concern for their flanks. The Seventeenth

Army's LII Army Corps captured a bridgehead at Derievka just south of Kremenchug on 31 August and by 10 September had moved the bulk of the LII and LV and part of the XI Army Corps across the river.[43]

Understanding the threat that the German bridgehead near Kremenchug posed to his forces, Budenny, commander of the Southwestern Direction Command, immediately ordered the 38th Army, now commanded by Major General-of-Tank-Forces N.V. Feklenko, to liquidate the threat; however, Feklenko's army was too weak to do so. Worse still, on 4 September Rundstedt ordered Kleist's panzer group to enter and expand the bridgehead. General Hans Hube's 16th Panzer Division (of the XXXXVIII Motorized Corps) began crossing the Dnepr on 11 September, and the rest of his division completed the passage the following night in a pouring rain. The next morning it attacked north, smashed Colonel P.P. Chubashev's defending 297th Rifle Division and by evening approached Khorol', 20km to the north, while the 14th Panzer prepared to join its northward thrust. Hube's division reached Lubna, 30km (18 miles) deep, at midday on 13 September, where a scratch force of anti-aircraft artillerymen and a home defense detachment halted its advance. Meanwhile, the 9th Panzer Division was tracking in the 16th Panzer's wake and the 14th Panzer Division had advanced 20km (12 miles) to the Khorol' river on Hube's left flank. By this time, Kleist's advancing panzers had carved a 20km-wide wedge between the defending 38th and 6th Armies.

To the north, impending disaster loomed ever larger for Kirponos. On 10 September Kirponos reported by telegraph to the *Stavka*, 'The enemy tank group has penetrated to Romny and Gaivoron. The 21st and 40th Armies are not able to liquidate this group. They request that forces be immediately transferred from the Kiev Fortified Region to the path of the enemy advance and a general withdrawal of *front* forces.'[44] In a telegraph exchange with Shaposhnikov late on 10 September, Kirponos again requested permission to withdraw his *front* to the east. Shaposhnikov responded that it was necessary to continue to fight along existing positions. Knowing full well that the 3rd and 4th Panzer Divisions were in the Romny region, Shaposhnikov labeled it a 'sortie' and declared that the *front* could cope with it by moving forces from the Dnepr line. However, he forbade the transfer of forces from Kiev even though Vlasov's 37th Army was the *front's* strongest and the Germans had clearly decided not to storm Kiev from the west.[45]

After hearing of Kirponos's exchange with Shaposhnikov, early on 11 September Budenny telegraphed Stalin from Poltava, stating, 'The withdrawal of the Southwestern Front is completely imminent,' and that any delay would only lead to 'the loss of forces and a huge quantity of logistical units.'[46] He added that the withdrawn forces were necessary to prevent an even larger encirclement. That day, Stalin informed Kirponos, 'Do not abandon Kiev and do not blow up the bridges without *Stavka* permission.'[47] Two days later, the impending disaster loomed ever larger. Late on 13 September, General Walter Model's 3rd Panzer Division from Guderian's Second Panzer Group approached Lokhvitsa from the north, leaving a gap of only 40km (24 miles) between his forces and the 16th Panzer Division's tanks approaching Lubna.[48] Although Kirponos's entire *front* (the 5th, 37th, 26th and 38th Armies and part of the 21st Army) was almost entirely encircled in a 200km (120-mile) deep sack anchored on Kiev and west of Lokhvitsa and Lubna, they still had an opportunity to escape eastward through the gap. However, the *Stavka* categorically forbade them to do so and, on 13 September, appointed Timoshenko to replace the hapless Budenny as the commander of the Southwestern Direction High Command.[49] Even then, Stalin and the *Stavka* overestimated the Briansk Front's capability for forestalling disaster.

Timoshenko's first act was to assure the *Stavka* that his command could hold Kiev. Despite Timoshenko's bravado, during the day on 13 September, Model's 3rd and Hube's 16th Panzer Divisions captured Lubna and Lokhvitsa, and the 9th Panzer Division captured Mirgorod to the southeast and began establishing blocking positions at the eastern end of the 40km (24-mile) gap between Guderian's and Kleist's forces. That night, Major-General V.I. Tupikov, the Southwestern Front's chief of staff, radioed Shaposhnikov, 'The catastrophe that is clear to you will occur in a matter of several days.'[50] Stalin responded to Shaposhnikov:

> Major-General Tupikov has submitted a panicky report to the General Staff. On the contrary, the situation requires the maintenance of extreme coolness and steadfastness on the part of commanders at all levels. Avoiding panic, it is necessary to take all measures to hold occupied positions and especially to hold on to the flanks. You must compel Kuznetsov and Potapov to cease their withdrawal. You must instill the entire front with the necessity to fight on stubbornly, and, without looking back, it is necessary to fulfill the orders given to you by Stalin on 11 September.[51]

However, the unthinkable had already occurred. On 16 September the German cordon around Southwestern Front closed when Guderian's and Kleist's forces linked up near Lokhvitsa, trapping the entire Southwestern Front between the Second and Sixth Armies in the west and the Second and First Panzer Groups in the east. Worse still, the fall rains turned the Russian roads into canals of mud. Despite reduced Luftwaffe air support and the haggard condition of Guderian's forces, the fate of Kirponos's *front* was sealed.[52] As the spearheads closed, Timoshenko and his commissar Khrushchev finally gave Kirponos permission to withdraw his forces from the Kiev region new defenses along the Psel' river line, but did so orally though their chief of staff, Bagramian. Recalling Stalin's strict prohibition against doing so, Kirponos refused to give the orders until written confirmation arrived. Since communications had lapsed between Timoshenko's command and Kirponos, Kirponos finally received the much-awaited confirmation from Shaposhnikov late on the night of 17-18 September, but only to abandon Kiev and not to withdraw to the Psel' river.[53]

Only hours before, Kirponos decided to act on his own volition and ordered the 5th, 21st, 26th and 37th Armies to attack eastward through the German armoured cordon, while the 38th and 40th Armies protected the flanks of the cordon by attacking toward Romny and Lubna. However, an organized withdrawal was impossible since Kirponos's forces were under assault from all sides. Suffering immense casualties, deprived of supplies and without any command and control, Kirponos's forces were chopped into separate isolated segments and destroyed piecemeal by the tightening German cordon. The remnants of Kostenko's 26th Army struggled the longest, fighting encircled in the Orzhitsa region up to 26 September. Meanwhile, Vlasov's 37th Army held out encircled in two regions, 10-15km (6-9 miles) and 40-50km (24-30 miles) southeast of Kiev until 21-23 September. The Piriatin Group, composed of Potapov's 5th and Lieutenant-General V.I. Kuznetsov's 21st Armies fought on until 25 September. Thereafter, a portion of the 5th Army with Potapov's headquarters joined up with Kirponos's staff and tried to penetrate to Piriatin, while the armies' remnants tried to escape the trap as they could in small groups.[54]

While the drama played out in the swamps and marshlands east of Kiev, the *Stavka* dispatched frantic messages, demanding Kirponos clarify the situation:

> *Stavka VGK* Directive No. 002202 to the Southwestern Front
> Military Council, 21 September 1941

> The *Stavka* of the Supreme High Command *demands* that you report immediately:
>
> 1. Whether or not your units have abandoned Kiev?
>
> 2. If Kiev has been abandoned, whether or not the bridges been blown up?
>
> 3. If the bridges have been blown up, then who will vouch for the fact the bridges have been blown up?
>
> Shaposhnikov[55]

The response was deafening silence. Having lost all communications with its subordinate armies, Kirponos's headquarters and accompanying 5th Army troops managed to reach Driukovshchina Farm, 15km (9 miles) southwest of Lokhvitsa late on 20 September. There, the 3rd Panzer Division attacked the column, capturing General V.N. Sotensky, the 5th Army's artillery commander, and driving the remainder of the column into nearby Shumeikovo Woods. Kirponos, Potapov, their principal staff officers, and about 2,000 troops fought on for several hours, but Kirponos, Tupikov and many other perished and Potapov and the remaining forces fell captive to the Germans.[56]

Certainly, the German Kiev encirclement was not airtight and for days after the German trap snapped shut small groups of Red Army troops managed to escape the cauldron, including Budenny, Timoshenko, and Khrushchev. Nevertheless, the Kiev disaster was an unprecedented defeat for the Red Army, exceeding even the Minsk tragedy of June–July 1941. On 1 September the Southwestern Front numbered 752–760,000 men (850,000 including reserves and rear service organs), 3,923 guns and mortars, 114 tanks, and 167 combat aircraft. The ensuing encirclement contained 452,700 men, 2,642 guns and mortars, and 64 tanks, of which scarcely 15,000 escaped from the encirclement by 2 October. Overall, the Southwestern Front suffered 700, 544 casualties, including 616,304 killed, captured, or missing during the Battle for Kiev.[57] As a result, four Soviet field armies (5th, 37th, 26th, and 21st), consisting of 43 divisions, virtually ceased to exist. Like the Western Front before it, the Southwestern Front had to be recreated from scratch. In the meantime, the door was wide open to the Khar'kov and Donbas regions, as well as the southern approaches to Moscow, a fact that the German command soon appreciated and exploited.

While the high drama was playing out at Korosten', Uman', and Kiev, the German Eleventh and Rumanian Fourth Armies drove the Southern Front's 9th and 18th Armies eastward through the southern Ukraine. By 7 August the advancing Axis forces had captured, in succession, Kotovsk, Pervomaisk, Kirovograd and Vosnesensk, trying but failing to cut off the Southern Front's withdrawal. Although the 9th and 18th Armies escaped to the relative safely of the River Dnepr, beginning on 8 August, the two axis armies cut off and besieged Sofronov's Coastal Army in the port of Odessa. Supported by the Black Sea Fleet, Sofronov's force consisted of one rifle division, two naval infantry brigades, several sailors' detachments, and six destroyer detachments raised locally. Within days, Soviet forces erected three fortified defensive belts around the city and many barricades within, protected by naval gunfire.

On 19 August the *Stavka* organized the so-called Odessa Defensive Region made up of the Coastal Army and Odessa Naval Base under the command of Admiral G.V. Zhukov.[58] In addition to holding off the Rumanian Fourth Army for more than a month, on 22 September the defenders mounted and amphibious and airborne assault at Grigor'evka that expanded the defense perimeter 5-8km (3-4.8 miles).[59] Nonetheless, in late September, when German Eleventh Army began an invasion of the Crimea, the *Stavka* ordered the Odessa garrison to evacuate and join the defense of Crimea. Subsequently, from 2-16 October the Black Sea Fleet evacuated the force fully intact to Sevastopol', although the gallant escapees were soon encircled once again, this time terminally in that famous Crimean city. Nevertheless, the defense of Odessa offered inspiration to the Soviet population and Red Army at a time when it was most needed.

Reflections

The prolonged struggle in the Ukraine with its dramatic and catastrophic encirclements at Uman' in late July and at Kiev in September seriously damaged the Red Army and destroyed the coherence of Soviet strategic defenses. Over a period of almost three months, German eliminated upwards of 1 million soldiers, the entire Southwestern Front, and the better part of the Southern Front from the Red Army's order of battle. By late September, Kiev and the entire Ukraine eastward to the Dnepr river were in German hands, and German forces had captured Poltava north of the Dnepr bend and were pressing into the Crimean peninsular.

Numerous historians have since argued that, tangentially, the Kiev encirclement produced distinctly positive results for the Soviet Union. First and foremost, they claim that the stubborn defense of Kiev during July and August, particularly by Potapov's 5th Army, convinced Hitler to shift his main strategic offensive effort to the south to destroy a more lucrative target – the Southwestern Front – and capture the economically vital Ukraine. Further, they argue, Guderian's southward turn and subsequent operations east of Kiev delayed the German advance on Moscow for roughly one month, perhaps fatally.

While true in part, it is only part of the answer, since an impatient Hitler also diverted sizeable forces from Army Group Centre to assist in the capture of Leningrad. In fact, Hitler decided to complete his self-ordained tasks at Leningrad and in the Ukraine at least in part due to the fierce Soviet resistance Army Group Centre encountered at and east of Smolensk along the Moscow axis. Thus, in retrospect, the delay in Army Group Centre's advance along the Moscow axis seemed to pave the way for the subsequent German defeat at Moscow.

At the same time, however, Guderian's Kiev diversion also removed from the battlefield most of the impediments to German Operation Typhoon. First and foremost, it eliminated four armies and over 600,000 men that, had they not been destroyed, would have threatened Army Group Centre's extended right flank as it advanced on Moscow. Furthermore, by late September Timoshenko's Western, Zhukov's Reserve, and Eremenko's Briansk Fronts had shot their bolts in futile and costly offensives north and south of Smolensk. If unaided from other quarters, these severely weakened forces could scarcely resist the renewed German offensive onslaught. Worse still, Guderian's path toward Moscow via Briansk was also virtually clear. Finally, the destruction of the Southwestern Front and dismemberment of the Southern Front left Rundstedt's army group virtually unopposed as they began their equally dramatic advance toward Khar'kov and across the southern Ukraine through the Donbas to Rostov.

In every respect, the Wehrmacht's achieved signal victories at Uman' and Kiev, victories that in no way diminished German hopes or capabilities for success in Operation Barbarossa. If Barbarossa were to fail, the blame did not belong to Hitler's Kiev venture.

VIAZ'MA, BRIANSK, TIKHVIN AND ROSTOV
30 SEPTEMBER—30 OCTOBER

Operation Typhoon

Undeniably, the Wehrmacht had won an unprecedented series of spectacular victories during the first three months of Operation Barbarossa. By 30 September it had advanced over 800km (480 miles) deep into the Soviet Union along a front of 1,650km (990 miles). In the process it destroyed two Red Army *fronts* at Minsk and Kiev, savaged three others, captured Smolensk and Kiev, besieged Leningrad, and was poised to strike at Moscow, the heart of the Soviet State. Despite these victories, however, in early fall Hitler's Barbarossa objectives – to capture Moscow by 15 August and end the war by 1 October – remained unfulfilled. Leningrad was still in Red Army hands and Moscow and Rostov remained over 300km (180 miles) distant. Nevertheless, Hitler was confident that victory was at hand. On 3 October 1941, the day after he unleashed his forces for the final drive on Moscow, Hitler announced triumphantly, 'The enemy has been broken and will never rise again.'[1] Given his army's recent victories, few including the Soviets, questioned his optimism.

On 6 September Hitler signed the document he believed would seal the Soviet Union's fate. Führer Directive No. 35 declared:

The initial operational successes against enemy forces between the Army Group South's and Centre's adjoining flanks and additional successes in encircling enemy forces in the Leningrad region, have created the prerequisites for conducting a decisive operation against Army Group Timoshenko, which is conducting unsuccessful offensive operations on Army Group Centre's front. It must be destroyed decisively before the onset of winter within the limited time indicated in existing orders... To this end we must concentrate all of the efforts of ground and air forces earmarked for the operation, including those that can be freed up from the flanks and transferred in timely fashion.[2]

The directive required the Wehrmacht to attack decisively along all three strategic axes, destroy enemy forces before the onset of winter, capture the Crimea, Kiev, Khar'kov, and Leningrad, and link up with the Finnish Karelian Army. Most important, the directive shifted the German main effort back to the Moscow axis. There, no later than the end of September, Army Group Centre was to:

Launch an operation against Army Group Timoshenko as quickly as possible so that we can go on the offensive in the general direction of Viaz'ma and destroy the enemy located in the region east of Smolensk by a double envelopment by powerful panzer forces concentrated on the flanks.

To that end, form two shock groups: the first – on the southern flank, presumably in the region southeast of Roslavl' with an attack axis to the northeast. The composition of the group [will include] forces subordinate to Army Group Centre and the 5th and 2nd Panzer Divisions, which will be freed up to fulfill that mission; the second – in the Ninth Army's sector with its attack axis presumably through Belyi. In so far as possible, this group will consist of large Army Group Centre formations.

After destroying the main mass of Timoshenko's group of forces in this decisive encirclement and destruction operation,

Army Group Centre is to begin pursuing enemy forces along the Moscow axis, while protecting its right flank to the Oka river and its left to the upper reaches of the Volga.[3]

Pursuant to Hitler's directive, on 16 September Bock, the commander of Army Group Centre, issued his directive for the capture of Moscow and assigned the codename 'Typhoon' to the operation.[4] While Hitler ordered two thrusts toward Moscow (by the Third and Fourth Panzer Groups), Bock capitalized on the recent Kiev victory by adding a third, an advance by Guderian's Second Panzer Group from Shostka through Orel toward Moscow from the southwest. Guderian's thrust offered the opportunity to carry out a second major encirclement operation against Soviet forces deployed in the Briansk region. If successful, the three-pronged advance would completely liquidate all three Red Army *fronts* (Western, Reserve, and Briansk) defending the approaches to Moscow, leaving the city utterly defenseless.

To this end, in late September the OKH transferred the headquarters and most of the Fourth Panzer Group's divisions from Army Group North to Army Group Centre. This concentrated the bulk of German mechanized forces (three panzer groups) on a 400km (240-mile) front, with Hoth's Third Panzer Group in the north, Hoepner's Fourth in the Centre, and Guderian's Second in the south. Initially, Bock's plan required the Third and Fourth Panzer Groups, under the operational control of German Ninth and Fourth Armies, respectively, to encircle Soviet forces in the Viaz'ma region, thereby tearing a gap in the Western Front and clearing the main highway to Moscow.[5] Guderian's Second Panzer Group, which had been weakened both by the Kiev operation and the transfer of some units to Fourth Panzer Group, would attack to the northeast through the Briansk area toward Tula in cooperation with Second Army.[6] Strauss's Ninth, Kluge's Fourth, and Colonel-General Maximilian von Weich's Second Armies were to liquidate encircled Soviet forces and the Second Air Fleet was to provide air support.

Once assembled, the German assault force numbered 1,929,406 men excluding the Luftwaffe personnel, organized into 3 armies, 3 panzer groups, and 78 divisions, including 14 panzer and 8 motorized divisions. This force fielded 14,000 artillery pieces, over 1,000 tanks, and 1,390 combat aircraft.[7] It was the largest armada the Wehrmacht had yet assembled.

Three Red Army *fronts* defended the 800km (480-mile) sector opposite Army Group Centre. The Western Front, consisting of the 22nd, 29th, 30th, 19th, 16th, and 20th Armies, defended the sector from Lake Seliger to south of Iartsevo. Its commander was the 43-year-old Colonel-General I.S. Konev, the former 19th Army commander, who had assumed command of the Western Front on 10 September from Timoshenko when the latter was assigned command of the Southwestern Direction. The Reserve Front, commanded by Marshal Budenny, who had replaced Zhukov when Stalin dispatched the latter to Leningrad on 10 September, consisted of six armies arrayed in depth between north of El'nia and Frolovka east of Roslavl'. Rakutin's 24th Army and Major-General P.P. Sobennikov's 43rd Army occupied forward positions along the Desna river south of Konev's forces, and the 31st, 49th, 32nd, and 33rd occupied second echelon positions 35km (21 miles) to the east protecting the approaches to Viaz'ma. The Briansk Front, under Eremenko's command, consisted of the 50th, 3rd, and 13th Armies and Operational Group Ermakov, which were deployed from east of Roslavl' southward to the Seim river. The three *fronts*, which comprised 40 percent of the Red Army's forces between the Baltic and Black Seas, numbered 1,250,000 men, supported by 7,600 guns and mortars, 990 tanks, and 667 combat aircraft.[8]

The divisions assigned to all three *fronts* were a mixture of veteran units worn down in previous battles and new, poorly trained and equipped People's Volunteer formations. Most rifle divisions were at half-strength (5-7,000 men) and many lacked their necessary artillery and machineguns. The 193,000 replacements the three *fronts* received to make up for previous losses fell far short of requirements. Only 45 of Konev's 479 tanks were new models, and all three *fronts* had severe shortages in trained officers, modern aircraft, and effective anti-aircraft and antitank weapons.[9] Except for a reserve in Konev's *front*, the available tanks and other weapons were widely dispersed, and a continuing shortage of motor vehicles made the defenders far less maneuverable than the attackers.

The complex command structure and incessant reshuffling of commanders between the *fronts* and direction commands fostered a climate of confusion and uncertainty. All of these headquarters were short on trained staff officers and long-range radios. In any event, the widespread fear of German signals intercept operations made many commanders avoid radios, relying on liaison officers to communicate their desires to higher and lower headquarters. Needless to say, this system was slow and tenuous, and communications broke down rapidly once the battle began.

The *Stavka*'s defensive concept required the three *fronts* to erect deeply echeloned defenses to prevent German forces from advancing on Moscow. The heaviest defenses were along the Smolensk-Moscow road (the Minsk Highway) and the Roslavl'-Moscow road (the Warsaw Highway). The defending forces were arrayed in two groupings, the most important of which consisted of the Western and Reserve Fronts' 12 armies protecting the Moscow axis. To the south, the Briansk Front's three armies and Group Ermakov defended the approaches to Moscow along the Briansk and Orel axes. The entire three-*front* force had 11 armies and an operational group in first echelon and 4 armies in second echelon.[10]

The *Stavka* had begun construction defensive works on the approaches to Moscow in early July using military engineers, construction troops, and civilian levies. The forward defense line, extending along the Desna and Sudost' rivers west of Viaz'ma, became the forward edge of the Western, Reserve, and Briansk Fronts' defense in August. To the east, the Rzhev–Viaz'ma Defense Line consisted of two separate belts, the first extending Lake Seligar through Selizharov and Olenino to Dorogobuzh and the second 35-45km (21-27 miles) to the east. The most important defense system west of Moscow was the Mozhaisk Defense Line, which the *Stavka* began erecting on 16 July. This line's main belt was anchored on four fortified regions at Volokolamsk, Mozhaisk, Maloiaroslavets, and Kaluga and was protected by a second belt several kilometres to the west. Both defense lines consisted of field rather than concrete and steel fortifications, and by 30 September both were only 40-50% complete.

None of the three *fronts* were particularly well prepared to conduct a skillful defense since all had been actively engaged in offensive operations through mid-September. On 10 September the *Stavka* ordered the Western Front to 'go over to the defense, firmly dig in, and withdraw six-seven divisions into reserve at the expense of secondary axes and the firm defense in order to create a powerful maneuver group for an offensive in the future.'[11] Konev proceeded to form a reserve that was larger than a normal army, a main defensive belt, and a security belt 4-20km (2.4-12 miles) deep.[12]

After receiving intelligence reports during the last 10 days of September concerning an impending German offensive, on 27 September the *Stavka* warned the Western and Briansk Fronts, 'the course of combat with the enemy has made it apparent that our forces are still not prepared for a serious offensive operation.'[13] It then specified precisely what was to be done to prepare an adequate defense. However, Konev had anticipated the order and took preventative measures such as intensifying reconnaissance, strengthening antitank and anti-aircraft defenses, and ordering preparation of an artillery counter-preparation in the 16th and 19th Armies' sectors to disrupt any enemy offensive. Eremenko began issuing similar orders on 28 September.[14] Nevertheless, as one recent Russian source put it, 'the *Stavka* failed to divine German intentions along the Moscow axis. It failed to concentrate its forces along the Germans' intended main attack axes, it issued its warning of an impending attack too late, and when it did, it never ordered the Reserve Front to prepare its defenses.'[15] As late as 29 September, Stalin directed the chief of the General Staff to inform Red Army forces how to organize and conduct offensive operations.[16] The *front* commanders too shared some of the blame for what resulted by accepting the *Stavka*'s guidance when intelligence told them to do otherwise.[17]

Viaz'ma and Briansk

Guderian's Second Panzer Group began its thrust along the Orel axis on 30 September, and Army Group Centre's assault followed on 2 October along the Viaz'ma axis. The mobility differential between German and Soviet forces became apparent the moment Operation Typhoon began. Guderian's XXXXVII and XXIV Motorized Corps struck Group Ermakov on the Briansk Front's left wing just as Ermakov was preparing an attack of his own toward Glukhov. Unprepared for defense, Ermakov's five divisions withdrew in disorder, exposing the flanks of the two divisions defending the left flank of Major-General A.M. Gorodniansky's 13th Army. By day's end, Guderian's spearheads had driven a 15-20km (3-13-mile) deep wedge between Gorodniansky's and Ermakov's forces.[18] At that time, however, Eremenko's headquarters assessed that the attack was only a diversion mounted by a single corps and that the main attack would occur later along the Briansk axis in the Second Army's sector. Eremenko so informed the *Stavka*, leaving his left flank forces to their own devices.[19]

Ermakov's group launched a counterattack to close the breech on 1 October, but the effort failed because he committed his forces piecemeal along several axes and without proper armour and air support. By noon, Lemelsen's XXXXVII Motorized Corps had captured Sevsk and wheeled to the north, while Geyr's XXIV Motorized Corps penetrated 80km (48 miles) toward Orel. By day's end, the thrust had cut off two of Gorodniansky's divisions and separated Group Ermakov from the rest of the Briansk Front.

Although Eremenko was now convinced that Guderian's thrust was not a diversion, the quiet that reigned elsewhere along the front calmed his fears. He notified the *Stavka* that the situation was not critical and ordered Ermakov to renew his counterattacks toward Sevsk.[20]

After a short artillery preparation laid a dense smokescreen along the front, at first light on 2 October, Bock's massive main force sprung into action along the 600km (360-mile) front from the Western Dvina to the Desna. Shortly before the attack, Hitler declared to his assembled troops:

> Today begins the last great decisive battle of this year. In it we will destroy the enemy and, in so doing, England, the instigator of this whole war… We are thus lifting from Germany and Europe the danger that has hovered over the continent ever since the times of the Huns and later the Mongol invasion.[21]

By day's end on 2 October, Hoth's Third Panzer Group had shattered Soviet defenses at the junction of Lukin's 19th Army and Khomenko's 30th Army and advanced 5–10km (3–6 miles) into the depths. South of the Warsaw Highway, Hoepner's 12 divisions likewise smashed the defenses of Sobennikov's 43rd Army, penetrated 40km (24 miles), and struck the defenses of General D.P. Onuprieko's 33rd Army in the Reserve Front's second echelon. Konev unleashed his artillery counter-preparation against Hoth's armoured spearheads and began assembling reserves to parry the German armoured strike. He released three rifle divisions and a motorized group to Khomenko and ordered him to restore the situation.[22] To the south, Eremenko moved part of his *front*'s reserve to the Nerussa river to block Guderian's advance. However, all of these measures were in vain, since the regrouping was too slow and the advancing German panzers were already too deep into the Soviet defenses.

The *Stavka*, however, was preoccupied with the situation to the south along the Orel, Kursk, and Khar'kov axis, which it considered most dangerous. On 1 October Stalin ordered the Reserve Front to transfer Lieutenant-General I.G. Zakharkin's 49th Army by rail to protect this axis. In addition, the next day it ordered Major-General D.D. Leliushenko's newly forming 1st Guards Rifle Corps, supported by a special aviation group, to liquidate enemy forces penetrating from Glukhov through Sevsk toward Orel.[23]

The situation along the Moscow axis worsened sharply on 3 October as German forces increased the depth of their penetration to 50km (30 miles) in the Western Front's sector and 80km (48 miles) in the Reserve Front's sector. To the south Guderian's panzers were approaching Orel, 200km (120 miles) deep, prompting Guderian to note, 'Our seizure of the town took the enemy so completely by surprise that the electric trams were still working as our tanks drove in.'[24] Simultaneously, the XXXXVII Motorized Corps' 17th and 18th Panzer Divisions slashed northward toward Karachev across the rear of Gorodniansky's 13th Army and into the rear area of Major-General Ia.G. Kreizer's 3rd Army, threatening to encircle the entire Briansk Front. Eremenko responded by counterattacking toward Seredina Buda with the 6th and 298th Rifle Divisions in an attempt to halt the XXXXVII Motorized Corps' advance and ordering Group Ermakov to attack eastward to protect Dmitriev-L'govskii. Hard pressed from front, flank, and rear, at day's end Eremenko requested but was denied permission by Shaposhnikov to withdraw to new defenses.[25]

The situation was no better in the Western and Reserve Fronts' sectors. The 3 October OKH daily summary noted that, late in the day, Hoth's Third Panzer Group 'penetrated to the Dnepr east of Kholm'-Zhirkovskii and captured two undestroyed bridges. South of the town a tank battle is raging with approaching Russian tank units.'[26] This meant that the panzer group had driven a wedge into the defenses of Major-General S.V. Vishnevsky's 32nd Army in Konev's second echelon. The complete penetration of Khomenko's 30th and Lukin's 19th Armies and the arrival of German forces at the Dnepr threatened Konev's rear area as well. In response, although heavily damaged, Soviet forces attempted to strike back, primarily with an operational group under the command of Lieutenant-General I.V. Boldin, Konev's deputy, who had performed the same mission for the Western Front in late June.[27] Boldin's operational group consisted of the 126th and 152nd Rifle and 101st Motorized Divisions and the 126th and 128th Tank Brigades. On 3 October, while the 30th Army's 207th Motorized and 242nd Rifle Divisions counterattacked southward from Belyi against Hoth's right flank, Boldin's 128th Tank Brigade struck Hoth's forces from the south.

Boldin committed the remainder of his force on 4 October, precipitating heavy fighting that slowed but did not halt Hoth's advance in the 19th and 32nd Armies' sectors.[28] To the south, Hoepner's panzers completed destroying Sobennikov's 43rd Army, dispersed Onuprienko's 33rd Army, turned the left flank of Major-General A.N. Ershakov's 20th and Rakutin's 24th Armies, and tore a 100–115km (60–69 mile) gap between the Reserve and Briansk Fronts. By day's end, the 10th and 2nd Panzer Divisions were lunging toward Viaz'ma and Iukhnov deep in the Reserve and Western Fronts' rear areas. Konev later recalled:

> On 4 October I reported to Stalin about the situation in the Western Front and about the enemy penetration of the Reserve Front... and also about the threat of a large enemy grouping reaching our forces' rear area... Stalin listened to me, however, made no decision. Communications were disrupted and further conversation ceased.[29]

Stalin's decision not to order a withdrawal played into the Wehrmacht's hands. As Konev's and Budenny's forces continued to cling to their defenses between the two penetration sectors, Hoth's and Hoepner's armoured spearheads approached to within 45km (15 miles) of Viaz'ma in the deep Soviet rear. Konev, however, did not sit idly by. Late on 5 October he ordered Group Boldin to block the German advance on Viaz'ma from the north and Rokossovsky's 16th Army to do the same from the south.[30]

Less than an hour later, Shaposhnikov informed Konev that 'The *Stavka VGK* has permitted you to begin withdrawing tonight in accordance with your request.'[31] Similar orders went to the Reserve and Briansk Fronts. On the same day, Stalin directed Zhukov to return to Moscow from Leningrad and ordered reserves from the Northwestern and Southwestern Fronts and the depth of the country to assemble at Moscow.

Early on 6 October, Konev ordered Rokossovsky's 16th and Lukin's 19th Armies to begin withdrawing toward Viaz'ma, followed the next day by his other armies.[32] Once assembled north of Viaz'ma, Rokossovsky's army was to protect both the northern and southern approaches to the city. However, the deteriorating situation and Rokossovsky's untenable position made it impossible for him to fulfill Konev's utterly unrealistic order.[33] Late on 6 October Rokossovsky received word that Viaz'ma had fallen to the Germans.[34]

If the looming disaster in the Viaz'ma region was not bad enough, Guderian's 17th Panzer Division approached the city of Briansk late on 6 October and captured the headquarters of Eremenko's Briansk Front, 11km (6.6 miles) south of the city. After a sharp firefight, the *front's* operational, intelligence, and communications departments escaped northeast, ultimately reaching Belev by circuitous route. With only his adjutant, after several hectic days of flight, Eremenko managed to reach the 3rd Army headquarters, where he continued to fight encircled with only one army at his disposal. During the next two days, the 17th Panzer Division captured Briansk and the 18th Panzer Division linked up with Second Army's forces near Zhizdra, northeast of Briansk, in effect encircling Kreizer's 3rd and Gorodniansky's 13th Armies (with Eremenko) south of the city and Petrov's 50th Army to the north.[35]

Farther north, as ordered, the 19th, 20th, and 24th Armies began withdrawing from their forward defenses on 6 October as ordered, protected by rear guards. While Lukin's 19th and Ershakov's 20th Armies withdrew in fairly good order, the Germans encircled and destroyed large chunks of Rakutin's

24th Army in several small encirclements east and northeast of El'nia. By the morning of 7 October, German forces had erected blocking positions west of Viaz'ma entrapping the 16th, 19th, 20th, 24th, and part of the 32nd Armies in the Viaz'ma caldron west of the city. The next day, the Western, Reserve, and most of the Briansk Fronts' armies all faced the same gruesome fate. Elated by Bock's initial success, the German radio announced Hitler's declaration that, 'The enemy has been broken and will never rise again.'[36] German propaganda posters soon proudly proclaimed, 'Penetration of the Eastern Front's Centre!', 'The Outcome of the March to the East has been Decided!' and 'The Last Combat-capable Soviet Divisions are Sacrificed!'[37] While it remained to be seen whether these words were prophetic, the initial indications were indeed encouraging.

The encirclement of its forward forces struck Moscow like a thunderclap. German forces had carved a 500km (300-mile) breech in the front and no strategic reserves were available to close it, since the *Stavka* had dispatched all to the southwestern axis. After his arrival in Moscow, early on 8 October Zhukov informed the *Stavka*:

> The chief danger is that almost all routes to Moscow are open and the weak protection along the Mozhaisk Line cannot guarantee against the surprise appearance of enemy armoured forces before Moscow. We must quickly assemble forces from wherever we can at the Mozhaisk Defense Line.[38]

Fearing the loss of the capital, the same day the GKO began preparing plans to destroy key Moscow installations and evacuate key governmental organs from the city, the *Stavka* frantically worked to strengthen its defenses to the west.[39] The latter ordered the Western and Reserve Fronts' 110th and 113th Rifle Divisions to man the Mozhaisk Line and began forming a new 5th Army under Leliushenko, which consisted of *Stavka* reserve units and forces already at the Mozhaisk Line. It also created the Moscow

Reserve Front, under Lieutenant-General P.A. Artem'ev, the Moscow Military District commander, and assigned him control of all forces in the Mozhaisk Defense Line. Finally, it formed Lieutenant-General G.G. Sokolov's 26th Army under its control to defend the Orel-Tula axis.[40] This new army's nucleus was the 1st Guards Rifle Corps, which, under Leliushenko's command, had temporarily halted Guderian's advance at Mtsensk.[41] Two days later, the *Stavka* combined what little was left of the Western and Reserve Fronts into a new Western Front with Zhukov in command and Konev as his deputy. Finally, the *Stavka* ordered the forces encircled at Viaz'ma, 'To penetrate the enemy's defense lines on 10–11 October and escape encirclement at all cost.'[42] It assigned Lukin command of the combined force and ordered him to break out to the east either toward Sychevka or Gzhatsk with the 19th, 24th, and 32nd Armies and Ermakov to break out to the southeast.

Although Konev ordered his forces to break out as separate shock groups and maneuver around German blocking forces, such an operation was impossible.[43] German forces were too strong, and they had erected a virtual wall of panzer divisions west of Viaz'ma.[44] Making matters worse, beginning on 7 October the weather turned cold and wet, transforming the roads into quagmires. Nonetheless, the encircled force agonizingly made their way eastward toward Viaz'ma suffering immense losses in the process. On 10 October Lukin reported:

> The situation of the encircled forces has worsened sharply. There are few shells, bullets are running out, and there is no food. They eat that which the population can provide and horseflesh. Medicines and dressing materials are used up. All tents and dwellings are overflowing with wounded.[45]

As the encirclement front shrank and the German cordon tightened, Lukin ordered the force to break out northeastward through Bogoroditskoe toward Gzhatsk.[46] During the break out attempt, which began on 11 October and lasted for several bloody and frustrating days, only elements of the 91st Rifle Division managed to run the gauntlet of fire successfully. Thereafter, Lukin's and Ershakov's forces fought encircled in two separate groups northwest and southwest of Viaz'ma, making one last desperate attempt to break out late on 12 October.[47] The end had indeed come for the Western and Reserve Fronts. On 13 October the Germans announced, 'The enemy encircled west of Viaz'ma has been completely destroyed.'[48] Despite this proclamation, the remnants of the once strong but now 'destroyed' Soviet forces continued to tie down five German divisions until the end of the month.

While the Briansk Front's situation was serious, it was not as critical as that faced by the two *fronts* in the Viaz'ma region. Late on 8 October Eremenko's armies began to withdraw. Kreizer's 3rd and Petrov's 50th Armies managed to thrust almost 50km (30 miles) to the east by first light before encountering significant opposition, but Gorodniansky's 13th Army had to gnaw its way southeast through successive cordons of blockading German forces. After several unsuccessful escape attempts, on 9 October Gorodniansky's army turned south through Suzemka and a major portion of his forces managed to break through the first line of German blocking positions.[49]

When the Second Army's 113th Infantry Division linked up with Guderian's 18th Panzer Division northeast of Briansk on 9 October, Eremenko's *front* was split in two with the 3rd and 50th Armies encircled at Diat'kovo and the 13th Army at Trubchevsk, Suzemka, and Navlia south of Briansk. Soon after, on 13 October, Eremenko was wounded in a German air strike and evacuated to Moscow by aircraft, leaving his chief of staff, Zakharov, in temporary command.[50] Petrov's 50th Army began withdrawing to the northeast on 10 October and, despite changes in march-route mandated by Shaposhnikov and near constant combat, about 10 percent of the force made it to Soviet lines at Belev. Kreizer's 3rd Army fought its way from south of Briansk to north of Dmitrovsk-Orlovskii, where on 17–20 October it again fought fully encircled.[51] Ultimately about

13,000 men of Kreizer's army made it to Soviet lines near Ponyri and were immediately assigned rear defensive positions. With the assistance of relief attacks mounted by Ermakov's group, the remnants of Gorodniansky's 13th Army, 10,000 men in all, made it back to Red Army lines and occupied defenses 45km (27 miles) northwest of Kursk on 22 October.[52]

The massive Viaz'ma and Briansk encirclements virtually destroyed the Western and Reserve Fronts and severely damaged the Briansk Front. The encirclements cost the three *fronts* 7 of their 15 armies, 64 of 95 divisions, 11 of 15 tank brigades, and 50 of 62 attached artillery regiments.[53] Equipment losses totalled 6,000 guns and mortars and 830 tanks. It is difficult to determine accurately the personnel losses from the two encirclements. An estimated 85,000 men escaped the Viaz'ma caldron and 23,000 from the Briansk encirclement, and 98,000 men from the 29th and 33rd Armies, Group Ermakov, and the 22nd Army also made it to safety. Counting those that reached other units, the total escapees numbered about 250,000. Therefore, it is likely that one million troops were lost at Viaz'ma and Briansk, of which 688,000 fell captive to the Germans. By any measure, the results were truly catastrophic.[54]

Exploiting Typhoon

Overestimating the scale and impact of their victory, on 10 October the OKH altered its plans by deciding to expand its offensive to the north and destroy the Northwestern Front, while its main forces advanced eastward to capture Moscow.[55] Accordingly, it ordered the Third Panzer Group, now commanded by Reinhardt, to advance northward to capture Kalinin, Torzhok, and Vyshnii Volochek and link up with Army Group North's forces advancing southward from Chudovo and eastward through the Valdai Hills. This thrust would give the Germans control of the Leningrad–Moscow railroad and also help to seal Leningrad's fate. Bock's final plan required Strauss's Ninth Army and Third Panzer Group to thrust northward and then veer southeastward toward Moscow, Kluge's Fourth Army and Hoepner's Fourth Panzer Group to advance eastward toward Moscow, and Guderian's Second Panzer Army with Weich's Second Army to envelop Moscow from the southeast.[56] Quite naturally, the decision to commit such large forces on the flanks weakened the power of Army Group Centre's drive directly on Moscow.

On the heels of the Viaz'ma and Briansk disasters, on 12 October the GKO ordered defenses be constructed on the immediate approaches to Moscow and in the city itself. It assigned the NKVD the responsibility for security in the city and east of the Kalinin, Rzhev, Mozhaisk, Tula, Kolomna, and Kashira line. The NKVD did so with about 6,000 NKVD forces supplemented with militia units, destroyer (local defense and security) battalions, and blocking detachments. The GKO also mobilized 440,000 inhabitants of Moscow *oblast'* (region) to construct defenses lines in a period of 20 days.[57] Four days before, on 8 October the GKO had issued warning orders to prepare 1,119 industrial, administrative, and educational institutions for destruction and, on 15 October, ordered government organs, leaders, the General Staff, and tens of other institutions be evacuated from Moscow to Kuibyshev and other cities to the east. Other orders instituted Draconian measures to prevent panic and insure order in the city. In essence, Moscow was under a state of siege.

On 10 October Reinhardt's Third Panzer Group began its northeastward drive.[58] Although it took several days to overcome stiff resistance by Major-General V.A. Iushkevich's 22nd and Lieutenant-General I.I. Maslennikov's 29th Armies, which had successfully withdrawn to a portion of the Rzhev-Viaz'ma defense line, Reinhardt's forces soon made spectacular progress. By 12 October SS 'Reich' had captured Gzhatsk and was halfway to Mozhaisk, the 36th Motorized Division had captured Pogoreloe, Lehr Brigade 900 had seized Zubtsov, and the 1st Panzer Division had taken Rzhev and Staritsa and was approaching Kalinin.[59] By doing so, they carved an 80km (48-mile) gap between Zubtsov and Gzhatsk in which there were no defenders. Two days later, Reinhardt's forces occupied the vital city of Kalinin.

The situation was so serious that Zhukov ordered the forces on his *front*'s right wing to withdraw north of the Volga and sent his deputy Konev to organize the defense and assemble a force with which to counterattack.[60] At the same time, the *Stavka* ordered Vatutin, the Northwestern Front's chief of staff, to organize a special operational group, consisting of two rifle and two cavalry divisions, one tank brigade, and one motorcycle regiment, and expel German forces from Kalinin.[61] Heavy fighting raged in the region from 15-29 October, and, although the Germans were able to maintain their grip on the city, the counterattacks forced them to abandon any idea of advancing on Torzhok and Vyshnii Volochek. During this fighting, on 17 October the *Stavka* subordinated all forces in the region (the 22nd, 29th, 30th, and 31st Armies and Operational Group Vatutin) to the newly formed Kalinin Front under Konev's command.[62]

After reducing the Viaz'ma encirclement, on 24 October the Ninth Army's forces joined the Third Panzer Group at Kalinin and tried to revive their offensive on Torzhok. However, the Kalinin Front managed to contain the advance in seven days of heavy fighting. Thereafter the front stabilized with Konev's *front* perched precariously over Army Group Centre's long left flank.[63]

To the south, Kluge's Fourth Army, at full combat strength, began advancing along the Minsk, Warsaw and Kiev highways toward the Mozhaisk Line on 10 October, even before the Viaz'ma encirclement had been liquidated. By this time, only scratch forces formed around the nucleus of four rifle divisions manned the Mozhaisk Defense Line, and these forces had wide open flanks.[64] To strengthen its defenses west of Moscow, on 13 October the *Stavka* merged the Moscow Reserve Front into the Western Front and formed the 16th, 5th, 43rd, and 49th Armies to defend the Volokolamsk, Mozhaisk, Maloiaroslavets, and Kaluga axes, respectively. German forces reached and began fighting for all four points between 11 and 16 October.[65] Combat developed in fragmented fashion as both sides continued to feed fresh forces into desperate struggles for possession of the four towns, all the while struggling to overcome appalling terrain conditions produced by the intermittent freezes, thaws, and rains.

In heavy and often confused fighting throughout the remainder of October, German forces finally captured Volokolamsk, Mozhaisk, Maloiaroslavets, and Kaluga and advanced to the outskirts of Kubinka and Naro-Fominsk in the Centre and Serpukhov and Tula in the south. During this period, the *Stavka* reinforced Zhukov's Front with Lieutenant-General M.G. Efremov's newly formed 33rd Army, which went into action near Naro-Fominsk. Inexorably, a combination of stiff and at times desperate Soviet resistance and heavy rains brought the German offensive to a temporary halt.[66] By 30 October, Operation Typhoon had lost its momentum along and east of the Mozhaisk Defense Line.

On the Flanks

While German and Soviet attention was fixed on the Wehrmacht's dramatic drive on Moscow, operations of near equal significance were unfolding along the northwestern and southern strategic axes. Struggling to satisfy Hitler's strategic ambitions, Army Groups North and South recorded spectacular achievements in October.

In the north, after Zhukov thwarted Leeb's attempts to capture Leningrad from the march, Army Group North sought to isolate Leningrad by cutting it off from the remainder of the country. Deprived of Hoepner's Fourth Panzer Group, which Hitler had ordered to join Operation Typhoon, Leeb decided to encircle Leningrad from the east with his last motorized corps, Schmidt's XXXIX. Schmidt's panzers and an accompanying army corps were to advance northeastward, capture Tikhvin and Volkhov, link up with the Finns along the Svir river east of Lake Ladoga to encircle Leningrad, and starve the city into submission.

Simultaneously, other army group forces were to advance eastward north and south of Lake Il'men' to cut the Moscow-Leningrad railroad and link up with Army Group Centre's Third Panzer Group at Vyshii Volochek.[67]

Preempting the Soviet counteroffensive at Siniavino, Schmidt's motorized corps advance rapidly eastward across the Volkhov river on 16 October, split apart the defending Soviet 52nd and 4th Armies and captured Malaia Vishera on 23 October and Tikhvin on 8 November. At the same time, Group Boeckmann approached Volkhov from the south. The German seizure of Tikhvin cut the Leningrad Front's last land route to Lake Ladoga along which supplies flowed to the already beleaguered city of Leningrad. However, by this time winter had set in, snows arrived, and the temperatures fell to −40 degrees Fahrenheit, locking the advancing German forces in an icy grip.[68] At this critical juncture, the *Stavka* reinforced its forces and ordered a series of counterstrokes to restore the situation. In early November, however, the outcome was unclear and Soviet forces in the Leningrad and Tikhvin region were indeed imperiled.

Nor was the situation much better in the south, where the destruction of the Southwestern Front at Kiev had savaged Red Army defenses. In the wake of its Kiev victory, the OKH ordered Rundstedt's Army Group South to launch simultaneous attacks toward Khar'kov, the Donbas, and Rostov. His left wing (the Sixth and Seventeenth Armies) were to advance on Khar'kov and the Northern Donets river, while his right wing (the First Panzer, Rumanian Third, and Eleventh Armies) were to advance from Dnepropetrovsk to encircle the Southern Front, advance on Rostov and invade the Crimea. On 27 September the *Stavka* ordered Timoshenko's Southwestern Front and Lieutenant-General D.I. Riabyshev's Southern Front (Lieutenant-General Ia.T. Cherevichenko replaced Riabyshev on 5 October) to defend their positions, and on 30 September ordered its Odessa garrison to evacuate and reinforce the Crimean defenses.[69] Neither *front*, however, was able to erect a sound and continuous defense.

Attacking from the march south of Poltava, Kleist's First Panzer Army quickly smashed the defenses of Major-General I.V. Galanin's 12th Army. Kleist's armour raced on to Melitopol', encircling six of divisions of Major-General F.M. Kharitonov's and Smirnov's 9th and 18th Armies on 7 October, the same day that the trap shut on Soviet forces at Viaz'ma. After suffering heavy losses, including Smirnov, who was killed in action, on 10 October the remnants of the two armies fought their way out of encirclement, the former to Stalino and the later to Taganrog.[70] The First Panzer Army pursued along the coast of the Sea of Azov, reaching the Mius river opposite Taganrog on 13 October where it halted temporarily to regroup.[71]

Meanwhile, to the north, Reichenau's Sixth and Stuelpnagel's Seventeenth Armies began their advance from the Mirgorod and Poltava regions on 6 October. Their assault shattered the Malinovsky's 6th and Major-General V.V. Tsiganov's 38th Armies, which were just reforming after the Kiev disaster. With its attention fixed on Viaz'ma and Briansk and lacking any reserves, the *Stavka* had no choice but to order Timoshenko and Cherevichenko to withdraw their *fronts'* forces to the Oskol', Northern Donets, and Mius rivers between 17-30 October.[72] At the same time, it ordered the North Caucasus Military District to deploy Lieutenant-General F.M. Remezov's new 56th Army to protect the approaches to Rostov and block access to the Caucasus region.[73] Subsequently, the Sixth Army drove Tsiganov's 38th Army from Khar'kov on 25 October after five days of heavy fighting. On 28 October the Southwestern Front and the Southern Front's right wing occupied defenses 70-80km (42-48 miles) east of those designated by the *Stavka* and the Southern Front's weak centre and left wing withdrew to defenses 30-35km (18-21 miles) west of the designated line. There the front temporarily stabilized. By this time, the Germans had occupied the vital Khar'kov industrial region and the southwestern portion of the Donbas and had reached within striking distance of Rostov, the gateway into the Caucasus.

As Army Group South advanced deep to the Northern Donets river and deep into the Donbas, its Eleventh Army, followed by the Rumanian Third Army, wheeled southward and invaded the Crimea. The peninsula was a vital objective because it contained the Black Sea Fleet's principal naval base, Sevastopol', and its Kerch peninsula was yet another entrance into the vital Caucasus region. Lieutenant-General F.I. Kuznetsov's 51st Separate Army, recently evacuated from Odessa, defended the peninsula with 12 rifle and 4 cavalry divisions, a force the *Stavka* deemed more than adequate for a stout defense. However, fearing an amphibious assault, Kuznetsov deployed his forces uniformly along the coast and failed to defend the northern approaches through Perekop adequately.[74]

Attacking on 18 October, von Manstein's Eleventh Army easily broke into the peninsula and within 12 days drove Soviet forces back into the city of Sevastopol' and the narrow Kerch peninsula. By the month's end, part of the 51st Army was besieged in Sevastopol' and the remainder abandoned Kerch and reached the Taman' peninsula on 16 November. The Crimean fiasco added yet another entry to the growing list of *Stavka* October disasters.

Reflections

The disasters the *Stavka* witnessed and the Red Army suffered in October exceeded those of June, August, and September in nearly every respect. Worse still, since they occurred on the threshold of Leningrad, Moscow, Rostov, and the Caucasus, once they occurred the *Stavka* had no more room for maneuver. The fact that the three *fronts* operating along the Moscow axis in late September had five times more strength than Zhukov possessed along the same axis at the end of November indicated the full measure of the Red Army's defeats at Viaz'ma and Briansk. On 2 November Zhukov wrote to Zhdanov, Commissar of the Leningrad Front, 'We are now operating in the West [the Western Front] – on the approaches to Moscow. The main thing is that Konev and

Budenny are missing all of their armed forces. I received from them only a trace – a headquarters and 98 men from Budenny and a headquarters and two reserve regiments from Konev.'[75]

In the north, German forces held the gateway to Lake Ladoga and Leningrad with two panzer divisions at Tikhvin and faced three severely shaken Soviet armies gripped by the same bone chilling cold. In the south, Khar'kov, the Donbas, and most of the Crimea were in German hands, and Kleist's panzers were poised to strike at Rostov and the Caucasus and Stalingrad beyond. Having lost well over one million soldiers in the course of one month of fighting, the *Stavka* had every reason to question its forces' capacity for continuing the struggle and successfully defending Moscow, Leningrad, and Rostov. Nor did the Wehrmacht question its ability to seize all three cities. Furthermore, by 30 October the Soviet Union had lost immense territories and well over half of its productive capacities.

Yet, for a variety of reasons, the Wehrmacht was unable to exploit the tremendous successes it achieved during the first half of October, and, in all critical sectors, its offensives faltered by the end of the month. In the case of Army Group Centre, the twin encirclements forced Bock to commit over half of his forces (48 of 75 divisions) for 7-14 days in order to eradicate the encircled forces, thereby losing the opportunity to exploit the empty defenses west of Moscow. Thereafter, overconfidence and utter contempt for what it thought was left of the Red Army governed German actions. Considering Moscow as available for the taking, it spread its forces too broadly by dispatching the Third Panzer Group to the north and the Second Panzer Army to the south, thus weakening its critical blow in the Centre. In addition, the arrival of the autumn *rasputitsa* [rainy season] deprived the Germans of their dearest advantage, mobility, and brought Blitzkrieg to a standstill in the mud, where Red Army troops could fight more equal battles with the bogged down German tanks and infantry. Finally, as the Germans slowly advanced on Moscow, the first Soviet reserves reached Moscow from the hinterland. The unsuspecting Germans soon encountered the first dribblets of what would become a significant flood of reinforcements from the vast Red Army strategic reserve.

The same mosaic emerged in the north and south as the Germans seemed on the verge of total triumph. Having been stripped of the bulk of his armoured forces, Leeb advanced on Tikhvin 'on a shoestring' with a single motorized corps and without a significant reserve, only to find his penetrating armour locked in winter's icy grip. At the same time, Rundstedt's forces swallowed up immense terrain only to find Kleist's panzer army outrun its logistics along the Mius river, bereft of support by Manstein's excursion into the Crimea and his vastly expanding front. On 1 November 1941 the Wehrmacht was indeed tantalizingly close to achieving Hitler's goal of victory over Stalin's Red Army and mastery of the Soviet Union. Whether it could achieve that goal, however, remained to be seen.

TO THE GATES
OF MOSCOW
NOVEMBER

The Situation on 1 November

As the month of October came to an end, Hitler, the OKH, and German commanders and soldiers of all ranks confronted and tried to reconcile four contradictory realities. First and foremost, it was clear to all that the Wehrmacht had won stunning victories across the entire front, which it was essential to exploit. Second, the arrival of the *rasputitsa*, after which winter would surely follow, would complicate that exploitation. Third, the increasingly debilitated state of the Wehrmacht, in particular its mechanized forces, tempered German optimism and congenital contempt for their Soviet foes. Fourth, and most sobering, as they sought to capitalize on their victories at such places as Tikhvin, Volokolamsk, Mozhaisk, Maloiaroslavets, Naro-Fominsk and the Tula region, many Germans finally began to appreciate the resilience and staying power of the Red Army and Soviet soldier.

Most German commanders understood that the Eastern Campaign had already exacted a heavy toll on their forces. The Wehrmacht had suffered 686,000 casualties by 1 November 1941, 20% of their original Barbarossa force plus all replacements received since 22 June, and it now fielded 2.7 million men.[1] Only one third of all motor vehicles were still operational, panzer divisions were at 35 percent of their required strength, and the Wehrmacht's 136 divisions were equivalent to 83 full-strength divisions.[2]

While an advance farther to the east might succeed on the tactical level, it would do so only at a cost of greater strains on logistics. The scarce railroad trains that brought up fuel and ammunition for a renewed offensive would not be available to carry warm clothing and construction materials, both of which were vital for winter survival regardless of how successful the offensive might be. For all of these reasons, on 4 November Field Marshal von Rundstedt asked that Army Group South be allowed to halt immediately and rebuild for an offensive in 1942. Other field commanders expressed similar concerns.

The Red Army, however, seemed to be in an even more parlous state. German intelligence placed Red Army strength at 160 divisions and 40 brigades, most at below 50 percent strength.[3] In reality, on 1 November the Red Army in the West fielded 269 divisions and 65 brigades in its field forces and the *Stavka* reserve, with an overall strength of 2.2 million men. One month later, these numbers rose to 343 divisions and 98 brigades, whose strength with replacements increased to over 4 million men.[4]

These realities dictated that, if the Wehrmacht wished to capture Moscow and Rostov and isolate Leningrad, it would have to do so before winter arrived. While Hitler remained optimistic, his OKH chief Halder tempered his usual optimism. Halder assessed that the Red Army's limited capabilities prevented it from defending a continuous front and would force it to concentrate its forces for the defense of Moscow and the Caucasus. The *Stavka*, he argued, would have to muster forces to defend Moscow, protect its communications with the country's northern ports and raise new forces necessary to take the offensive in 1942. Therefore, in Halder's judgement, it was essential that the Red Army be deprived of its vital communications routes and industrial regions.[5]

To do so, on 7 November Halder prepared a plan entitled, 'Concerning the Continuation of Operations against the Enemy

Grouping between the Volga and Lake Ladoga.'⁶ Neglecting to mention Moscow by name, Halder's plan recommended the Wehrmacht concentrate on enveloping Red Army forces along the northeastern strategic axis with an advance by the Third and Fourth Panzer Groups to Iaroslavl' and Rybinsk.⁷ Halder's plan offered 'maximum' and 'minimum' variants. The former, which called for an advance to the Vologda, Gorki, Stalingrad and Maikop line, would deprive the Soviet Union of access to its northern ports and the vital Moscow and north Caucasus industrial regions, but probably would not end the war. The latter, which required German forces to advance to a line extending from 50km (30 miles) east of Lake Ladoga through a point 275km (165 miles) east of Moscow to Rostov, would require subsequent operations to reach these economically vital centres.

Opposing Plans

On 13 November Halder, his principal OKH staff officers and the three army groups' chiefs of staff met at Orsha to discuss future offensive options.⁸ The conference convinced Halder that the army was even weaker than he had feared and that the most it could accomplish in 1941 was to encircle Leningrad and threaten Moscow. Hitler, however, was already convinced that Moscow must fall. Driven by his own hatred of Bolshevism and his appreciation that the seizure of Moscow would raise popular morale, which was beginning to flag, Hitler personally ordered Army Group Centre to capture Moscow.⁹ He timed the offensive to coincide with the onset of cold weather so that his panzers would have frozen ground to traverse rather than impenetrable mud. What he had not reckoned with, however, was the winter's unprecedented severity in 1941. Even before the offensive began, the temperature fell precipitously to 5 degrees Fahrenheit (-15°C) on 12 November and −8 degrees (-22°C) the next day; and the worst was yet to come.

The final plan, which Hitler had already approved on 30 October, required two mobile groupings to strike the Western Front's flanks no later than 15 November, envelop Moscow from the north and south and encircle Red Army forces in Moscow by linking up near Orekhova–Zueva and Kolomna.[10] Reinhardt's Third Panzer Group and Strauss's Ninth Army were to spearhead the northern pincer by advancing through Klin and across the Volga-Moscow Canal, and Guderian's Second Panzer Army was to thrust northeastward through Tula and Kashira to unite with its sister group east of Moscow. Hoepner's Fourth Panzer Group and Kluge's Fourth Army were to march directly eastward toward Moscow and support the advance of the two pincers.

Stalin and other *Stavka* members faced the grim possibility that, once the first hard frost restored mobility, the invaders would be able to capture or at least encircle Leningrad, Moscow, Stalingrad and Rostov. Even if the Soviet regime could survive such a blow politically, the loss of manpower, transportation hubs and manufacturing capacity might well prove fatal militarily. This was especially true at a time when the evacuated factories were still being reassembled in the Urals. Therefore, Stalin chose to concentrate his main efforts on the Moscow defense. In the meantime, he orchestrated counterstrokes on the distant flanks to stabilize the situation in those regions and, in so far as possible, distract German attention and forces from the Centre.

The *Stavka* expected the Germans to launch their main attack from Volokolamsk and Serpukhov. Therefore, it concentrated the 16th, 5th, 33rd, 43rd, 49th and 50th Armies of Zhukov's Western Front, most of which had been severely shaken in earlier battles, in new defensive positions from north of Volokolamsk to south of Tula to protect the approaches to Moscow. The 22nd, 29th, 31st and 30th Armies of Konev's Kalinin Front were to tie down German forces on the Western Front's right flank from Ostashkov to south of Kalinin. Finally, the 3rd and 13th Armies of Timoshenko's Southwestern Front, which had been assigned to his *front* on 10 November after the Briansk Front was disbanded, were to block any German advance toward Moscow from the south via Efremov or Elets.[11] The *Stavka* hastily dispatched reserve formations to the Western Front from the Far East, Siberia, Central Asia and other internal military districts and ordered the formation of 9 reserve armies consisting of 59 rifle and 13 cavalry divisions and 75 rifle and 20 tank brigades.[12]

In addition, the *Stavka* ordered militia and security forces to man the extensive defenses in and around Moscow and farther east. By late November, a force of 65,000 men defended Moscow proper, consisting primarily of peoples' militia and destroyer detachments.[13] The city's defenses comprised three defense zones ringing the city, including an outer belt 30km (18 miles) distant, a ring defense in the city's suburbs and a series of rear defensive belts arrayed east of the city. Within the city itself, security forces erected and manned a complex system of barricades and strong points.[14] To a considerable extent, Muscovites exploited the Leningraders' defensive experiences of August and September 1941.

Finally, based on intelligence received on the eve of the offensive, on 14 November Stalin personally ordered a reluctant Zhukov to mount multiple spoiling attacks to disrupt German offensive preparations.[15] Although Zhukov objected that it was too late to do so, Stalin insisted, and the Western Front commander ordered Rokossovsky's 16th and Lieutenant-General I.G. Zakharkin's 49th Armies to attack the flanks of German Fourth Army north of Volokolamsk and east of Serpukhov, respectively. Zhukov's reservations were indeed correct. In addition to failing miserably, the unjustified attacks only served to weaken and disrupt the Red Army's defenses once the German offensive began.

Rokossovsky attacked with his right flank on 16 November in an attempt to exploit local victories he had achieved during the previous five days. His 126th Rifle, 17th and 24th Cavalry and 58th Tank Divisions struck the 14th Motorized and 7th Panzer Divisions at the junction of Ninth Army's XXVII Army Corps and LVI Motorized Corps, which were themselves preparing to attack. Even though the attack bogged down with heavy

Clockwise from top left:

GERMAN
1 Adolf Hitler.
2 Colonel-General Franz Halder, chief of OKH.

SOVIET
3 Joseph Stalin.
4 Army-General G.K. Zhukov, Chief of the Red Army General Staff, commander Reserve
  Front, commander Leningrad Front and commander Western Front.
5 Marshal-of-the-Soviet-Union B.M. Shaposhnikov, Chief of the Red Army General Staff.
6 Lieutenant-General A.M. Vasilevsky, deputy chief of the General Staff's Operational
  Directorate, deputy chief of the General Staff and Stavka representative.
7 Lieutenant-General N.F. Vatutin, deputy chief of the General Staff and chief of staff
  Northwestern Front.

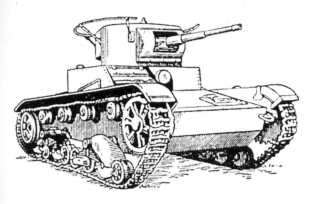

8 Red Army T-26 light tank.

9 Red Army BT-7 tank.

10 Red Army T-34 medium tank.

11 Red Army KV-1 heavy tank.

12 Hitler (centre), Halder (left) and von Brauchitsch.

13 Red Army artillery on parade in Red Square, 1 May 1941.

14 German
infantry on
the attack in a
Soviet village.

15 German
artillery
moving
forward.

16 German
troops fighting
on the
outskirts of
Brest.

17 Red Army mechanized corps counterattack.

18 Red Army infantry deploying to the front, June 1941. The sign reads: 'Our cause is just. The enemy will be defeated. The victory will be behind us.'

19 Red Army soldiers taking the oath, summer 1941.

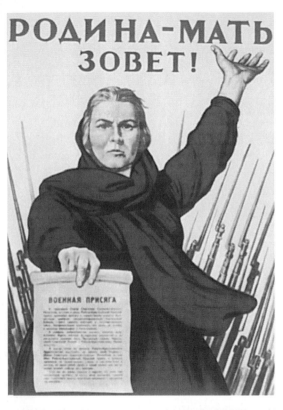

20 Red Army poster, 1941: 'The Motherland Calls!'

21 Women manning the arms industry assembly lines.

22 Colonel-General Herman Hoth (centre) with junior officers.

23 The 'Road of Life' across Lake Ladoga.

24 (Below) A Katiusha multiple rocket launcher battery in firing position.

25 Workers at
the Kirov factory
erect a barricade.

26 German
troops and
Russian roads.

27 German
artillery in firing
position near
Kiev.

28 Soviet heavy artillery firing.

29 Soviet infantry on the attack with grenades.

30 Red Army cavalry on the attack, November 1941.

31 Russian civilians constructing defensive lines west of Moscow.

32 Troops passing in review for Stalin during the Red Square parade, 7 November 1941.

33 The 1st Guards Tank Brigade attacking German positions near the Volokolamsk road.

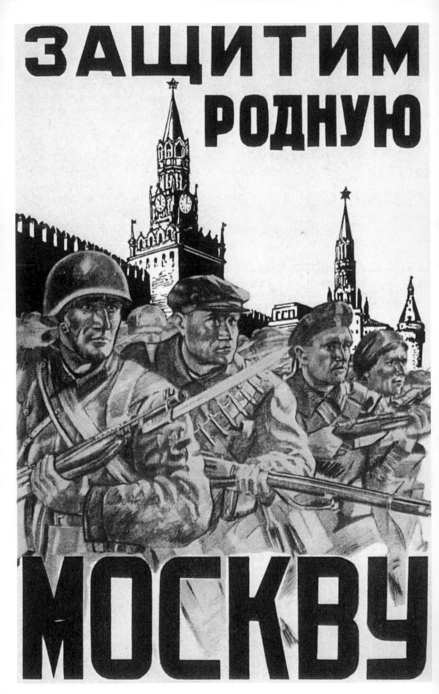

34 Soviet placard, 1941: 'We will defend Mother Moscow.'

35 Red Army troops deploying into winter positions.

36 A captured German artillery position, December 1941.

37 Red Air Force fighters defend the skies over Moscow, December 1941.

38 On the forward edge of Moscow's defense, December 1941.

39 Soviet placard entitled 'Pincers in pincers'. The torn document reads, 'OKH Plan for the Encirclement and Seizure of Moscow'.

40 Red Army infantry assault, December 1941.

41 Zhukov (right) meets with Rokossovsky, commander of the 16th Army.

losses after a meager 3-4km (1.8-2.4 mile) advance, on Zhukov's orders, Rokossovsky committed Major-General L.M. Dovator's 20th and 44th Cavalry Divisions into combat to exploit.[16] The consequences were disastrous. The inexperienced 44th Mongolian Cavalry Division conducted a mounted charge across an open, snow-covered field during which it lost 2,000 cavalrymen and their horses to artillery and machine-gun fire of the German 106th Infantry Division, which suffered no casualties. With his left flank under heavy attack and his right nearly surrounded, Rokossovsky ordered his forces to withdraw to new defenses on 17 November.[17]

To the south Zakharkin's 49th Army attacked the XII and XIII Army Corps' 98th, 13th, 17th and 137th Infantry Divisions defending northeast of Serpukhov early on 14 November. Zakharkin led his assault with the 415th, 5th Guards, and 60th Rifle Divisions, supported on the left by the 194th Rifle Division and on the right by the 17th Rifle Division. After achieving small penetrations north and south of Voronino, Major-General P.A. Belov's 2nd Cavalry Corps and the fresh 112th Tank Division attempted to exploit but were halted by the Fourth Army's 263rd and 268th Infantry Divisions, which counterattacked and restored the front.[18]

In addition, Zhukov ordered Zakharkin's 49th Army and the 50th Army, now commanded by Lieutenant-General I.V. Boldin, to attack Guderian's spearheads north and south of Tula.[19] The newly arrived 413th Rifle Division and 32nd Tank Brigade did so beginning on 8 November in a running battle near Uslovaia south of Tula in conjunction with the newly arrived 239th Rifle Division and other 3rd Army forces attacking from the south. Although the attack proved unsuccessful, it produced temporary consternation in Guderian's headquarters and delayed his advance. During the fighting on 17 November, elements of the German 112th Infantry Division, which lacked antitank weapons that were ineffective against the attacking T-34 tanks, broke and ran and had to be rescued by the 167th Infantry Division.[20] The panicky retreat was almost unprecedented in the German Army.

Further north, on 11 November the 49th Army's 238th Rifle Division and the 50th Army's 258th Rifle and 31st Cavalry Divisions mounted a concentric attack against the XXXXIII Army Corps' 31st and 131st Infantry Divisions, which were attempting to envelop Tula from the north. In five days of heavy fighting, during which the 194th Rifle Division joined the fray, the Soviet forces halted the German attacks short of the Moscow–Tula road, thus thwarting the German envelopment effort.

Even though most Soviet accounts claim that these local offensives accomplished little and even undermined the Red Army's defenses, they had a clear impact on the Germans. Halder thought them significant enough to note their occurrence in his now famous diary, in which he echoed Bock's prophetic warning:

> Army group orders provide for a long-range and short-range objective. Attaining even the latter appears doubtful to von Bock in view of the condition of his troops. He had given them as interim objective the line of the Mosvka river through Moscow and the Volga Canal…. Von Bock argues that even if we were content to reach the interim objective ('the bird in hand'), we would have to commence the attack immediately, for every day was bringing us closer to the critical date for deep snowfall. If we were to wait until we had enough striking power for a more distant goal, we might well be overtaken by winter weather and immobilized for good.
>
> The time for spectacular operational feats is passed. Troops cannot be shifted around anymore. The only course lies in the purposeful exploitation of tactical opportunities.[21]

Far more important, the failed operations ordered by Stalin and Zhukov between 11 and 16 November indicated that the Red Army was prepared to contest every inch of Soviet soil along the approaches to Moscow, making it exceedingly difficult for German forces to exploit their tactical opportunities. Worse still, while the Wehrmacht was thinking tactically, Stalin, Zhukov and the *Stavka* were already thinking operationally. Within days the *Stavka* ordered the formation and forward deployment of three new reserve armies, the 1st Shock, 20th and 10th.[22] While the Western Front's forward armies contested the Wehrmacht tactically, a Soviet operational counterstroke was already in the offing.

The Final Drive on Moscow

While Zhukov's spoiling attacks continued, the ground froze rock hard. Bock's army group resumed its offensive on 15 November with a force estimated by the Soviets at 233,000 men, 1,880 guns, 1,300 tanks and 60–800 aircraft. By this time, the Western Front's forces, reinforced by the Kalinin Front's 30th Army on its northern flank, numbered 240,000 men supported by 1,254 guns and mortars, 502 tanks and 600–700 combat aircraft.[23] Zhukov's defenses were anchored on well-prepared defenses extending from Kalinin in the north to Tula in the south.

In the north, where Reinhardt's Third Panzer Group and Strauss's Ninth Army posed the most immediate threat to the Russian capital, a desperate fight developed for control of the highway running from Kalinin through Klin to Moscow. The initial German assault split apart Rokossovsky's 16th Army from the 30th Army, now commanded by Leliushenko. When the German assault began, Leliushenko's army withdrew to defenses along the Volga north of the Volga Reservoir, followed closely by Strauss's Ninth Army. Strauss's forces secured bridgeheads north of the river and went over to the defense on 19 November to protect the left flank of Reinhardt's panzer group as it advanced to the east. Reinhardt's panzers then swept eastward toward Klin, the Volga-Moscow Canal and the northern approaches to Moscow.

Zhukov assigned Rokossovsky's deputy, Major-General F.D. Zakharov, to cover the gap near Klin with the 126th and 17th Cavalry Divisions and the 30th Army's 107th Motorized (Rifle) Division and 8th and 25th Tank Brigades. Along the Volokolamsk and Istra axis to the south, the 316th, 18th and 78th Rifle

Divisions, Dovator's 50th and 53rd Cavalry Divisions and Major-General M.E. Katukov's 1st Guards Tank Brigade struggled to hold back the advance by Hoepner's Fourth Panzer Group.[24] While Reinhardt's forces advanced steadily along the Klin axis, Hoepner's advance was slow and costly. His forces advanced only 4-6km in three days against fierce resistance, but finally managed to penetrate Rokossovsky's main defensive belt. Discouraged by his slow progress, Hoepner committed all three of his corps on 19 November, broke the stalemate and advanced 18-23km (11-14 miles) by late on 20 November.[25]

Several factors facilitated the Third Panzer Group's success. First, the assault struck at the junction of the 30th and 16th Armies, where Zhukov's defenses were the weakest. Second, the ill-advised preemptive attacks used up almost all of Zhukov's reserves, which prevented him from orchestrating counterattacks at the proper time or place. By the time he did generate reserves, Rokossovsky's flanks had been turned and Klin was in jeopardy.

The slow but steady German advance against fierce resistance led to a seesaw battle that decimated both sides. By late November both Soviet and German regiments had been reduced to the size of companies, with only 150 to 200 riflemen left in each. Nevertheless, Reinhardt's 7th Panzer Division (of LVI Motorized Corps) captured Klin at 1600 hours on 23 November and, on its right flank, Hoepner's 2nd Panzer Division (of XXXX Motorized Corps) seized Solnechnogorsk. As the V Army Corps pulled up alongside Hoepner's armour, the way was open for German forces to advance both eastward toward the Moscow-Volga Canal and directly toward Moscow from the northwest.

With yet another climax at hand, the *Stavka* and Zhukov took immediate action to counter or eliminate the threat to Moscow. They ordered Rokossovsky to withdraw his 16th Army to a new defense line from south of Solnechnogorsk along the Istra Reservoir and river to Istra in line with the forces of Lieutenant-General of Artillery L.A. Govorov's 5th Army, which was withdrawing to new positions from Istra to Zvenigorod. The *Stavka* covered

Rokossovsky's withdrawal with a scratch force made up of anti-aircraft gunners from Moscow, engineer obstacle troops and reserves hastily gathered from quiet sectors of the front.[26]

While Rokossovsky withdrew his forces, Reinhardt's panzers exploited eastward from Klin against only light resistance. The left flank of Leliushenko's 30th Army withdrew to the north, leaving a breech that Third Panzer Group quickly exploited late on 28 November. Late that night the 14th Motorized and 7th Panzer Divisions reached the western bank of the Moscow-Volga Canal at and south of Iakhroma, and the latter captured several small bridgeheads on the canal's west bank, less than 35km (21 miles) from the Kremlin.[27] Reinforcing its assault, Hoepner's Fourth Panzer Group smashed Rokossovsky's resistance at Solnech-nogorsk and Istra and pushed on toward the capital. By 30 November his 2nd Panzer Division captured Krasnaia Poliana within artillery range of Moscow. German officers claimed they could see the spires of the city through their field glasses. Heavy fighting then ensued from Kriukovo to Dedovsk southeast of Istra as the remainder of Hoepner's XXXXVI and XXXX Motorized Corps and Reinhardt's V Army Corps closed on Rokossovsky's and Govorov's defenses northwest of Moscow.[28]

Despite categorical orders to hold in place, Rokossovsky's 16th Army had been forced back step by step. In an effort to stem the tide, on 30 November the *Stavka* released its strategic reserves, General V.I. Kuznetsov's 1st Shock Army and General A.I. Liziukov's 20th Army, to Zhukov's Western Front and ordered Zhukov to hold the Moscow-Volga Canal.[29] Zhukov immediately inserted the two armies into the breach between the 30th and 16th Armies and ordered Kuznetsov's army to throw German forces back across the canal near Iakhroma and Liziukov's army to protect the Krasnaia Poliana sector.

The situation was equally perilous south of Moscow, where, on 18 November, after recovering from the brief panic caused by the Soviet attack of the previous day, Guderian's Second Panzer Army resumed its offensive. Striking at the junction of the Western and Southwestern Fronts, Guderian's forces had eroded to such an extent that he had to concentrate his remaining armour into one brigade, commanded by Colonel Eberbach of the weakened 4th Panzer Division. By mid-November this brigade had only 50 tanks left, but it was the spearhead for the XXIV Motorized Corps and, in effect, for the entire army. Eberbach forced his way forward slowly and penetrated through the weak cordon of forces south of Tula in an attempt to encircle Tula from the east as a stepping-stone to Moscow.[30]

Guderian's initial spectacular progress belied his army's actual strength and capabilities. On 18 November the XXXXVII Motorized Corps captured Epifan' and the XXIV Motorized Corps' 4th Panzer Division seized Dedilovo and prepared to march northward toward Venev on the Moscow road. At the same time, on the 4th Panzer Division's left flank, the 17th Panzer Division began to advance toward Venev and Kashira. By 24 November, the 10th Motorized Division had captured Mikhailov deep in the steppes on Guderian's left flank, while his 29th Motorized Division screened the Second Panzer Army's lengthening right flank. Ominously, as the temperatures plummeted, Guderian's intelligence began detecting fresh Siberian troops detraining in the Riazan' region to the east.

General Boldin's 50th Army, defending tenaciously the outskirts of Tula, launched counterattack after counterattack against Guderian's front and flank. With temperatures well below freezing and troops running out of fuel, ammunition and functioning vehicles, the German advance slowly shuddered to a halt. Guderian repeatedly asked that the offensive be canceled, but no one in OKH had the authority to take such an action without Hitler's consent.[31]

With Tula almost encircled and the Second Panzer Army still pushing slowly north in late November, Zhukov again turned to Belov, the commander of the 2nd Cavalry Corps, to 'restore the situation at any cost.' From the very small reserves available, Stalin and Zhukov gave Belov half of the 112th Tank Division, the 35th and 127th Separate Tank Battalions, some anti-aircraft gunners from Moscow, a combat engineer regiment, one of the new '*Katiusha*' multiple-rocket launcher units and the instructors and students from several military schools. On 26 November it redesignated this composite force 1st Guards Cavalry Corps and ordered it to attack Guderian's spearhead 17th Panzer Division near Kashira. Considering the desperate equipment shortages of the time, this corps represented one of the first Soviet efforts to revive their pre-war doctrine of a 'cavalry-mechanized group' for deep penetrations. The German advance guards were so scattered that Belov was able to infiltrate his squadrons forward virtually undetected. On 27 November he counterattacked, drove back the 17th Panzer Division and relieved the pressure on Tula. Thus began the odyssey of the 1st Guards Cavalry Corps, which would continue its long exploitation and, ultimately, operate in the German rear areas for the next five months.[32]

The Crisis

At the end of November, when the situation seemed equally critical north and south of Moscow, Bock decided to unleash the Fourth Army for an attack on Moscow directly from the west. He did so, at least in part, because in late November Zhukov had ordered all divisions defending west of Moscow to send one platoon to reinforce Rokossovsky's beleaguered 16th Army.[33] Driven by a combination of apprehension and confidence that Soviet defenses west of the city had been weakened, Bock believed that the time had come for a decisive assault on Moscow. Therefore, he ordered Kluge's Fourth Army to strike Soviet defenses south of Zvenigorod and at Naro-Fominsk, and envelop Govorov's 5th Army and Efremov's 33rd Army by advancing concentrically to Kubinka and Golitsyno. Subsequently, Kluge's forces were to advance into Moscow along the Minsk and Kiev Highways.[34]

   Kluge formed three shock groups for the attack: the 267th Infantry Division southwest of Zvenigorod, the XX Army Corps'

258th and 292nd Infantry and 3rd Motorized Divisions north of Naro-Fominsk, and the 183rd Infantry and 20th Panzer Divisions and one regiment of the 15th Infantry south of Naro-Fominsk. All three groups attacked toward Golistyno on 1 December, but the attack had only limited armoured support and ran directly into a carefully planned Soviet antitank defensive region. The 5th Army repelled the 267th Infantry Division's thrust and drove the division back to its starting positions. To the south, the systematic defense by Colonel V.I. Polosukhin's 1st Guards Motorized Rifle Division at Naro-Fominsk became a legend of tenacity. The 258th Infantry and 3rd Motorized Divisions managed to penetrate 4-9km north and south of the 1st Guards Motorized Rifle Division's defenses at Naro-Fominsk and reached positions just south of Golitsyno. This prompted Bock to inform his army commanders on 2 December that the enemy was close to breaking.

Bock's optimism, however, was unwarranted. A scratch force consisting of the 18th Rifle Brigade, the 5th and 20th Tank Brigades, and the 23rd and 24th Ski Battalions from Efremov's 33rd Army struck the penetrating German force in the flanks, nearly encircling it near Aprelevka. The next day, the 258th and 3rd Motorized Divisions managed to fight their way back to Fourth Army lines along the River Nara, ending Kluge's gambit.[35]

Worse still for Bock, his other attacks were also floundering. Hoepner, who was trying in vain to pry the 16th and 20th Armies from their defenses northwest of Moscow, reported that his panzer group's strength was 'in the main exhausted.' On his left flank, Reinhardt's Third Panzer Group was now struggling against the 1st Shock Army at Iakhroma, slowly giving ground southwest of that town. By early on 5 December the advance by both panzer groups inexorably and finally ground to a halt astride the Leningrad, Piatitskoe and Volokolamsk roads, 15-28km (9-14 miles) from Moscow's main defense lines. The incredibly cold weather, which set new records, did not help matters.[36]

To the south, Guderian's Second Panzer Army, now blocked from advancing on Moscow proper by a blizzard and Belov's cavalry corps, was still trying to find a way to encircle the 50th Army in Tula. To do so, Guderian combined all of his army's remaining armour into two small shock groups under the XXIV Motorized Corps' control. The two shock groups, formed from the 3rd and 4th Panzer Divisions and Infantry Regiment Grossdeutschland, were to attack westward north of Tula to sever the Moscow–Tula road. There they were to link up with a third shock group formed from the XXXXIII Army Corps' 31st and 296th Infantry Divisions, which were to attack eastward northwest of the city. Together, the three groups were to encircle the 50th Army in Tula.[37] Attacking early on 2 December, the panzer shock groups managed to cut the vital road, but then encountered heavy counterattacks by the 112th Tank and 340th Rifle Divisions, the 31st Cavalry Division and several rifle and tank regiments. At the same time, the 194th and 258th Rifle Divisions repelled the 31st Infantry Division's attack, bringing the entire venture to an abrupt end and forcing Guderian to withdraw his exhausted forces and go over to the defense.

Despite these setbacks, Bock was not yet ready to admit defeat. On 4 December he informed General Jodl, Hitler's operations chief in the OKW chief that, 'although his troop strength was almost at an end, he would stay on the attack,' to hold on 'with tooth and claw' rather than withdraw to a defense with weakened forces holding exposed positions.[38] To make matters worse, on 4 December the temperature fell to minus 31 degrees Fahrenheit (minus 35°C), only increasing the misery of German forces struggling across the front. By this time it was clear to everyone, German and Soviet alike, that the Wehrmacht had been stretched to the breaking point and was no longer capable of continuing the offensive. Although it had advanced 80–110km (48–66 miles) in 20 days and had reached the very threshold of the Soviet capital, its strength had ebbed to dangerously low levels.[39] Unbeknownst to German commanders, while their strength was eroding, the Red Army's strength was increasing. Within hours German field commanders would have to contend with far more than the bitter cold because Zhukov's reserve armies were about to make their presence felt.

It is now clear that strategic reserves raised and deployed in accordance with *Stavka* orders of 24-25 November played a decisive role in the defeat of German forces at Moscow.[40] During the 67-day advance of Bock's Army Group Centre along the Moscow axis, the OKH and OKW were unable to provide the army group with a single reinforcing division. During the same period, however, the *Stavka* raised and deployed 75 division-equivalents, including 24 division-equivalents assigned to the 10th, 26th and 61st Armies, which were concentrating in the Riazan', Noginsk and Rzhev regions. Counting the 271,395 Red Army soldiers sent to the front as individual replacements, the *Stavka* formed and committed to combat in early December a new strategic grouping whose strength was at least equivalent to the entire Red Army force that had been attacked by Army Group Centre on 1 October.[41] Worse still for the Germans, the Red Air Force was able to achieve air superiority by early December.

Unlike the case in early October, by early December the *Stavka*, *front* and army commands had sorted out and corrected the chaotic command and control systems that contributed to the October disaster. The chain of command from *Stavka* through Western Front to individual armies was now clear and crisp, and these improvements helped Red Army forces first slow and then stop the German advance. Better cooperation between Zhukov's Western, Konev's Kalinin and Timoshenko's Southwestern Fronts created real threats to Bock's flanks and forces him to allocate 22 divisions to their defense, depriving his main thrust toward Moscow of 30 percent of its strength.[42] All the while, the Red Army's counterstrokes at Tikhvin in the north and Rostov in the south deprived Bock of any reinforcements from Army Groups North and South on the strategic flanks.

On the Flanks

Even before the Wehrmacht's advance ground to a halt on the outskirts of Moscow, Hitler and the OKH witnessed ominous indicators on the distant flanks that Barbarossa was indeed faltering. In fact, well before 5 December, the offensives by Army Groups North and South had experienced sharp reverses in the Leningrad and Rostov regions.

In the north, by 8 November the forward divisions of Leeb's XXXIX Motorized Corps were locked by the icy grip of winter in Tikhvin and south of Volkhov. The *Stavka* responded by assigning Army-General K.A. Meretskov, just released from NKVD captivity, to command the defeated 4th Army and ordered his army, which it then reinforced, to counterattack and drive German forces from Tikhvin. The Tikhvin counterstroke, which also involved the Leningrad Front's 54th Army and the 52nd Army under *Stavka* control, developed in piecemeal fashion between 12 November and 3 December. Klykov's 52nd Army began the assault southeast of the Volkhov river on 12 November, and, although the attacks failed, they forced Leeb to dispatch forces from Tikhvin to defend its XXXIX Motorized Corps' threatened flanks. Employing three shock groups, Meretskov's 4th Army struck the XXXIX Motorized Corps' overextended panzer and motorized divisions at Tikhvin on 19 November, creating a new crisis for Leeb.[43]

As the weather deteriorated further, Meretskov's forces closed on Tikhvin as the incessant attacks and bitter cold eroded the defenders' forces. After repeatedly failing to obtain Hitler's permission to withdraw from Tikhvin, on 8 December, exactly one month after they had triumphantly entered the town, the Germans abandoned the town. With it they also abandoned all hopes of capturing Leningrad in 1941. The retreat, which replicated in microcosm Napoleon's dramatic but costly retreat from Moscow in 1812, was not complete until late December, when German forces dug in along the Volkhov. By this time, the *Stavka* had reorganized its victorious 4th and 52nd Armies into the new Volkhov Front under Meretskov's command and reinforced it with the fresh 26th (soon re-designated 2nd Shock) and 59th Armies. Within days, acting on Stalin's orders, Meretskov was attempting to turn his successful Tikhvin counterstroke into a fully-fledged counteroffensive to relieve besieged Leningrad. The Red Army's signal victory at Tikhvin materially assisted its defense at Moscow both by tying down significant German forces and by convincing the Soviet leadership and Red Army that the Wehrmacht was indeed not invincible.

If this was not evidence enough of the Wehrmacht's deteriorating situation, during the same period, Red Army forces dealt Army Group South a signal reverse at Rostov in southern Russia. After a short delay to refit, on 5 November Kleist's First Panzer Army resumed its offensive toward Rostov. However, his panzers advanced to envelop the city from the northeast by way of Shakhty and Novocherkassk rather than along the shortest route to Rostov from the northwest. Despite driving a 30km (18-mile) deep wedge into the defenses of Lieutenant-General F.M. Kharitonov's defending 9th Army, heavy German losses and increasing Soviet resistance forced Kleist to halt his advance on 11 November.[44] In accordance with OKH orders, Kleist spent the next eight days preparing for a fresh advance on Rostov from the north.

While Kleist was preparing for his new attack, the *Stavka* significantly reinforced Cherevichenko's Southern Front by assigning him Major-General A.I. Lopatin's newly formed 37th Army and ordered Cherevichenko to hold Rostov at all costs. Cherevichenko concentrated his new army in the Shakhty region with orders to prepare a counterstroke to block and repel any German advance on Rostov. By this time, Cherevichenko's forces outnumbered German forces in every combat category except armour. However, the *front* commander failed to exploit his superiority by neglecting to concentrate his forces sufficiently.[45]

The battle for Rostov began on 17 November with both sides attacking simultaneously; the Germans assaulting Rostov from the north and the 37th Army striking Kleist's advancing forces in the flanks and rear. From the very start, the Southern Front's attack suffered from poor command and control and a host of other problems.[46] As a result, Kleist's forces captured Rostov on 21 November. The next night Halder wrote prophetically in his diary:

> Rostov is in our hands… North of Rostov, First Panzer Army was forced into the defense by the Russian attack with superior forces, and will have a hard time seeing it through.[47]

He was indeed correct.

Although victorious, Kleist's forces found themselves in an untenable position, occupying a major city and facing heavy attacks from front, flanks and rear. After regrouping his forces, Cherevichenko attacked once again on 27 November, this time from both northwest and south. The concerted Red Army assaults left Kleist with no choice but to evacuate the city and withdraw to new defenses along the River Mius from which he had begun the Rostov offensive only weeks before. The 56th and 9th Armies reoccupied Rostov and pursued German forces to the Mius. Kleist's defeat ended all German hopes for major gains along the southern axis. At a cost of 158,577 dead, captured and missing suffered since 29 September, the Southern Front had brought Army Group South's advance in southern Russia to an abrupt halt.[48] Thereafter, the front stabilized along the Mius as the fate of Barbarossa was being determined at Moscow.

Reflections

By 4 December 1941, the Red Army had achieved what many had thought unimaginable by halting and even driving back Wehrmacht offensives in northern and southern Russia. In so doing it had denied Hitler two of his most enticing strategic objectives, Leningrad and Rostov, and blocked the eastern gate into the Caucasus. Contrary to expectations, it had also halted the German juggernaut on the outskirts of Moscow, although it remained to be seen whether it could expel the Germans from their still threatening advanced positions within sight of the Kremlin's spires.

Despite these significant feats, the human costs the Red Army paid for its victories were significantly higher than the 145,000 casualties suffered by the Wehrmacht during its October and November lunge at Moscow.[49] From 1 October through 31 December 1941, official data indicates that the Red Army lost 1,656,517 men across the expanse of the entire front, including 636,383 killed, captured, or missing.[50] However, this figure is too low given the likely loss of one million men at Viaz'ma and Briansk. The final figure for losses during the Wehrmacht's ensuing advance on Moscow is probably closer to several hundred thousand men out of a total loss across the front of over two million. Russian sources now candidly attribute these catastrophic losses to serious mistakes on the part of the Soviet strategic and operational level leaderships direction of the defense, inexperienced command cadre and poor soldier training.[51]

The loss of 2.8 million soldiers in the first three months of the war and another 2 million by 31 December virtually eradicated the peacetime Red Army and forced the NKO to raise new largely untrained forces led by relatively inexperienced command cadre. The education of the 'new Red Army' took place on the battlefield in a real 'blooding' process. Fortunately, a number of experienced formations, such as the 32nd, 78th and 316th Rifle Divisions, the 1st Guards and 82nd Motorized Rifle Divisions and the 112th Tank Division, were available to participate in the fighting at Moscow and similar forces did so elsewhere along the front. As for the remainder of the Red Army, their contribution was a vivid demonstration that quantity has a quality of its own. Through their combined efforts and sacrifices and the rigors of the most severe Russian winter in recollection, the Red Army brought the German juggernaut to an abrupt halt at the gates of Moscow. On 5 December, however, it remained to be seen whether the Red Army could do more.

BARBAROSSA
CONTAINED
DECEMBER

The Situation on 5 December

After enduring just over five months of brutal and costly war, the Soviet Union and its Red Army teetered on the edge of an awful abyss in early December 1941. German officers perched in church steeples in the villages of Katiushka, Puchki and Krasnaia Poliana could observe the traffic in Moscow's streets through binoculars. The victorious Wehrmacht had advanced 900–1,200km (540–720 miles) deep into Mother Russia, occupied 1.5 million square kilometres of its soil, enslaved 77.6 million of its inhabitants and deprived it of well over half of its economic base and one third of its agriculture.[1] Despite its failure to capture the city by early December, the Wehrmacht's presence at the gates of Moscow menaced the country's survival, and Stalin, the *Stavka* and every Red Army soldier knew it. Therefore, the Red Army's sole mission in December was to eradicate the threat to Moscow at all costs.

If halting the Wehrmacht had been a Herculean task, then driving it back was almost unimaginable. Yet that is what the *Stavka* set about doing and it did so by mobilizing every ounce of strength remaining to the State and its people. Despite its weakened industrial base and resulting shortages in military equipment, the

Stavka marshaled to that task all of its own resources and some of its allies' (through Lend Lease).[2] All the while, the *Stavka* had to keep a wary eye on the Japanese and Turks as potential foes, leaving sizeable forces and over half of its tanks and aircraft to deal with eventualities in the Far East and Caucasus.[3]

The *Stavka* first began contemplating a counteroffensive in early November after the German advance faltered temporarily against the Mozhaisk line in the fall rains. From 21 October through 2 November the *Stavka* ordered the formation of 9 reserve armies and, simultaneously, 9 tank brigades, 49 separate tank battalions and more than 100 ski battalions by 1 December along with 90,000 individual replacements for the Western and Kalinin Fronts.[4] However, when Army Group Centre resumed its offensive in mid-November, the *Stavka* temporarily postponed the counteroffensive and employed its existing reserves to slow and then halt the German advance, particularly after Solnechnogorsk fell on 23 November.

Since German forces were only 40-45km (24-27 miles) from Moscow and where they would strike was only conjecture, in the next two days the *Stavka* ordered the 10th, 26th and 61st Armies to deploy forward to Riazan', Riazhsk and Ranenburg, respectively, 'to prevent the enemy advance.'[5] In addition, it reinforced its 30th, 5th and 16th Armies and, on 29 November, inserted the 1st Shock and 20th Armies from the *Stavka* reserve into the gap between the 16th and 30th Armies.[6]

After Kluge's Fourth Army began its assault at Naro-Fominsk, on 2 December the *Stavka* assigned additional reinforcements to Artem'ev's Moscow Military District with which to man Moscow's outer defense lines.[7] The following day, it also formally organized the Moscow Defense Zone (*Moskovskaia zona oborony* – MZO), consisting of the 24th and 60th Armies, which formed a second strategic echelon behind the Western Front.[8] While the *Stavka* assembled and assigned reserves and dealt with the immediate crisis at Moscow, Shaposhnikov's General Staff planned all aspects of the actual counteroffensive.[9]

Throughout this period the weather changed dramatically. By Russian standards, temperatures had been relatively mild throughout November and snowfall was light. In early December, however, the snow and cold finally arrived with a vengeance and the temperature fell precipitously to well below zero. German troops, who were ill equipped to withstand harsh winter conditions, were strung out along the few roads, and the Luftwaffe was operating from improvised forward airfields. Both vehicle and aircraft engines had to be heated for hours before attempting to start them. By contrast, the Red Air Force had heated hangers at permanent airfields. The Wehrmacht could do no more, and the initiative passed to the Soviets. The *Stavka* initiated a counteroffensive that ultimately became the first phase of a fully-fledged winter campaign.

On 29 November Zhukov requested the *Stavka* authorize him to commence the counteroffensive, stating:

> The enemy is exhausted. But if we do not now liquidate the dangerous enemy penetration, the Germans will be able to reinforce their forces in the Moscow region with large reserves at the expense of their northern and southern groups of forces, and then a serious situation can result. I.V. Stalin says that he agrees with the General Staff.[10]

The *Stavka* accepted Zhukov's advice and assigned the Western and Southwestern Fronts their respective missions later that evening. After the two *fronts* presented the *Stavka* their specific plans the next day, the *Stavka* ordered Konev's Kalinin Front to join the counteroffensive and, at 0330 hours on 1 December, issued its attack directives.[11]

Ultimately, the *Stavka*'s offensive concept required the Western Front's right and left wings, in conjunction with the Kalinin and Southwestern Fronts, to destroy the main enemy groupings that were attempting to envelop Moscow from the north and south.[12] Zhukov's Western Front was to play the main role. The plan anticipated an advance of 60km (36 miles) north of Moscow and 100km (60 miles) to its south. The Western Front's 30th, 1st Shock, 20th and 16th Armies were to attack on 3-4 December and the Kalinin Front's 29th and 31st Armies on 5-6 December.[13]

Zhukov ordered the armies on his *front*'s right and left wings, which were 200km (120 miles) apart, to destroy enemy forces operating north and south of Moscow. Simultaneously, the 5th, 33rd, 43rd and 49th Armies in the *front*'s central sector were to tie down enemy forces and prevent them from reinforcing their flanks.[14] Konev ordered his centre and right flank armies to defend the Selizharevo-Torzhok sector 'actively,' and his left flank armies were to attack and destroy the enemy Klin grouping in cooperation with the Western Front's right flank.[15] At the same time, Timoshenko's forces were to encircle and destroy the enemy Elets-Livny grouping, threaten the rear of Guderian's Second Panzer Army and destroy German forces in cooperation with Western Front's left flank.[16]

According to official Soviet count, by 6 December the three *fronts* had received 27 additional divisions, bringing their strength up to 1,100,000 troops supported by 7,652 guns and mortars, 774 tanks and 1,000 aircraft. These forces faced an estimated 1,708,000 German soldiers equipped with 13,500 artillery pieces, 1,170 tanks and 615 aircraft.[17] However, this count clearly overestimates both German and Soviet strength and falsely claims German numerical superiority in all categories except aircraft. In fact, formerly classified Soviet studies estimate Red Army effective combat strength on 5 December at 388,000 combat troops supported by 5,635 guns and mortars and 550 tanks opposing 240,000 German troops equipped with 5,350 artillery pieces and 600 tanks.[18] This documents the stark reality that both sides were at the end of their tether, and the opposing forces were often mere skeletons of their former selves.[19] The vast majority of Soviet troops, however, were poorly trained, only partially equipped and led by inexperienced command cadre.[20] Given the circumstances, the reserve forces went into combat from the march and through heavy snow without proper assembly or offensive preparations.[21]

Worse still for the Germans, their forces were woefully overextended, poorly equipped for winter, lacked reserves and occupied unprepared positions, while the Soviets were temporarily concentrated at a few critical points. The Wehrmacht had lost 830,000 men by 6 December, although Hitler admitted to only half a million.[22] Thus, on the Western Front's right wing attacking north of Moscow Zhukov was able to achieve a better than two to one superiority over the Germans in personnel and lesser superiority in artillery and mortars. But the Germans were superior in armour. Moreover, German intelligence estimates believed that Stalin had no more reserves and that it would take an additional three months before the Red Army could raise new forces. For example, an OKH intelligence estimate prepared on 4 December optimistically noted, 'At present, the enemy in front of Army Group Centre are not capable of conducting a counteroffensive without significant reserves.'[23] The reserves, however, were present. Consequently, the Soviet counterattacks achieved surprise and the shock of the blow was all the greater.[24]

Despite Hitler's optimism and obstinacy, on 5 December a more prudent Bock at Army Group Centre began working on a plan to withdraw his exposed forces to more favorable defensive positions and so informed his subordinate armies. The next day, Hitler reluctantly approved the withdrawal, which was supposed to take two days, but only as a prudent measure to 'shorten the front lines.'[25] In the midst of this withdrawal and before retreating German forces could dig in, Zhukov's armies struck.

The Moscow Counteroffensive

The Red Army's counteroffensive began at first light on 5 December in the Kalinin Front's sector and, over the next two days, spread inexorably across the entire front from Kalinin southward to Kastornoe.[26] The counterattack began in the north early on Friday, 5 December, when the temperature was minus 15 degrees Fahrenheit (minus 26°C) and the snow was more than a metre deep. The 29th and 31st Armies of Konev's Kalinin Front attacked the northern flank of the Klin bulge and were joined by the 5th Army at 1600 hours. The 30th, 1st Shock and 20th Armies joined the battle north of Moscow on 6 December, while the 10th and 13th Armies went into action against Guderian's forces south of the city the same day. The forces in the centre and on the right flank of Rokossovsky's 16th Army and Kostenko's Operational Group far to the south attacked on 7 December, and, finally, Rokossovsky's remaining forces, Operational Group Belov and the 3rd and 50th Armies joined the fray on 8 December. By that time, combat was raging along the Kalinin, Klin, Solnechnogorsk, Istra, Tula and Elets axes.

During early December, the *Stavka*'s highest priority goal was to eliminate the threatening German pincers north and south of Moscow. To do so, Maslennikov's 29th and Iushkevich's 31st Armies attacked west and east of Kalinin at 0300 hours on 5 December, but made only limited progress against Ninth Army's prepared defenses.[27] The next day Leliushenko's 30th Army, Kuznetsov's 1st Shock Army and Vlasov's 20th Army struck from positions north and south of Dmitrov on the Volga-Moscow Canal. Penetrating the Third Panzer Group's defenses, Leliushenko's 8th Tank Brigade and 365th Rifle Division advanced 13km (7.8 miles) and approached Klin from the northeast.[28] German resistance at Klin was fierce because control of its road junction was vital to Reinhardt's ability to withdraw forward elements of his panzer groups from Dmitrov and Solnechnogorsk, where they were under heavy assault by the 1st Shock and 20th Armies. Therefore, after notifying Bock of his intentions, at noon on 6 December Reinhardt ordered his 1st, 2nd, 6th and 7th Panzer Divisions and the 14th Motorized Division to conduct a fighting withdrawal back to Klin against the advancing 1st Shock and 20th Armies. This meant that the left flank of Hoepner's Fourth Panzer Group would soon be uncovered.

Kuznetsov's 1st Shock and Vlasov's 20th Armies pressed westward in the Iakhroma and Krasnaia Poliana sectors early on 7 December. Although they made only slow progress (1-1.5km per day), they generated a massive traffic jam among Reinhardt's forces which, under the most trying conditions, were struggling to reach Klin before Soviet troops cut off their withdrawal routes. The scene was an unaccustomed one for the Wehrmacht:

> Sunday, 7 December, dawned clear and cold at the front. Early morning Luftwaffe reconnaissance flights brought back reports of continuing heavy rail traffic toward Moscow and toward Tikhvin. At ground level, plumes of blowing snow restricted visibility and the roads drifted shut. During the night, the roads running east and southeast from Klin had filled with Third Panzer Group rear echelon trucks and wagons all heading west. How far west nobody knew. The front had already begun to pull back from the Moscow-Volga Canal. First Shock Army was following hesitantly behind the panzer group which because of the weather had already abandoned fifteen tanks, three heavy howitzers, a half-dozen anti-aircraft guns and dozens of trucks and passenger cars – more material than would ordinarily be lost in a week's heavy fighting. Troops could not tow the guns out of their emplacements. The motors of some vehicles would not start; the grease on the bearing and in transmissions in others froze while they were running. The 1st Panzer Division, which had been headed toward Krasnaya Polyana, had turned around during the night with orders to block the Soviet thrust toward Klin. In the morning it was extended over forty miles, bucking snowdrifts on jammed roads, with its tanks low on fuel.[29]

To increase Reinhardt's misery, Rokossovsky's 16th Army also went into action on 7 December. The 8th and 9th Guards' and 18th Rifle Division's assault threatened to crumble the 35th Infantry Division's defenses on the Third Panzer Group's right flank and cut off Reinhardt's force from Hoepner's group on his right.[30] By nightfall, the most serious threat to Reinhardt's panzer group was Leliushenko's force, whose lead elements were only 8km (5 miles) from Klin. That night Bock put out a call for 'even for the last bicyclist' to assist Reinhardt.[31]

Heavy fighting raged around Klin through 8 December, while Leliushenko's 379th Rifle Division severed the Klin–Kalinin railroad and the remainder of Rokossovsky's army assaulted westward toward Istra against Hoepner's now sagging defenses. Major-General A.P. Beloborodov's 9th Guards Rifle Division, manned by seasoned Far Easterners, smashed against the SS 'Reich' Motorized Division's defenses at Snegiri and, after a full day of brutal fighting, enveloped the defenders' flanks, forcing SS Reich to withdraw. Hoepner reinforced the sector with part of the 10th Panzer Division, but the next day had to send the bulk of the 10th Panzer northward to help Reinhardt hold on to Klin as SS 'Reich' withdrew, according to Soviet accounts, 'in disorder' to the Istra river.[32]

In the absence of any meaningful reinforcements, over Reinhardt's objections, Bock had no choice but to subordinate the Third Panzer Group to Fourth Panzer Group (and thus Fourth Army) since, as he reasoned, it would make both Hoepner and Kluge more responsive to Reinhardt's needs. For the moment, however, the priority task of all three commanders was to extract Reinhardt's panzer group from the Klin region so that Hoepner could withdraw and, in turn, protect Kluge's right flank.[33]

Despite these initial successes, not everything was going smoothly for the *Stavka* and Zhukov. By late on 8 December Red Army forces had advanced from 3-20km (2-12 miles) along a 290km (174-mile) front, but the advance was uneven. Leliushenko's 30th Army hung threateningly over Reinhardt's left flank and, with it, Klin, while Kuznetsov's 1st Shock, Vlasov's 20th and Rokossovsky's 16th Armies were compressing German forces back toward Klin and Istra from the east and south. To the north, Konev's forces had achieved only mixed success. West of Kalinin, Maslennikov's 29th Army had struck in three sectors up to 7 or 8km apart instead of a single sector, and each attack had faltered in the face of heavy flanking fire and Ninth Army counterattacks. Attacking east of Kalinin, Iushkevich's 31st Army attacking east of Kalinin had achieved greater success. His forces captured a bridgehead over the Volga and penetrated 10-12km (6-7.2 miles), severing the Kalinin–Turginovo road and threatening to envelop German forces in Kalinin from the east. So serious was the threat that Strauss, the Ninth Army commander, shifted two divisions southeast of Kalinin to contain Iushkevich's advance.[34]

Frustrated over the slow rate of advance, on 9 December Zhukov issued a directive to correct the situation:

> I order:
> 1. Categorically forbid you to conduct frontal combat with enemy covering units and to conduct frontal combat against fortified positions. Leave small covering forces against rear guards and fortified positions and seek to envelop them, while reaching as deep as possible along the enemy's withdrawal routes.
> 2. Form several shock groups in the armies consisting of tanks, submachine gunners and cavalry and, under the direction of brave commanders, throw them into the enemy's rear area to destroy fuel and artillery tractors.
> 3. Strike the enemy day and night. In the event units become exhausted, create pursuit detachments.
> 4. Protect of forces' operations with antitank defenses, reconnaissance and constant security, bearing in mind that, when withdrawing, the enemy will search for opportunities to counterattack...
>
> [Signed] Zhukov, Sokolovsky, Bulganin[35]

Over the next several days, Zhukov's right flank armies tightened the noose around Klin as an increasingly desperate Reinhardt struggled to extract his forces from the looming trap.[36] By late on 12 December, the 30th and 1st Shock Armies closed in on Klin from the north and east, while Vlasov's 20th Army captured Solnechnogorsk and Rokossovsky's 16th Army, Istra. German forces blew up the dam at the Istra Reservoir, inundating man, beast and equipment and forming a 60m (65-yard) wide water barrier in Hoepner's sector that stopped the 16th Army's forward progress in its tracks.[37] At the same time, Reinhardt's 1st,

6th and 7th Panzer Divisions and 14th Motorized Divisions clung desperately to their shrinking defense lines east of the town, while the 2nd Panzer attempted to hold open the road to the west. His goal was to extract his forces to the safety of the new Volokolamsk-Russa defense line, then under construction to the west.

Urged on by Zhukov, the 30th and 1st Shock Armies tried to envelop German forces defending Klin. While Leliushenko's and Kuznetsov's forces attacked the town from all sides, the former committed a mobile group, consisting of the 18th and 82nd Cavalry Divisions and the 107th Motorized Rifle Division under the command of Colonel P.G. Chanchibadze, to cut German escape routes to the west. Chanchibadze's force managed to penetrate to Diatlovo, 35km (21 miles) west of Klin by late on 14 December, but was blocked just short of the Klin-Volokolamsk road by the withdrawing 6th Panzer and 14th Motorized Divisions. During the dramatic attempt to cut German withdrawal routes, at 0200 hours on 15 December, the 30th Army's 365th and 371st Rifle Divisions and the 1st Shock Army's 348th Rifle Division and 50th and 84th Rifle Brigades captured the town. The fall of Klin also settled Kalinin's fate and the next day Strauss's forces abandoned the city to Konev's forces.[38]

While Leliushenko's and Kuznetsov's forces were capturing Klin, Rokossovsky's 16th Army tried in vain to surmount the massive water obstacle along his front. Through sheer sacrifice and heroism, soldiers from the 18th and 354th Rifle Divisions tried to seize a bridgehead over the swollen River Istra, but were stopped in their tracks by devastating artillery fire. Rokossovsky reacted by forming two mobile groups under Generals Remizov and Katukov to envelop the reservoir from the north and the river from the south. In addition, Zhukov ordered Govorov's 5th Army to join the assault and assigned him General Dovator's 2nd Guards Cavalry Corps, reinforced by two separate tank battalions, to serve as a third mobile group.[39]

The 16th and 5th Armies and their three mobile groups attacked on 13 December and achieved immediate success. In the 5th Army's sector, Govorov first committed a 'shock group' of three rifle divisions (the 19th, 329th and 326th) and several tank brigades on a narrow front toward Russa. Dovator's 2nd Guards Cavalry Corps then charged into the gap. Hard on the heels of Dovator marched a mobile tank group consisting of the 20th Tank Brigade and 136th Separate Tank Battalion. Dovator's force advanced 16km (9.6 miles) in two days, cut the German withdrawal routes west of Zvenigorod early on 15 December and forced Fourth Panzer Group to accelerate its westward withdrawal.[40]

Meanwhile, by late on 16 December, 30th Army's Group Chanchibadze was 17km (10.2 miles) northeast of Volokolamsk, Remizov's Group, now under 20th Army's control, was 16km (9.6 miles) west of the Istra Reservoir, and Katukov's group had advanced 24km (14.4 miles) west of Istra. Abandoning much of its heavy weaponry and forced by the deep snow to keep to the roads, the Fourth Panzer Group's XXXXVI Motorized Corps withdrew westward at a rapid rate, destroying roads and bridges alike as it withdrew. Even though Dovator was killed in action on 20 December, Zhukov's shock group tactics finally unhinged German defenses, albeit slowly. The Germans frantically moved their few available reserves back and forth along lateral routes to shore up threatened sectors, while other units tried to withdraw from the trap.

In a period of 11 days, the armies on Zhukov's right flank advanced 30-65km (18-39 miles) at a rate of almost 6km (3.6 miles) per day, while Konev's armies had covered 10-22km (6-13 miles) at a much slower rate. While limited in scope, the Red Army's offensive had cleared German forces from the northern and northeastern approaches to Moscow and forced the Third and Fourth Panzer Groups to withdraw in unprecedented disorder to new defenses farther west.[41]

Far to the south, Red Army forces experienced even greater success. There, Zhukov's left flank armies attempted to carry out a similar pincer movement against Guderian's Second Panzer Army. A cavalry-mechanized group commanded by Belov, Boldin's 50th

Army and Lieutenant-General F.I. Golikov's new 10th Army launched concentric attacks to cut off and encircle Guderian's forward elements in the Venev and Stalinogorsk region.

Guderian's forces were indeed vulnerable to such a blow. First, his army occupied a vulnerable salient east of Tula. Seventy-five per cent of his forces faced the 50th Army at Tula or Group Belov north of Venev, and only four divisions were deployed along an extended broken front defending his long right flank.[42] Second, Zhukov had concentrated Golikov's 10th Army against the weak easternmost segment of Guderian's advance, creating a more than three-fold superiority over the German defenders. Third, Golikov's attack, which he launched from the march through deep snow, caught Guderian's forces by surprise, 'causing panic among the German forces.'[43]

Striking on 6 December, in two days of heavy fighting, Golikov's forces captured Mikhailov and Serebrianye Prudy and advanced 30km (18 miles) into the depth of Guderian's defenses, threatening to encircle one third of Guderian's forces. Zhukov then ordered Boldin's 50th Army to strike south and southeast from Tula to complete the encirclement. Guderian responded by ordering part of his forces to withdraw to the Shat and Don rivers, while the remainder held off the advancing Soviet forces. Exploiting their superior mobility, four of Guderian's divisions withdrew 17-25km (10.2-15 miles) by late on 8 December, reaching the Dedilovo region. Boldin's forces then struck toward the south, but were halted by the 296th Infantry Division after insignificant gains. Although Red Army ski battalions harassed the Germans withdrawing in the snow, Soviet main forces were too weak and immobile to encircle the bulge completely before the Germans escaped. Renewed attacks on 11 December got nowhere, because the 50th Army had been severely weakened in manpower and equipment after the earlier Briansk encirclement and the battles around Tula. The Soviet attacks in the north were also inconclusive, although several German rear-guard divisions were cut up in both pincers.[44]

Understanding the reasons for Boldin's failure, Zhukov reported:

The 50th Army's forces, which have been defending Tula, suffered great losses during the last few days. There are no reserves... I request one rifle brigade and one tank battalion be sent on auto-transport to Tula to assist Comrade Boldin. The assistance is necessary since, apparently, the operations by Golikov and Belov will not develop so quickly.[45]

By late on 9 December the German 112th Infantry Division and other withdrawing forces managed to halt the 10th Army's advance along the Shat and Don rivers. Golikov's army had advanced 60km (36 miles) but could advance no farther. However, Guderian's forces were also reaching the limits of their endurance and were, in fact, attempting to avoid disaster. As early as 8 December, the Second Panzer Army reported that one of its corps had suffered 1,500 frostbite cases, 350 requiring amputations, many vehicles and guns had to be abandoned, supplies were running short and a 'serious crisis in confidence had broken out among the troops and the NCOs.'[46]

The situation on Guderian's left flank and centre was little better. Northeast of Tula, Cavalry-Mechanized Group Belov, which consisted of two cavalry divisions, one rifle and one tank division and a tank brigade, attacked on 8 December, captured Venev on 9 December, raced to the south and captured Stalinogorsk from the withdrawing Germans on 11 December.[47] Once again Zhukov ordered Belov and Boldin's forces to encircle the Germans, the former by advancing south from Tula and the latter by advancing to Plavsk.[48] At the same time, Golikov also reoriented his 10th Army's advance from Stalinogorsk to Plavsk in an attempt to effect an even larger encirclement. However, the regrouping took Golikov three days, Boldin's attack encountered stiff resistance and only Belov's force achieved any notable success. By 16 December Belov's forces had captured Dedilovo and Golikov's army seized Bogoroditsk. More important, Zakharkin's

49th Army joinéd the attack north of Tula and advanced 5-50km (3-30 miles) on Boldin's right flank. By this time, Guderian's army was withdrawing across its entire front.

Similar disasters befell the German Second Army, which was deployed on Guderian's right flank and was now under the command of Colonel-General Rudolf Schmidt. Since Schmidt's army had been attacking continuously right up to 6 December, it had not been able to occupy substantial defensive positions when Timoshenko began his counteroffensive. Delivering Timoshenko's supporting attack, Gorodniansky's 13th Army struck Schmidt's positions forward of Elets on 6 December, drawing German reserves away from the region where Timoshenko's intended to deliver his main attack.[49] The following morning, Lieutenant-General F.Ia. Kostenko's operational group, formed around the nucleus of Major-General V.D. Kriuchenkin's 5th Cavalry Corps, struck Schmidt's weakened defenses along the Kastornoe-Livny axis south of Elets. Gorodniansky's forces captured Elets on 9 December and the next day Group Kostenko cut off the withdrawal routes of the Second Army's XXXIV Army Corps to Livny.

During the ensuing days, Kreizer's 13th and Lieutenant-General K.P. Podlas's 40th Armies joined the offensive north and south of Elets. The fighting reached ever-higher intensity when the XXXIV Army Corps, already encircled, managed to encircle Kriuchenkin's 5th Cavalry Corps. By 21 December, the attacking Soviet forces had decimated the encircled German corps, prompting the OKH to disband the unfortunate force. According to Soviet sources:

> The commander of the 134th Infantry Division was killed....The division lost most of its equipment... The 134th Infantry Division was no longer combat capable.[50]

A German account vividly confirmed the XXXIV Army Corps' defeat:

On 7 December, Second German Army stopped after taking Yelets, the last town of any consequence within fifty miles. The army's commander, General Rudolph Schmidt, proposed in the next several days to devastate a ten-mile strip parallel to his entire line and then pull back behind that ready-made no-mans-land to settle in for the winter.

The next day, even more suddenly than it had dropped, the temperature rose to above freezing along the entire Army Group Centre front. At the Second Army centre north of Yelets, in snow and rain that froze when it hit the stone-cold ground, half-a-dozen Soviet tanks [from the 150th Tank Brigade] created a hole between the 45th and 95th Infantry Divisions and a Soviet cavalry division [the 55th] galloped through.

The two German divisions' self-propelled assault guns could barely negotiate the ice and by the next morning after heavy fresh snow had fallen and blown into drifts during the night, they could not move at all, which was immaterial since both divisions had by then also run out of motor fuel. In another day, two more cavalry divisions and a rifle division [the 5th Cavalry Corp and 121st Rifle Division] had opened a gap to sixteen miles and had driven a fifty-mile-deep wedge northwest toward Novosil and Orel. The 95th Division had lost half its strength. The 45th had lost more. Nobody knew how much. Both were out of motor fuel and short on ammunition and rations. Air supply was promised, but the airplanes could not fly in the snow and rain. Schmidt told Bock that Second Army was about to be cut in two and driven back on Kursk and Orel leaving an 85-mile gap in between.[51]

The cumulative effect of the Red Army's incessant offensives during the first half of December reinforced the on-going crisis in German command circles, bringing Hitler's long-standing distrust of his senior commanders into the open. The Wehrmacht's defeats at Tikhvin in the north and Rostov in the south only exacerbated the situation. The first act had begun in the south on 29 November, when SS Division *Liebstandarte Adolf Hitler* withdrew from Rostov under Soviet pressure. By the time the dictator attempted to reverse this decision, the leading elements of First Panzer Army had begun a general withdrawal back to a more defensible line along the Mius river. The Army Group South commander, Rundstedt, insisted that this withdrawal was essential and requested that he be relieved unless he was allowed to continue. Hitler took him at his word on 1 December, only to be forced the next day to approve the withdrawal that Rundstedt had demanded. Bowing to the inevitable, on 8 December Hitler issued his Führer Directive No. 39, which grudgingly admitted all was not well with Barbarossa.[52]

By 16 December the Soviet counteroffensive at Moscow had forced Army Group Centre commander Bock to make a similar request for authority to withdraw and adjust positions as necessary. Late that night, Brauchitsch, the German Army commander, and Halder explained the situation to Hitler, who insisted that a general withdrawal was out of the question. On 18 December Bock surrendered his command to Kluge, ostensibly because of genuine ill health. Hitler then forbade any further major withdrawals, ordering Army Group Centre to use 'fanatical resistance' to stem the tide until reinforcements could arrive. The next day a disgusted Hitler accepted Brauchitsch's resignation and personally assumed command of the Wehrmacht. He told Halder that the Wehrmacht should emulate the positive, enthusiastic approach of the Luftwaffe and forbid any preparation or discussion of 'rear positions' in the event of a Soviet breakthrough.[53]

Heinz Guderian was the next victim. Like many field commanders before and since, he was convinced that higher headquarters were out of touch with the real gravity of the situation. Throughout December he had used Hitler's personal adjutant and other acquaintances as back door channels to convey his concerns to Hitler and the OKH. On 14 December, one of Brauchitsch's last acts as Wehrmacht commander had been to place the Second Army under the control of the Second Panzer Army and to authorize Guderian to withdraw so long as he held Orel. Ordered to stand fast, Guderian flew back to Rastenburg on 20 December to explain his desperate situation to Hitler. Although the general's account of this conversation naturally is biased, he undoubtedly insisted his forces lacked clothing, equipment and shelter and needed to withdraw to more defensible lines. On Christmas Day, after a final pointless argument with his new army group commander, Kluge, Guderian in turn found himself relieved.[54]

Within the context of the savaging of the twin concepts of Blitzkrieg and presumed German military invincibility at Moscow, it came as no surprise that the heads of those who had nurtured such concepts would roll.

Reflections

On 16 December, the Red Army's offensive had only just begun. Zhukov committed his remaining armies (the 33rd and 43rd) into the maelstrom west of Moscow by the end of the month. During the same period, the *Stavka* committed its fresh 39th and 61st Armies into combat on the northern and southern flanks of what by now had become a fiery cauldron in the midst of the frigid cold. Having liberated Kalinin and breached the Germans' Volga defenses, Konev's armies were approaching Staritsa and Rzhev, and Zhukov's right flank armies (the 30th, 1st Shock, 20th and 16th) were driving the shaken Third and Fourth Panzer Groups inexorably west toward the Lama and Russa rivers north and south of Volokolamsk. Having already retreated 100-125km (60-75 miles), German forces were hard-pressed to retain control of positions from which they had begun their mid-November advance on Moscow.

While Kluge's Fourth Army held firm against the 33rd and 43rd Armies in Zhukov's centre, Guderian's Second Panzer was struggling to hold onto his defenses north and south of Kaluga against Group Belov and the 49th, 50th and 10th Armies. Further south, Schmidt's decimated Second Army tried frantically to cover a yawning gap between his and Guderian's armies. South of Moscow,

German forces had withdrawn 250km (150 miles) westward, well beyond the positions from which they had begun their offensive in mid-November. By every measure, the German defeat was real, sobering and by no means at an end.

In addition to shaking the concept of Blitzkrieg to its very foundations, the first 10 days of the Red Army's Moscow counteroffensive punctured forever the myth of German military invincibility for both German and Russian alike. Moreover, it thwarted Operation Barbarossa and placed the strategic initiative firmly in Soviet hands. It was understandable, therefore, that when its initial series of counterattacks north of Moscow achieved success, the *Stavka*'s ambitions soared. Within only weeks, the initial, limited counterattacks were replaced with far more extensive offensive missions for *fronts* and armies deployed from Leningrad southward to the Black Sea.

Ultimately, by early January 1942, an overall concept had emerged that governed subsequent Soviet operations throughout the entire winter. However, because of its hasty formulation and the often-clumsy execution of the concept, in the end the spectacular early gains did not produce the desired strategic results. In particular, the *Stavka*'s winter campaign failed to destroy Army Group Centre. The offensive did, however, prove immensely sobering for the German High Command and, for the first time, raised doubts among some German commanders as to whether the war could indeed be won.

CONCLUSIONS

When Hitler unleashed his Wehrmacht against the Soviet Union in Operation Barbarossa, neither the Red Army nor the Soviet State were prepared for Blitzkrieg or perhaps any other sort of war. The Red Army was beset with a host of problems, most of which were products of misguided state policy. Internally, the army had experienced and was still experiencing brutal waves of purges, ruthless and often indiscriminate repression, inflicted by Stalin in the name of cleansing the military of any disloyal elements, real or imagined. The purges physically tore the heart and brain from the army by eliminating the best, brightest and most capable military theorists and leaders at virtually every level of command. Stark intimidation deadened initiative and original thought among those who survived. Tangentially, the purges also struck Soviet defense industries, liquidating weapons designers and developers and inhibiting the design, production and fielding of new weaponry. This, coupled with the Red Army's massive expansion from 1937 to 1941, which was a byproduct of Stalin's concern with the deteriorating international situation in Europe and the Far East, thrust thousands of officers into command positions for which they were clearly unqualified.

Externally, the Red Army's dismal military performance in the 1939-1940 Russo-Finnish War and in its clumsy occupation of eastern Poland, prompted Stalin to reform, reorganize and reequip the Red Army, an ambitious program that was only partially complete when Barbarossa commenced. As a result, although massive, in June 1941 the Red Army was a Colossus with feet of clay. With few exceptions, its five million troops were poorly trained, badly led, inadequately supplied and equipped and mal-deployed. Worse still, echoing the situation in 1914, the cumbersome Soviet mobilization system did not meet the requirements of modern war. As a result, rather than losing 2 armies and 245,000 men as the Tsarist Army had done in one month of battle at Tannenberg and the Masurian Lakes in 1914, the Red Army lost 3 armies and 747,850 men during the first two weeks of Operation Barbarossa.¹ In 1914 A.V. General Samsonov, the commander of the defeated Russian 2nd Army, committed suicide on the battlefield. In 1941 Stalin had General Pavlov, his defeated *front* commander, shot for treason.

The Red Army's occupation of Poland, Bessarabia and the Baltic States in 1939 and 1940 undermined the coherence of Soviet strategic defenses, and new defenses were incomplete when the German Army struck. Finally, Stalin's policy of accommodation with Germany, whether or not it was designed to gain time to prepare the country for war, provided the prerequisites for the Wehrmacht's achievement of strategic, operational and tactical surprise. Even though Stalin was cautious enough to mobilize the Red Army partially in April 1941, the tyrant in him never allowed for the possibility that Hitler, his brother tyrant, might betray him:

> Believing completely in the correctness of his estimate of the political situation, Stalin was in no position to assess objectively the conditions in the prewar months and neither managed to exploit those possibilities accorded him by the non-aggression pact nor was able to turn the state's control rudder suddenly enough to repulse Fascists aggression in timely fashion, which, in turn, led to false conclusions and incorrect diplomatic actions.²

In June 1941 Stalin was clever to a fault, but his cleverness nearly undid both him and the Soviet Union.

As a result, the Red Army that the Wehrmacht encountered when it attacked in June 1941 was a peacetime army – and it showed. The Wehrmacht's subsequent Barbarossa victories were, by every possible measure, as unprecedented as they were massive. While the Red Army struggled desperately to save itself from utter destruction, for weeks Stalin and the *Stavka* adhered slavishly to an ill-advised and inappropriate strategy of 'offensiveness.' They ordered their increasingly threadbare and disorganized forces to undertake repeated counterattacks, counterstrokes and counter-offensives in an attempt to fulfill the unrealistic demands of Soviet war plans. Most of these actions were simply suicidal. At Raseinai, Brody, Dubno, Sol'tsy, Staraia Russa, Siniavino, Smolensk, Korosten', Dukhovshchina, Novozybkov, El'nia and countless other battlefields, loyal officers and brave troop sacrificed themselves in search of illusive victories against the most efficient killing machine modern Europe had yet produced.

On the positive side of the ledger, the incessant, seemingly irrational and usually futile Soviet attacks imperceptibly eroded German combat strength, exacting a toll that prompted Hitler to alter his strategy and, ultimately, conditioned the Wehrmacht for defeat at Moscow. Those Soviet officers and soldiers who survived their severe and costly baptism of fire eventually exploited their harsh education to exact a terrible toll on their tormentors.

Despite the congenital 'spirit of offensiveness' that permeated Soviet military theory in the 1930s and dominated *Stavka* actions during the first several months of war, the Wehrmacht forced the Red Army to conduct a strategic defense throughout the entire summer-fall campaign. The Germans seized and maintained the initiative along all three strategic axes, compelling the *Stavka* to find ways to alter the course of war. Throughout most of this period, in every respect, the Red Army was ill suited and unable to do so. To a considerable degree, Stalin and his *Stavka* associates were responsible for the Red Army's defensive disasters. They failed to order the

Red Army over the defense at the appropriate time and place, and their numerous attempts to halt the German Army and regain the strategic initiative failed miserably, often with catastrophic results.

Only at Smolensk in late July and August 1941 did the Red Army successfully halt the German advance and force Hitler to alter his strategic offensive plan. Even in this case, however, Soviet success was only fleeting. Hitler's decision to turn Guderian's forces south led directly to the loss of the entire Southwestern Front at Kiev. At the same time, the Smolensk counteroffensives weakened Red Army forces defending the Moscow axis and paved the way for the subsequent disasters at Viaz'ma and Briansk, which decimated the Western, Reserve and Briansk Fronts and left Moscow vulnerable and nearly defenseless in November.

Clearly the Red Army was not capable of organizing and conducting a deep strategic defense in summer 1941. Exploiting its superior command and control, firepower and mobility, the Wehrmacht conducted Blitzkrieg in ruthlessly efficient fashion, repeatedly penetrating, enveloping, encircling and destroying large Soviet forces and creating immense gaps in the front that the *Stavka* could close only by committing large numbers of hastily raised strategic reserves.

Nevertheless, even in these extremely unfavorable circumstances, operationally at least, the Red Army was able to erect sound defenses along selected axes for brief periods. In addition to doing so at Smolensk in August and September, it slowed German forward momentum at Sol'tsy and Staraia Russa along the Leningrad axis and on the approaches to Kiev in July and August and, for brief periods, successfully defended the cities of Odessa and Sevastopol'.[3] In a strategic sense, however, even these operational successes proved inexpedient given the Red Army's heavy losses. Stalin's tardy decision to withdraw his forces from Belorussia in June, from the western Ukraine in July and from Kiev in September led directly to the encirclement and destruction of entire *fronts* and the loss of immense territories with large populations and valuable industrial and agricultural resources. Similar catastrophes on a smaller scale occurred at Uman', Luga and in the Donbas region.

Only during the Moscow defense in late fall was the Red Army able to seize and hold the strategic initiative. When it finally did so in December, it was due primarily to German strategic errors, the greatest of which was Hitler's insatiable appetite for victory and congenital over-optimism that impelled him to commit Wehrmacht forces too far along too many strategic axes. The successful Red Army counteroffensives at Tikhvin and Rostov accentuated Hitler's errors and signaled the sharp turn about to take place in the fortunes of war. The twin victories in both north and south played a vital role in the defense of Moscow and created the necessary prerequisites for the Red Army to conduct its decisive Moscow counteroffensive.

In conjunction with the continuing counteroffensive at Tikhvin, the Moscow counteroffensive soon developed into a general offensive along the entire Soviet-German front. With it, the Red Army seized and maintained the strategic initiative for more than five months and, in retrospect at least, created the first great turning point in the war. Thereafter, it was clear that Germany could not destroy the Soviet Union. Operation Barbarossa failed at Moscow and with that failure, Hitler's hope of destroying the Soviet Union forever faded.

The Moscow counteroffensive proved to be a turning point in several other respects, particularly in the realm that the Soviets termed 'military art' [*voennoe iskusstva*]. For the first time in the war, at Moscow the *Stavka* managed to raise, assemble, deploy and commit strategic reserves into combat secretly and successfully.[4] It selected the proper time to conduct its counteroffensive, at that critical juncture when the Wehrmacht's offensive momentum had ebbed but before it occupied well-prepared defenses, and it chose appropriate axes along which to concentrate its main attacks. The counteroffensive surprised German forces and denied them the opportunity to regroup and counter the Soviet attacks. Thus, 'The fact that the German command was caught unaware bore witness to the skillful Russian deployment of their forces and their correct selection of the time for the counteroffensive.'[5]

A recent Russian assessment of the Moscow counteroffensive correctly notes:

> The Battle for Moscow completed the failure of Hitler's Blitzkrieg. It signified the ruin of all of the Nazi leadership's military-political and strategic plans and doomed Germany to a prolonged war, which it could not successfully conduct. The Red Army's operations in the Battle for Moscow, which influenced the further course of the Second World War and peaceful coexistence, was regarded as an outstanding victory that facilitated the strengthening of the anti-Fascist struggle in the entire world. Certainly, it also produced tremendous moral and political elan in the USSR, both in the rear and at the front.[6]

The numerous disasters the Red Army experienced during the first six months of the war resulted from many factors, some of which the Soviet leadership had begun correcting by the fall of 1941. These included incompetent leadership within the army and navy, poorly trained command cadre and soldiers, inadequate mastery of modern weaponry and hasty commitment to combat of poorly trained and equipped reserves. In short, the Red Army was not prepared to fight a modern war against a strong and well-trained enemy that was constantly on the attack. Excessive turbulence in command assignments, continuing repression by the state and the state's resort to unfounded propaganda to inspire its soldiers only compounded these difficulties.

Frequent breakdowns in command, control and communications led to poor and often tardy command decisions, which, in turn, resulted in many costly encirclements and massive personnel and equipment losses. Severe command turbulence forced newly assigned commanders to reach hurried and often incorrect decisions. For example, the Western Front had four commanders

(Pavlov, Timoshenko, Konev and Zhukov) in less than six months and the Briansk Front three (Eremenko, Zakharov and Cherevichenko). To a lesser extent, the Leningrad, Northwestern and Southern Fronts experienced the same turbulence, which utterly shattered command continuity and the sound planning and conduct of operations.

Throughout the entire period, Stalin 'turned the screws' on Red Army troops, issuing directives that demanded absolute obedience to orders under threat of censure, arrest and even execution. The *Stavka* authorized the establishment and employment of blocking detachments to enforce discipline by brute force and Stalin often accused and prosecuted unsuccessful commanders for treason, unleashing against them the full power of state security organs. The raw fear that had kept the Red Army obedient in the late 1930s did not improve Red Army combat performance during wartime.

The Red Army's poor combat performance was also the result of faulty force organization, which was only exacerbated by the *Stavka*'s and NKO's 'extraordinary fascination with the quantity of formations.'[7] To its credit, the NKO quickly abolished the rifle corps and repeatedly restructured its rifle and cavalry divisions to make them lighter and easier to command and control. However, it did so primarily because the Wehrmacht had already demolished these forces in combat. In addition, while it dramatically increased the quantity of rifle and cavalry divisions, virtually all of these new formations lacked adequate armour, artillery and other means of combat and combat service support. Simultaneously, the NKO disbanded its cumbersome mechanized corps (most of which the Wehrmacht had already destroyed) and replaced them with numerous tank brigades and battalions that it also lacked the means to equip adequately.

Both prior to the war and throughout its initial period, the NKO and *Stavka* also woefully underestimated the role and importance of artillery, engineers and communications forces throughout the force structure and this, too, significantly decreased the resilience of the army's strategic, operational and tactical defenses. Making matters worse, the number of available combat aircraft decreased dramatically from 5,952 planes in June 1941 to 2,436 on 31 December.[8] Consequently, while the force restructuring the Stavka mandated in 1941 did facilitate the training of command cadre in the conduct of modern war, it also contributed to the Red Army's many catastrophic defeats and tragic personnel and equipment losses. It was no coincidence, therefore, that, in early 1942, the Stavka and NKO began hastily restructuring its forces to create an army that could fight and win against the Wehrmacht.

The effects of the Red Army's defeats in 1941 were appalling. In six months of war, the Wehrmacht advanced up to 1,200km (720 miles) along a 1,000km (600-mile) front.[9] The precipitous advance deprived the Soviet Union of up to 40% of its population and 35% of its productive capacity and inflicted a minimum of 4.5 million military casualties, including over 3.1 million dead, captured, or missing.[10] At the same time, the Red Army lost 20,500 tanks, 101,100 guns and mortars, 17,900 aircraft and 6,290,000 rifle weapons.[11] To the GKO's credit, its evacuation of industry eastward and the extraordinary measures it took to continue production, combined with Lend-Lease aid from its Allies, permitted the Red Army and Soviet State to survive.

During 1941 a combination of factors converted the State-against-State war into a people's war, a struggle that also ultimately undermined Operation Barbarossa. The heavy-handed treatment by the Wehrmacht and German occupation authorities of the populations in German-occupied territory undercut frequent popular enthusiasm over the demise of Communist authority and impelled the population to take up arms. Although it would take over a year to fully mature and those who fought often did so against both Soviet and Nazi, the ensuing partisan war added a new dimension to the war overall and, ultimately, kindled a partisan struggle that would reach unprecedented proportions.

The evolving people's war reflected another reality that sharply differentiated the Soviet-German War from warfare in other theatres; namely, the sheer brutality of the struggle. Hitler had set the tone as early as the 1920s when he wrote his memoir, *Mein Kampf*. In Hitler's perspective, the war against the Soviet Union was also a crusade, a 'culture war' [*kulturkampf*] designed to subjugate or eradicate an entire people (or race) aimed at obtaining 'living space' [*lebensraum*] for the German nation. These attitudes fostered a 'no holds barred' approach to the war, which was only reinforced by such pronouncements as his 'Commissar Order,' the brutal behavior of the SS toward the Soviet population and a host of other harsh and repressive measures. Within months, to much of the Soviet population the Soviet-German War became the 'Great Patriotic War,' a term that would endure.

Understandably, the Soviets reciprocated. As evidenced by his treatment of Polish Army officers at Katyn before the war and the treatment of his own population during the 1930s, Stalin was not a reluctant participant in this struggle. In fact, his security, intelligence and counterintelligence organs (such as the NKVD and 'SMERSH') worked feverishly to foster intense hatred of the German invaders. German repression and atrocities made it easier for the Red Army and the population as a whole (in the form of partisans and the underground) to join the effort. What resulted was a struggle where no quarter was asked for or expected, and atrocities on both sides became routine. Unlike other theatres of war, where German officers referred to combat as sport, in Russia it was not.

The Wehrmacht did not emerge from the first six months of war unscathed. During this period it suffered over one million military casualties, an unprecedented number for an army that had never before tasted defeat.[12] Worse still, despite its spectacular string of victories, the Red Army survived and was able to inflict an equally unprecedented defeat on the Wehrmacht at Moscow. Once defeated, the Wehrmacht began experiencing the same command turbulence that had plagued the Red Army. The sad fact for the Germans was that Hitler and the German Army had embarked on its Barbarossa crusade employing forces, military techniques and a logistical structure perfected to prosecute war in western and central Europe. The German Army was not suited to wage war in the vast 'peasant rear' of the eastern theatre, militarily or psychologically.

General Gotthard Heinrici, the commander of German Fourth Army's XXXXIII Army Corps at Moscow and, by war's end, the Wehrmacht's premier defensive specialist, cogently assessed the reasons for the German failure even before the Red Army's Moscow counteroffensive began, stating:

> The goal set for the Eastern Campaign was not achieved. The enemy's armed forces were defeated, but the Russian State structure did not collapse. The threat of a two-front war stood at the door. The attack on Russia did not prevent this from happening; on the contrary, it conjured up its possibility.
>
> The basis of this failure rested on the following:
>
> 1. Politically, Hitler had underestimated the inner stability of the Bolshevik system. It proved to be tenacious and consolidated. The spirit within the Russians to defend 'Mother Russia' was stronger than their rejection of the Communist dictatorship. The improper treatment of the population in the occupied areas, above all, in the Ukraine and the Baltic States, only increased this feeling.
> 2. Economically, Russia was also better established than Hitler was willing to admit.
> 3. Militarily, the Russian armed forces were surprisingly capable. They often defended with a stubborn tenacity, and they had an astounding ability to improvise, even in the technical arena. These qualities consistently made up for the inability of the senior Russian leadership. However, all of this does not explain away the failure. German negligence and omission may make it easier to understand.
> 4. Most decisive was the operational decision of August 1941, which shifted the main emphasis of the operation from Army Group Centre to Army Group South and, in part, to the north. This forfeited the best chance to conduct a decisive battle with

the enemy during a direct attack on Moscow. I stress 'best chance,' because there has been no evidence to the contrary.

5. The motorized problem must also be considered. The German Army did not have the necessary motorized units and air transport formations or the required fuel reserves for a campaign in an area with the depth of Russia. The result was the necessity of having to stop the panzer formations until the infantry could catch up, instead of exploiting the opportunity to attack into the depth. Secondly, complete dependence on the railroads for supply, with all of the ensuing problems, was no way to tackle the East.

6. The width and depth of Russia had a decisive significance. After the rapid defeat of the Russian armed forces was not accomplished, the German Army was still faced by these two factors, and they did not have the means to overcome them.

7. The Russian climate and terrain also complicated matters. The effect of the mud period was surprising in its significance. The coming of the Russian winter did not correspond with German expectations. And the difficulty of the terrain, with its wide marshes and impassible regions, the great primeval-like forests complexes, the few good roads and the wide, unregulated river courses may not have stopped the offensive, but they did cause considerable delays.

8. Therefore, the Germans had to fight a constant battle with time. The end of June start time, in conjunction with the time lost during the battle of Kiev, took bitter revenge upon the Germans. If the incorrect decision of August 1941 were not made, the time left before the beginning of the mud period would have been sufficient for a decisive success. However, it would still have been very close.

In summary, it can be established that the decisive factor in the failure of the operation was the August 1941 decision. In addition, however, there was also the underestimation of the enemy, German weakness, above all in the realm of motorization, the depth of the area, the climate, the terrain and time factors.

With this in mind, the efforts made by the German soldiers takes on special significance.[13]

Heinrici went on to say that the Red Army's successes during the first three weeks of their Moscow counteroffensive were only 'tactical' in nature. He admitted, however, that the next three weeks on the counteroffensive produced a clear 'operational' crisis.

While providing superb perspectives on the root causes for German defeat in Operation Barbarossa, Heinrici also highlights one of many controversies that have since dogged historians as they ponder how the Wehrmacht might have conducted the campaign differently. Discounting the fact that, 'What has been has been,' and 'Speculation must remain pure speculation,' new information now available casts considerably more light on this controversy.

The most heated controversy associated with Operation Barbarossa was the wisdom of Hitler's order to cease the advance on Moscow in August 1941 and turn Guderian's panzer group southward toward Kiev in September. Most German generals and many historians as well have sharply criticized Hitler's August decision, arguing that Guderian's diversion into the Ukraine thwarted the German capture of Moscow in 1941 and, perhaps, also prevented German victory in the war. Significant new evidence now exists that contradicts their arguments and, at the least, supports Heinrici's judgment that the seizure of Moscow in 1941 'would still have been very close.'

It is now apparent that the Wehrmacht's best opportunity for capturing Moscow occurred in October 1941 rather than September. This was so because Red Army opposition to a German thrust toward Moscow in October was far weaker than it had been in September, for three basic reasons. First, the Western, Reserve and Briansk Fronts, which had halted the German juggernaut east of Smolensk in late July and early August, dissipated much of their strength during August and September by conducting numerous futile and costly assaults on German defenses north and south of Smolensk. By late September, all three *fronts* were primed for sudden and irrevocable collapse. Second, the elimination of much of the Southwestern Front from the Red Army's order of battle in September meant that Guderian's panzer group faced only token resistance on its October lung through Orel to Tula. Third, by severely damaging the Central Front in August and, then, smashing the Briansk Front in September, Army Group Centre could attack toward Moscow in October with impunity and without concern for its right flank.

Had Army Group Centre advanced on Moscow in September, before clearing its flanks, it would have had to deal with far stronger Soviet forces protecting Moscow and significant forces positioned along its vastly over-extended northern and southern flanks. Although it is conceivable it could have captured the city, as was the case with Napoleon's army over a century before, it would have then faced the grim prospects of wintering in a devastated city with immense forces operating against its extended and exposed flanks and rear. If the German Army could not defend its relatively short flanks in December 1941 against a Red Army force of 4.1 million men, it would have found it far more difficult to defend vastly longer ones in November against one of at least 5 million men. Roughly the same argument applies to criticism of Bock for spreading his forces so far during his October advance toward Moscow. In this case, Bock well understood the necessity for anchoring his northern flank on the Volga and the critical city of Kalinin for largely the same reasons.

Finally, in the last analysis, the most significant factor in the Red Army's ability to defeat Operation Barbarossa was its ability to raise and field strategic reserves, a fact unknown to all those who postulated the 'what ifs' mentioned above. As slow and cumbersome as it was and as poorly trained and ill equipped the forces it generated were, the mobilization system produced a seemingly endless array of armies and divisions. Furthermore, it served as the trigger mechanism for mobilizing the full power of the massive multi-ethnic Soviet State. Inevitably, the dull bludgeon representing the mobilized mass Soviet Army blunted the surgically precise, deadly, but fragile rapier thrusts that the German Army relied on to power Blitzkrieg War. In addition, unlike Hitler, Stalin realized that victory in a 'culture war' to the death required complete and ruthless total mobilization of the countries' entire resources. Stalin did so by December 1941; Hitler failed to do so until 1944. In these circumstances the defeat of Barbarossa was utterly understandable and, perhaps, even predictable.

Almost 800 years before 1941, Frederick Barbarossa's Third Crusade foundered in Asia Minor, before his armies reached and liberated Jerusalem from the infidels. Like his ancestral model, who drowned in the River Seleph (Calicadnus) on 10 June 1190, Hitler, too, failed, and perished in May 1945 in the crumbling ruins of Berlin.[14]

MAPS AND TABLES

Map 1 The Disposition of German and Soviet Forces on 22 June 1941.

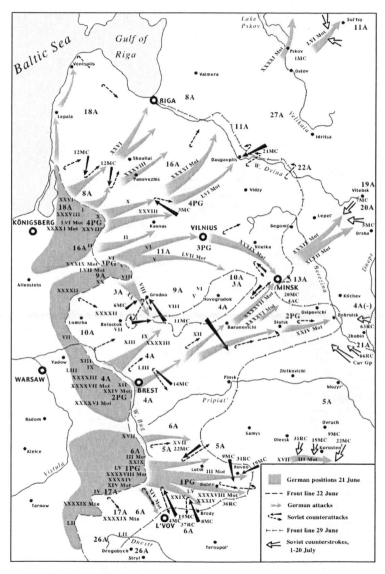

Map 2 The Border Battles, 22 June–9 July 1941.

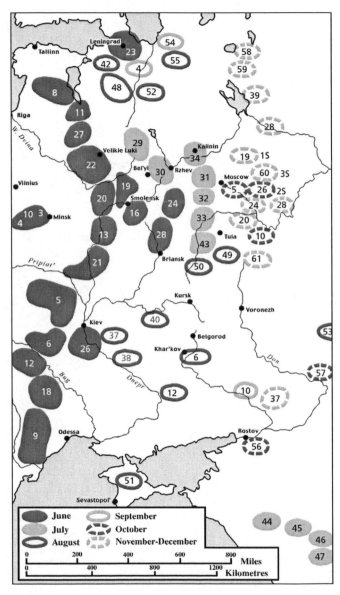

Map 3 Soviet Dispositions on 31 July and Armies Mobilized by
31 December 1941.

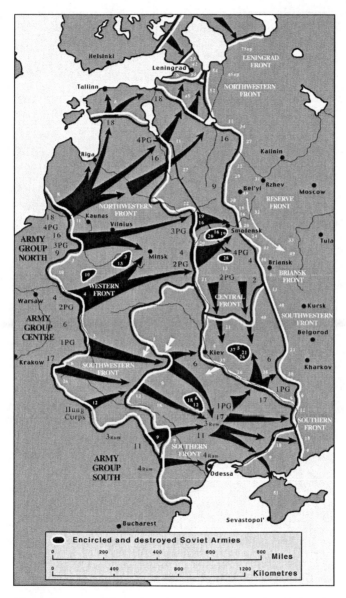

Map 4 Summary of Operations, 22 June – 30 September 1941.

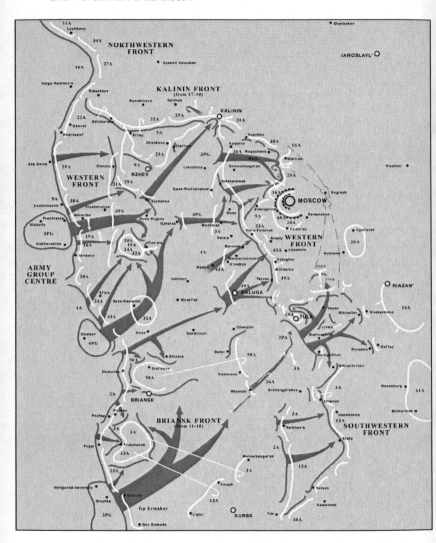

Map 5 The German Advance on Moscow, 30 September–4 December 1941.

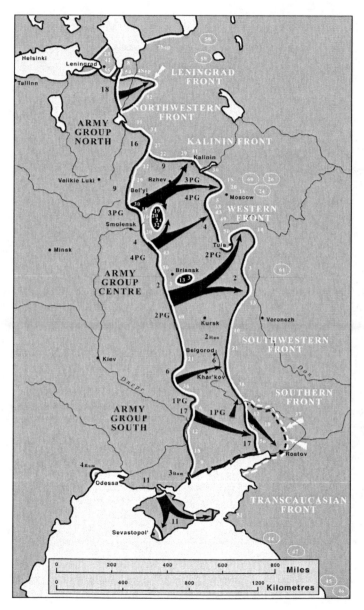

Map 6 Summary of Operations, 1 October–5 December 1941.

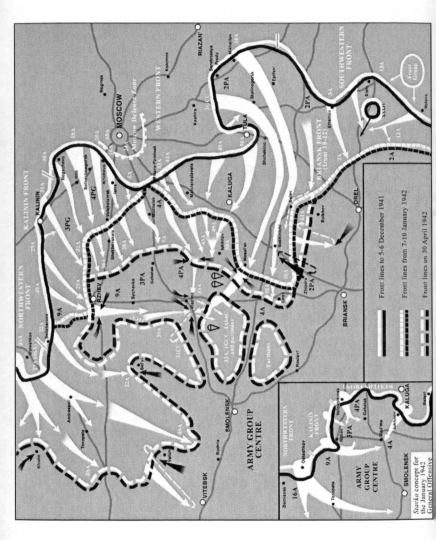

Map 7 The Soviet Winter Offensive, December 1941–April 1942.

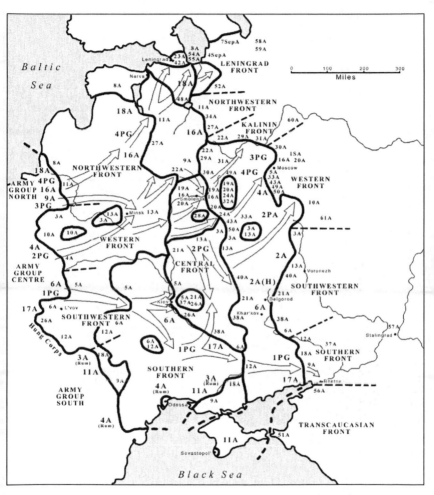

Map 8 Summary of Operation Barbarossa, 22 June–5 December 1941.

Table 1 Red Army wartime mobilization, 1941.

Date	Armies	Deployment Region
June	16th Army*	Trans–Baikal MD
	18th Army**	Khar'kov MD
	19th Army* (1st Shock Army in November)	North Caucasus MD
	20th Army*	Orel MD
	21st Army*	Volga MD
	22nd Army*	Ural MD
	24th Army*	Siberian MD
	25th Army	Far Eastern Front
	28th Army*	Arkhangel'sk MD
July	29th Army (30th Rifle Corps)	Moscow MD
	30th Army	*Stavka* reserve
	31st Army	Moscow MD
	32nd Army	Moscow MD
	33rd Army	Moscow MD
	34th Army	Moscow MD
	35th Army	Far Eastern Front
	36th Army	Transbaikal MD
	43rd Army (33rd Rifle Corps)	*Stavka* reserve
	44th Army (40th Rifle Corps)	Transcaucasus MD
	45th Army (25th Rifle Corps)	Transcaucasus MD
	46th Army (3rd Rifle Corps)	Transcaucasus MD
	47th Army (28th Mechanized Corps)	Transcaucasus MD
August	6th Army (second formation – 48th Rifle Corps)	Southern Front
	12th Army (second formation – 17th Rifle Corps)	Southern Front
	37th Army (Kiev FR)	Southwestern Front
	38th Army	Southwestern Front
	40th Army	Southwestern Front
	42nd Army (Krasnogvardeisk FR)	Leningrad Front
	48th Army (Novgorod Army Group)	Northwestern Front
	49th Army	Moscow MD
	50th Army (2nd Rifle Corps)	Briansk Front
	51st (Separate) Army	Crimea
	52nd (Separate) Army (25th Rifle Corps)	Northwestern Front
	53rd Army	Central Asian MD
	55th Army (Slutsk-Kolpino FR)	Leningrad Front
	6th Army (second formation)	Southern Front (Khar'kov)
	12th Army (second formation)	Southern Front (Pavlograd)
September	4th (second formation)	*Stavka* reserve
	10th Army (second formation – disbanded on 17 October)	Southern Front
	54th Army (44th Rifle Corp)	Moscow MD

October	5th Army (second formation – Mozhaisk Combat Sector)	Western Front
	10th Army (third formation)	Volga MD
	26th Army (second formation – 1st Guards Rifle Corps)	Moscow MD
	56th (Separate) Army	North Caucasus MD
	57th Army	North Caucasus MD (Stalingrad)
November	1st Shock Army (former 19th Army)	Western Front
	20th Army (second formation – Op. Gp Liziukov)	Western Front
	26th Army (third formation – 2nd Shock Army in December)	Volga MD
	28th Army (second formation)	Moscow Military District
	37th Army (second formation)	Southern Front
	39th Army	Arkhangel'sk MD
	58th Army	Siberian MD
	59th Army	Siberian MD
	60th Army (3rd Shock on December 25)	Moscow MD
	61st Army	Volga MD
December	3rd Shock Army (former 60th Army)	*Stavka* reserve
	4th Shock Army (former 27th Army)	Northwestern Front
	24th Army (second formation)	Moscow Military District
	20th Army (second formation)	Western Front (Moscow)

* Formed in accordance with a 13 May NKO mobilization order
** Headquarters only

NOTES

1. OPPOSING PLANS AND FORCES

1. Gotthardt Heinrici, *The Campaign in Russia, Volume 1* (Washington, DC: United States Army G-2, 1954). Unpublished National Archives manuscript in German (unpublished translation by Joseph Welch), 85.
2. Franz Halder, *The Halder War Diary 1939-1942*. Eds. Charles Burdick and Hans-Adolf Jacobsen (Novato, Calif.: Presidio Press, 1988), 294.
3. The original Plan Marcks had called for a force of 147 divisions, including 24 panzer and 12 motorized divisions. The total force deployed for combat in the East included 138 divisions (104 infantry and 34 mobile) in the 3 forward army groups, 9 security divisions, 4 divisions in Finland, 2 divisions under OKH control and a separate regiment and motorized training brigade. The most recent Soviet sources place German strength at 153 divisions and 3 brigades manned by 4.1 million men and equipped with 4,170 tanks, 40,500 guns and mortars and 3,613 combat aircraft. See V.A. Zolotarev, ed., *Velikaia Otechestvennaia voina 1941-1945, Kn. 1* [The Great Patriotic War 1941-1945, Book 1] (Moscow: 'Nauka,' 1998), 95. Hereafter cited as *VOV* with appropriate page. See also *Schematische Kriegsgliederung, Stand: B-Tag 1941 (22.6) 'Barbarossa.'* The original German order of Battle for Operation Barbarossa.
4. *Ibid.* Army Group South's Eleventh Army controlled the forward Rumanian forces and Rumanian Third and Fourth Armies controlled the remaining forces.
5. In July 1940, B.M. Shaposhnikov, Chief of the Red Army General Staff approved a plan drafted by his deputy, Major-General A.M. Vasilevsky. Vasilevsky's plan assumed an attack by Germany, supported by Italy, Finland, Rumania and possibly Hungary and Japan. The total enemy force would be 270 divisions, 233 of which would be massed along the Soviet Union's new western borders. Vasilevsky assumed that the main German effort, 123 infantry divisions and 10 panzer divisions, would deploy north of the Pripiat' Marshes and advance toward Minsk, Moscow and Leningrad. He therefore planned to put the bulk of Red Army forces in the same region. For details on Soviet prewar military planning see David M.

Glantz, *The Stumbling Colossus: The Red Army on the Eve of World War* (Lawrence, Ks: The University Press of Kansas, 1998), 90-98.

6. Defense Commissar Marshal of the Soviet Union S.K. Timoshenko rejected this plan, probably because he anticipated Stalin's objections. When K.A. Meretskov became Chief of Staff in August 1940, he had Vasilevsky and the rest of the General Staff draft a new plan. The second draft provided for two variants, concentrating the bulk of Soviet forces either north or south of the Pripiat' Marshes, depending on the political situation. On 5 October Stalin reviewed this draft. He did not openly reject the northern option but remarked that Hitler's most likely goals were the grain of the Ukraine and the coal and other minerals of the Donbas region. The General Staff therefore presented a new plan, approved on 14 October 1940, in which the basic orientation of forces was shifted to the southwest.

7. *VOV*, 108.

8. *Ibid.*

9. The Western border military districts fielded 170 divisions, 2 separate rifle brigades and 12 airborne brigades. The first operational echelon, deployed 10-50km from the border, consisted of 56 divisions (53 rifle and 3 cavalry) and 2 separate rifle brigades. The second operational echelon, deployed 50-100km from the border, contained 52 divisions (13 rifle, 3 cavalry, 24 tank and 12 motorized)). The third operational echelon, deployed 100-400km from the border, consisted of 62 divisions constituting the military district reserve deployed along the Dvina and Dnepr rivers. See *VOV*, 108-109.

10. For example, 13 divisions designated for assignment to the Southwestern Front and reserve armies and the 21st Mechanized Corps' three divisions assigned to the 22nd Army (in the High Command Reserve – RGK) had not yet assembled and another 10 divisions were still moving forward from the internal military districts.

11. As the tension increased in 1941, Zhukov tried to persuade Stalin of the need for a preemptive attack. The new chief of staff wrote a 'Report on the Plan of Strategic Deployment of Armed Forces of the Soviet Union to the Chairman of the Council of People's Commissars on 15 May 1941' and convinced Timoshenko to co-sign the document. In this hand-written proposal, Zhukov argued for an immediate offensive, using 152 divisions to destroy the estimated 100 German divisions assembling in Poland. The Southwestern Front would attack across southern Poland to separate Germany from her southern allies, while the Western Front would grapple with the main German force and capture Warsaw. Given the many problems that the Red Army was experiencing at the time, however, such an attack would have been a desperate gamble. Stalin was probably justified in ignoring Zhukov's proposal. See David M. Glantz, *The Military Strategy of the Soviet Union: A History* (London: Frank Cass, 1992), 87-90.

12. See Jonathan M. House, *Toward Combined Arms Warfare: A Survey of 20th Century Tactics, Doctrine, and Organization* (Fort Leavenworth, Ks: Combat Studies Institute, 1984), 81-83 and 96-97 and F.W. von Senger und Etterlin, *Die Panzergrenadiere: Geschichte und Gestalt der mechanisierten infanterie 1930-1960* (Munich: J.F. Lehmanns Verlag, 1961), 72-77.

13. Timothy Wray, *Standing Fast: German Defensive Doctrine on the Russian Front During World War II: Prewar to March 1943* (Fort Leavenworth, Ks.: Combat Studies Institute, 1986), 1-21.

14. To avoid telegraphing German intentions, many of these aircraft had remained in the West, continuing the air attacks on Britain until a few weeks before the offensive.

15. Similarly, the May 1941 airborne invasion of Crete had devastated German parachute formations and air transport units; 146 Ju-52s had been shot down and another 150 were seriously damaged. See Williamson Murray, *Luftwaffe* (Baltimore, Md.: Nautical and Aviation Publishing Co. of America, 1985), 79, 83.

16. For the best German assessment of the first six months of the war, see Klaus Reinhardt, *Moscow – The Turning Point: The Failure of Hitler's Military Strategy in the Winter of 1941-1942*, trans. Karl B. Keenan (Oxford and Providence: Berg Publisher, 1992), 26-28.

17. For a detailed description of the state of the Red Army in June 1941, see Glantz, *Stumbling Colossus*.

18. The tank division consisted of two tank regiments, one motorized infantry regiment, and reconnaissance, antitank, anti-aircraft, engineer and signal battalions. For details on the structure of the Red Army's mechanized forces, see O.A. Losik, ed., *Stroitel'stvo i boevoe primenenie sovestskikh tankovykh voisk v gody Velikoi Otechestvennoi voiny* [The formation and combat use of Soviet tank forces during the Great Patriotic War] (Moscow: Voenizdat, 1979) and, in English, David M. Glantz, *Soviet Military Operational Art: In Pursuit of Deep Battle* (London: Frank Cass, 1991), 74-121.

19. The actual strength of the mechanized corps varied widely. Some had a considerable amount of new equipment. For example, the Baltic Front's 3rd Mechanized Corps had 651 tanks, of which 110 were new KV-1 heavy and T-34 medium tanks. Other corps, especially those farther away from the frontier, were far weaker. In the Western Front's 4th Army, for example, the 14th Mechanized Corps had only 518 aging T-26 light tanks instead of its authorized complement of 1,031 medium and heavy tanks. Draconian factory discipline could only do so much to make up for past neglect in weapons production. The Southwestern Front's 19th Mechanized Corps had only 453 of its authorized tanks, all but 11 of them obsolete models. Moreover, this corps was expected to use requisitioned civilian trucks for its wheeled transportation; when the war actually began, the 'motorized rifle' regiments in its two tank divisions had to march on foot 120 miles to battle, slowing the movement of the available tanks. As new equipment became available from the production lines, that equipment was distributed to select corps among those in the forward area. The paucity of new machines (1,861), however, was such that even full-strength mechanized corps included a hodgepodge of different vehicles. All this complicated maintenance to an enormous extent. In addition, Soviet formations remained notoriously weak in radio communications and logistical support, making coordinated maneuver under the chaotic conditions of the surprise German invasion almost impossible. For details on Red Army strength on 22 June 1941, see *Boevoi i chislennyi sostav vooruzhennykh sil SSSR v period Velikoi Otechestvennoi voiny (1941-1945 gg.): Statisticheskii sbornik No. 1 (22 iiunia 1941 g.)* [The combat and numerical composition of the USSR's armed forces in the Great Patriotic War (1941-1945); Statistical collection No. 1 (22 June 1941) (Moscow: Institute of Military History, 1994). Hereafter cited as *BICS*.

20. Most Soviet rifle divisions lacked the tank battalion, since all available tanks were used to fit out the mechanized corps.

21. See *BICS*.

22. At the time, most German armoured units were equipped with the Mark III and Mark IV medium tanks, dependable second-generation vehicles that were more than a match for lightly armoured opponents like the Soviet T-26. In 1941 Germany was in the process of re-arming all Mark III's with a medium-velocity 50mm main gun, while the Mark IV's still retained a low-velocity 75mm gun. The velocity of these weapons was at least as important as the size of the shell because high velocity was necessary for effective armour penetration. Neither German weapon could penetrate the thick frontal armour of the T-34 medium tanks and KV-1 heavy tanks that were just coming off the assembly lines in Russia.

23. At least one designer was shot for 'sabotage' when an experimental aircraft crashed, and many other engineers were put to work in prison design shops. To put it mildly, such sanctions did not encourage innovative design solutions.

24. On 12 April 1941, Timoshenko and Zhukov complained to Stalin that training accidents were destroying two or three aircraft each day and demanded the removal of several senior Air Force officers. For the best English coverage of the state of the Red Air Force in 1941, see Van Hardesty, *Red Phoenix: The Rise of Soviet Air Power, 1941-1945* (Washington, DC: The Smithsonian Institution Press, 1982).

25. Throughout the disastrous summer of 1941, Soviet bombers stubbornly attacked at an altitude of 8,000 feet, too high to ensure accurate bombing but high enough for German fighters to locate and attack them. Despite the bravery of individual Soviet fighter pilots that repeatedly rammed German aircraft, their combat formations were too defensive to be effective against their dog-fighting opponents.

26. See Glantz, *Stumbling Colossus*, 233-257.

27. Alexander Werth, *Russia at War, 1941-1945* (New York: E.P. Dutton and Co.: 1964), 113.

28. In a June 1941 newspaper article, Propaganda Minister Joseph Goebbels 'leaked' the 'news' that a British invasion was imminent. Goebbels then had the newspaper ostentatiously withdrawn from circulation and put himself in simulated disgrace for this 'mistake.'

29. For example, Colonel General Kirponos, commander of the Kiev Special Military District, maintained close liaison with NKVD border troops and alerted his units when the Germans massed at the border.

2. THE BORDER BATTLES

1. The best German-based account of operations during the first six months of Barbarossa is found in Charles V.P. von Luttichau, *The Road to Moscow: The Campaign in Russia 1941, Unpublished Centre for Military History Project 26-P* (Washington, DC: Office of the Chief of Military History, 1985). Hereafter cited as Luttichau with appropriate manuscript page. For the best survey narrative from the Soviet perspective see, V.A. Anfilov, *Proval 'Blitskiga'* [The Failure of Blitzkrieg] (Moscow: 'Nauka,' 1974), now published in unexpurgated form. Extensive documents related to Red Army *front*, army, corps and division operations during the first four months of war are contained in the series, *Sbornik boevykh dokumentov Velikoi Otechestvennoi voiny, vypusk 33-43* [Collection of combat documents of the Great Patriotic War, issues

34-43] (Moscow: Directorate for the Study of War Experiences, The General Staff of the USSR's Armed Forces, 1958-1960). These formerly classified volumes are hereafter referred to as *SBDVOV* with appropriate issue and page.

2. Van Hardesty, *Red Phoenix*, 11.

3. The Brest Citadel was defended by seven battalions of the 6th and 42nd Rifle Divisions, elements of the 17th Red Banner Border Guards Detachment and specialized elements of the 28th Rifle Corps, numbering about 3,500 men. See V.I. Anikin, *Brestskaia krepost': Krepost'-geroi* [The Brest Fortress: Hero fortress] (Moscow: Stroiizdat, 1985).

4. Less the Third Panzer Group, which was attacking in the Northwestern Front's sector, Army Group Centre numbered approximately 635,000 men and attacked with 28 divisions, including 4 panzer divisions, forward. Bock's army group fielded 51 divisions and a third army headquarters (the Second) and 15 divisions in OKH reserve. These forces encountered Pavlov's 678,0000-man Western Front, which had only 13 rifle divisions deployed near or along the border.

5. Heinrici, 87-88.

6. Kluge's force consisted of ten army and five motorized corps, backed up by three security divisions and two army corps in reserve for a total of 20 infantry, 3 panzer and 3 motorized divisions. See *Schematische Kriegsgliederung*.

7. The 13th Army had no combat forces assigned. Pavlov's military district fielded 671,165 men (including 71,715 in schools), 14,171 guns and mortars, 2,900 tanks (2,192 operational) and 1,812 combat aircraft (1,577 operational) on 22 June 1941. See *Boevoi i chislennyi sostav*, 16-17. Only 13 of Pavlov's rifle divisions manned border defenses and most of these divisions had only one regiment forward and the remaining two in garrison.

8. For a detailed account of the hectic first days of war in the Western Front's sector, see *SBDVOV*, Issue 35 and I.V. Boldin, *Stranitsy zhizni* [Pages of a life] (Moscow: Voenizdat, 1961).

9. *VOV*, 138. The appendices to this volume (498-499) contain the full texts of Directives Nos. 1, 2 and 3.

10. Hoth's Third Panzer Group consisted of the XXXIX and LVII Motorized Corps and V and VI Army Corps. The XXXIX Motorized Corps fielded the 7th and 20th Panzer Divisions and the 14th and 20th Motorized Divisions and the LVI Motorized Corps, the 12th and 19th Panzer Divisions and 18th Motorized Division. See *Schematische Kriegsgliederung*.

11. Khatskilevich's 6th Mechanized Corps, the best equipped in the Red Army, was equipped with 1,022 tanks, including 352 new T-34 and KVs. However, it lost most of its tanks during its movement to forward assembly areas, largely because of air attacks and mechanical breakdowns. Complicating the situation, the estimated 200 tanks that made it to their attack positions ran out of fuel by the end of the day. Mostovenko's 11th Mechanized Corps, which received order to attack toward Grodno the next day, had 243 mostly older model tanks and suffered the same fate. Zolotarev, *VOV*, 139.

12. The Second Panzer Group consisted of the XXIV, XXXXVI and XXXXVII Motorized Corps and the XII Army Corps. The XXIV Motorized Corps fielded the 3rd and 4th Panzer, 10th Motorized, 1st Cavalry and 267th Infantry Divisions. The XXXXVI Motorized Corps consisted of the 10th Panzer and SS 'Reich'

Motorized Divisions and the 'Grossdeutschland' Infantry Regiment. Finally, the XXXXVII Motorized Corps contained the 17th and 18th Panzer, 29th Motorized and 167th Infantry Divisions.

13. The Western Front lost 738 aircraft, fully 40 percent of its total strength, on the first day of the war.

14. Filatov's order were to assemble the 21st Rifle Corps, 50th Rifle Division and other withdrawing forces and mount an effective defense protecting the approaches to Minsk, while the reserve 44th Rifle Corps defended Minsk proper.

15. *SBDVOV*, Issue 35, 344.

16. The 20th Mechanized Corps, whose divisions were scattered about the Minsk region, was to attack southward and link up with the airborne forces, which were to conduct an air-assault into the region. The mechanized corps dutifully attacked with its 94 older model tanks, but since they lacked the aircraft necessary to launch the air-assault, the airborne corps deployed forward on foot. Neither force posed any threat whatsoever to Guderian's panzers and the advancing German armoured tide swept both forces aside.

17. For the sordid tale of Pavlov's arrest and execution, see 'Delo No. P-240000 generala Pavlova Dmitriia Grigor'evicha' [Case no. P-24000 of General Dmitri Grigor'evich], *Kommunist voruzhennykh sil* [Communist of the armed forces] 8 (April 1991): 70-75; 9 (May 1991): 68-73; 11 (June 1991): 54-60; 13 (July 1991): 63-68; and 14 (July 1991): 57-67.

18. *VOV*, 147. During this period, 24 divisions of Pavlov's initial force of 44 divisions perished entirely and the other 20 lost from 30 to 90 percent of their men.

19. Halder, 432-435.

20. Leeb's force totalled 21 infantry, 3 panzer, 3 motorized divisions and 3 security divisions with another two divisions in OKH reserve. See *Schematische Kriegsgliederung*.

21. The XXXXI Motorized Corps contained the 1st and 6th Panzer and 36th Motorized Divisions and the LVII Motorized Corps, the 8th Panzer and 3rd Motorized Divisions. See *Schematische Kriegsgliederung*

22. The Eighteenth Army consisted of the XXVI, XXXVIII and I Army Corps, and the Sixteenth Army, the X, XXVIII and II Army Corps. See *Schematische Kriegsgliederung*.

23. Kuznetsov's military district fielded 369,702 men (including 44,143 in schools), 7,019 guns and mortars, 1,549 tanks (1,274 operational) and 1,344 combat aircraft (1,150 operational) on 22 June 1941. See *Boevoi i chislennyi sostav*, 16-17.

24. Kurkin's 3rd Mechanized Corps, whose strength was 651 tanks, including 110 new models, threw a fright into the 6th Panzer Division, which led the XXXXI Motorized Corps' advance. Attacking just east of Raseinai with its 2nd Tank Division, two battalions of T-34 and KV tanks crushed the 6th Panzer Division's reconnaissance elements and drove the division to the outskirts of the town. After the Soviets failed to exploit their success, German sappers systematically destroyed the Soviet tanks with explosive charges. Later they learned that the Soviet tanks ran out of fuel and had orders to 'ram' the German tanks, since the T-34s and KV's had not been bore-sighted and thus could not fire a round. Within 24 hours after the engagement, German forces bypassed, encircled and destroyed the immobile Soviet tank division.

25. Lieutenant-General F.A. Ershakov's 22nd Army and Major-General D.D. Leliushenko's 21st Mechanized Corps had been in *Stavka* Reserve.

26. Once at Daugavpils on the Dvina, Hitler ordered Hoepner's Fourth Panzer Group to advance on Ostrov, but von Leeb ordered a 12-hour delay to permit the Sixteenth Army to catch up with his advancing panzers. See Luttichau, Chapter VII, 57-58

27. The *Stavka* reinforced Kuznetsov with the 41st Rifle and 1st Mechanized Corps and the 234th Rifle Division from its reserve with which to erect new defenses. By this time, however, the 3rd Mechanized Corps had only the 84th Motorized Rifle Division combat capable and the 12th Mechanized Corps had lost 600 of its 750 tanks. Kuznetsov's entire *front* had only 150 tanks and 150 aircraft operational. See *VOV*, 152-153.

28. Popov's Northern Front, formed on 24 June from the Leningrad Military District, consisted of the 14th Army defending the Murmansk axis, the 7th Army defending the border north of Lake Ladoga and the 23rd Army defending from the Gulf of Finland to west of Lake Ladoga. Popov formed the Luga Operation Group of three rifle divisions on 9 July with orders to defend the Luga line. On 22 June, Popov's military district numbered 404,470 men (including 49,227 in schools), 7,901 guns and mortars, 1,857 tanks (1,543 operational) and 1,342 aircraft (1,222 operational). See *Boevoi i chislennyi sostav*, 16-17. However, by this time, Popov had dispatched sizeable reinforcements to the Northwestern Front.

29. The best sources for action in the Southwestern Front's sector are A.V. Vladimirsky, *Na kievskom napravlenii* [On the Kiev axis] (Moscow: Voenizdat, 1985), David M. Glantz, ed., *The Initial Period of War on the Eastern Front, 22 June-August 1941* (London: Frank Cass, 1993) and *SBDVOV*, Issue 36.

30. Army Group South numbered 797,000 men and 715 tanks north of the Carpathians and another 175,000 men in the Eleventh Army to the south, roughly one third of the 3 million men and one fifth of the 3,350 tanks committed in Barbarossa. See Luttichau, Chapter VIII, 4.

31. Kirponos's military district fielded 907,046 men (including 142,105 in schools), 16,997 guns and mortars, 5,465 tanks (4,788 operational) and 5,465 combat aircraft (4,788 operational) on 22 June 1941. See *Boevoi i chislennyi sostav*, 16-17.

32. With Zhukov's approval, Kirponos planned to attack the German penetration from the north and south with two shock groups of three mechanized corps each, with a total of 3,700 tanks. See *VOV*, 156.

33. Karpezo's armour fought without infantry support since a lack of trucks had forced him to leave his motorized division behind, a common problem throughout this period. Swampy ground and German air strikes slowed the advance of the two tank divisions and the German 297th Infantry Division established a strong antitank defense on its open flank. The handful of T-34 tanks in this attack gave the Germans a momentary fright, but by evening the 11th Panzer Division had resumed its advance to the east, leaving the 197th to hold the Soviets off.

34. For details on this complex action, see *VOV*, 156-158 and A. Vladimirsky, 'Nekotorye voprosy provedeniia kontrudarov voiskami Iugo-Zapadnogo fronta 23 iiunia-2 iiulia 1941 goda' [Some aspects of the conduct of counterstrokes by the Southwestern Front's forces between 23 June and 2 July 1941], *Voenno-istoricheskii zhurnal*, No. 7 (July 1981): 21-28. Hereafter cited as *VIZh* with appropriate issue and pages.

35. Together, the 4th and 8th Mechanized Corps fielded 1,877 tanks, but 979 of these, including 414 new models, were assigned to the 4th Corps. On the other hand, the 9th and 19th Mechanized Corps fielded 298 and 453 tanks respectively, on 5 of which were new types. See Glantz, *Stumbling Colossus*, 156. By 27 June, the 4th Mechanized Corps' tank strength had fallen to 65 tanks, largely due to technical breakdowns and only 564 tanks from the 9th and 19th Mechanized Corps, all older models, made it to the battlefield. See *VOV*, 157.

36. For details see, K.K. Rokossovsky, *Soldatskii dolg* [A Soldier's Duty] (Moscow: 'GOLOS,' 2000), 42-54. This is the unexpurgated version of Rokossovsky's earlier censored biography.

37. See *VOV*, 161.

38. The 27th Rifle Corps's two divisions numbered only 1,500 men apiece and the 22nd Mechanized Corps fielded only 153 operable tanks. After several days of fighting, the mechanized corps' strength fell to 58 serviceable tanks. See *VOV*, 161 and Vladimirsky, *Na kievskom napravlenii*, 110-125.

39. See *VOV*, 161 for this and other orders designed to restore discipline.

40. Prior to this date, Rundstedt's southern group limited its activities to bombing Soviet cities in Moldavia, southern Ukraine and the Crimea.

41. *VOV*, 162-164.

42. *Ibid.*, 164.

43. Many older residents of European Russia remembered the hard but bearable and 'correct' German occupation of 1917-19 and were inclined to wait on events rather than abandoning their homes to become refugees.

44. Many German officers later insisted that the Wehrmacht never implemented such policies and that atrocities were largely the work of SS, genocidal *Einsatzkommando* units and other Nazi party occupation forces who followed behind the army.

45. One analysis of three combat divisions in 1941 indicates that 29 per cent of the officers were Nazi Party members and that these officers, who had a higher education and social status than their peers, set the tone of those divisions. See Omar Bartov, *The Eastern Front, 1941-1945: German Troops and the Barbarization of Warfare* (New York: St. Martin's Press, 1986), 51 and 66.

46. *Ibid.*, 153. Regardless of the circumstances, these prisoners were the moral responsibility of the German Army. In fact, in 1941 that Army made so little provision for the huge mass of prisoners that many of those who survived the act of surrender died in a matter of months for lack of food and shelter. Once winter approached, the poorly equipped German soldiers often deprived their prisoners of coats and boots.

47. From a statement to the author during the 1984 Art of War Symposium held at the US Army War College in Carlisle, PA, 26-30 March 1984.

48. *VOV*, 164-165 and G.F. Krivosheev, ed., *Grif sekretnosti sniat: Poteri vooruzhennykh sil SSSR v voinakh, boevykh deistviiakh, i voennykh konfliktakh* [The secret classification has been removed: The losses of the USSR's armed forces in wars, combat operations and military conflicts] (Moscow: Voenizdat, 1992), 164 and 368.

3. THE SOVIET RESPONSE

1. The *Stavka* formed its first group of reserve armies, consisting of the 19th, 20th, 21st and 22nd Armies, on 25 June. Commanded by Marshal of the Soviet Union S.M. Budenny, these armies occupied defenses from Nevel' southward along the Desna and Dnepr rivers to Kremenchug. After occupying their defenses, the armies were to 'be prepared to conduct a counteroffensive on order of the High Command.' By the end of June, the *Stavka* deployed the 16th, 24th and 28th Armies at and east of Smolensk. After the German's smashed the bulk of these armies along the Dnepr, the *Stavka* assembled a new reserve east of Smolensk, which, by 14 July, included the 24th, 28th, 29th, 30th, 31st and 32nd Armies. After most of these armies were drawn into combat around Smolensk, by 1 August the Reserve Front had evolved to include the 24th, 31st, 32nd, 33rd, 34th and 43rd Armies. See *Boevoi sostav Sovetskoi armii, chast' 1 (iiun'-dekabr' 1941 goda)* [The combat composition of the Soviet Army, Part 1 (June–December 1941)] (Moscow: VAGSh, 1963). Prepared by the Military-scientific Directorate of the General Staff [*Voenno-nauchnoe Upravlenie General'nogo Shataba*] and classified secret. Hereafter cited as *Boevoi sostav*.
2. Along with the General Staff and the People's Commissariat of the Navy, the Peoples' Commissariat of Defense provided the working apparatus for the *Stavka*.
3. As an interim measure, of 10 July the *Stavka* of the Main Command was reorganized as the *Stavka* of the High Command [*Stavka Verkhovnogokomandovaniia − SVK*] with Stalin as chairman and B.M. Shaposhnikov as a new member.
4. V.A. Zolotarev, ed., *Prikazy Narodnogo Komissara Oborony SSSR 22 iiunia 1941 g. − 1942 g, T-13 2, (2).* [Orders of the People's Commissar of Defense of the USSR 22 June 1941-1942] in *Russkii arkhiv: Velikiaia Otechestvennaia* [The Russian archives: The Great Patriotic] (Moscow: 'TERRA,' 1997), 387.
5. N.A. Voznesensky, L.M. Kaganovich and A.I. Mikoian joined the GKO in 1942 and N.A. Bulganin in 1944
6. 'Gosudarstvennyi komitet oborony' [The State Defense Committee] in *Sovetskaia voennaia entsiklopediia T-3* [Soviet military encyclopaedia, Vol. 3] (Moscow: Voenizdat, 1976), 621-627 (hereafter cited as *SVE* with appropriate volume and page) and *Krasnaia zvezda* [Red Star], 5 May 1975.
7. The GKO continued its work until 4 September 1945 when an order of the Presidium of the USSR's Supreme Soviet disbanded the organization.
8. The General Staff was responsible for the strategic planning and direction of the armed forces at the front. At the beginning of war, the General Staff consisted of operational (1st), intelligence (2nd), organizational and mobilization (3rd), transport and communications (4th), logistics and supply (rear installations and supply) (5th) and military-topographical (6th) directorates and departments for general matters, fortified regions and military history. On 29 July 1941, the Organizational and Mobilization Directorate was removed from the General Staff and given to the Commissariat of Defense as the Main Directorate for the Formation and Manning of the Red Army [*Glavnoe upravlenie formirovaniia i ukomplektovaniia Krasnoi Armii − GUFUKA*]. However, this action was premature and proved unworkable. Consequently, in April 1942 the NKO formed a new Organizational Directorate in the General Staff responsible for tracking troop distribution and losses and training officer cadres in the vast military school system throughout the Soviet Union.

The general and specific duties of the General Staff included:

– Collection and analysis of data concerning the situation at the front;

– Preparing conclusions and recommendations for the *Stavka*;

– Working out plans for campaigns and strategic operations on the basis of *Stavka* decisions;

– Organizing strategic cooperation between the Armed Force's services and the *fronts*;

– Maintaining constant communications with the *fronts* and armies;

– Preparing and transmitting *Stavka* directives, orders and instructions to the *fronts* and fleets; and

– Controlling the fulfillment of *Stavka* directives, orders and instructions.

9. Based on documents released thus far, Stalin's signature appears on no *Stavka* orders issued prior to 29 June, but began signing such orders beginning that day.

10. Shaposhnikov served until poor health forced him to relinquish his position to his deputy Vasilevsky in May 1942.

11. V.A. Zolotarev, ed., 'Stavka VGK: Dokumenty i materialy, 1941 god, T-16-5, (1). [*Stavka* VGK: Documents and materials, 1941] in *Russkii arkhiv: Velikiaia Otechestvennaia* [The Russian archives: The Great Patriotic] (Moscow: 'TERRA,' 1996), 62. Hereafter cited as Zolotarev, 'Stavka VGK.'

12. For example, former Chief of the General Staff K.A. Meretskov was imprisoned, interrogated and beaten by the NKVD in Moscow in late summer 1941, but later returned to army and then *front* command.

13. 'Lev Zakharovich Mekhlis,' *SVE, Tom-5* [Vol. 5] (Moscow: Voenizdat, 1978), 273. Although his official biography avoids criticism of him, Mekhlis remains one of the very few wartime leaders bitterly criticized by his fellow senior officers in their memoirs.

14. These and other problems are candidly addressed in General Staff war experience studies in the archival series *SMPIOV* (*Sbornik materialov po izuchenie opyta voiny* [Collections of materials for the study of war experience]) and *STPPOVOV* (*Sbornik takticheskikh primerov po opytu Otechestvennoi voiny* (Collection of tactical examples base on the experience of the Fatherland War]). They are covered in more general terms in numerous open-source, formerly classified studies of operational art and tactics. For example, see A.A. Strokov, *Istoriia voennogo iskusstva* [History of military art], (Moscow: Voenizdat, 1966), 388-392.

15. The full directive is found in Zolotarev, 'Stavka VGK,' 72-74. The number '0' in the directive meant that the document was secret. The annotation '00' meant top secret.

16. By 31 December 1941, only 6 of the original 62 rifle corps remained.

17. The full scope of these changes in force structure are found in Iu.P. Babich and A.G. Baier, *Razvitie vooruzheniia i organizatsii Sovetskikh sukhoputnykh voisk v gody Velikoi Otechestvennoi voiny* [Development of the Soviet ground forces in the Great Patriotic War] (Moscow: Izdanie akademii, 1990) and David M. Glantz, *The Red Army in 1943: Strength, Organization, and Equipment* (Carlisle, PA: Self-published, 1999).

18. See David M. Glantz, *Red Army Ground Forces in June 1941* (Carlisle, PA: Self-published, 1997) to track the evolution of Red Army tank divisions and other types of formations.

19. NKO order No. 0063 dated 12 August 1941 ordered the formation of 170 new tank brigade by 1 January 1942. Each brigade was to contain 91 tanks (7 KV, 20 T-34 and 64 T-40 or T-60s). See V.A. Zolotarev, ed., *'Prikazy Narodnogo Komissara Oborony SSSR, 22 iiunia 1941 g. – 1942 g. , T-13-2, (2).* [Orders of the Peoples' Commissariat of Defense, 22 June 1941-1942] in *Russkii arkhiv: Velikiaia Otechestvennaia* [The Russian archives: The Great Patriotic] (Moscow: 'TERRA,' 1997), 51-53.

20. Glantz, *The Red Army in 1943*, 116.

21. Zolotarev, 'Stavka VGK,' 94-96.

22. *VOV*, 259.

23. David M. Glantz, 'Soviet Mobilization in Peace and War, 1924-42: A Survey,' *The Journal of Slavic Military Studies*, Vol. 5. No. 3 (September 1992), 351.

24. For details on mobilization, see Glantz, *Stumbling Colossus*, 205-232.

25. For details on the evolution of GUFUKA, see S.A. Il'enkov, 'Concerning the Registration of Soviet Armed Forces' Wartime Irrevocable Losses, 1941-1945,' *The Journal of Slavic Military Studies*, Vol. 9, No. 2 (June 1996), 440-441. However, this action was premature and proved unworkable. Consequently, in April 1942 the NKO formed a new Organizational Directorate in the General Staff responsible for tracking troop distribution and losses and training officer cadres in the vast military school system throughout the Soviet Union.

26. The Soviet mobilization plan (MP-41) called for mobilizing 344 divisions and 7.85 million men, 6.5 million of which were to be deployed to the Western Theatre. In actuality, by 22 June 1941, MP-41 produced an initial combat force of 2,901,0000 men organized into 171 divisions. For details, see A.G. Khor'kov, *Boevaia i mobilizatsionnaia gotovnost' prigranichnykh voennykh okrugov nakanune Veliokoi Otechestvennoi voiny* [Combat and Mobiization readiness on the eve of the Great Patriotic War] (Moscow, Voroshilov Academy of the General Staff, 1985), 34-42 and *Nachal'nyi period Velikoi Otechestvennoi voiny* [The initial period of the Great Patriotic War] (Moscow: Voroshilov Academy of the General Staff, 1989), 39 and 97.

27. For mobilization orders, see Zolotarev, 'Stavka VGK,' and for the mobilization cites, see respective army histories in all eight volumes of the *SVE*. Some of these armies formed in the Transcaucasus and Transbaikal Military Districts and Far Eastern Front. Seventeen of the armies formed on the base of existing corps, fortified regions, or operational groups.

28. See Glantz, *Stumbling Colossus*, 101-107 and 205-226; *Boevoi sostav*, A.I. Evseev, 'Manevr strategicheskimi reservami v pervom period Velikoi Otechestvennoi voiny' [Maneuver of strategic reserves during the first period of the Great Patriotic War], *VIZh*, No. 3 (March 1986), 11-13; and V. Golubovich, 'Sozdanie strategicheskikh reservov' [The creation of strategic reserves], *VIZh*, No. 4 (April 1977), 12-19.

29. By 31 December, the Red Army lost a total of 4,308,94 men and 229 divisions.

30. For details on economic dislocations and industrial evacuations and reconstruction, see *VOV*, 385-414 and Dimitri Volkogonov, *Stalin: Triumph and Tragedy*, trans. and ed., Harold Shukman (Rocklin, CA: Prima Publishing, 1992), 415 and 418.

31. Specially formed aviation groups transported many of the technicians and skilled workers to new industrial sites.

32. A. Nikitin, 'Perestroika raboty promyshlennosti SSSR v pervom periode Velikoi Otechestvennoi voiny' [Rebuilding the work of military industry of the USSR

during the first period of the Great Patriotic War], *VIZh*, No. 2 (February 1963), 11-20.

33. Reinhardt, *Moscow – The Turning Point*, 32, 146-147.

4. THE BATTLE FOR SMOLENSK

1. Halder, 446.

2. The *Stavka* appointed Marshal Budenny and Lieutenant-General A.I. Eremenko as Timoshenko's deputies. The Group of Reserve Armies had been formed on 29 June under Budenny's command. See Zolotarev, 'Stavka VGK,' 31.

3. Additionally, 29th, 30th, 31st, 32nd and 33rd Armies, formed around a nucleus of NKVD border guards and peoples' militia from the Moscow region, mobilized and deployed into positions from Staraia Russa to south of Viaz'ma to protect the approaches to Moscow. See Evseev, 'Manevr strategicheskiimi reservami,' 9-20. The parlous condition of these armies is described in Glantz, *Stumbling Colossus*, 214-26.

4. B. Bytkov, 'Kontraudar 5-go mekhanizirivannogo korpusa na lepel'skom napravlenii (6-11 iiulia 1941 goda)' [The counterstroke of the 5th Mechanized Corps along the Lepel' axis (6-11 July 1941)], *Voenno-istoricheskii zhurnal* [Military-historical journal], No. 9 (September 1971), 60. Hereafter cited as *VIZh* with appropriate number and date.

5. *Sbornik boevykh dokumentov Velikoi Otechestvennoi voiny, vypusk 33* [Collection of combat documents of the Great Patriotic War, issue 33] (Moscow: Voenizdat, 1957), 80. Prepared by the Military-scientific Directorate of the General Staff and classified top secret. Hereafter cited as *SBDVOV* with appropriate volume. Kurochkin's army included the 128th, 153rd, 229th, 233rd, 73rd, 18th and 137th Rifle Divisions and the 5th and 7th Mechanized Corps, which numbered 1,036 tanks each, although many of the tanks were older BT-7 and T-26 models. The day before Timoshenko's assault, early on 5 July the *Stavka* issued yet another directive that underscored its optimism and reflected its concern over the sagging defenses further south along the Dnepr river. It read:

> Existing information indicates that there is no enemy in front of the 2nd and 4th Rifle Corps, 20th Mechanized Corps and the airborne corps [the 4th]. Only reconnaissance has been observed. Comrade Stalin believes that the 2nd and 44th Rifle Corps must attack toward Borisov, crush the enemy and reach the Lepel' and Dokshiny region to encircle the enemy LVII Motorized Corps. Unless it makes these attacks, the 5th and 7th Mechanized Corps will achieve no success. Leave the airborne corps to protect the crossings over the Berezina River. Liquidate the enemy crossing at Rogachev; otherwise it will disrupt our plan.
>
> [signed] Zhukov.

6. The two mechanized corps attacked the 7th Panzer Division's well-prepared antitank defenses without conducting adequate reconnaissance and without organizing effective infantry-armour cooperation.

7. *VOV*, 147.

8. The 13th Army's commander, General Filatov, was fatally wounded on 8 July and replaced by Lieutenant-General F.N. Remezov.

9. The GKO later designated Mogilev as the first 'hero city' because of its tenacious defense.

10. See also, Heinz Guderian, *Panzer Leader* (New York: E.P. Dutton, 1952), 167-174 and K. Cheremukhin, 'Na smolenskom-moskovskom strategicheskom napravlenii letom 1941 goda' [On the Smolensk-Moscow strategic axis in summer 1941], *VIZh*, No. 10 (October 1966), 3-18.

11. 'Direktiva Stavki VK No. 00290 glavnokomanuiushchemy voiskami Zapadnogo Napravleniia o plane likvidatsii proryva protivnika u Vitebska' [*Stavka* VK Directive No. 00290 to the High Commander of forces along the Western Direction concerning the plan to liquidate the enemy penetration at Vitebsk] in Zolotarev, 'Stavka VGK,' 65. Timoshenko commanded both the Western Direction Command and the Western Front.

12. For additional details on the opening stages of the Battle of Smolensk, see David M. Glantz, ed., *The Initial Period of War on the Eastern Front: 22 June-August 1941* (London: Frank Cass, 1993), 345-454.

13. Heinz Guderian, *Panzer Leader* (New York: Ballantine, 1965), 144.

14. The 63rd Rifle Corps consisted of the 61st, 167th and 154th Rifle Divisions. For details see, *VOV*, 175-176 and G. Kuleshev, 'Na Dneprovskom rubezhe' [On the Dnepr line], *VIZh*, No. 6 (June 1966), 16-28. The rank of *komkor* was a prewar designation that some commanders still retained.

15. The cavalry group consisted of the 32nd, 43rd and 47th Cavalry Divisions. For details see *SBDVOV*, Issue 34.

16. Bartov, 20. For graphic day-by-day development of the Smolensk operation, see David M. Glantz, *Atlas of the Battle of Smolensk* (Carlisle, PA, Self-published, 2001). For further details on the fighting, see *VOV*, 178-182.

17. For additional details on this stage of the Smolensk operation, see Glantz, *The Initial Period of War*, 345-454.

18. The *Stavka* created the Front of Reserve Armies on 14 July to back up the Western Front and provide depth to its defenses along the Moscow axis. Initially deployed along a 750km (450-mile) front from Staraia Russa through Ostashkov, Belyi and El'nia to Briansk. Commanded by Lieutenant-General I.A. Bogdanov, the *front* consisted of the 29th, 30th, 24th and 28th Armies in first echelon and the 31st and 32nd Armies in reserve. On 20 July the *Stavka* assigned 14 divisions from its first echelon armies to participate in the Smolensk counterstrokes. The *Stavka* disbanded the *front* on 25 July, assigning its armies to the Western and new Reserve Front. See Zolotarev, 'Stavka VGK,' 70-72 and 90-91.

Zhukov's order for the Smolensk counterstroke read,

> In order to conduct an operation to encircle and destroy the enemy Smolensk grouping, the *Stavka* ORDERS:
> 1. Group Maslennikov, consisting of the 252nd, 256th and 243rd Rifle Divisions and Armoured Trains No. 53 and 82, will reach the Chikhachi (40km northwest of Toropets) and Lake Zhizhitskoe (at Artemovo station) line by the close of 23 July and prepare a defense protecting the Toropets axis. Dispatch a detachment of no more

than a battalion to protect the group's flank in the Kniazhovo region (25km north of Chikhachi). Deploy the group's headquarters in Selishche (22km west of Toropets).

2. Group Khomenko, consisting of the 242nd, 251st and 250th Rifle Divisions, will move to the Maksimovka (22km southwest of Belyi) and Petropol'e line by the end of 22 July and attack in the general direction of Dukhovshchina on the morning of 23 July. Establish communications with the 50th and 53rd Cavalry Divisions, which have been ordered to concentrate in the Zhaboedovo, Shchuch'e and Zharkovskii Station region (40-50km west of Belyi) and which are subordinated to a group for a joint blow against Dukhovshchina. Deploy the group headquarters in the Belyi region.

3. Group Kalinin, consisting of the 53rd Rifle Corps (the 89th, 91st and 166th Rifle Divisions), will move to the Vop' River in the Vetlitsy (30km northeast of Iartsevo) and the mouth of the Vop' River line by the close of 22 July in readiness to exploit the success of Group Khomenko's offensive. The 166th Rifle Division will concentrate in the Miakishevo (20km southeast of Belyi), Petropol'e and Nikitinka Station region by the end of 22 July to operate as Group Khomenko's second echelon.

4. Group Kachalov, consisting of the 149th and 145th Rifle and 109th Tank Divisions, will concentrate in the Krapivenskii, Vezhniki and Roslavl' region by the close of 21 July to launch an attack in the direction of Smolensk on the morning of 22 July.

5. The commander of the Red Army Air Force will attach [the following] aviation by the end of 21 July:

a) The 31st Aviation Division for Group Maslennikov

b) The 190th Assault Aviation regiment and the 122nd Fighter Aviation regiment for Group Khomenko.

c) The 209th Assault Aviation Regiment and the 239th Fighter Aviation regiment for Group Kachalov.

6. All groups will become subordinate to Comrade Timoshenko, the Western Direction High Commander, when they reach their jumping-off positions. They will receive all of their orders from him. Report receipt and fulfillment of this directive.

Army General Zhukov
Chief of the General Staff.

From 'Direktiva *Stavka* VK komanuiushchemu voiskami Fronta Rezervnykh Armii o sozdanii operativnykh grupp voisk, ikh razvertyvsanii dlia operatsii po razgromu smolenskoi gruppirovki protivnika' [*Stavka* VK directive to the commander of the Front of Reserve Armies about the creation of operational groups of forces and their deployment for an operation to destroy the enemy Smolensk grouping] in Zolotarev, 'Stavka VGK,' 85.

Rokossovsky, who had been reassigned to Western Front headquarters to command the 16th Army after the border battles in the Ukraine, had been sent on 17 July to defend the Dnepr River crossing at Iartsevo against Third Panzer Group. He assembled a motley collection of shattered units and stragglers around the cadres of the 38th Rifle and 101st Tank Divisions, the latter reduced to only 40 obsolete tanks.

19. See V. Shevchuk, 'Deistviia operativnykh grupp voisk v Smolenskom srazhenii (10 iiulia-10 sentiabria 1941 g.' [The actions of operational groups of forces in the battle of Smolensk (10 July-10 September 1941], *VIZh*, No. 12 (December 1979), 10-13 and appropriate documents in *SBDVOV*, Issue 36 (Moscow: Voenizdat, 1960).

20. Rokossovsky, 58-68.

21. For the parameters of the strategic debate, see Luttichau, Chapter XVI, 44-45. The full text of this and other Hitler directives are found in *Sbornik voenno-istoricheskikh materialov Velikoi Otechestvennoi voiny, vypusk 18* [Collection of military-historical materials of the Great Patriotic War, Issue 18] (Moscow: Voenizdat, 1960). The Military-historical Department of the General Staff's Military-scientific Directorate compiled this formerly classified volume. Hereafter cited as *SVIMVOV*.

22. Führer Directive, No. 34 of 30 July, provided even more precise instruction regarding the capture of Leningrad.

23. *SVIMVOV*, 242-245.

24. For a breakdown of these figures, see Luttichau, Chapter XVI, 41-43. By way of contrast, from 22 June through 30 September, the Red Army and Fleet lost 2,129,677 soldiers, including 236,372 killed, 40,680 died of wounds, 153,526 died from illness and other non-combat causes, and 1,699,699 were missing and prisoners-of-war. Another 687,626 soldiers were wounded sufficiently to cause hospitalization. All told the casualty figure equals more than 50% of the armed forces' prewar strength. See Krivosheev, 146-153.

25. Reinhardt, 26-27 and Halder, 480 and 487-495.

26. Halder, 506.

27. Guderian, 190.

28. See the full order in Zolotarev, 'Stavka VGK,' 88-89.

29. The *Stavka* formed the Reserve Front on 30 July on the base of the former Front of Reserve Armies and the Mozhaisk Defense Line. The *front* consisted of the 24th, 31st, 32nd, 33rd, 34th, 43rd (added on 6 August) and 49th (added on 7 August) Armies. The *front* backed up the Western Front and, ultimately, occupied defenses in the El'nia sector between the Western and Central Fronts. See Zolotarev, 'Stavka VGK,' 98 and 106-108.

30. The *Stavka* order read,

> 1. For the sake of convenience I am organizing the Briansk Front and subordinating it directly to the Supreme High Command. Lieutenant-General Eremenko is appointed as commander of the Briansk Front, Major-General Ermakov as deputy *front* commander, and Major-General Zakharov as *front* chief of staff. Employ the command and control [organs] of the 20th Rifle Corps and the 25th Mechanized Corps to form the *front* headquarters. The *front* headquarters will be in the Briansk region...
>
> 2. The Briansk Front consists of:
> a) The 50th Army, consisting of the 217th, 279th, 258th, 260th, 290th, 269th and 280th Rifle Divisions, the 55th Cavalry Division, the 2nd and 20th Rifle Corps corps artillery regiments and the 761st and 753rd Antitank Artillery Regiments.
> b) The 13th Army, consisting of the 137th, 121st, 148th, 132nd, 6th,

155th, 307th and 285th Rifle Divisions, the 50th Tank Division, the 52nd and 21st Cavalry Divisions and an airborne corps.

c) The *front* reserve consists of the 229th, 287th and 283rd Rifle divisions and the 4th Cavalry Division.

> [signed] The Supreme High Commander, I. Stalin
> and The Chief of the General Staff, B. Shaposhnikov.

See Zolotarev, 'Stavka VGK,' 116.

31. The directive read:

2. a) The 22nd Army will liquidate enemy mobile units that have penetrated into Velikopol'e Station, Nazimovo, Zhilitsa and Zamosh'e region and, exploiting aviation and tanks and an active and firm defensive line from Nasva Station, Velikie Luki and Lake Velinskoe to achieve that end, will protect the attacking *front* forces from the north and the direction of Opochka. When the 29th and 30th Armies reach the Velizh, Demidov front, the armies' left wing will advance to the Lake Usmynskoe line.

b) While developing its ongoing offensive, the 29th Army will make the main attack on Velizh.

c) The 30th Army will facilitate the attack by the 19th Army on Dukhovshchina and further to Smolensk by attacking Toikhovitsy, Eliseevichi and Kholm.

d) The 19th Army will develop an offensive with the immediate mission of capturing Dukhovshchina and, subsequently, capture the Smolensk region by a blow from the southwest without making a frontal attack on Smolensk.

e) The 16th Army will assist the 19th and 20th Armies' destruction of the enemy Smolensk-Iartsevo grouping by an attack on Kardymovo Station and Smolensk.

f) The 20th Army will destroy the enemy Smolensk grouping together with the 19th and 16th Armies by an initial blow in the general direction of Kliukova Station and Riabtsevo Station and subsequently to the northwest.

3. *On the right* – the Northwestern Front has the mission of halting the enemy on the Lovat' River by an active defense... *On the left* – The Reserve Front will launch an offensive on the morning of 30 August, liquidate the enemy El'nia grouping and attack Propiosk with 24th Army and Roslavl' with 43rd Army to defeat the enemy, capture these points and reach the Dolgie, Nivy, Khislavichi and Petrovichi front by 8 September 1941. The main forces will continue to develop the defensive belt along the Ostashkov, Selizharovo, Olenino, Dnepr River (west of Viaz'ma), Spas-Demensk and Kirov line. The boundary with it is the Bol. Nezhoda, Peresna Station and Krasnyi line, all points inclusive for the Western Front.

> [signed] I. Stalin, B. Shaposhnikov.

See Zolotarev, 'Stavka VGK,' 135–136.

32. Zhukov's directive read:

> 2. a) The 24th Army, consisting of eight rifle divisions, one tank division and one mechanized division, will destroy the enemy El'nia grouping by concentrated attacks and will reach the Bol'shaia Nezhoda Station, Petrovo and Stroila front by 1 September. Subsequently, while developing the offensive, it will attack in the direction of Pochinok and, having captured the latter, will reach the Dolgie Nivy and Khislavich front by 8 September;
>
> b) Having left its 222nd and 53rd Rifle Divisions along their occupied defensive front and the army's main forces to defend positions at Spas-Demensk and Kirov, on 30 August the 43rd Army will attack in the general direction of Roslavl' with two rifle and two tank divisions. Having captured Roslavl' [the army] will reach the Khislavichi (inclusive) and Petrovichi front by 8 September;
>
> c) Remaining in place, the 31st, 49th, 32nd and 33rd Armies will continue their work to develop their occupied defensive sectors.
>
> d) Retain one rifle division per army in *front* reserve from the reserves of people's militia divisions in order to strengthen the defenses along the Sukhinichi and Zhizdra axes and to protect the junction with the Briansk Front in the Kirov and Liudinovo region.
>
> e) Transfer the 298th Rifle Division to the Briansk Front and move it by rail to the Diat'kovo region by 1 September.
>
> 3. *On the right* – The Western Front is continuing to develop an offensive with the mission of reaching the Velizh, Demidov and Smolensk front by 8 September. Its left-flank 20th Army has the mission of initially attacking in the general direction of Klokovo and Riabtsevo Stations and subsequently to the northwest together with the 16th and 19th Armies to defeat the enemy Smolensk grouping and capture the Smolensk region... *On the left* – The Briansk Front will launch an offensive on 2 September with the missions of destroying the enemy groupings concentrated in the Dubrovka, Pochep and Surazh regions and, subsequently, reaching the Petrovichi, Osmolovichi, Belaia Dubrava and Guta-Koretskaia front.
>
> [signed] I. Stalin, B. Shaposhnikov

See Zolotarev, 'Stavka VGK,' 136-137.

33. Soviet historiography has focused on the July battles around Smolensk and mentioned the El'nia operation only within the context of the late August offensive. It has been virtually silent on the immense scope and ambitious aims of the 30 August Western Front offensive.

34. *VOV*, 181.

35. *Ibid*, 182. More detail is found in the operational reports associated with these operations found in *SBDVOV*, Issue 41 (Moscow: Voenizdat, 1960).

36. See *Boevoi sostav*, 41.

37. 'Zapis' peregovorov po priamomu provodu Verkhovnogo Glavnokoman-duiushchego i nachal'nika General'nogo Shtaba s komanduiushchim voiskami

Rezervnogo Fronta' [Notes of a conversation by direct line between the Supreme High Commander, the chief of the General Staff and the Reserve Front commander] in Zolotarev, 'Stavka VGK,' 162-163.

38. 'Direktiva Stavki No. 001805 komanuiushchemu voiskami Zapadnogo Fronta o perekhode k oborony' [*Stavka* VGK Directive No. 001805 the Western Front commander concerning a transition to the defense] in Zolotarev, 'Stavka VGK,' 171.

39. Krivosheev, 224.

40. 'Direktiva Stavki VGK No. 001941 komanduiushchemu voiskami Rezervnogo Fronta o nedostatakh v organizatsii nastupleniia' [*Stavka* VGK Directive No. 001941 to the Reserve Front commander concerning the shortcomings in the organization of the offensive] in Zolotarev, 'Stavka VGK,' 181-182. This was not the first time that Zhukov was rebuked for crudely organizing an operation and suffering heavy casualties. The General Staff had done so in late 1939 after his victory at Khalkhin Gol. Nor would it be the last time. The fact was, however, that Zhukov fought, and, as often as not, his forces won despite the heavy casualties. When they lost, the enemy also suffered greatly. In 1941 that was a quality Stalin could not easily dispense with.

41. 'Direktiva Stavki VGK No. 001296 komanuiushchemu voiskami Brianskogo Fronta o razgrome protivnika v raoine Staroduba' [*Stavka* VGK Directive No. 001296 to the Briansk Front commander about the destruction of the enemy in the Starodub region] in Zolotarev, 'Stavka VGK,' 138.

42. 'Prikaz Verkhovnogo Glavnokomanduiushchego No. 0077 komanduiushchim voiskami Brianskogo i Rezervnogo Frontov o provedenii vozdushnoi operatsii po razgromu tankovoi gruppirovki protivnika' [Supreme High Command Order No. 0077 to the Briansk and Reserve Front commanders concerning the conduct of an air operation to destroy the enemy tank grouping] in Zolotarev, 'Stavka VGK,' 146.

43. The directive read:

a) Having left the 217th, 279th, 258th and 290th Rifle Divisions to defend their positions, on 3 September the 50th Army will launch an offensive with 4 rifle divisions and tanks from the Viazovsk and Vereshovskii front toward Peklina, Nov. Krupets and Roslavl' and, together with the Reserve Front's 43rd Army, will destroy the enemy grouping in the Zhukovka and Zubarovka region. Subsequently, capture the Roslavl' region and reach the Petrovichi, Klimovichi front by 13 September;

b) The 3rd Army will deliver a blow from the Menki, Vitovka and Semtsy front on Starodub and Novozybkov with not less than two rifle divisions reinforced by tanks and, together with the 13th Army, will smash the enemy mobile group in the Starodub, Novgorod-Severskii and Trubchevsk region. The army will reach the Klimovichi, Belaia Dubrovka front by 15 September;

c) The 13th Army, consisting of 5 divisions with tanks, will continue its offensive and, while attacking in the general direction of Zheleznye Mosty and Semenovka, will destroy the enemy Novgorod-Severskii grouping in cooperation with the 3rd Army. Reach the Belaia Dubrovka (exclusive) and Guta-Karetskaia front by 15 September.

d) While firmly defending its left flank, the 21st Army will continue its offensive, delivering its main attack from the Koriukovka, Pereliub and Novaia Barovichi front toward Semenovka and Starodub, and, together with the 13th Army, will destroy the enemy in the Semenovka, Starodub and Novgorod-Severskii region;

e) Keep the 298th Rifle Division in *front* reserve in the Diat'kovo region to protect the junction with the Reserve Front. On the right – On 30 August the Reserve Front will launch an offensive to destroy the enemy in the Pochinok and Roslavl' region, capture Roslavl' and reach the Dolgie Nivy, Khislovichi (exclusive) and Petrovichi front.

See *SBDVOV,* Issue 41, 12-13 and Zolotarev, 'Stavka VGK,' 148-149.

44. First, Eremenko had to fill in a growing gap of more than 20km (12 miles) between the former Central Front's right flank 21st Army and the Briansk Front's newly assigned 13th Army. This task fell to the newly and hastily formed 40th Army, whose forces were drawn from other *front* sectors. Formed on 28 August, the 40th Army's lead elements joined combat against Guderian's panzer spearheads in piecemeal fashion. Worse still, the Briansk Front's command cadre lacked necessary experience. The *front* commander, Eremenko, had just relinquished command of 43rd Army, the commanders of the 3rd and 13th Armies, Generals Ia.G. Kreizer and A.M. Gorodniansky, had just commanded divisions, and the commander of the 50th Army, General M.P. Petrov, had just commanded a corps. The *front* staff was likewise green and inexperienced, since it was formed from the staff of the just disbanded 20th Rifle and 25th Mechanized Corps. See A.A. Volkov, *Kriticheskii prolog: Nezavershennye frontovye nastupatel'nye operatsii pervykh kampanii Velikoi otechestvennoi voiny* [Critical prologue: Incomplete *front* offensive operations in the first campaign of the Great Patriotic War] (Moscow: AVIAR, 1992), 74.

45. Specifically, the order stated:

a) On the 50th Army's front: the 299th, 278th, 290th and 279th Rifle Divisions, the 121st Tank Brigade and one tank battalion are assigned to attack from the Viazovsk and Vereshovskii front along the Roslavl' axis and two High Command Reserve regiments and one guards-mortar regiment [will attack] from Diat'kovo.

b) On the 3rd Army's front: the 282nd and 269th Rifle Divisions, the 108th Tank Division, the 4th Cavalry Division and one High Command Reserve regiment are assigned to attack from the Pochep and Semtsy front along the Starodub axis;

c) On the 13th Army's front: the 155th, 307th and 6th Rifle Divisions, the 147th Tank Division, the 50th Tank Division (without tanks) and two High Command Reserve regiments are assigned to attack from the Pogar, Gremiach and Pushkary front along the Semenovka axis;

d) On the 21st Army front: while firmly defending the Karpovichi and Gorodnia sector along the Snov River line, three divisions will attack from the Sidorkin and Pereliub front toward Semenovka.

See 'Doklad komanuiushchego voiskami Brianskogo Fronta No. 349 Verkhovnomu Glavnokomanduiushchemu plana operatsii po razgromu protivnika v raione Pochep, Trubchevsk, Novgorod-Severskii, Novozybkov' [Report No. 349 of the Briansk Front commander to the Supreme High Commander on the operational plan to destroy the enemy in the Pochep, Trubchevsk, Novo-Severskii and Novozybkov region] in Zolotarev, 'Stavka VGK,' 369.

46. 'Direktiva Stavki VGK No. 001482 komanduiushchemu voiskami Brianskogo Fronta ob uskorenii podgotivki nastupleniia 50-i armii' [*Stavka* VGK Directive No. 001482 to the Briansk Front commander about accelerating the preparations of the 50th Army's offensive] in Zolotarev, 'Stavka VGK,' 151.

47. 'Direktiva Stavki VGK No. 001540 komanduiushchemu voiskami Brianskogo Fronta, zamestiteliu komanduiushchego VVS Krasnoi Armii o neudovletvoritel'nykh resultatakh deistvii po razgromu gruppy Guderiana i zadachakh aviatsii' [*Stavka* VGK Directive No. 001540 to the Briansk Front commander and the deputy commander of the Red Army Air Force concerning the unsatisfactory results of operations to destroy Group Guderian and the missions of aviation] in Zolotarev, 'Stavka VGK,' 155.

48. *Ibid.,* 69. See the Briansk Front's daily situation report for 2 September.

49. 'Rasporiazhenie Verkhovnogo Glavnokomanduiushchego komanduiushchemu voiskami Brianskogo Fronta ob uluchshenii organizatsii boevykh deistvii I vyvode iz okruzheniia 108-i tankovoi divizii' [Supreme High Command order to the Briansk Front commander about the improvement in the organization of combat operations and the withdrawal of the 108th Tank Division from encirclement] in Zolotarev, '*Stavka VGK,*' 165.

50. *Ibid.,* 82. See the Briansk Front's daily report for 6 September. By 7 September the 108th Tank Division reported the loss of a total of 53 tanks throughout the operation and the 141st Tank Brigade 24 tanks. The 108th Tank Division's after-action-report prepared on 17 September summarized the gruesome results of the operation and typified the losses in other Briansk Front forces. The division, which had begun the operation with a strength of about 72 tanks and about 4,500 personnel, ended the operation with only 11 tanks (2 KV's, 7 T-34's and 2 T-40's) and 1,200 men.

51. 'Direktiva Stavki VGK No. 001650 komanduiushchemu voiskami Brianskogo Fronta, razreshaiushchaia sozdanie zagraditel'nikh otriadov' [*Stavka* VGK Directive No. 001650 to the Briansk Front commander permitting the creation of blocking detachments] in Zolotarev, 'Stavka VGK,' 164.

52. *Ibid.,* 16. See also 'Direktiva Stavki VGK No. 001918 komanduiushchemu voiskami Brianskogo Fronta o likvidatsii proryva 2-i tankovoi gruppy protivnika' [*Stavka* VGK Directive No. 001918 to the Briansk Front commander concerning the liquidation of the enemy 2nd Tank Group penetration] in Zolotarev, '*Stavka VGK,*' 179-180.

53. *Ibid.,* 76-78.

54. Volkov, 81-82.

55. From the historiographical standpoint, the immense scale, scope and success of German Operation Barbarossa largely masked from public view the numerous *Stavka* attempts to halt the German advance and regain the strategic and operational initiative. Understandably, therefore, since war's end German and

Soviet accounts of combat during this period have accentuated the successful and spectacular aspects of the campaign, while ignoring the rest. From the Germans' perspective, the many Soviet counteractions were but temporary episodes in a nearly seamless successful advance to the gates of Moscow, Leningrad and Rostov. These episodes warranted brief mention but little more. Only when the Soviets halted the German juggernaut at the gates of Moscow in early December did German commanders and military analysts begin to reflect on what had occurred during the previous six months, as if to discover the basic flaws and weaknesses in their obviously over-ambitious strategic plans.

5. THE BATTLE FOR LENINGRAD

1. To the north, the Finnish Army was to assault Leningrad from the northwest between Lakes Onega and Ladoga and assist Army Group North in capturing Leningrad.
2. S.P. Platonov, ed., *Bitva za Leningrad, 1941-1944* [The Battle for Leningrad, 1941-1944] (Moscow: Voenizdat, 1964), 27-28.
3. Zolotarev, 'Stavka VGK,' 47-48. The Luga Defense Line was intended to be a 10-15km (6-9-mile) deep defense of barriers, minefields and antitank guns behind the Luga River 100km (60 miles) south of Leningrad. At the same time, Popov had to defend the city's northern approaches with his 23rd Army and the approaches into central Karelia and Murmansk in the far north with his 7th (Separate) and 14th Armies.
4. Platonov, 28. Initially, the LOG consisted of the 70th, 171st, 177th and 191st Rifle Divisions, the 1st, 2nd and 3rd Peoples' Militia Divisions (DNO), the 1st Separate Mountain Rifle Brigade and supporting artillery.
5. When the first of the LOG's divisions, the 177th Rifle, arrived south of Luga on 4 July, the line was so incomplete that an additional 25,000 laborers were mobilized to accelerate its construction. Thereafter, additional forces occupied the defenses, while the front inched perilously northward toward it. The 191st Rifle Division occupied the Kingisepp sector; the 111th Rifle Division, which had been shattered in fighting east of Pskov, withdrew to back up the 177th south of Luga, and the remaining forces filtered into position from 10 to 14 July. As of 14 July, the LOG consisted of the 177th and 191st Rifle Divisions, Major-General I.S. Kosobutsky's 41st Rifle Corps (the 90th, 111th, 118th and 235th Rifle Divisions), the 1st Mountain Rifle Brigade, the 1st, 2nd and 4th DNOs and the Leningrad 'S.M. Kirov' infantry and rifle-machine gun school. See Platonov, 28 and *Boevoi sostav*, 22.
6. The Rear Line Construction Directorate (USTOR), which hastily constructed the Luga line, was commanded by Major-General P.A. Zaitsev, Popov's Deputy Commander for Fortified Regions and employed construction forces and 30,000 civilians to work round-the-clock on the new defenses. See John Erickson, *The Road to Stalingrad* (New York: Harper and Row, 1975), 144.
7. A.A. Zhdanov, Secretary of the Communist Party's Central Committee and Leningrad Party Chief, served as the High Command Member of the Military Council (Commissar) and Major-General M.V. Zakharov as its Chief of Staff. See Zolotarev, 'Stavka VGK,' 62-63.

8. On 10 July the LOG consisted of the 191st and 177th Rifle Divisions, the 1st and 2nd DNOs, the 1st Separate Mountain Rifle Brigade and the 41st Rifle Corps (the 111th, 90th, 235th and 118th Rifle Divisions), the latter refitting east of Luga.

9. Reinhardt faced the 2nd DNO and two companies of the Leningrad Red Banner Infantry School that Popov had hastily dispatched to that sector to stem the German tide. For details on the German advance, see Luttichau, Chapter XXVIII.

10. For details on the Sol'tsy battle see also, Erich von Manstein, *Lost Victories* (Chicago, Henry Regnery, 1958), 194-195 and Platonov, 36-37. Only days before, an angry Stalin had scathingly criticized Voroshilov's conduct of the defense and ordered Vatutin, the Northwestern Front's new chief of staff, to savage the exposed German panzer force. See Zolotarev, 'Stavka VGK,' 61-62. Vatutin orchestrated a two-pronged assault on Sol'tsy from the north and east by two Northwestern Front shock group's. His plan called for the Northwestern Front's 11th Army to counterattack along the Sol'tsy-Dno axis with two shock groups. The northern group's 21st Tank Division of the 1st Mechanized Corps and the 70th and 237th Rifle Divisions of the 16th Rifle Corps were to attack the 8th Panzer Division's exposed positions around Sol'tsy from the north. Other LOG's forces to the west and the 1st DNO and 1st Mountain Rifle Brigade defending along the Novgorod axis were to support and reinforce the northern group's assault. The southern group, which consisted of the 22nd Rifle Corps' 180th, 182nd and 183rd Rifle Divisions, was to attack Sol'tsy from the east with the 183rd Rifle Division the 8th Panzer Division's communications routes to the southwest with its other two divisions.

11. While the bulk of Leeb's army group was attacking toward Leningrad, Eighteenth Army elements were clearing Soviet forces from the army group's left flank in Estonia and along the Baltic coast to deprive the Soviets of vital naval and air facilities in the region. Between 11 July and 28 August, the Eighteenth Army's XXVI and XXXXII Army Corps defeated the 8th Army and occupied Tartu, Parnu and Tallinn. The *Stavka* ordered Tallinn evacuated on 26 August. At a cost of heavy losses, including roughly 20,000 prisoners, the Soviet defense of Estonia tied down four German divisions and marginally weakened the German Luga and Novgorod groupings. Thereafter, in September and October, German forces seized the Moon Islands off the Estonian coast while Finnish forces eliminated the Soviet naval base at Hango.

12 The LOG's 1st DNO and 1st Separate Mountain Rifle Brigade defended the Shimsk-Novgorod axis.

13. While Soviet critiques of the so-called Sol'tsy-Dno counterstroke recognize its impact on the German offensive timetable, they also lamented the attacking forces' poor command, control and coordination that prevented the operation from accomplishing far more.

14. The command transferred the 272nd Rifle Division to the 7th Army at Petrozavodsk, the 265th Rifle Division to the 23rd Army on the Karelian Isthmus, the 268th Rifle Division to the 8th Army in Estonia and the 281st Rifle Division to the Kingisepp defensive sector. Voroshilov positioned his 1st Tank Division at Krasnogvardeisk.

15. *Stavka* Directive No. 1, dated 15 July, to the Northern Front abolished the rifle corps link within armies and created smaller armies, consisting of five to six divisions

each, presumably, armies that the commanders could better control. The Kingisepp Sector, made up of Baltic Fleet coastal units, the 90th and 191st Rifle Divisions, the 2nd DNO and 4th Light DNO, the Leningrad Infantry School, the 14th Anti-Tank Brigade, Armoured Train No. 60 and the 519th RVK (Stavka reserve) Howitzer Artillery Regiment, was responsible for defending the Kingisepp axis. The Luga Sector had the mission of protecting the Luga highway axis with the 111th, 177th and 235th Rifle Divisions, the 2nd Tank Division, the 1st Rifle Regiment, 3rd DNO, the 260th and 262nd Machine gun-Artillery Battalions and the Leningrad Artillery School's Rifle-machine Gun School and Battalion. Finally, the Eastern Sector, consisting of the 1st DNO, the 1st Separate Mountain Rifle Brigade and the 261st and 263rd Machine gun-Artillery Battalions, was to protect the Novgorod axis. Major-General V.V. Semashko commanded the Kingisepp Sector and Majors General A.N. Astanin and F.N. Starikov commanded the Luga and eastern Sectors, respectively. Presumably, General Piadyshev was arrested for dereliction of duty. See Platonov, 49-50.

16. Zolotarev, 'Stavka VGK,' 107-108. The *Stavka* had already dispatched nine rifle and two cavalry divisions to the Northwestern Front by early August. The 48th Army consisted of the 1st DNO, the 70th, 128th and 237th Rifle Divisions, the 1st Separate Mountain Rifle Brigade and the 21st Tank Division.

17. Führer Directive, No. 34 of 30 July provided even more precise instruction regarding the capture of Leningrad.

18. Luttichau, Chapter XXIX and Platonov, 47-48. The Eighteenth Army's XXXXII Army Corps was to join the advance after they captured Tallinn and completed operations in Estonia.

19. The Sixteenth Army consisted of the X, II, L and XXIII Army Corps deployed from north to south. Leeb retained only three security divisions in reserve.

20. For planning details, see Zolotarev, 'Stavka VGK,' 107-108, 111-112 and 116-117 and Volkov, 64-70.

21. The 202nd and 163rd Motorized and 25th Cavalry Divisions spearheaded the 34th Army's advance.

22. For details from the German perspective, see Manstein, 200-201 and Luttichau, Chapter XXIX, 7-13. The Germans reported capturing 18,000 Russians and capturing or destroying 200 tanks, 300 guns and mortars, 36 anti-aircraft guns, 700 vehicles and the first '*Katiushas*' to fall intact into their hands.

23. By this time, Army Group North's losses had reached 80,000 men. See Luttichau, Chapter XXIX, 15.

24. OKW claimed the operation destroyed the 11th, 34th and 27th Armies (18 divisions) and captured or destroyed 53,000 men, 320 tanks and 659 guns during the month and 35,000 men, 117 tanks and 334 guns during the operations in the Valdai Hills. After the operation ended, OKH ordered the LVI and LVII Motorized Corps to join Army Group Centre's advance on Moscow. See Luttichau, Chapter XXIX, 16-17.

25. *Ibid.*, 4-5 and Platonov, 53-55. The Germans suffered 1,600 casualties in the intense fighting.

26. Voroshilov sent the 1st Tank Division and the 1st Guards DNO to reinforce the Kingisepp sector on 9 August and the 281st Rifle Division on 13 August. Popov reinforced Krasnogvardeisk with the 2nd and 3rd Guards DNOs on 17 August and

the 291st Rifle Division on 18 August and formed a Separate Aviation Group to centralize control of his *front*'s aircraft. See Platonov, 53-55.

27. The 8th Army reported losing all of its regimental and battalion commanders and their staffs in the vicious fighting around Kingisepp. See Erickson, 189.

28. This threatening force included the remnants of the 8th Army's 48th, 125th, 191st, 268th, 11th and 118th Rifle Divisions and the 1st Naval Infantry Brigade, and the Kingisepp Defensive Sector's 2nd DNO, 1st Guards DNO and the 1st Tank and 281st Rifle Divisions.

29. The Eighteenth Army reported it captured 9,774 prisoners and destroyed or captured 60 tanks and 77 guns during the period from 21 August-9 September. See Luttichau, Chapter XXIX, 47.

30. The LVI Motorized Corps had only the 3rd Motorized Division and the L Army Corps', the 269th and SS Police Division.

31. The bag of captured reached a reported 16,000 men, 51 tanks, 171 guns and 1,000 vehicles. See Luttichau, Chapter XXIX, 47.

32. Platonov, 62. In two weeks of heavy fighting, the XXVIII and I Army Corps reported capturing 16,000 prisoners and destroying or capturing 74 tanks and 300 guns.

33. *Ibid.*, 60, Zolotarev, 'Stavka VGK,' 126, and *Boevoi sostav*, 39. The Leningrad Front controlled the 8th, 23rd and 48th Armies, the Kopor, Southern and Slutsk-Kolpino Operational Groups, the Baltic Fleet and *front* air forces and the Karelian Front, which was responsible for operations north of Lake Ladoga, the 7th and 14th Armies and the Northern Fleet.

34. Voroshilov, who had displayed his military incompetence on numerous occasions prior to and during the war, would not feel the directive's full effects until almost two weeks later. In the interim, on 5 September the GKO appointed Voroshilov to command the Leningrad Front with Popov as his Chief of Staff, ostensibly to foster unity of command.

35. Zolotarev, 'Stavka VGK,' 129 and Platonov, 60. The 54th Army was formed in late August and early September. Under *Stavka* control, the army formed around the nucleus of the 44th Rifle Corps and consisted of the 285th, 286th, 310th and 314th Rifle Divisions, the 27th Cavalry Division, the 122nd Tank Brigade and the 119th Separate Tank Battalion. Its mission was to defend along the Volkhov River. The 4th Army formed in late September under *Stavka* control. It consisted of the 285th, 292nd and 311th Rifle Divisions and the 27th Cavalry Division, the 285th Rifle and 27th Cavalry Divisions from the 54th Army. It deployed along the Volkhov River in early October. The 52nd Army formed in August 1941 on the base of the 25th Rifle Corps as a separate army under *Stavka* control. It consisted of the 276th, 285th, 288th, 292nd, 312th, 314th and 316th Rifle Divisions and occupied defenses along the Volkhov river at the end of August.

36. For details of the assault, see Luttichau, 48-60. The XXXIX Motorized Corps consisted of the 12th and 18th Panzer and 20th Motorized Divisions. The First Air Fleet and VII Air Corps were to support Schmidt's thrust.

37. The NAG consisted of the remnants of the 16th Rifle Corps' 237th Rifle Division, the 1st Mountain Rifle Brigade and the fresh 305th Rifle Division. See *Boevoi sostav*, 39.

38. A frantic *Stavka* allocated the Leningrad Front four days worth of Leningrad's tank production, four aviation regiments and ten march battalions with which to reinforce its defenses. See Platonov, 62.

39. Platonov, 63 and *Boevoi sostav*, 39. The 55th Army was to defend the western portion of the sector with its 168th, 70th, 90th and 237th Rifle Divisions, the 4th DNO and the Slutsk-Kolpino Fortified Region. The 42nd Army was to defend the eastern sector and Krasnogvardeisk proper with the 2nd and 3rd DNOs, the 291st Rifle Division and the Krasnogvardeisk Fortified Region.

40. Popov ordered 48th Army to employ the refitted 311th and 128th Rifle Divisions, the 1st Separate Mountain Rifle Brigade and the NKVD division in the counterattack.

41. The NKVD Rifle Division withdrew to the Neva River and the 1st Separate Mountain Rifle Brigade to defenses east of Siniavino.

42. The encircled forces included the 41st Rifle Corps' 111th, 177th, 90th, 70th, 235th, 237th Rifle Divisions, the 1st and 3rd DNO and the 24th Tank Division. During the LOG's attempted escape, the 8th Panzer, SS Police, 269th and 96th Infantry Divisions hounded the encircled forces unmercifully by constant converging attacks, inflicting estimated losses of roughly 30,000 men, 120 tanks and 400 guns on the beleaguered Soviet force. See Luttichau, 47.

43. Halder, 524.

44. The directive went on to state:

> First and foremost, however, it is necessary to strive to encircle Leningrad completely, at least from the east and, if weather conditions permit, conduct a large-scale air offensive on Leningrad. It is especially important to destroy the water supply stations.
>
> As soon as possible, Army Group North's force must begin an offensive northward in the Neva River sector to help the Finns overcome the fortifications along the old Soviet-Finnish border, and also to shorten the front lines and deprive the enemy of the ability to use the air bases. In cooperation with the Finns, prevent enemy naval forces from exiting Kronshtadt into the Baltic Sea (Hango and the Moonzund Islands) by using mine obstacles and artillery fire.
>
> Also isolate the region of combat operations at Leningrad from the sector along the lower reaches of the Volkhov as soon as forces necessary to perform this mission become available. Link-up with the Karelian Army on the Svir River only when enemy forces have been destroyed in the Leningrad region.

The full order is found in *SVIMVOV*, Issue 18, 242-243.

45. For example, at a time when Popov most needed reserves, Finnish operations forced him to transfer the 265th Rifle Division, the 48th Army's reserve and the 291st Rifle Division from the Krasnogvardeisk Fortified Region to bolster the 23rd Army's defense against the Finns.

46. See Luttichau, Chapter XXIX, 52-54. Originally, Leeb planned to encircle Leningrad by sealing off access routes to it from east and west. Hoepner's panzer group was to establish a tight inner encirclement line around the city with Reinhardt's and Schmidt's XXXXI and XXXIX Motorized Corps, while Kuechler's Eighteenth Army formed a broader encirclement line extending from Koporskii Bay to Lake Ladoga. At the time, the XXXXI Motorized Corps

consisted of the 1st, 6th and 8th Panzer and 36th Motorized Divisions and the XXXIX Motorized Corps, the 12th Panzer and 18th and 20th Motorized Divisions. Eighteenth Army consisted of the XXVI, XXXVIII, L and XXVIII Army Corps. However, Hitler's decision to transfer the XXXXI, LVI and LVII Motorized and VIII Air Corps to Army Group Centre, effective 15 September, left Leeb with only the XXXIX Panzer Corps and, as a later concession, the 8th Panzer Division. Thus, Leeb decided to envelop the city from the east with the XXXIX Motorized Corps and attack with the Eighteenth Army south and west of Leningrad. The XXXXI Motorized Corps would spearhead his advance on Leningrad from the southwest before its departure to Army Group Centre.

47. The XXXVIII Army Corps consisted of the 1st, 58th, 291st and later the 254th Infantry Divisions and the L Army Corps, the SS Police and 269th Infantry Divisions. The 8th Panzer Division was refitting after suffering heavy losses the previous month.

48. The XXVIII Army Corps consisted of the 121st, 96th and 122nd Infantry Divisions.

49. The 42nd Army consisted of the 2nd and 3rd Guards DNOs and the Krasnogvardeisk Fortified Region. The 55th Army consisted of the 90th, 70th, 168th Rifle Divisions, the 1st and 4th DNOs, the Slutsk-Kolpino Fortified Region and the 84th and 86th Tank Battalions. The 8th Army's 191st, 118th, 11th and 281st Rifle Divisions defended opposite the XXXVIII Army Corps and two other divisions defended further west. See Platonov, 66-79 for a detailed account of the action from the Soviet perspective.

50. Voroshilov's reserve consisted of the 10th and 16th Rifle Divisions, the 5th DNO, the 8th Rifle and 1st Naval Infantry Brigades, the 48th Tank Battalion and the 500th Rifle Regiment. In addition, the 155th Rifle and 1st NKVD Rifle Divisions defended the Neva River front east of Leningrad.

51. 'State Committee of Defense Decree of 11. 9. 41,' *Central Party Archives of the Institute of Marxism and Leninism, TsPA UML* f. 644, op. 1, d. 9. The 48th Army was disbanded on 14 September and its forces were transferred to the 54th Army.

52. See Dmitri V. Pavlov, *Leningrad 1941: The Blockade* (Chicago: The University of Chicago Press, 1965), 24-25. The artillery fire's effectiveness, however, was limited since it could not range the heart of the city. The Luftwaffe dropped 8,000 incendiary bombs during the air strikes, causing heavy damage and many fires and destroying the Badaev Warehouses where most of Leningrad's foodstuffs were stored.

53. These included the 500th Rifle Regiment on 10 September, the 1st Naval Infantry Brigade on 12 September and the newly formed 5th DNO on the same day.

54. The 2nd DNO and 500th Rifle Regiment defended Dutergov, the 3rd DNO and 1st Naval Infantry Brigade Krasnoe Selo and the 5th DNO Pulkovo.

55. The 168th Rifle Division defended the Fedorovskoe sector east of Slutsk.

56. Luttichau, Chapter XXIX, 55.

57. The reported presence of the 27th Cavalry Division on Schmidt's flank was incorrect.

58. When the 8th Panzer arrived at XXXIX Corps three days later, it was no longer needed.

59. Zolotarev, 'Stavka VGK,' 175 and G.K. Zhukov, *Reminiscences and Reflections, Vol. 1* (Moscow: Progress, 1985). 398-400. Stalin was particularly angry over

Voroshilov's failure to inform him about the fall of Shlissel'burg, a fact which Stalin first read about in a German communiqué. Stalin also learned of the Leningrad Military Council's decision to demolish Leningrad's military installations in anticipation of city's fall to the Germans. While meeting with Admiral Kuznetsov, whom he had summoned to Moscow to prepare preliminary instructions for scuttling the Baltic Fleet, Stalin admitted, 'It is possible that it (Leningrad) may have to be abandoned.' Before Zhukov's departure to Leningrad, Stalin informed him, 'It is an almost hopeless situation. By taking Leningrad and joining up with the Finns the Germans can strike Moscow from the northeast and then the situation will become even more critical.' Handing Zhukov a slip of paper, Stalin said, 'Give this to Voroshilov.' The paper read, 'Hand over command of the *front* to Zhukov and fly back to Moscow immediately.' Indicative of his mood, Stalin had sent a letter to Churchill on 3 September describing the deteriorating situation in the Ukraine and at Leningrad, lamenting the absence of a second front and large-scale material aid and describing the effects on Britain of Soviet defeat. In the letter, Stalin suggested that Churchill send 25-30 divisions to Arkhangel'sk or via Iran to help the Red Army. Churchill noted the letter's 'utter unreality,' in a remark of 15 September. See Luttichau, Chapter XXIX, 45.

60. In August 1939, Zhukov had commanded Soviet forces that defeated a Japanese inclusion into Mongolia at Khalkhin Gol.

61. The Military Council was enlarged on 17 September by the addition of Admiral I.S. Isakov, Chief of the Main Naval Staff and *Stavka* representative.

62. The 3rd Guards DNO's and 1st Naval Infantry Brigade defended north of Krasnoe Selo and the villages of Sosnovka and Finskoe Koirovo changed hands several times during the fighting. Zhukov reinforced the 42nd Army with the 10th and 11th Rifle Divisions.

63. Platonov, 69.

64. *Ibid.* Zhukov also ordered his *front* 'to form five rifle brigades and two rifle divisions by 18 September and concentrate them in four defense lines for the immediate defense of Leningrad.'

65. The 42nd Army's 10th and 11th Rifle Divisions defended Uritsk.

66. The new defense line extended from Ligovo through Miasokombinat to Rybatskoe. Zhukov forbade commanders from removing forces from this line without his expressed permission, and Stalin reinforced Zhukov's prohibition by issuing a Draconian order of his own dealing mercilessly with 'saboteurs and German sympathizers' who retreated without authorization. The new reserves were the newly formed 21st NKVD Rifle Division, the 6th DNO, two naval rifle brigades and PVO troops.

67. When Fediuninsky arrived at army headquarters, he found General Ivanov sitting with his head in his hands, unable to report where his troops were located. Major-General Larionov, the Ivanov's chief of staff, reported that the 42nd Army was holding, 'literally by a miracle.' Ivanov requested permission to move his headquarters to the rear, but Fediuninsky categorically refused. Later, Fediuninsky also reported that Ivanov had relocated his headquarters to a safer locale further behind the lines in the basement of the Kirov factory, See Erickson, 192.

68. Shcherbakov was to attack with the 191st and 281st Rifle Divisions, reinforced by the 10th and 11th Rifle Divisions and the remnants of the 42nd Army's 3rd DNO.

While doing so, he was to protect his extended right flank by withdrawing the 5th Naval Infantry Brigade to new defenses along the Kovashi River and retain the 125th and 286th Rifle Divisions in reserve

69. The 8th Army's front finally stabilized along the Novyi Petergof, Tomuzi and Petrovskaia line and remained stable through early 1944.

70. Platonov, 69-75. Soviet accounts claim that intelligence forewarned the Leningrad Front and its army commands of the impending attack, permitting them to deal effectively with it.

71. The 5th DNO, the 500th Rifle Regiment and the 5th Separate Machine-gun Artillery Battalion defended Pulkovo Heights.

72. See the caustic exchanges between the *Stavka* and Kulik in, Zolotarev, 'Stavka VGK,' 186-187 and 193-194. The NOG had been organized on 2 September from the 46th and 115th Rifle Divisions and the 4th Armoured Car Regiment. Kulik's 54th Army consisted of the 128th and 310th Rifle Divisions, the 21st Tank Division and the 1st Mountain Rifle Brigade from the former 48th Army, reinforced in late September by the 3rd and 4th Guards and 286th and 294th Rifle Divisions and the 16th and 122nd Tank Brigades. Its strength was 85,000 men.

73. See Kulik's dismissal order in Zolotarev, 'Stavka VGK,' 200. Although court-martialed for his failure and reduced to the rank of Major-General, later the politically loyal Kulik would return to army command with predictably poor results.

74. The NOG's 115th Rifle Division and the 4th Naval Infantry Brigade seized the bridgehead.

75. The Germans transferred two parachute regiments of the 7th Parachute Division from Germany, one infantry regiment from Army Group Centre, the Spanish 250th 'Blue' Division and the 72nd Infantry Division from Western Europe to the Leningrad region. In addition, it forced Leeb to transfer the 8th Panzer and part of the 96th Infantry Division from south of Leningrad to the Siniavino sector.

76. Luttichau, Chapter XXIX, 71. Soviet sources claim that Leeb's forces fighting for the coastal bridgehead and the Krasnogvardeisk 77 Krivosheev, 167-168.

78. The XXXIX Motorized Corps took with it the 1st, 6th and 8th Panzer and the 36th Motorized Divisions. To compensate for this loss, the OKH also began transferring the 227th and 212th Infantry Divisions from France to Army Group North.

79. The 6th Panzer Division departed late on 15 September, the 1st Panzer Division on 19 September, the 36th Motorized Division on 20 September and the corps' headquarters on 20 September.

80. Erickson, 195 and Luttichau, Chapter XXIX, 71.

81. The front north of Leningrad also stabilized on the Karelian Isthmus and along the Svir River.

82. *SVIMVOV*, 244.

6. THE BATTLE FOR KIEV

1. For detailed coverage of the fighting during July, see, Luttichau, Chapter IX; *VOV*, 184-187; Vladimirsky, 110-171; and documents in *SBDVOV,* Issues 36 and 38 (Moscow: Voenizdat, 1958 and 1959) and Zolotarev, 'Stavka VGK,' 38-98.

2. For Rundstedt's rationale see, Luttichau, Chapter IX, 9-11.
3. Zolotarev, 'Stavka VGK,' 58. The *Stavka*'s directive read:

> Based upon information received from the Southwestern Front commander, enemy tanks have penetrated through the fortified region at Novoe Miropol'. If this accords with reality, then the enemy has disrupted our regrouping and the reorganization of the Southwestern Front's forces behind the fortified regions.
>
> The *Stavka* ORDERS the Southwestern Front commander to be personally responsible for immediately protecting the fortified region and preventing any further development of the penetration through the fortified region by the enemy tanks. Immediately destroy the penetrating group.
>
> The Southern Front commander will immediately move the 16th Mechanized Corps to Berdichev and assist the Southwestern Front's reserve in destroying the enemy. After the liquidation of the enemy, in accordance with this directive, the corps will immediately move to Mozyr' so as to maintain close contact with the corps.
>
> Retain the 18th Mechanized Corps in full readiness to operate in a northerly axis. The Southern and Southwestern Front commanders will maintain close contact and cooperate with one another without further *Stavka* instructions....
>
> [signed] Zhukov

4. *SBDVOV*, Issue 38, 85. Kirponos's Order No. 0053 dated 9 July 1941 read:

> 1. While covering the Novgorod-Volynskii Fortified Region from the east, the 5th Army will attack from the Serby and Guta Station region in the direction of Broniki and Chernitsa with its 31st Rifle Corps and the 9th and 22nd Mechanized Corps. I charge you with conducting the attack.
> 2. While holding on to the fortified region line within the army's boundaries, on 9 July 1941 the 6th Army will attack northward from the Liubar region with its 49th Rifle Corps.
> 3. The boundary line between the armies is Kozarovichi (exclusive), Radomyshl' (exclusive), Markhlevsk and Annopol; − for the 6th Army.
>
> [signed] Kirponos, Purkaev

5. *Ibid.*, 100. The heavy fighting reduced the strength of the *front*'s mobile forces, leaving the 9th Mechanized Corps with 7 BT and 25 T-26 tanks, the 19th Mechanized Corps with 4 KV, 7 T-34 and 22 T-26 tanks, and the 22nd Mechanized Corps with 2 BT and 28 T-26 tanks.
6. *VOV*, 185-186.
7. Zolotarev, 'Stavka VGK,' 79.
8. *VOV*, 186-187.
9. For details on the Uman' encirclement, see Luttichau, Chapters X and XI.

10. *VOV*, 186.

11. *Ibid.* The initial German force consisted of the 297th, 125th, 295th and 257th Infantry, the 97th, 100th and 101st Jäger [Light], the 1st and 4th Mountain and SS 'Reich' and 11th Panzer Divisions, plus the 11th Cavalry Brigade and several Hungarian divisions. In early August, the Germans committed the 297th, 295th and 257th Infantry, the 97th, 100th and 101st Jager, the 1st and 4th Mountain, and the SS 'Adolf Hitler' and 11th Panzer Divisions to liquidate the encirclement. See the operational maps of First Panzer Group and Seventeenth Army.

12. Zolotarev, 'Stavka VGK,' 91.

13. *Ibid.* Ponedelin's combat reports are found in *SBDVOV*, Issue 38, 241-254.

14. *SBDVOV*, Issue 38, 147-148.

15. *VOV*, 187.

16. Zolotarev, 'Stavka VGK,' 96.

17. Luttichau, Chapter XI, 23-24.

18. *SBDVOV*, Issue 39 (Moscow: Voenizdat, 1959), 252.

19. *Ibid.*, 162.

20. *VOV*, 188.

21. Luttichau, Chapter XI, 26-27. *VOV*, 188, claims that 103,000 men were lost by German count. In addition to Lieutenant-Generals Muzychenko and Ponedelin, the captured included Major-Generals M.G. Snegov and I.A. Kornilov, the commanders of the 8th and 49th Rifle Corps and Major-Generals S.A. Tkachenko, N.I. Pronin, V.I. Prokhurov, P.I. Abramidze and Ia.I. Tonkonogov, the commanders of the 44th, 58th Mountain, 80th Rifle, 72nd Mountain and 141st Rifle Divisions.

22. The dead generals included Major-General N.N. Belov, the commander of the 12th Army's 15th Rifle (former motorized) Division. See Aleksander A. Maslov, *Fallen Soviet Generals: Soviet General officers killed in battle, 1941-1945* (London: Frank Cass, 1998), 24-25.

23. *VOV*, 189 and A.A. Maslov, 'Tried for Treason against the Motherland: Soviet Generals Condemned after Release from German Captivity, Part 1,' *The Journal of Slavic Military Studies, Volume 13, No. 2* (June 2000), 111-115.

24. *SBDVOV*, Issue 39, 7. See the full order in Zolotarev, 'Stavka VGK,' 96.

25. See Vladimirsky, 194-196 and David M. Glantz, *Forgotten Battles of the German-Soviet War (1941-1945), Volume 1: The Summer-Fall Campaign (22 June-4 December 1941)* (Carlisle, PA: Self-published, 1999), 71-73.

26. Soviet historians have written very little about the Uman encirclement and the subsequent withdrawal of Southern Front forces eastward to the Dnepr River. Soviet records now indicate that the defensive operation was identified as the Tiraspol'-Melitopol' Defensive Operation, which lasted from 27 July-28 September 1941. At its outset, the Southern Front's 9th and 18th Armies and the *front* air forces and supporting units numbered 280,510 men. The *front* suffered 121,650 casualties during the entire operation, including 75,424 irrecoverable (killed, mortally wounded, captured and missing) and 46,226 sick and wounded.

Subsequent to the encirclement of the Southwestern Front at and east of Kiev, the *front*'s remnants also conducted a defensive operation that has been largely ignored by Soviet historians. Termed the Sumy-Khar'kov Defensive operation, the defense lasted from 30 September through 30 November 1941. During its course,

German Army Group South drove the Southwestern Front's 21st, 38th and 40th Armies eastward through Sumy and Khar'kov to Soviet defensive positions along the eastern bank of the Northern Donets River. The weakened Southwestern Front began the operation with 147,110 men, most of whom were survivors of the Kiev encirclement. During the operation, which included a short defense of Khar'kov proper, the *front* lost 96,509 men including 75,720 irrecoverable losses and 20,789 sick and wounded. Reinforcement sent by the *Stavka* to the front included several NKVD divisions and brigades that fought as regular ground units. See V.V. Gurkin, 'Liudskie poteri Sovetskikh Vooruzhennykh Sil v 1941-1954 gg.: Novye aspekty' [Personnel losses of the Soviet Armed Forces in 1941-1945: New aspects], *VIZh*, No. 2 (March-April 1999), 4, for details on the identity of the operations and Soviet strength and loss figures.

27. *VOV*, 191.
28. *Ibid.* Shaposhnikov had been serving as Chief of Staff of Timoshenko's Western Direction High Command.
29. *Ibid.* Intelligence information, in particular, reports from agent Rado in Switzerland, maintained that the Germans would advance on Moscow via Briansk.
30. *Ibid.*, 189. For the German debate, see Luttichau, Chapter XII, 1-5.
31. Luttichau, Chapter XII, 11-13.
32. *VOV*, 192 and Luttichau, Chapter XII, 17-21. Halder, 512-516 tracks the controversy.
33. Halder, 515-516 and Guderian, 152-156.
34. *VOV*, 192-193.
35. Zolotarev, 'Stavka VGK,' 120-121.
36. *VOV*, 193.
37. For details on the German advance to the Dnepr River, see Luttichau, Chapter XII.
38. Zolotarev, 'Stavka VGK,' 148-149.
39. The German Second Army also captured a bridgehead east of Chernigov from the 5th Army, threatening to separate it from the 21st Army.
40. Zolotarev, 'Stavka VGK,' 164. The *Stavka* directive read, 'The *Stavka* has familiarized itself with your report and will permit you to create blocking detachments in those divisions that show themselves to be unreliable. The purpose of the blocking detachments is to prevent the unauthorized withdrawal of units and, in instances of flight, to halt them using all necessary weaponry.'
41. A.M. Vasilevsky, *A Lifelong Cause* (Moscow: Progress, 1974), 106-107.
42. *Ibid.*, 107. See also Luttichau, Chapter XXI.
43. By 11 September the 257th, 239th and 125th Infantry, the 101st Jager, 100th Jager and 97th Jager, and the 76th Infantry Divisions were deployed from west to east in the bridgehead. See Luttichau, Chapter XII and XXII and Army Group South's and First Panzer Group's daily situation maps (originals).
44. *VOV*, 193. Full text in *SBDVOV*, Issue 40 (Moscow: Voenizdat, 1959), 176-178.
45. Zolotarev, 'Stavka VGK,' 171-172.
46. *VOV*, 193-194.
47. Zolotarev, 'Stavka VGK,' 176-177.
48. On 11 September the *Stavka* ordered Kirponos to commit two rifle divisions from the 26th Army to halt the 3rd and 4th Panzer Divisions advance to Romny and also ordered heavy air strikes on the advancing Germans.

49. Zolotarev, 'Stavka VGK,' 176.

50. *Ibid.*, 380 and *SBDVOV*, Issue 40, 192-193.

51. *VOV*, 194.

52. For example, the lead regiment of Model's 3rd Panzer Division was down to an effective strength of 10 tanks.

53. *VOV*, 194 and Zolotarev, 'Stavka VGK,' 191.

54. *VOV*, 195.

55. Zolotarev, 'Stavka VGK,' 198. Over the next five days, the *Stavka* repeatedly dispatched instructions to Kirponos's individual armies on how to break out, but in vain.

56. *VOV*, 195-196. See vivid accounts of the last days of Kirponos's encircled forces in Maslov, *Fallen Soviet Generals*, 25-27; S. Osipov and K. Golunbovsky, 'Sentiabr' 10941-go: Iugo-zapadnyi front, Gibel' komandovaiia' [September 1941: The Southwestern Front, the destruction of the command], *Armiia*, No. 16 (August 1991), 5-17; and 'Pravda o gibeli generala M.P. Kirponos' [The truth about the death of General m.P. Kirponos], *VIZh*, No. 9 (September 1964), 61-69.

57. Krivosheev, 166. These figures include the 6th and 12th Armies' losses during August and September. German sources claim a figure of 665,000 prisoners in the Kiev encirclement, but this figure also includes Soviet losses at Uman' and Briansk.

58. Zhukov's force totalled 34,500 men, 303 guns and mortars, 2 tanks and 19 combat aircraft. *VOV*, 196. The most detailed account of the siege in found in *SVIMVOV*, Issue 14 (Moscow: Voenizdat, 1954). Unclassified accounts include N.I. Krylov, *Ne pomerknet nikogda* [It never grows dark] (Moscow: Voenizdat, 1969) and I.I. Azerov, *Osazhdennaia Odessa* [Besieged Odessa] (Odessa, 1975).

59. David M. Glantz, *A History of Soviet Airborne Forces* (London: Frank Cass, 1994), 305-308.

7. VIAZ'MA, BRIANSK, TIKHVIN AND ROSTOV

1. Luttichau, Chapter XXX, 1.

2. *SVIMVOV*, Issue 18, 242-243.

3. *Ibid.*

4. For the complete text of Bock's Directive No. 1300, see V.A. Zolotarev, 'Bitva pod Moskvoi: Sbornik dokumentov,' T-15-4 (1) ['The Battle for Moscow: A collection of documents, Vol. 15-4 (1)] in *Russkii arkhiv: Velikaia Otechestvennaia* [The Russian archives: The Great Patriotic] (Moscow: 'TERRA,' 1997), 10-14. Hereafter cited as Zolotarev, 'Bitva pod Moskvoi.'

5. The Third Panzer Group was to attack from Dukhovshchina and the Fourth Panzer Group from Roslavl'.

6. The Second Panzer Group was to attack from the Shostka region.

7. See Army Group Centre *Kriegstagebuch* (KTB), 2 October 1941 and Reinhardt, 57, n. 51. German infantry divisions were roughly 1,500 men short each, giving them a strength of roughly 15,500 men each. Guderian had roughly 50 percent of his required tanks, Hoth had 70-80 percent and Hoepner roughly 100 percent. *VOV*, 213 placed German strength at 1,800,000 men, 14,000 guns and mortars, 1,700 tanks and 1,300 combat aircraft.

8. *VOV*, 213. The three *fronts* consisted of 83 rifle divisions, 1 rifle brigade, 9 cavalry divisions, 1 tank division, 1 motorized rifle division, 2 fortified regions and 13 tank brigades. See *Boevoi sostav*. German intelligence accurately estimated that Bock faced a force of 80 divisions with another 10 in reserve, which were equivalent to 54 full-strength divisions.

9. M. Lukin, 'V Viazemskoi operatsii' [In the Viaz'ma operation], *VIZh*, No. 9 (September 1981), 32.

10. *VOV*, 213.

11. Zolotarev, 'Bitva pod Moskvoi,' 66.

12 Konev's reserve consisted of four rifle and two motorized rifle divisions, one cavalry division, four tank brigades and five artillery regiments.

13. See Zolotarev, 'Bitva pod Moskvoi,' 73-74 for the full text.

14. *Ibid.*, 74-76.

15. *VOV*, 215.

16. Zolotarev, 'Stavka VGK,' 210-211.

17. Hence, the *front* commanders failed to concentrate their forces along the most critical axes. For example, Konev concentrated his forces along the Smolensk-Viaz'ma axis, where the *Stavka* anticipated the attack, but failed to do so in the 16th and 19th Armies' sectors where the Germans concentrated 17 divisions against two armies' 8 divisions, even after intelligence confirmed this was the case. Having recently commanded an army, the Konev still lacked requisite experience and, as the fighting at Smolensk had indicated, the lesson he learned was, first and foremost, that the *Stavka* required his forces to fight to the death and not abandon their positions. When Rokossovsky, the 19th Army commander, submitted his defense plan to Konev on 27 September, it contained some variants for a forced withdrawal. Konev ordered Rokossovsky, 'Fight on stubbornly. Exclude any and every notion of a mobile defense. Revise your operational plan.' See *VOV*, 215.

18. Ermakov's group consisted of the 2nd Guards, 160th and 283rd Rifle Divisions, the 21st and 52nd Cavalry Divisions, the 121st and 150th Tank Brigades and the 113th Separate Tank Battalion. It totalled 33,500 men, 158 tanks and 132 guns and mortars. See *Boevoi sostav*, 52. See German and Soviet archival maps depicting the day-by-day development of the German offensive in David M. Glantz, *Atlas of the Battle of Moscow: The Defensive Phase: 1 October-5 December 1941* (Carlisle, PA: Self-published, 1997).

19. Zolotarev, 'Bitva pod Moskvoi,' 79.

20. *Ibid.*, 81-82.

21. Luttichau, Chapter XXX, 1.

22. Zolotarev, '*Bitva pod Moskvoi,*' 83-84.

23. Zolotarev, 'Stavka VGK,' 214-215 and 217. The aviation group consisted of five aviation divisions from the *Stavka* reserve commanded by Colonel I.N. Rukhle, the *Stavka* representative to the Briansk Front.

24. Guderian, 178.

25. *VOV*, 219.

26. *Ibid.*

27. Lukin, 34-35.

28. *VOV*, 219 claims that Boldin's forces destroyed 38 German tanks on 4 October.

29. *Ibid.*, 220. See Konev's now unexpurgated account of the action around Viaz'ma in I.S. Konev, *Zapiski komanduiushchego frontom* [Notes of a *front* commander] (Moscow: 'GOLOS,' 2000), 52-74.

30. *Ibid.* Konev's order read:

> To the 16th Army commander Rokossovsky – I order you to turn the 16th Army's sector over to Ershakov, the 20th Army commander, immediately. You, your army headquarters and necessary equipment will reach Viaz'ma by forced march no later than 6 October. The army's mission is to halt the enemy advancing on Viaz'ma from the Spas-Demensk region in the south.

31. *Ibid.*

32. Zolotarev, 'Bitva pod Moskvoi,' 89-90.

33. The order was unrealistic because Rokossovsky's forces were themselves hard-pressed and could not move the required distance and German forces had already occupied some of his intended positions.

34. Initially, General I.S. Nikitin, the commander of the Viaz'ma garrison radioed Rokossovsky that, 'There are no forces in Viaz'ma and its environs. I have only militia.' Moments later, Rokossovsky learned that German forward units had reached the city. See *VOV*, 220.

35. *Ibid.*, 220-221 and Glantz, *Atlas of the Battle of Moscow*, 17-23. See Eremenko's account of the action in A.I. Eremenko, *V nachale voiny* [In the beginning of the war] (Moscow: 'Nauka,' 1965), 331-392.

36. *VOV*, 221 quoting from the *Volkischer Beobachter* (9 and 10 October 1941).

37. *Ibid.*

38. A.M. Samsonov, ed., *Proval gitlerovskogo nastuplenia na Moskvu* [The defeat of the Hitlerite offensive on Moscow] (Moscow: 'Nauka,' 1966), 20-21.

39. Initially, the GKO ordered 1,119 installations and other objectives be prepared for destruction.

40. See appropriate documents in Zolotarev, 'Stavka VGK,' 231-233 and Zolotarev, 'Bitva pod Moskvoi,' 96.

41. Major-General Dmitrii D. Leliushenko's 1st Guards Rifle Corps had rushed to Mtsensk to block the Second Panzer Group's advance. Leliushenko's troops included two tank brigades, the 4th and 11th, and two airborne brigades, the 10th and 201st of the 5th Airborne Corps, which flew into a nearby airfield. Colonel Mikhail E. Katukov's 4th Tank Brigade, equipped with newly-produced T-34s, displayed tactical proficiency that the Germans had not encountered before. Katukov concealed his armour in the woods while the German advance guard rolled by. Leliushenko's patchwork collection of infantry and airborne troops blocked the 4th Panzer Division from the front, and, soon after, Katukov's tanks ambushed the Germans from the flanks. The under-gunned, under-armoured German Mark IV's attempted to break out of the ambush by manoeuvring around Katukov but were quickly halted by quick counterattacks. By the end of the day, most of the 4th Panzer Division's armour had been reduced to smoking hulks. This shock to Second Panzer Group, which had just been re-designated

Second Panzer Army, was so great that a special investigation was conducted. Even Guderian grudgingly acknowledged that his opponents were learning. See Guderian, 232-235 and D. Leliushenko, 'Boi pod Mtsenskom' [The battle of Mtsensk], *VIZh*, No. 12 (December 1960), 34-44.

42. *VOV*, 222.

43. Konev noted:

> Having made the decision to withdraw from encirclement, we assigned the armies' shock groups the mission to penetrate the enemy's front... neither combining the army into a single group nor designating a continuous breakthrough sector. Our aim was to prevent the enemy from narrowing the encirclement ring and, given the extensive territory, to maneuver forces and hold off the superior enemy forces by an active defense.

See *VOV*, 222.

44. When the German encirclement at Viaz'ma was complete, the circumference of the encircled forces' internal front was 320km (192 miles) defended by 24 German divisions. Six panzer divisions (the 6th, 7th, 10th, 2nd, 11th and 5th) formed an 80km (48-mile) 'tank front,' which blocked Soviet egress to the east. See Glantz, *Atlas of the Battle of Moscow*, 19.

45. *VOV*, 222.

46. *Ibid.*, 223. Lukin's intelligence indicated that the 7th Panzer Division occupied the swampy terrain in the break out sector, when in fact, the 5th and 35th Infantry Divisions were also in his path.

47. *Ibid.* Lukin's force tried to break out along three separate routes from south of Viaz'ma towards Bykovo, but the Germans blocked all three routes. After failing to break out, Ershakov's final message to the Western Front was, 'With only two divisions [the day before he had reported having seven] and while experiencing shortages in ammunition and fuel, we will continue to fight... The army's units are ready to penetrate toward Bykovo.'

48. *Ibid.*, 224.

49. The 132nd and 143rd Rifle Divisions and the 141st Tank Brigade escaped via Suzemka along with much of the army staff. For documents related to Eremenko's defense, see *SBDVOV*, Issue 43 (Moscow: Voenizdat, 1960).

50. For details on Eremenko's hegira, see, Eremenko, 360-371.

51. *VOV*, 225. Kreizer's 137th and 269th Rifle Divisions and the 42nd Tank Brigade made it to this point.

52. *Ibid.*, 225. The 13th Army successfully withdrew with 10,000 men, 32 heavy and 34 light machine guns, 130 PPSh submachine guns and 11 guns from the encirclement. See also, M.A. Kozlov, ed., *V plameni srazhenii: Boevoi put' 13-i armii* [In the flames of battle: The combat path of the 13th Army] (Moscow: Voenizdat, 1973), 41.

53. *VOV*, 225-226. A total of 4 field armies (the 19th, 20th, 24th and 32nd), 37 divisions, 9 tank brigades and 31 artillery regiments were encircled at Viaz'ma, and 5 rifle divisions and 4 artillery regiments were encircled outside of the larger encirclement. The remaining armies (the 3rd, 13th and 50th), 22 rifle divisions, 2 tank brigades and 15 artillery regiments were encircled and destroyed at Briansk.

54. *Ibid* and Krivosheev, 171-172. The Germans reported capturing 663,000 Soviet troops at Viaz'ma and another 100,000 at Briansk. See Earl F. Ziemke and Magna E. Bauer, *Moscow to Stalingrad: Decision in the East* (Washington, DC: Centre of Military History United States Army, 1987), 37. The *Stavka* was unable to mount any relief effort to save the encircled forces. On the positive side, the encirclements tied up from 26 to 48 German divisions for 3 weeks. In addition, 3 army headquarters, 32 division remnants and 13 artillery regiments made it back to Soviet lines and were soon restored to some semblance of strength.

55. Ziemke and Bauer, 37 and Zolotarev, '*Bitva pod Moskvoi,*' 22.

56. Guderian's panzer group became the Second Panzer Army on 5 October. The Third and Fourth Panzer Groups would not achieve that status until 1 January 1942.

57. *VOV*, 226-227 and Zolotarev, 'Bitva pod Moskvoi,' 103-105. During this period the *Stavka* ordered its forward *fronts* to construct rear defense lines, an order which was totally unrealistic given what the three *fronts* faced.

58. Reinhardt replaced Hoth of 5 October.

59. See the Third Panzer Group's daily progress, see Glantz, *Atlas of the Battle of Moscow*, 24-32.

60. *VOV*, 227 and Zolotarev, 'Stavka VGK,' 246-247. A very detailed account of Kalinin operation is found in *SVIMVOV*, Issue 7 (Moscow: Voenizdat, 1952).

61. Initially, the 29th Army's 174th, 178th, 250th, 243rd, 252nd, 246th, 119th and 133rd Rifle Divisions defended the Kalinin region. Vatutin's force consisted of the 183rd and 185th Rifle Divisions, the 46th and 54th Cavalry Divisions and the 8th Tank Brigade.

62. *VOV*, 228 and Zolotarev, 'Stavka VGK,' 248. Operational Group Vatutin was disbanded on 19 October and its forces were absorbed into General V.A. Iushkevich's 31st Army. Iushkevich had just replaced General V.N. Dolmatov, who was arrested and tried by a military tribunal for his lackluster performance in the defense of Rzhev.

63. During the seven days of fighting, the Ninth Army had advanced 30-40km (12-16 miles).

64. Defending forces included 4 rifle divisions (the 32nd, 322nd, 5th Guards and 113th), 6 military schools, 3 reserve rifle regiments, 5 machine gun battalions, 7 tank brigades and 10 artillery regiments.

65. Combat began on 10 October at Maloiaroslavets, 11 October at Kaluga, 13 October at Mozhaisk and 16 October at Volokolamsk.

66. *VOV*, 229-230. During this period, heavy fighting occurred at numerous locations in which many formations distinguished themselves. These included: Colonel P.V. Mironov's 5th Guards Rifle Division at Kaluga, Colonel A.S. Griaznov's 7th Guards Rifle Division at Serpukhov, Major-General I.V. Panfilov's Kazakh 316th Rifle Division at Volokolamsk, Colonel V.I. Polosukhin's 32nd Rifle Division and, later, Colonel G.P. Karamyshev's 82nd Motorized Rifle Division at Mozhaisk and Major-General A.I. Liziukov's 1st Guards Moscow Motorized Rifle Division at Maloiaroslavets. The entire 50th Army and numerous tank brigades distinguished themselves at Tula.

67. Details of the Tikhvin defense are found in Platonov, 97-107, Luttichau, Chapter XXIX, I.P. Barbashin and A.D. Kharitonov, *Boevye deistviia Sovetskoi armii pod Tikhvinom v 1941 godu* [The Red Army's combat operation at Tikhvin in 1941]

(Moscow: Voenizdat, 1958) and *Tikhvin god 1941* [Tikhvin, 1941] (Leningrad: Lenizdat, 1974).

68. *VOV*, 235.

69. Zolotarev, 'Stavka VGK,' 212.

70. *VOV*, 236 and Maslov, 22 and 44.

71. *VOV*, 236-237. Kleist's panzer resumed their assault on 5 November, attempting to capture Rostov by a deep envelopment from the northeast via Shakhty and Novocherkassk. However, Kleist encountered stiff resistance from Lieutenant-General F.M. Kharitonov's 9th Army, which forced him to postpone his advance for eight days.

72. Zolotarev, 'Stavka VGK,' 245.

73. *Ibid.*, 245-246.

74. *VOV*, 237. See also, Manstein, 204-260.

75. *VOV*, 234.

8. TO THE GATES OF MOSCOW

1. See Albert Seaton, *The Battle for Moscow* (New York: Playboy Press, 1971), 131. This included 145,000 dead and 29,000 missing. *VOV*, 239 claims the German Army lost 88,000 men just in October 1941.

2. Ziemke and Bauer, 44.

3. *Ibid.*, 48.

4. See *Boevoi sostav*, 60-82. Forces available to the Red Army on 1 November included 193 rifle, 5 cavalry and 6 tank divisions, 1 motorized rifle division, 3 fortified regions and 14 rifle, 5 airborne and 44 tank brigades in operating forces. Another 22 rifle and 8 cavalry divisions, 1 tank division and 2 tank brigades were in *Stavka* reserve. By 1 December operating forces included 230 rifle, 43 cavalry and 5 tank divisions, 1 motorized rifle division and 38 rifle, 5 airborne and 47 tank brigades. By this time the *Stavka* reserve included 44 rifle and 14 cavalry divisions, 7 rifle brigades and 1 tank brigade.

5. Halder, 551-555.

6. *VOV*, 238, Ziemke and Bauer, 43-44, and Halder, 545-555.

7. The plan rejected the concept of a Ninth Army attack on Vyshnii Volochek in co-operation with the southern wing of Army Group North.

8. Ziemke and Bauer, 44.

9. An SS Security Services report underscored German popular bewilderment over the Wehrmacht's inability to capture Moscow in late October. It read:

> A certain disappointment still exists in wide circles of the population concerning the fact that the destruction of the Bolsheviks is not being realized as quickly as hoped and that the end of the campaign in the East is not in sight. The absence of further reports about victories at Moscow raises doubts among the population as to whether the reports transmitted 14 days ago stating that German forces were 60km [36 miles] from Moscow, were really correct.

See *VOV* 238.

10. See Zolotarev, 'Bitva pod Moskva,' 63-64 for the full text of the order.

11. *VOV*, 239. See the full *Stavka* order to Zhukov in Zolotarev, 'Bitva pod Moscow,' 132-133.

12. The *Stavka* orders are found in Zolotarev, 'Stavka VGK,' 270-274.

13. *VOV*, 239. These forces included the 332nd Rifle and 2nd, 3rd, 4th and 5th DNOs, 25 tank destroyer detachments and 169 special combat detachments for street fighting, equipped with 623 guns and mortars.

14. *Ibid.*, 240.

15. *Ibid.* The most detailed Soviet account of the fighting from 15 November through 31 December is found in B.M. Shaposhnikov, ed., *Razgrom nemetskikh voisk pod Moskvoi (Moskovskaia operatsiia zapadnogo fronta 16 noiabria 1941 g. – 31 ianvaria 1942 g) v 3 chasti* [The destruction of German forces at Moscow (the Western Front's Moscow operation 16 November 1941-31 January 1942) in 3 parts] (Moscow: Voenizdat, 1943). Prepared by the Voroshilov Academy of the General Staff and classified secret. Hereafter cited as Shaposhnikov, *Razgrom.*

16. Shaposhnikov, *Razgrom*, 42. Rokossovsky later recalled, 'As expected, the local counterattack begun on 16 November by order of the *front* brought little benefit. At first, by exploiting surprise we even wedged 3km [1.8 miles] into the German dispositions. At that time, however, they began a general offensive across the entire front. Our advancing units had to turn back hastily. Cavalry Group L.M. Dovator was in an especially difficult situation. The enemy set upon him from all sides. The cavalry commander escaped full encirclement thanks only to his mobility and native wit.' Earlier, Rokossovsky had noted that the 17th, 20th, 24th and 44th Cavalry Divisions, which had recently arrived from Central Asia, were 'not accustomed to operating in such broken and forested swampy terrain… during the winter.' See Rokossovsky, 103-104. For other details on the action, see M.G. Grigorenko, ed., *Skvoz' ognennye vikhri: Boevoi put' 11-I gvardeiskoi armii v Velikoi Otechestvennoi voine 1941-1945* [Through a fiery whirlwind: The combat path of the 11th Guards Army in the Great Patriotic War], 63. See also Seaton, 152, who dismisses this and other Soviet attacks as insignificant.

17. *VOV*, 240-241 notes that the 58th Tank Division, which possessed a full complement of T-26 tanks, lost 139 tanks in the failed operation and the 17th Cavalry Division lost 75% of its strength. The 44th Cavalry Division had just arrived by rail from Tashkent. See also, A.Ia. Soshnikov, ed., *Sovetskaia kavaleriia* [Soviet Cavalry] (Moscow: Voenizdat, 1984), which states, 'On 16 November, as a result of combat with units of the 35th Infantry and 2nd Panzer Divisions, [the 44th Cavalry] suffered heavy losses and withdrew to new defensive positions.'

18. Shaposhnikov, *Razgrom*, 113 and A. Getman, '112-ia tankovaia diviziia v bitve pod Moskvoi' [The 112th Tank Division in the battle of Moscow], *VIZh*, No. 11 (November 1981), 49. See also Glantz, *Atlas of the Battle of Moscow.*

19. Boldin was assigned command of the 50th Army shortly after he escaped from the Viaz'ma encirclement.

20. Shaposhnikov, *Razgrom*, 109 and F.D. Pankov, *Ognennye rubezhi: Boevoi put' 50-i armii v Velikoi Otechestvennoi voine* [Firing lines: The combat path of the 50th Army in the Great Patriotic War] (Moscow: Voenizdat, 1984), 53. The 239th Rifle Division, which arrived at Uzlovaia Station from the Far East on 17 November, and elements of the 32nd Tank Brigade made up the force that attacked the 112th

Infantry Division. In his memoirs Guderian noted:

> Before judging their [the 112th Infantry Division's] performance, it should be borne in mind that each regiment had already lost some 500 men from frostbite, that as a result of the cold the machine guns were no longer able to fire and that our 37-mm anti-tank gun had proved ineffective against the T-34. The result of all this was a panic which reached back as far as Bogorodisk. This was the first time that such a thing had occurred during the Russian campaign, and it was a warning that the combat ability of our infantry was at an end and that they should no longer be expected to perform difficult tasks.

See Guderian, 190.

21. As early as 11 November Halder wrote, 'There can be no doubt that Guderian is under heavy attack,' and five days later, he added, 'On the right wing of Fourth Army, heavy enemy attacks against XIII Corps. Situation tight.' See Halder, 555-556.

22. The *Stavka* issued the formation orders for the 1st Shock (the former 19th Army), 20th and 10th Armies on 20 November. See Shaposhnikov, *Razgrom*, 28-34 for details on the formation of the armies and Zolotarev, 'Stavka VGK,' 308-310 for the subsequent mobilization of the 26th and 61st Armies.

23. Shaposhnikov, *Razgrom*, 22. The *Stavka* transferred the 30th Army to Zhukov's control on 17 November.

24. After his failed offensive on 16 November, Rokossovsky pulled his shattered 20th, 24th, 44th Cavalry Divisions and the 58th Tank Division back into reserve positions, and they did not participate in the fighting for Klin.

25. *VOV*, 242 and Seaton, 154-156. See Glantz, *Atlas of the Battle for Moscow* for the day-to-day progress of the German advance. When they attacked, the 12 divisions of Hoepner's Fourth Panzer Group had only three-quarters of their ammunition and sufficient fuel for an advance of 200 miles. His group consisted of the IX and V Army Corps and the XXXX Motorized Corps. See Seaton, 153.

26. *VOV*, 242 and Shaposhnikov, *Razgrom*, 47-54.

27. Shaposhnikov, *Razgrom*, 63-65. A counterattack by the 29th and 50th Rifle Brigade (of the 1st Shock Army) drove the German forces back to the western bank of the canal, but was unable to recapture Iakhroma.

28. *VOV*, 242 and Shaposhnikov, *Razgrom*, 64-67. Heavy fighting also took place near present-day Sheremet'evo Airport just east of Kriukovo, where the 2nd Panzer engaged the right flank of Rokossovsky's army (Group Remizov, which consisted of the 282nd Rifle Regiment, the 145th Tank Brigade and a cavalry brigade).

29. Shaposhnikov, *Razgrom*, 68-69. Many of these reserves were well-trained units, but they had to counterattack almost as soon as they disembarked from the trains that had brought them forward. By late November Zhukov's dwindling mobile forces consisted of 3 tank divisions, 3 motorized rifle divisions, 12 cavalry divisions and 14 separate tank brigades. These units were often well under strength, however, and still included numerous obsolete light tanks.

30. *VOV*, 243 and Guderian, 242-256. Guderian's army consisted of the XXIV and XXXXVII Motorized and the XXXXIII and LIII Army Corps with a total of 12 divisions. See Seaton, 158; Guderian, 201; and Glantz, *Atlas of the Battle of Moscow*.

31. Guderian, 161-162. See Shaposhnikov, *Razgrom*, 113-116 for details.

32. For further details, see P.A. Belov, *Za nami Moskva* [Behind us Moscow] (Moscow: Voenizdat, 1963). Belov's force initially included 129 tanks, mostly light models. Shaposhnikov, *Razgrom*, 117-119, identifies the 9th Tank Brigade with Belov's force.

33. *VOV*, 243.

34. For details of the operation, see Seaton, 165-166, Shaposhnikov, *Razgrom*, 91-95, and A. Surchenko, 'Likvidatsiia proryva v raione Naro-Fominska [The liquidation of the Naro-Fominsk penetration], *VIZh*, No. 12 (December 1962), 49-57.

35. Seaton, 165-166 reports heavy German losses, including 600 soldiers in the 292nd Infantry Division.

36. Shaposhnikov, *Razgrom*, 7-8. Average Moscow temperatures in winter 1942 were: November -5°C; December -12°C, and January -19°C; as opposed to normal -3°, -8° and -11°, respectively.

37. Guderian, 194-195 and Shaposhnikov, *Razgrom*, 113-121.

38. Ziemke and Bauer, 63.

39. On 30 November Halder noted in his diary that 'The eastern army has a shortage of 340,000 men, i.e., 50% of the combat strength of the infantry. Company combat strength is 50 to 60 men.' See Halder, 571.

40. Zolotarev, 'Bitva pod Moskvoi,' 151-153.

41. *VOV*, 244.

42. *Ibid.*

43. Platonov, 110-112 and Luttichau, Chapter XXIX, 74-78.

44. For details on the 9th Army's defense, see A.K. Oreshkin, *Oboronitel'naia operatsiia 9-i armii (oktiabr'-noiabr' 1941 g)* [The 9th Army's defensive operation (October-November 1941)] (Moscow: Voenizdat, 1969).

45. *VOV*, 237. See also N. Kirpichenko, 'V boiakh pod Rostovom-na-Donu (oktiabr'-dekabr' 1941 g.)' [In the battles at Rostov (October-November 1941)], *VIZh*, No. 12 (December 1983), 10-17 and I. Bagramian, 'Razgrom 1-i tankovoi armii generala Kleista [The defeat of General Kleist's First Panzer Army], *VIZh*, No. 11 (November 1969), 60-69 and No. 12 (December 1969), 65-74.

46. Despite its poor beginning, the Southern Front's counterstroke captured Halder's attention and prompted him to write, 'On the northeastern front of First Panzer Army (XIV Corps), hard fighting and threat of an enemy breakthrough. Also the mountain corps, which is opposed by a strong enemy, was subjected to violent attacks; all were expelled.' See Halder, 559.

47. See Halder, 561.

48. *VOV*, 237.

49. Reinhardt, 381.

50. Krivosheev, 143.

51. *VOV*, 244-245.

9. BARBAROSSA CONTAINED

1. *VOV*, 248.

2. *Ibid.*, 249. According to Russian official figures, since 22 June 1941 the Red Army had lost over 20,000 tanks, 17,000 combat aircraft, 60,000 guns and mortars and 20% of its

ammunition and fuel. At the same time, the number of workers decreased from 31.5 to 18.5 million and its industrial production decreased by over 50% and metallurgy by 68% to 1931-32 levels. In addition, the government uprooted and evacuated 10 million workers and 1,523 industrial plants to the country's interior to remove them from harm's way. Understandably, arms production fell between 30 and 80%. In November 1941 Soviet industry produced 2,575 guns, 880 tanks and 448 combat aircraft. Despite every effort, the production of tanks did not reach prewar levels until January 1942 and rifles, guns and ammunition until February, March and May 1942 respectively.

The Lend Lease Agreement, signed with the United States and Great Britain in October 1941, provided considerable assistance during this difficult period. By 31 December 1941, Lend Lease had provided the Red Army with 669 tanks and 873 combat aircraft, 24.1 and 43.3%, respectively, of Soviet production. The quantities would increase dramatically in the future and the foreign equipment, particularly the trucks, strategic metals and foodstuffs, would add such terms as 'Willies,' 'Studebaker' and 'Spam' to the average Russian's vocabulary.

3. *Ibid.*, 249 and *Boevoi sostav*, 81-82. On 1 December 1941, the *Stavka* retained 587 tanks and 716 aircraft in the Far East and Transcaucasus regions, amounting to 57 and 56% of its tanks and aircraft. The 45th and 47th Armies with 9 rifle and 2 cavalry divisions, 1 fortified region and 2 tank brigades were stationed in the Transcaucasus and Iran. The 58th Rifle and 4thh Cavalry Corps with 4 rifle and 17 cavalry divisions and 4 rifle brigades were in the Central Asian Military District. The 1st and 2nd Red Banner, 15th, 17th, 25th and 35th Armies were stationed in the Transbaikal and Far Eastern Fronts with a total force of 24 rifle, 4 tank and 2 cavalry divisions, 15 fortified regions, 9 rifle, 6 tank and 2 motorized brigades and 1 airborne brigade. Despite the Japanese threat, the *Stavka* managed to transfer some of the best of these formations, such as the 32nd and 78th Rifle and 82nd Motorized Rifle Divisions, to Moscow in December 1941.

4. The *Stavka* ordered the formation of the following armies at the time and location indicated:
    10th Reserve Army (21 October, Volga and Moscow Military Districts – MDs);
    57th Reserve Army (22 October, North Caucasus MD);
    26th Reserve Army (24 October, Volga and Ural MDs);
    58th Reserve Army (2 November, Siberian MD);
    59th Reserve Army (2 November, Siberian and Ural MDs);
    61st Reserve Army (2 November, Volga and Central Asian MDs);
    60th Reserve Army (2 November, Volga MD);
    39th Reserve Army (2 November, Ural MD); and
    28th Reserve Army (2 November, Ural MD).

See Zolotarev, 'Stavka VGK,' 253 and 270-274 for specific *Stavka* orders.

5. *VOV*, 250 and Zolotarev, 'Stavka VGK,' 308-310.

6. Zolotarev, 'Stavka VGK,' 312-313. The *Stavka* reinforced the 30th Army with four rifle divisions and one cavalry division and the 5th and 16th Armies with two rifle divisions and five rifle brigades.

7. *Ibid.*, 321. The *Stavka* assigned Artem'ev the 201st, 329th, 358th and 360th Rifle Divisions, the 11th Cavalry Division and the 19th, 20th, 21st, 26th, 27th, 30th and 31st Rifle Brigades.

8. *Ibid.*, 322.

9. *VOV*, 250-251. To do so the General Staff had to return to Moscow in late November from Arzamas, the location to which it had been evacuated in October. Planning involved selection of main attack axes and moving, concentrating, supporting and protecting the deploying forces. The movement of the 10th, 26th and 61st Armies alone involved over 60,000 railroad cars and 7-10 days.

10. Zhukov, 254.

11. Zolotarev, 'Stavka VGK,' 316, contains the initial directive to the Western and Kalinin Fronts to 'attack toward Truginovo' with the mission of destroying the German Klin grouping.

12. The Western Front's left wing included the 30th, 1st Shock, 20th and 16th Armies and the left wing, the 50th and 10th Armies and the 1st Guards Cavalry Corps. The Kalinin Front's 29th and 31st Armies and the Southwestern Front's 3rd and 13th Armies and Operational Group Kostenko were to support the Western Front's assault.

13. *VOV*, 251-252. The plan was drawn on a 1:200,000 scale map classified Top Secret [*osobo vazhno*]. It was signed by Zhukov, his commissar, Bulganin, and his chief of staff, Sokolovsky, and authenticated by Stalin on 30 November 1941. The plan appeared 'local' in nature and not strategic since it involved only one *front* and did not include cooperation as to aim, place and time with the other two *fronts*. This was so since the *Stavka* issued separate directives to the other *fronts* and closely coordinated all three *fronts'* operations. Therefore, there was no formal counter-offensive plan. Instead the counteroffensive developed gradually over the course of time as circumstances permitted. Thus, Zhukov later wrote:

> In our concepts, there was still no clear cut well-founded idea that we were undertaking such a grandiose counteroffensive as later occurred. The first assignment of missions on 30 November... pursued an important but limited aim – to repel the most threatening enemy penetration toward Moscow... As I recall, a special order or general directive for a counteroffensive was not given. The combat missions to the forces... were assigned consecutively, in separate directives of the *front* headquarters.

See G. Zhukov, 'Kontrnastuplenie pod Moskvoi' [The Moscow counteroffensive], *VIZh*, No. 10 (October 1966), 70 and 72. The attack orders indicated only *front* immediate missions for the subordinate armies and set no time limits on their achievement. Zhukov later noted, 'We would need more forces to assign farther-going and more categorical missions. As it was, our purpose was to throw the enemy as far away from Moscow as we could, causing him maximum casualties.' See Zhukov, 47. Ultimately, delays in regrouping forced Zhukov to change the actual attack dates to those indicated in the text.

14. The 30th, 1st Shock, 20th and 16th Armies, on Zhukov's right wing, were to attack the German Third Panzer Group, while the 50th and 10th Armies on his left attacked the Second Panzer Army. His 5th, 33rd, 43rd and 49th Armies in the centre were to tie down German Fourth Army and Fourth Panzer Group.

15. Konev's 22nd Army was to defend the sector from Selizharevo to Torzhok, and his 29th and 31st Armies were to attack west and east of Kalinin. The 30th Army, which had been transferred to Zhukov's control, was to attack between the Moscow Sea and the Moscow-Volga Canal.

16. Timoshenko's 3rd and 13th Armies and Operational Group Kostenko were to attack at Elets and Livny, and his 21st, 40th, 38th and 6th Armies were to defend the remainder of the Southwestern Front's sector to the south.

17. *VOV*, 252.

18. Shaposhnikov, *Razrom*, Part 2, 12.

19. For example, on the German side, many infantry divisions were at 40-50% strength with companies numbering 30-60 instead of their required 100-120 men. The 106th Infantry Division's 240th Infantry Regiment was down to 600 men and the 35th Infantry Division's infantry companies numbered from 50-60 men. At the same time, the 6th Panzer Division had lost almost all of its tanks in November and December and had 30-35 men in its panzer companies and 600-700 men in its regiments. See Shaposhnikov, *Razgrom*, Part 2, 13-14. On the other hand, many Soviet formations were in a similar state. For example, the 108th Tank Division, for example, was down to 15 out of 217 authorized tanks, and many rifle divisions had less than 3,000 men. See 'Moskovskaia bitva 1941-1942' in *Velikaia Otechestvennaia voina 1941-1945: Entsiklodediia* ['The battle of Moscow 1941-1942' in the Great Patriotic War; An encyclopedia] (Moscow: 'Sovetskaia entsiklopediia, 1985), 465. According to Krivosheev, 174, however, Soviet strength at Moscow was 1,021,700 soldiers, including Western Front, 748,000; Kalinin Front, 192,000; and the right wing of the Southwestern Front, 80,800.

20. *VOV*, 253. Many attacking rifle divisions lacked up to 40% of their establishment rifle weaponry and had to arm themselves with equipment from units they relieved.

21. *Ibid.*, 253-254. Since the Western and Kalinin Fronts' armies received their orders on 2 December (4 December for the 10th Army) and the Southwestern Front received its orders on 4 December, the attacking armies had only two or three days to prepare for the attack. When formed for the attack, the Soviets committed 1 division per 8.7km (5.22 miles) of front supported by 10-11 guns and mortars and 0.8 tanks per 1km of front, which was quite low for a penetration operation and required considerable concentration of forces in main attack sectors.

22. Seaton, 180.

23. *Das Deutsche Reich und der Zweite Weltkrieg*, Vol. 4, 599.

24. The OKH's *Lage Ost* (situation in the East) map for 6 December failed to identify many Soviet divisions and the Western Front's three reserve armies, which were about to enter combat.

25. Ziemke and Bauer, 67, explains, stating:

> Along the front around Moscow at daybreak on 6 December, the temperature dropped as low as −38 degrees F. During the night, Bock at Army Group Centre had approved Guderian's proposed withdrawal of Second Panzer Army, and had told Reinhardt and Hoepner to 'adjust' their plans for Third and Fourth Panzer Groups to pull back from Yakhroma and in Krasnaia Poliana to a line covering Klin. He had also called General der Panzertruppen Rudolf Schmidt at Second Army, which had been drifting slowly eastward toward Yelets for the past several days, and had told him he had better come to a stop; otherwise, his army would soon find itself standing further east than any of the others.

This adjustment required Guderian's forces to pull back to the Shat and Don River lines and Hoepner's panzer group to withdraw behind the Nara River. Reinhardt's forces, already hard-pressed along the Moscow-Volga Canal, were to withdraw to Klin.

26. In reality, it began as an expansion of the 1st Shock and 20th Armies' offensive, which was already underway in the region north of Moscow. For details maps covering on the day-by-day development of the counteroffensive, including translated maps from Shaposhnikov's *Razgrom*, see David M. Glantz, *Atlas of the Battle of Moscow: The Soviet Offensive, 5 December 1941-20 April 1942* (Carlisle, PA; Self-published, 1998).

27. For details see, A.A. Zabaluev, S.G. Goriachev, *Kalininskia nastupatel'naia operatsiia* [The Kalinin offensive operation] (Moscow: Voroshilov Higher Military Academy, 1942) and 'Operativnye itogi razgroma nemtsov pod moskvoi' [Operational results of the destruction of the Germans at Moscow], *SPMPOIV*, No. 5 (Moscow: Voenizdat, 1943), 3-22.

28. Shaposhnikov, *Razgrom*, Part 2, 13-14. According to Shaposhnikov, the Western Front' right wing (the 30th, 1st Shock, 20th and 16th Armies), numbered 152,000 men, 2,295 guns and mortars, 360 antitank guns and 270 tanks. Opposing German forces numbered 75,000 men, 1,410 guns and mortars, 470 antitank guns and 380 tanks.

29. Ziemke and Bauer, 70.

30. Shaposhnikov, *Razgrom*, Part 2, 16-18.

31. Ziemke and Bauer, 70.

32. *VOV*, 258 and Shaposhnikov, *Razgrom*, Part 2, 19-22.

33. Seaton, 194-195.

34. *VOV*, 259-260.

35. Zolotarev, 'Bitva pod Moskvoi,' 176-177.

36. Ziemke and Bauer, 77, describes the scene:

> Discipline was breaking down. More and more soldiers are heading west on foot without weapons, leading a calf on a rope or pulling a sled loaded with potatoes. The road is under constant air attack. Those killed by the bombs are no longer being buried. All the hanger-ons (corps troops, Luftwaffe, supply trains) are pouring to the rear in full flight. Without rations, freezing, irrationally they are pushing back. Vehicle crews that do not want to wait out the traffic jams in the open are drifting off the roads and into the villages. Ice, inclines and bridges create horrendous blockages. Traffic control is working day and night and barely maintaining some movement. The panzer group has reached its most dismal hour.

Ziemke and Bauer added, 'A general retreat, possibly of Napoleonic proportions, appears the most likely.'

37. *VOV*, 260.

38. Shaposhnikov, *Razgrom*, Part 2, 25-33 and Seaton, 195. Stalin was dissatisfied with the performance of Konev's forces, which he thought could have encircled German forces in Kalinin. He accused Konev of employing 'pedantic' rather than

'decisive offensive' tactics. In reality, Konev failed because his forces were far weaker than Zhukov's. See *VOV*, 261.

39. *VOV*, 261-262, Shaposhnikov, *Razgrom*, Part 2, 35-39, and Seaton, 205-207.

40. Shaposhnikov, *Razgrom*, Part 2, 57-60. A German IX Army Corps report stated, 'The IX Army Corps' divisions have been forced to cast off the greater part of their heavy weapons and equipment...They have not succeeded in organizing a new front. There is no news from the 78th Infantry Division...It is encircled from the west.' Despite the parlous situation, the Fourth Panzer Group conducted a speedy withdrawal that was up to twice as fast as Dovator's cavalry advance. See *VOV*, 262.

41. *VOV*, 262.

42. *Ibid.*, 263. See also Glantz, *Atlas of the Battle of Moscow; The Soviet Offensive*, 54. The 29th and 10th Motorized, 112th Infantry and 18th Panzer Divisions were deployed from Serebrianye Prudy to Shishkino.

43. *Ibid.* For details on the 10th Army's preparations and assault, see F. Golikov, 'Rezervnaia armaia gotovitsia k zashchite stolitsy' [A reserve army prepares to defend the capital], *VIZh*, No. 5 (April 1966), 65-75.

44. *VOV*, 263 and Shaposhnikov, *Razgrom*, Part 2, 76-85. Shaposhnikov, *Razgrom*, Part 2, 6, places the strength of Zhukov's left wing armies (the 49th, 50th and 10th Armies and Group Belov) at 140,000 men, 1,605 guns and mortars, 200 antitank guns and 100 tanks. Opposing German forces were estimated as 78,000 men, 1,495 guns and mortars, 510 antitank guns and 300 tanks.

45. *VOV*, 264.

46. Ziemke and Bauer, 73.

47. By this time, Belov's group consisted of the 1st and 2nd Guards Cavalry, the 112th Tank and the 173rd Rifle Divisions, the 9th Tank Brigade, the 35th and 127th Separate Tank Battalions and the 15th Guards-Mortar [Katiusha] Regiment.

48. Shaposhnikov, *Razgrom*, Part 2, 86.

49. *VOV*, 265-266. See Zhukov's attack order in Zolotarev, 'Bitva pod moskvoi,' 178. For details on the Elets operation, see *Eletskaia operatsiia (6-16 dekabria 1941 g.)* [The Elets operation (6-16 December 1941)] (Moscow: Voenizdat, 1943). According to this formerly classified study, the 3rd and 13th Armies totalled 7,548 and 19,799 men and 119 and 21 guns, respectively, on 11 November. By 4 December, after the assignment of Group Kostenko, the force numbered 40,000 men, 245 guns and mortars and 16 tanks. Opposing German forces (the 262nd, 134th, 45th and 95th Infantry Divisions) numbered 31,500 men, 470 guns and mortars and 30-40 tanks.

50. *VOV*, 266.

51. Ziemke and Bauer, 74.

52. *VOV*, 257 and Seaton, 181. Issued under the heading, 'The Führer and Supreme Commander of the Armed Forces, OKW/WFSt./Abt.L (I) Nr. 442090/41 g.Kdos, Top Secret, Führer Headquarters, 8 December 1941,' the directive read:

> The early arrival of cold winter on the Eastern Front and resupply difficulties associated with it are forcing us to halt immediately all offensive operations and go on the defense. The manner of this defense's conduct depends on the aims that it pursues, namely:

a) Hold on to those regions that have important operational and military-economic importance for the enemy;
b) Rest and replenish the forces;
c) By doing so, create conditions necessary to resume large-scale offensive operations in 1942.

53. For details on the German high-level discussions, see Ziemke and Bauer, 80-84.
54. Guderian, 262-271 and Ziemke and Bauer, 85-86.

CONCLUSIONS

1. The 1941 campaign in East Prussia lasted from 18 August-21 September 1914. During the fighting against the German Eighth Army, the Northwestern Front's 1st Army under General P.V. Rennenkampf and the 2nd Army under General A.V. Samsonov lost 245,000 men, including 135,000 who fell captive to the Germans. See A.A. Strokov, *Vooruzhennye sily i voennoe iskusstkvo v Pervoi Mirovoi voine* [The armed forces and military art in the First World War] (Moscow: Voenizdat, 1974), 240.
2. *VOV*, 462-463.
3. Actually, the Red Army defended Sevastopol' from 30 October 1941 to 4 July 1942.
4. The *Stavka* had already demonstrated its ability to raise and deploy reserve armies secretly, but had never been able to employ them successfully.
5. Reinhardt, 204.
6. *VOV*, 465.
7. *Ibid*, 466.
8. *Ibid*.
9. The German advance was roughly equivalent to an advance from the Atlantic coast to the Mississippi River in the United States and from the French channel coast to Warsaw or Budapest in Europe.
10. *Ibid*, 467-468 and Krivosheev, 143.
11. Krivosheev., 367.
12. Halder, 599 states that the Wehrmacht lost 830,903 men (25.96% of its eastern army of 3.2 million men between 22 June and 31 December 1941. These figures included 7,120 officers and 166,602 NCOs and enlisted men killed, 19,016 officers and 602,292 NCOs and enlisted men wounded, and 619 officers and 35,254 NCOs and enlisted men missing in action.
13. Heinrici, 190. A veteran of the First World War, Heinrici commanded the Fourth Army's XXXXIII Army Corps at Moscow and the Fourth Army from 26 January 1942 to August 1944. During this period, he earned notoriety for his skilful defense at Moscow in 1942, at Viaz'ma and Smolensk in 1942-1943 and in Belorussia in late 1943 and early 1944. He commanded the First Panzer Army from August 1944 (as Group Heinrici with the First Hungarian Army) to March 1945, conducting a successful defense in the Carpathian region and Slovakia. Because of his fine reputation for tenacity of the defense, he was assigned command of Army Group Vistula in March 1945, to defend the Oder River front east of Berlin. He commanded Army Group Vistula during the Battle for Berlin, surrendering to the British on 28 May 1945.
14. Frederick drowned while either crossing or bathing in the Seleph River, which was located at Cilicia (Seleucia) in Asia Minor.

SELECTED BIBLIOGRAPHY

Akalovich, N.M. *Oni zashchitali Minsk* [They defended Minsk]. Minsk: 'Narodnaia Asveta,' 1982.

Alekseev, P.D., Makovsky, V.B. *Pervaia oboronitel'naia operatsiia 4-i armii v nachale Velikoi Otechestvennoi voiny* [The 4th Army's initial defensive operation in the beginning of the Great Patriotic War]. Moscow: Izdanie akademii, 1992.

Andriushchenko, N.K. *Na zemle Belorussii letom 1941 goda* [On Belorussian soil in the summer of 1941]. Minsk: 'Nauka i tekhnika,' 1985.

Anfilov, V.A. *Krushenie pokhoda Hitlera na Moskvy 1941* [The collapse of Hitler's march on Moscow in 1941]. Moscow: 'Nauka,' 1989.

Anfilov, V.A. *Nezabyvaemyi sorok pervyi* [Unforgotten forty one]. Moscow: 'Sovetskaia Rossiia,' 1989.

Anfilov, V.A. *Proval 'blitskiga'* [The failure of 'Blitzkrieg'] (Moscow: 'Nauka,' 1974).

Anikin, V.I. *Brestskaia krepost'-krepost'-geroi* [The Brest Fortress–Hero fortress]. Moscow: Stroiizdat, 1985.

Azarov, I.I. *Osazhdennaia Odessa* [Besieged Odessa]. Odessa: Maiak, 1975.

Aziassky, N.F. Ed. *Nachal'nyi period Velikoi Otechestvennoi voiny. Vyvody i uroki* [The initial period of the Great Patriotic War. Conclusions and lessons] (Moscow: Voroshilov General Staff Academy, 1989).

Babich, Iu.P., Baier, A.G. *Razvitie vooruzhenniia i organizatsii Sovetskikh sukhoputnykh voisk v gody Velikoi Otechestvennoi voiny* [Development of the Soviet ground forces' weaponry and organization in the Great Patriotic War]. Moscow: Izdanie akademii, 1990.

Bagramian, I. Kh. *Tak nachinalas' voina* [How the war began]. Kiev: Khudozhestvennoi literatury 'Dnipro,' 1975.

Barbashin, I.P., Kharitonov, A.D. *Boevye deistviia Sovetskoi armii pod Tikhvinom v 1941 godu* [The Soviet Army's combat operations at Tikhvin in 1941]. Moscow: Voenizdat, 1958.

Bartov, Omar. *The Eastern Front, 1941-1945: German Troops and the Barbarization of Warfare*. New York: St. Martin's Press, 1986.

Belov, P.A. *Za nami Moskva* [Behind us Moscow]. Moscow: Voenizdat, 1963.

Bezymenskii, L.A. *Ukroshchenie 'Taifuna'* [The taming of 'Typhoon']. Moscow: Moskovskii rabochii, 1987.

Bitva za moskvoi [The battle for Moscow]. Moscow: Moskovskii rabochii, 1968.

'Boevye deistviia Sovetskikh voisk na Kalininskom napravlenii v 1941 gody (s oktiabria 1941 g. po 7 ianvaria 1942 g)' [Combat operations of the Soviet Army on the Kalinin axis in 1941 (from October 1941 through 7 January 1942] in *Sbornik voenno-istoricheskikh materialov Velikoi Otechestvennoi voiny, vypusk 7* [Collection of military-historical materials of the Great Patriotic War, issue 7]. Moscow: Voenizdat, 1952. Classified secret.

'Boevye dokumenty po oboronitel'noi operatsii v Litve i Latvii, provedivsheisia s 22 iiunia po 9 iiulia 1941 g. voiskami Severo-zapadnogo fronta' [Combat documents on the operations in Lithuania and Latvia conducted by the Northwestern Front from 22 June-9 July 1941] in *Sbornik boevykh dokumentov Velikoi Otechestvennoi voiny, vypusk 34* [Collection of combat documents of the Great Patriotic War, issue 34]. Moscow: Voenizdat, 1958. Classified secret.

Boevoi sostav Sovetskoi armii, Chast' 1 (Iun'-dekabr' 1941 goda) [Combat composition of the Soviet Army, Part 1 (June-December 1941]. Moscow: Voroshilov General Staff Academy, 1963.

Boldin, I.V. *Stranitsy zhizni* [Pages of a life]. Moscow: Voenizdat, 1961.

Buiskikh, B.N. Ed. *Kievskii krasnoznamennyi: Istorii krasnoznamennogo Kievskogo voennogo okruga 1919-1972* [Red banner Kiev: A history of the Red Banner Kiev Military District 1919-1972]. Moscow: Voenizdat, 1974.

Burdick, Charles and Jacobsen, Hans-Adolf. *The Halder War Diary, 1939-1942*. Novato, CA: Presidio, 1988.

Carell, Paul. *Hitler Moves East 1941-1943*. Boston: Little, Brown and Company, 1963.

Clark, Alan. *Barbarossa: The Russian-German Conflict 1941-1945*. New York: Signet, 1965.

Das Deutsche Reich und der Zweite Weltkrieg, Band 4: Der Agriff auf der Sowjetunion. Stuttgart: Deutsche Verlags-Anstalt, 1983.

'Dokumenty nemetskogo komandovaniia po voprosam vedeniie voiny' [Documents of the German commands on the matter of the conduct of the war] in *Sbornik voenno-istoricheskikh materialov Velikoi Otechestvennoi voiny, vypusk 18* [Collection of military-historical materials of the Great Patriotic War, issue 18]. Moscow: Voenizdat, 1960. Classified secret.

'Dokumenty po boevym deistviiam voisk Brianskogo frontov na orlovskom i kurskom napravleniiakh s 16 avgusta po 29 oktiabria 1941 g.' [Documents on the Briansk Front's combat operations on the Orel and Kursk axes from 16 August through 29 October 1941] in *Sbornik boevykh dokumentov Velikoi Otechestvennoi voiny, vypusk 43* [Collection of combat documents of the Great Patriotic War, issue 43]. Moscow: Voenizdat, 1960. Classified secret.

'Dokumenty po boevym deistviiam voisk Iugo-Zapadnogo i Iuzhnogo frontov v Zapadnoi Ukraine i Moldavii s 22 iiunia po 11 iiulia 1941 g.' [Documents on the Southwestern and Southern Fronts' combat operations in western Ukraine and Moldavia from 22 June through 11 July 1941] in *Sbornik boevykh dokumentov Velikoi Otechestvennoi voiny, vypusk 36* [Collection of combat documents of the Great Patriotic War, issue 36]. Moscow: Voenizdat, 1958. Classified secret.

'Dokumenty po boevym deistviiam voisk Iugo-zapadnogo napravleniia s 11 po 25 iiulia 1941 g.' [Documents on the Southwestern direction's combat operations from 11 through 25 July 1941] in *Sbornik boevykh dokumentov Velikoi Otechestvennoi voiny, vypusk 38* [Collection of combat documents of the Great Patriotic War, issue 38]. Moscow: Voenizdat, 1959. Classified secret.

'Dokumenty po boevym deistviiam voisk Iugo-zapadnogo napravleniia s 26 iiulia po 6 avgusta 1941 g.' [Documents on the Southwestern direction's combat operations from 26 July through 6 August 1941] in *Sbornik boevykh dokumentov Velikoi Otechestvennoi voiny, vypusk 39* [Collection of combat documents of the Great Patriotic War, issue 39]. Moscow: Voenizdat, 1959. Classified secret.

'Dokumenty po boevym deistviiam voisk Iugo-zapadnogo napravleniia na pravoberezhnoi i levoberezhnoi Ukraine s 6 avgusta po 25 sentiabria 1941 g.' [Documents on the Southwestern direction's combat operations on the right and left bank of the Ukraine from 6 August through 25 September 1941] in *Sbornik boevykh dokumentov Velikoi Otechestvennoi voiny, vypusk 40* [Collection of combat documents of the Great Patriotic War, issue 40]. Moscow: Voenizdat, 1960. Classified secret.

'Dokumenty po boevym deistviiam voisk Iuzhnogo fronta v Donbasse s 26 sentiabria po 5 noiabria 1941 g.' [Documents on the Southern Front's combat operations in the Donbas from 26 September through 5 November 1941] in *Sbornik boevykh dokumentov Velikoi Otechestvennoi voiny, vypusk 42* [Collection of combat documents of the Great Patriotic War, issue 42]. Moscow: Voenizdat, 1960. Classified secret.

'Dokumenty po boevym deistviiam voisk Zapadnogo fronta s 22 iiunia po 5 iiulia 1941 g.' [Documents on the Western Front's combat operations from 22 June through 5 July 1941] in *Sbornik boevykh dokumentov Velikoi Otechestvennoi voiny, vypusk 35* [Collection of combat documents of the Great Patriotic War, issue 35]. Moscow: Voenizdat, 1958. Classified secret.

'Dokumenty po boevym deistviiam voisk Zapadnogo fronta na smolenskom napravlenii s 12 avgusta po 13 sentiabria 1941 g.' [Documents on the Western Front's combat operations on the Smolensk axis from 22 June through 5 July 1941] in *Sbornik boevykh dokumentov Velikoi Otechestvennoi voiny, vypusk 41* [Collection of combat documents of the Great Patriotic War, issue 41]. Moscow: Voenizdat, 1958. Classified secret.

'Dokumenty po boevym deistviiam voisk Zapadnogo fronta i Fronta rezervnykh armii (Rezervnogo fronta) s 3 iiulia po 7 avgusta 1941 g.' [Documents on the combat operations of the Western Front and the Front of reserve armies (Reserve Front) from 5 July through 7 August 1941] in *Sbornik boevykh dokumentov Velikoi Otechestvennoi voiny, vypusk 37* [Collection of combat documents of the Great Patriotic War, issue 37]. Moscow: Voenizdat, 1959. Classified secret.

'Dokumenty po ispol'zovanniiu bronetankovykh i mekhanizirovannykh voisk Sovetskoi armii v period s 22 iiunia po sentiabr' 1941 g. vkliuchitel'no' [Documents of the use of tank and mechanized forces of the Soviet Army in the period from 22 June–September 1941 inclusively] in *Sbornik boevykh dokumentov Velikoi Otechestvennoi voiny, vypusk 33* [Collection of combat documents of the Great Patriotic War, issue 33]. Moscow: Voenizdat, 1957. Classified secret.

Eletskaia operatsiia (6-16 dekabria 1941 g.) [The Elets operation (6-16 December 1941)]. Moscow: Voenizdat, 1943.

Eremenko, A.I. *V nachale voiny* [In the beginning of the war]. Moscow: 'Nauka,' 1975.

Erickson, John. *The Road to Stalingrad*. New York: Harper & Row, 1975.

Evstigneev, V.I. Ed. *Velikaia bitva pod Moskvoi* [The great battle at Moscow]. Moscow: Voenizdat, 1961.

Glantz, David M. *Atlas of the Battle of Moscow: The Defensive Phase, 1 October-5 December 1941*. Carlisle, PA: Self-published, 1997.

Glantz, David M. *Atlas of the Battle of Moscow: The Offensive Phase, 5 December 1941-20 April 1942*. Carlisle, PA: Self-published, 1998.

Glantz, David M. *Forgotten Battles of the German-Soviet War (1941-1945), volume I: The Summer-Fall Campaign (22 June-4 December 1941)*. Carlisle, PA: Self-published, 1999.

Glantz, David M. Ed. *The Initial Period of the War on the Eastern Front, 22 June-August 1941*. London: Frank Cass, 1993.

Glantz, David M. *The Military Strategy of the Soviet Union: A History*. London: Frank Cass, 1992.

Glantz, David M. *The Red Army in 1943: Strength, Organization, and Equipment*. Carlisle, PA: Self-published, 1999.

Glantz, David M. *Stumbling Colossus: The Red Army on the Eve of World War*. Lawrence, KS: University Press of Kansas, 1998.

Glantz, David M. *When Titans Clashed: How the Red Army Stopped Hitler*. Lawrence, KS: University Press of Kansas, 1995.

Goure, Leon. *The Siege of Leningrad*. Stanford, CA: Stanford University Press, 1962.

Grechko, A.A. Ed. *Istoriia Vtoroi Mirovoi voiny 1939-1945 v dvenadtsati tomakh* [A history of the Second World War 1939-1945 in twelve volumes]. Moscow: Voenizdat, 1973-1982.

Grechko, A.A. Ed. *Sovetskaia voennaia entsiklopediia v bos'mi tomakh* [Soviet military encyclopaedia in eight volumes]. Moscow: Voenizdat, 1976-1980.

Gribkov, A.I. Ed. *Istoriia Ordena Lenina Leningradskogo voennogo okruga* [A history of the Order of Lenin Leningrad Military District]. Moscow: Voenizdat, 1974.

Guderian, Heinz. *Panzer Leader*. New York: Ballentine Books, 1965.

Heinrici, Gotthard. *The Campaign in Russia, Volume 1*. Washington, D.C.: United States Army G-2, 1954. Unpublished national Archives manuscript translated by Joseph Welch.

Ivanov, S.P. Ed. *Nachal'nyi period voiny* [The initial period of war]. Moscow: Voenizdat, 1974.

Ivanovsky, E.F. Ed. *Krasnoznamennyi Belorusskii voennyi okrug* [Red Banner Belorussian Military District]. Moscow: Voenizdat, 1983.

Ivanovsky, E.F. Ed. *Ordena Lenina Moskovskii voennyi okruga* [Order of Lenin Moscow Military District]. Moscow: Voenizdat, 1971.

Karasev, A.V. *Leningradtsy v gody blokady 1941-1943* [Leningraders in the years of the blockade 1941-1943]. Moscow: Akademii Nauk SSSR, 1959.

Khametov, M.I. Ed. *Bitva pod Moskvoi* [The battle at Moscow]. Moscow; Voenizdat, 1989.

Khor'kov, A.G. *Analiz boeboi gotovnosti voisk zapadnykh prigranichnykh voennykh okrugov nakanune Velikoi Otechestvennoi voiny* [Analysis of the combat readiness of forces in the border military districts on the eve of the Great Patriotic War]. Moscow: Voroshilov General Staff Academy, 1985.

Khor'kov, A.G. *Boevaia i mobilizatsionnaia gotovnost' prigranichnykh voennykh okrugov nakanune Velikoi Otechestvennoi voiny* [The combat and mobilization readiness of the border military districts on the eve of the Great Patriotic War]. Moscow: Voroshilov General Staff Academy, 1984.

Khromov, S.S. Ed. *Na ognennykh rubezhakh Moskovskoi bitvy* [On the firing lines of the battle of Moscow]. Moscow: Moskovskii rabochii, 1981.

Kirsanov, N.A. *Po zovu Rodiny: Dobrovol'cheskie formirovaniia Krasnoi Armii v period Velikoi Otechestvennoi voiny* [At the call of the Homeland: Volunteer formations of the Red Army in the Great Patriotic War]. Moscow: 'Mysl',' 1974.

Kolesnik, A.D. *Narodnoe opolchanie gorodov-geroev* [The peoples' militia of hero cities]. Moscow: 'Nauka,' 1974.

Kolesnik, A.D. *Opolchenskie formirovaniia Rossiiskoi Federatsii v gody Velikoi Otechestvennoi voiny* [Militia formations of the Russian Federation in the Great Patriotic War]. Moscow: 'Nauka,' 1988.

Komandovanie korpusnogo i divizionnogo zvena Sovetskikh Vooruzhennykh Sil perioda *Velikoi Otechestvennoi voiny 1941-1945* [The Soviet Armed Force's corps and division level commanders during the Great Patriotic War]. Moscow: Frunze Military Academy, 1964.

Konev, I.S. *Zapiski komanduiushchego frontom* [Notes of a *front* commander]. Moscow: 'GOLOS,' 2000.

Krinov, Iu.S. *Luzhskii rubezh god 1941-i* [The Luga line in 1941]. Leningrad: Lenizdat, 1987.

Krivosheev, G.F. Ed. *Grif sekretnosti sniat: Poteri vooruzhennykh sil SSSR v voinakh, boevykh deistviiakh i voennykh konfliktakh* [The secret classification is removed: The losses of the Soviet armed forces in wars, combat operations and military conflicts]. Moscow: Voenizdat, 1993.

Krylov, N. Glory Eternal: *The Defense of Odessa*. Moscow: Progress, 1972.

Kudriashov, O.N., Ramanichev, N.M. *Boevye deistviia Sovetskikh voisk v nachal'nom periode Velikoi Otechestvennoi voiny (Po opytu 5-i armii i 8-go mekhanizirovannogo korpusa Iugo-zapadnogo fronta)* [Combat operations of Soviet forces in the initial period of the Great Patriotic War (Based on the experiences of the Southwestern Front's 5th Army and 8th Mechanized Corps)]. Moscow: Izdanie akademii, 1989.

Luttichau, Charles V.P. von. *The Road to Moscow: The Campaign in Russia 1941*. Washington, D.C.: Office of the Chief of Military History, 1985. Unpublished Centre for Military History Project 26-P.

Manstein, Erich von. *Lost Victories*. Chicago: Henry Regnery, 1958.

Maslov, A.A. *Fallen Soviet Generals: Soviet General Officers killed in battle 1941-1945*. London: Frank Cass, 1998.

Moskalenko, K.S. *Na iugo-zapadnom napravlenii, 1941-1943, kniga 1* [On the southwestern axis, 1941-1943, book 1]. Moscow: 'Nauka,' 1975.

Muller, Rolf-Dietr, Ueberschar, Gerd R. *Hitler's War in the East: A Critical Assessment*. Providence: Berghahn Books, 1997.

Muriev, D.Z. *Proval operatsii 'Taifun'* [The failure of operation 'Typhoon']. Moscow: Voenizdat, 1966.

Naumov, V.P. Ed. '1941 god v 2-x knigakh' [1941 in 2 books] in Iakovlev, A.N. Ed. *Rossiia XX vek: Documenty* [Russia in the 20th Century: Documents]. Moscow: Mezhdunarodnyi fond 'Demokratiia,' 1998.

Nevzorov, B.I. *Vozrastanie ustoichivosti oborony i osobennosti nastupleniia s khodu v bitve pod Moskvoi (noiabr'-dekabr' 1941 g.)* [The growth in the durability of defenses and the peculiarities of the offensive from the march in the battle at Moscow (November-December 1941)]. Moscow: Frunze Academy, 1982.

'Oborona Odessy v 1941 godu' [The defense of Odessa in 1941] in *Sbornik voenno-istoricheskikh materialov Velikoi Otechestvennoi voiny, vypusk 14* [Collection of military-historical materials of the Great Patriotic War, issue 14]. Moscow: Voenizdat, 1954. Classified secret.

Orenstein, Harold S. Trans. 'The Initial Period of War 1941' in *Soviet Documents on the Use of War Experience, Volume One*. London: Frank Cass, 1991.

Orenstein, Harold S. Trans. 'The Winter Campaign 1941-1942' in *Soviet Documents on the Use of War Experience, Volume II*. London: Frank Cass, 1991.

Orenstein, Harold S. Trans. 'Military Operations 1941-1942' in *Soviet Documents on the Use of War Experience, Volume III*. London: Frank Cass, 1993.

Oreshchkin, A.K. *Oboronitel'naia operatsiia 9-i armii (oktiabr'-noiabr' 1941 g)* [The defensive operations of the 9th Army (October-November 1941)]. Moscow: Voenizdat, 1960.

Platonov, S.P. Ed. *Bitva za Leningrada 1941-1944* [The Battle for Leningrad 1941-1944]. Moscow: Voenizdat, 1964.

Platonov, S.P. Ed. *Boevye deistviia Sovetskoi armii v Velikoi Otechestvennoi voine 1941-1945, tom 1* [Combat operations of the Soviet Army in the Great Patriotic War 1941-1945, volume 1]. Moscow: Voenizdat, 1958.

Pospelov, P.N. Ed. *Istoriia Velikoi Otechestvennoi voiny Sovetskogo Soiuza 1941-1945 v shesti tomakh* [A history of the Great Patriotic War of the Soviet Union 1941-1945 in six volumes]. Moscow: Voenizdat, 1960-1965.

Reinhardt, Klaus. Moscow: *The Turning Point: The Failure of Hitler's Military Strategy in the Winter of 1941-1942*. Trans. by Karl B. Keenan. Providence: Berg, 1992.

Rodionov, I.N. Ed. *Voennaia entsiklopediia v vos'mi tomakh* [A military encyclopaedia in 8 volumes]. Moscow: Voenizdat, 1997-1999.

Rokossovsky, K.K. *Soldatskii dolg* [A soldier's duty]. Moscow: 'GOLOS,' 2000.

Samsonov, A.M. Ed. *Proval gitlerovskogo nastupleniia na Moskvu* [The failure of Hitler's offensive on Moscow]. Moscow: 'Nauka,' 1966.

Samsonov, A.M. *Porazhenie vermakhta pod Moskvoi* [The defeat of the Wehrmacht at Moscow]. Moscow: Moskovskii rabochii, 1981.

Samsonov, A.M. *Velikaia bitva pod Moskvoi* [The great battle of Moscow]. Moscow: 'Nauka,' 1958.

Sandalov, L.M. *Na Moskovskom napravlenii* [On the Moscow axis]. Moscow: 'Nauka,' 1970.

Sandalov, L.M. *Pererzhitoe* [Survived]. Moscow: Voenizdat, 1961.

Schematische Kriegsgliederung, Stand: B-tag 1941 (22.6) 'Barbarossa.'

Seaton, Albert. *The Battle for Moscow*. New York: Playboy Press, 1971.

Seaton, Albert. *The Russo-German War 1941-1945*. New York: Praeger Publishers, 1970.

Shaposhnikov, B.M. Ed. *Razgrom nemetskikh voisk pod Moskvoi v trex chastei, chast' pervaia i vtoraia* [The defeat of German forces at Moscow in three parts, parts one and two]. Moscow: Voenizdat, 1943. Classified secret.

Savushkin, R.A. Ed. *Razvitie sovetskikh vooruzhennykh sil i voennnogo iskusstva v Velikoi Otechestvennoi voine 1941-1945 gg.* [The development of the Soviet armed forces and military art during the Great Patriotic War 1941-1945]. Moscow: Voroshilov General Staff Academy, 1988.

Sorokin, K.L. *Trudnye dni sorok pervogo* [Difficult days of forty one]. Moscow: Voenizdat, 1991.

Tikhvin god 1941-i [Tikhvin 1941]. Leningrad: Lenizdat, 1974.

Vasil'ev, A. *Velikaia pobeda pod Moskvoi* [The great victory at Moscow]. Moscow: Voenizdat, 1952.

Vasilevsky, A.M. *Delo vsei zhizni* [Life's work]. Moscow: Politicheskii literatury, 1983.

Valdimirsky, A.V. *Na kievskom napravleni* [On the Kiev axis]. Moscow: Voenizdat, 1989.

Volkhov, A.A. *Kriticheskii prolog: Nezavershennye frontovye nastupatel'nye operatsii pervykh kampanii Velikoi Otechestvennoi voiny* [Critical prologue: Incomplete *front* offensive operations on the Great Patriotic War's initial campaign]. Moscow: Aviar, 1992.

Volkogonov, Dmitri. *Stalin: Triumph and Tragedy*. Trans. and ed. by Harold Shukman. Rocklin, CA: Prima Publishing, 1992.

Werth, Alexander. *Russia at War, 1941-1945*. New York: E.P. Dutton and Co., 1964.

Wray, Timothy. *Standing Fast: German Defensive Doctrine on the Russian Front during World War II: Prewar to March 1943*. Fort Leavenworth, KS: Combat Studies Institute, 1986.

Zaitsev, L.A. *Voennoe iskusstvo Sovetskikh voisk pri oborone Odessy i sevastopolia* [The military art of Soviet forces during the defense of Odessa and Sevastopol']. Moscow: Izdanie akademii, 1989.

Zhilin, P.A. Ed. *Besprimernyi podvig* [Unparalled feat]. Moscow: 'Nauka,' 1968.

Zhukov, G. *Reminiscences and Recollections*, Volume 1. Moscow: Progress, 1974.

Ziemke, Earl F., Bauer, Magna E. *Moscow to Stalingrad: Decision in the East*. Washington, D.C.: Office of the Chief of Military History United States Army, 1987.

Zabaluev, A.A., Goriachev, S.G. *Kalininskaia nastupatel'naia operatsiia* [The Kalinin offensive operation]. Moscow: K.E. Voroshilov Higher Military Academy, 1942. Classified secret.

Zolotarev, V.A. Ed. 'Bitva pod Moskvoi: Sbornik dokumentov' [The Battle of Moscow: Collection of documents] in *Russkii arkhiv: Velikaia Otechestvennaia, 15, 4 (1)* [The Russian archives: The Great Patriotic War, vol. 15, 4 (1)]. Moscow: 'TERRA,' 1997.

Zolotarev, V.A. Ed. 'General'nyi shtab v gody Velikoi Otechestvennoi voiny: Dokumenty i materialy 1941 god' [The General Staff in the Great Patriotic War: Documents and materials from 1941] in *Russkii arkhiv: Velikaia Otechestvennaia, 23 12 (1)* [The Russian archives: The Great Patriotic War, vol. 23, no. 12 (1)]. Moscow: 'TERRA,' 1997.

Zolotarev, V.A. Ed. 'Stavka VGK: Dokumenty i materialy 1941 god' [The Stavka VGK: Documents and materials of 1941] in *Russkii arkhiv: Velikaia Otechestvennaia, 16 5 (1)* [The Russian archives: The Great Patriotic War, vol. 16, no. 5 (1)]. Moscow: 'TERRA,' 1996.

Zolotarev, V.A. Ed. *Velikaia Otechestvannaia voina 1941-1945: Voenno-istoricheskie ocherki v chetyrekh tomakh* [The Great Patriotic War 1941-1945: Military-historical essays in four volumes]. Moscow: 'Nauka,' 1998-1999.

Zolotov, N.P. Ed. *Boevoi i chislennyi sostav vooruzhennykh sil SSSR v period Velikoi Otechestvennoi voiny (1941-1945 gg.): Statisticheskii sbornik No. 1(22 iiunia 1941 g.)* [Combat and numerical strength of the USSR's armed forces in the Great Patriotic War (1941-1945): Statistical collection No. 1 (22 June 1941)]. Moscow: Institute of Military History of the Russian Federation's Ministry of Defense, 1994).

APPENDIX I

German Planning Documents Associated with Operation Barbarossa

Directive No. 21 'Plan Barbarossa'

The Führer and Supreme Commander
  of the Armed Forces
OKW/WFSt./Abt.L (I)
Nr. 33 408/40 g.Kdos Chefsache
Top Secret

Führer Headquarters
18 December 1940

Directive No. 21
Operation 'Barbarossa'

The German Wehrmacht [Armed Forces] must be prepared *to defeat Soviet Russia* in *one rapid campaign*, even before the war with England has been concluded.

The Army [*des Heeres*] must, in this case, be prepared to commit all available formations, with the proviso that the occupied territories must be secured against surprise attacks.

The Air Force [*Luftwaffe*] must make available for the support of the army in the Eastern Campaign forces of adequate strength to ensure a rapid termination of the land action and to give the East German territories maximum protection against enemy air raids. Making the main effort in the East must not be carried to the point where we can no longer adequately protect the totality of our battle and our armament zones against enemy air attacks, nor must the offensive against England, and in particular against England's supply routes, suffer as a consequence.

For the Navy [*Kriegsmarine*] the point of main effort will remain consistently against England, even while the Eastern Campaign is in progress.

I shall give the order for the *assembly* of troops, etc., for the proposed operation against

Soviet Russia, should the occasion arise, eight weeks before the operation is due to begin.

Preparations that require more time than this shall – so far as they have not already been made – be begun at once and are to be completed by 15 May 1941.

Great stress, however, must be laid on disguising any offensive intentions.

Preparations by the high commands are to be based on the following considerations.

1. General Intention

The mass of the army stationed in Western Russia it to be destroyed in bold operations involving deep and rapid penetrations by panzer spearheads, and the withdrawal of combat-capable elements into the vast Russian interior is to be prevented.

By means of a rapid pursuit, a line is to be reached from beyond which the Russian air force will no longer be capable of attacking the territory of the German Reich. The operation's final objective is the establishment of a defensive barrier against Asiatic Russia running along the general line of the Volga to Arkhangel. From such a line the one remaining Russian industrial area in the Urals can be eliminated by the Luftwaffe should the need arise.

During the course of this operation, the Russian's *Baltic Fleet* will quickly be deprived of its bases and thus will no longer be capable of continuing the struggle.

Effective intervention by the Russian *Air Force* is to be prevented from the very beginning of the operation by means of powerful strikes against it.

2. Anticipated Allies and their Tasks

1. On the wings of our operation we can count on active cooperation in the war against Soviet Russia by *Rumania* and *Finland*.

How exactly the combat forces of those two countries will be under German control when they go into action is a matter that the Armed Forces High Command will arrange and set forth at the proper time.

2. *Rumania's* task will be to pin down the enemy's forces opposite that sector and to provide assistance in rearward areas.

3. *Finland* will cover the movement in the Northern German Group coming from Norway (Elements of Group XXI) and will then operate in conjunction with this group. The elimination of Hangö will also be Finland's responsibility.

4. It may be anticipated that the *Swedish* railways and roads will be made available for the movement of the Northern German Group, at the latest when the operation has begun.

3. The Conduct of the Operations

(A) *Army* (in accordance with my operational concept):

The area of operations is divided into northern and southern halves by the Pripiat Marshes. The point of the main effort will be made north in the *northern* half. Here two army groups are to be committed.

The southern of these two army groups – in the Centre of the whole front – will have the mission of breaking out of the area around and to the north of Warsaw with exceptionally strong panzer and motorized formations and destroying the enemy forces in Belorussia. This will create a situation that will enable strong formations of mobile troops to swing north; such formations will then cooperate with the northern army group – advancing from East Prussia in the general direction of Leningrad – in destroying enemy forces in the area of the Baltic states. Only after the accomplishment of offensive operations, which must be followed by the capture of Leningrad and Kronshtadt, are further offensive operations with the objective of occupying the important Centre of communications and of armaments manufacture, Moscow.

Only a surprisingly rapid collapse of the Russian ability to resist could justify an attempt to achieve both objectives simultaneously.

The *primary task* of Group XXI, even during the Eastern operations, remains *the protection of Norway*. Forces available other than those needed for this task (Mountain Corps) will first of all be used to protect the Petsamo area and its mines, together with the Arctic road, and will then advance, in conjunction with Finnish forces, against the Murmansk railway and will cut the Murmansk area's land supply route.

Whether an operation of this nature can be carried out by *stronger* German forces (two to three divisions) coming from the Rovaniemi region and to the south depends on Sweden's willingness to make the Swedish railways available for such a move.

The mass of the Finnish Army will have the task, in accordance with the advance made by the northern wing of the German armies, of tying up maximum Russian strength by attacking to the west or on both sides of Lake Ladoga. The Finns will also capture Hangö.

The army group *south of the Pripiat Marshes* will make its point of main effort from the Lublin region in the general direction of Kiev, with the objective of driving into the deep flank and rear of the Russian forces with strong armoured formations and of then rolling up the enemy along the Dnepr.

The German-Rumanian group on the right flank will have the mission of:

(a) Protecting Rumanian territory and thus covering the southern flank of the entire operation.

(b) In cooperation with the attack by the northern wing of Army Group South, of tying up the enemy forces in its sector of the front; then, as the situation develops, of launching a second thrust and thus, in conjunction with the Luftwaffe, of preventing an orderly enemy withdrawal beyond the Dnestr.

Once the battles south or north of the Pripiat Marshes have been fought, the pursuit is to be undertaken with the following objectives:

In the south, the rapid occupation of the economically important Donetz Basin,

In the north, the speedy capture of Moscow.

The capture of this city would be a decisive victory both from the political and from the economic point of view; it would involve, moreover, the neutralization of the most vital Russian rail Centre.

(B) *Luftwaffe*:

It will be the task of the Luftwaffe, so far as possible, to damage and destroy the effectiveness of the Russian air force and to support the operations of the army at the points of main effort, that is to say in the sectors of Army Group Centre and in the area where Army Group South will be making its main effort. The Russian railways will either be destroyed, or, in the case of more important objectives close at hand (i.e., railway bridges), will be captured by the bold use of parachute or airborne troops. In order that maximum forces may be available for operations against the enemy air forces and for direct support of the army, the munitions industry will not be attacked while the major operation is in progress. Only after the completion of the mobile operations will such attacks, and in particular attacks against the industrial area of the Urals, be considered.

(C) *Kriegsmarine*

During the war with Soviet Russia, the Kriegsmarine's mission will be to protect the German coastline and to prevent any hostile naval force from breaking out of the Baltic. Since the Russian Baltic Fleet will have lost its last base and thus will be in a hopeless position once Leningrad has been reached, major naval operations previous to this are to be avoided. After the destruction of the Russian fleet the Kriegsmarine will be responsible for making the Baltic fully available for carrying sea traffic, including supplies by sea to the northern wing of the army. (The sweeping of minefields!)

4.

It is important that all of the Commanders-in-Chief make it plain that the taking of necessary measures in connection with this directive is being done as a precaution against the possibility of the Russians adopting an attitude toward us other than what it has been up to now. The number of officers engaged in the early stages of these preparations is to be kept as small as possible, and each officer is only to be given such information as is directly essential to him in the performance of his mission. Otherwise the danger will arise of our preparations becoming known, when a time for carrying out of the proposed operation has not even been decided on. This would cause us the gravest political and military disadvantages.

I anticipate further conferences with the Commanders-in-Chief concerning their intentions as based on this directive.

Reports on the progress made in the proposed preparations by all services of the armed forces will be forwarded to me through the Armed Forces High Command [OKW].

[signed] Adolf Hitler

Directive No. 33

The Führer and Supreme Commander   Führer Headquarters
  of the Armed Forces   19 July 1941
OKW/WFSt./Abt.L (I)
Nr. 441230/41 g.Kdos
Top Secret

Directive No. 33
The Further Conduct of the War in the East

1. The second offensive in the East has been completed by the penetration of the 'Stalin Line' along the entire front and by the further deep advance of the panzer groups to the east. Army Group Centre requires a considerable time to liquidate the strong enemy groups that continue to remain between our mobile formations.

The Kiev fortifications and the operations of the Soviet 5th Army's forces in our rear have inhibited active operations and free maneuver on Army Group South's northern flank.

2. The objective of further operations should be to prevent the escape of large enemy forces into the depth of the Russian territory and to annihilate them. To do so, prepare [as follows] along the following axes:

a) *The Southeastern sector of the Eastern Front.* The immediate mission is to destroy the enemy 12th and 6th Armies by a concentrated offensive west of the Dnepr, while preventing them from withdrawing beyond the river.

The Rumanian's main forces will cover that operation from the south.

The complete destruction of the enemy 5th Army can be carried out most rapidly by means of an offensive by the closely cooperating forces of Army Group Centre's southern flank and Army Group South's northern flank.

Simultaneously with the turn by Army Group Centre's infantry divisions southward, after they have fulfilled the missions assigned to them and have been re-supplied and protected their flank along the Moscow axis, commit new and primarily mobile forces into combat. These forces will have the missions of preventing Russian forces that have crossed to the eastern bank of the Dnepr River from withdrawing further to the east and destroying them.

b) *The Central sector of the Eastern Front.* After destroying the numerous encircled enemy units and resolving supply problems, the mission of Army Group Centre will be to cut the Moscow-Leningrad communications lines and, at the same time, protect the right flank of Army Group North advancing on Leningrad with mobile formations that will not participate in the advance to the southeast beyond the Dnepr line, while further advancing toward Moscow with infantry formations.

c) *The Northern sector of the Eastern Front.* Resume the advance toward Leningrad only after the Eighteenth Army has restored contact with the Fourth Panzer Group and the Sixteenth Army's forces are protecting its eastern flank. When that is accomplished, Army Group North must strive to prevent Soviet forces that are continuing to operate in Estonia from withdrawing to Leningrad. It is desirable to capture as rapidly as possible the islands in the Baltic Sea, which can be Soviet fleet strong points.

d) *The Finnish Front.* As before, the missions of the Finnish main forces, reinforced by the German 163rd Division, are to attack the enemy by delivering their main attack east of Lake Ladoga and, later, destroy him in cooperation with Army Group North's forces. The aims of the offensive operations being conducted under the command of the XXXVI Army and Mountain Infantry Corps remain unchanged. Since there is no possibility of providing strong support by air formations, one must expect the operation to be prolonged.

3. First and foremost, the Luftwaffe's mission is to support the advance of forces along the principal axes in the southern sector of the front as they are freed up in the central sector. Concentrate the required aircraft and anti-aircraft artillery in their respective regions by bringing up additional forces quickly and also by regroupings.

As quickly as possible, it is necessary to begin air raids on Moscow by forces of the Second Air Fleet, temporarily reinforced by bombers aircraft from the west, which must be 'retribution' for Russian air raids on Bucharest and Helsinki.

4. The Kriegsmarine's mission remains the defense of sea communications, particularly to protect ground operations in so far as the situation at sea and in the air effects them. To the degree possible, the fleet's efforts are to threaten the enemy's naval bases to prevent his fleet's combat forces from entering and being interned in Swedish ports.

As soon as naval forces (torpedo boats and minesweepers in groups of one flotilla each) are freed up from the Baltic Sea, they must be transferred to the Mediterranean Sea. It is necessary to dispatch some quantity of submarines to the Barents Sea to support German forces in Finland, whose operations are being hindered by the transport of reinforcements to the enemy by sea.

5. All three armed forces branches in the West and in the North must anticipate repelling possible English attacks against the islands in the Gulf of La Mancha [the English Channel] and the Norwegian coast. It is necessary to prepare Luftwaffe forces for rapid transfer from the West to any region of Norway.

Hitler

Addendum to Directive No. 33

The Chief of Staff of OKW   Führer Headquarters
The Chief of Staff of the   23 July 1941
   Operations Department
Nr. 442254/41 g.Kdos
Top Secret

Addendum to Directive No. 33

After the report of the OKW on 22 July 1941, I order [the following] as an addition to and broadening of Directive No. 33:

1. *The Southern sector of the Eastern Front.* The enemy still located west of the Dnepr must be completely and fully annihilated. As soon as the operational situation and material-technical support permit, the First and Second Panzer Groups, subordinate to Fourth Panzer Army headquarters, and the infantry and mountain infantry divisions that are following them, are to undertake an offensive across the Don into the Caucasus after capturing the Khar'kov industrial region.

The priority mission of the main mass of infantry divisions is the capture of the Ukraine, the Crimea and the territory of the Russian Federation to the Don. When that is accomplished, Rumanian forces will be entrusted with occupation service in the regions southwest of the Bug River.

2. *The Central sector of the Eastern Front.* After improving the situation in the Smolensk region and on its southern flank, Army Group Centre is to defeat the enemy located between Smolensk and Moscow with sufficiently powerful infantry formations of both of its armies and advance with its left flank as far as possible to the east and capture Moscow.

The Third Panzer Group is temporarily assigned to Army Group North with the mission of supporting the latter's right flank and encircling the enemy in the Leningrad region.

To fulfill the subsequent missions – the advance to the Volga – the intention is to return the Third Panzer Group's mobile formations to their former subordination.

3. *The Northern sector of the Eastern Front.* Having received control of the Third Panzer Group, Army Group North will be capable of allocating large infantry forces for the advance on Leningrad and thus avoid expending mobile formations on frontal attacks in difficult terrain.

Enemy force still operating in Estonia must be destroyed. While doing so, it is necessary to prevent their transport by ship and penetration through Narva toward Leningrad.

Upon fulfilling its mission, the Third Panzer Group must be once again transferred to Army Group Centre's control.

4. Subsequently, as soon as conditions permit, the OKW will fix its attention on withdrawing part of Army Group North's forces, including the Fourth Panzer Group, and also part of Army Group South's infantry force, to the Homeland.

While doing so, the combat readiness of the Third Panzer Group must be fully restored at the expense of transferring to it material and personnel from the Fourth Panzer Group. If necessary, the First and Second Panzer Groups must accomplish their missions by combining their formations.

5. The instructions contained in Directive No. 33 remain in force for the Fleet and Air Forces.

In addition, the Naval Fleet and Air Forces must ease the situation of the Mountain Infantry Corps. [It will do so] first, by decisive action of naval forces in the Barents Sea; and second, by transferring several groups of bomber aircraft into the region of combat operations in Finland, which will be carried out after the battle in the Smolensk region has ended. These measures will also deter England from attempts to join the struggle on the coast of the polar seas.

6. Forces allocated for the performance of security services in the occupied eastern regions will be sufficient to fulfill their missions only if the occupation authorities liquidate all resistance by employing extensive fear and terror to rid the population of any desire to resist rather than by legal judgement of the guilty.

Appropriate commands and the forces subordinate to them are entrusted with the responsibility for order in the occupied regions.

The commanders must find means to ensure order in the secured region, while employing appropriately Draconian measures and without requesting new security units.

Keitel

Directive No. 34

The Führer and Supreme Commander
  of the Armed Forces
OKW/WFSt./Abt.L (I)
Nr. 441298/41 g.Kdos
Top Secret

Führer Headquarters
30 July 1941

Directive No. 34

The course of events in recent days, the appearance of large enemy forces before the front, the supply situation and the necessity of giving the Second and Third Panzer Groups 10 days to restore and refill their formations has forced a temporary postponement of the fulfillment of aims and missions set forth in Directive Nr. 33 of 19 July and the addendum to it of 23 July.

Accordingly, I order:

I. Army Forces:

1. In the northern sector of the Eastern Front, continue the offensive toward Leningrad by making the main attack between Lake Il'men' and Narva to encircle Leningrad and establish contact with the Finnish Army.

North of Lake Il'men', this offensive must be limited by the Volkhov sector and, south of this lake, continue as deeply to the east as required to protect the right flank of forces attacking to the north of Lake Il'men'. In advance, restore the situation in the Velikie Luki region. All forces that are not being employed for the offensive south of Lake Il'men' must be transferred to the forces advancing on the northern flank.

Do not begin the anticipated offensive by the Third Panzer Group to the Valdai Hills until its combat readiness and the operational readiness of its panzer formations has been fully restored. Instead, the forces on Army Group Centre's left flank must advance northeastward to such a depth as will be sufficient to protect Army Group North's right flank.

The priority missions of all of the Eighteenth Army's forces are the clearing of all enemy forces from Estonia. After this, its divisions can begin to advance toward Leningrad.

2. Army Group Centre will go on the defense, while employing the most favorable terrain in its sector.

You should occupy favorable jumping-off positions for conducting subsequent offensive operations against the Soviet 21st Army and you can carry out limited objective offensive operations to this end.

As soon as the situation permits, the Second and Third Panzer Groups are to be withdrawn from battle and quickly refilled and re-equipped.

3. Continue operations in the southern sector of the front for the time being only with Army Group South's forces. The objective of these operations is to destroy the large enemy forces west of the Dnepr and create conditions for the subsequent crossing of the First Panzer Group to the eastern bank of the Dnepr by the seizure of bridgeheads at and south of Kiev.

The Soviet 5th Army, which is operating in the swampy region northwest of Kiev, is to be drawn into combat west of the Dnepr River and destroyed. It is necessary to avert the danger of a possible penetration by that army's forces northward across the Pripiat River.

4. *The Finnish Front*. Halt the offensive toward Kandalaska. Eliminate the threat of a flank attack from Motovskii Bay in the Mountain Infantry Corps' sector. Leave the commander of the XXXVI Army Corps only those forces necessary for defensive purposes and carry out preparations for a false offensive.

At the same time, attempt to cut the Murmansk railroad in the Finnish III Army Corps sector and, above all, along the Loukhi axis by transferring all forces necessary to fulfill that mission to that region. In the event the offensive in the III Army Corps' sector misfires due to the difficult terrain conditions, bring up German units and subordinate them to the Karelian Army. This particularly concerns motorized units, tanks and heavy artillery.

Place the 6th Mountain Infantry Division and all types of transport at the Mountain Infantry Corps's disposal.

The Ministry of Foreign Affairs will determine the possibility for using the Narvik-Luleo railroad on Swedish territory.

II. *Air Forces:*

1. The northern sector of the front.

The Luftwaffe will shoulder the main effort of the air offensive in the northern sector of the front and, to do so, the main forces of the VIII Air Corps are attached to the First Air Fleet. These forces must be transferred as quickly as possible so that they can support Army Group North's offensive along the main attack axis from the very beginning (the morning of 6 August).

2. The central sector of the front.

The mission of Luftwaffe forces remaining with Army Group Centre is to provide reliable anti-aircraft defense along the Second and Ninth Armies' fronts and support their offensive. Continue the air offensive against Moscow.

3. The southern sector of the Eastern Front.

Missions are unchanged. We do not anticipate a decrease in the air forces operating in Army Group South's area.

4. *Finland*

The primary mission of the Fifth Air Fleet is to support the Mountain Infantry Corps. In addition, it is necessary to support the Finnish III Army Corps' offensive along axes where the greatest success is achieved. It is necessary to conduct corresponding prepared measures in support of the Karelian Army.

Hitler

Addendum to Directive No. 34

OKW   Führer Headquarters
The Staff of the Operations Department   12 August 1941
Nr. 441376/41 g.Kdos
Top Secret

Addendum to Directive No. 34

The Führer has ordered the following on the further conduct of operations as an addition to Directive No. 34:

1. *The Southern sector of the Eastern Front.* As a result of the decisive battle in the Uman' region, Army Group South has achieved complete superiority over the enemy and has secured freedom of maneuver for the conduct of further operations on that side of the Dnepr. As soon as its forces firmly dig in on the eastern bank of that river and secure rear area communications, they will be able to achieve the large-scale operational aims assigned to them with their own forces with appropriate use of Allied forces and in cooperation with Rumanian ground forces.

Its missions are as follows:

      a) Prevent the enemy from creating a defensive front along the Dnepr. To do so, it is necessary to destroy the largest enemy units located west of the Dnepr and capture bridgeheads on the eastern bank of that river as rapidly as possible;

      b) Capture the Crimea, which, being an enemy air base, poses an especially great threat to the Rumanian oil fields; and

c) Seize the Donets Basin and the Khar'kov industrial region.

2. The battles to capture the Crimea may require mountain infantry forces. It is necessary to verify the possibility of their crossing the Kerch Straits for employment in a subsequent offensive toward Batumi.

Halt the offensive on Kiev. As soon as ammunition resupply permits, bombing from the air must destroy the city.

The entire range of missions depends on these actions being carried out sequentially rather than simultaneously by means of maximum massing of forces. In the first instance, achieve the greatest concentration of forces by committing additional groups of bomber aircraft to support combat operations in the region between Kanev and Boguslav and then to assist the creation of a bridgehead on the eastern bank of the Dnepr River.

3. *The Central sector of the Eastern Front.* The priority mission in this sector is to eliminate the enemy flank positions wedging to the west, which are tying down large forces of Army Group Centre's infantry. In the central sector of the front to the south, pay particular attention to the organization of the mixed flanks of Army Groups' Centre and South according to time and axis. Deprive the Soviet 5th Army of any operational capabilities by seizing the communications leading to Ovrich and Mozyr' and, finally, destroy its forces.

North of the central sector of the front, defeat the enemy west of Toropets as rapidly as possible by committing mobile forces into combat. Advance Army Group Centre's left flank far enough north that Army Group North will not fear for its right flank and will be capable of reinforcing its forces advancing on Leningrad with infantry divisions.

Regardless, undertake measures to transfer this or that division (for example, the 102nd Infantry Division) to Army Group north as a reserve.

Only after the threatening situation on the flanks has been completely eliminated and the panzer groups have been refitted will conditions be conducive for an offensive by deeply echeloned flank groupings across a broad front against the large enemy forces concentrated for the defense of Moscow.

The aim of this offensive is to capture the enemy's entire complex of state economic and communications Centres in the Moscow region before the onset of winter, by doing so, depriving him of the capability for restoring his destroyed armed forces and smashing the functioning of state control apparatus.

Complete the operation against Leningrad before the offensive along the Moscow axis begins and return the aircraft units transferred earlier by the Second Air Fleet to the First Air Fleet to their former subordination.

4. *The Northern sector of the Front.* The offensive being conducted here must lead to the encirclement of Leningrad and link-up with Finnish forces.

Insofar as the situation with airfields permits, in the interest of the effective employment of aviation it is important that it be employed as far as possible massed along distinct axes.

As soon as the situation permits, you should liquidate enemy naval and air bases on Dago and Ezel' Islands by the joint efforts of ground, naval and air forces. While doing so it is particularly important to destroy enemy airfields from which air raids on Berlin are carried out.

The High Command of the Ground Forces (OKH) is entrusted with coordinating the conducted measures.

The Chief of OKW
Keitel

Führer order

OKW   Führer Headquarters
The Staff of the Operations Department   15 August 1941
Nr. 441386/41 g.Kdos
Top Secret

Order

After a report by the OKH, the Führer orders:

1. *Army Group Centre* will halt its further advance on Moscow. Organize a defense in sectors whose nature will prevent any possibility of the enemy conducting enveloping operations and will not require air support to repel his offensive operations.

2. The offensive by *Army Group North* must lead to success in the immediate future. Only after this can we think about resuming the offensive on Moscow. Danger has arisen because the appearance of enemy cavalry in the Sixteenth Army's rear and the absence of mobile units in the I Army Corps' reserve, which, in spite of strong air support, has halted the promising offensive north of Lake Il'men'.

Without delay, allocate and transfer as great a quantity of mobile formations from General Hoth's panzer group (for example, one panzer and two motorized divisions) to Army Group North.

Chief of Staff of the OKW
Jodl

OKW order

21 August 1941

Order from the OKW to the OKH

The OKH's 18 August considerations regarding the further conduct of operations in the East do not agree with my intentions.

I order:

1. The most important missions before the onset of winter are to seize the Crimea and the industrial and coal regions of the Don, deprive the Russians of the opportunity to obtain oil from the Caucasus and, in the north, to encircle Leningrad and link up with the Finns rather than capture Moscow.

2. The favorable operational situation, which had resulted in reaching the Gomel' and Pochep line, must immediately by exploited by the conduct of an operation along concentric axes by the adjoining flanks of Army Groups South and Centre. Our objective is not to push the Soviet 5th Army back beyond the Dnepr by the Sixth Army's local attacks. Instead, [it is] the destruction of the enemy before he can withdraw to the Desna River, Konotop and Sula line.

Army Group South can do so only by digging-in in the region east of the middle reached of the Dnepr and continuing operations toward Khar'kov and Rostov with the forces operating in its Centre and on its left flank.

3. Army Group Centre is to allocate sufficient forces to that offensive to ensure the destruction of the Russian 5th Army's forces, and, at the same time, that it will be prepared to repel enemy counterattacks in the central sector of its front.

The decision to advance Army Group Centre's left flank to the hills in the Toropets region and tie it in with Army Group North's right flank is unchanged.

4. The seizure of the Crimean peninsula has colossal importance for the protection of oil supplies from Rumania. Therefore, it is necessary to employ all available means, including mobile formations, to force the lower reaches of the Dnepr rapidly before the enemy is able to reinforce its forces.

5. Only by encircling Leningrad, linking-up with the Finns and destroying the Russian 5th Army can we free up forces and create prerequisites for fulfilling the missions contained in the 12 August addendum to Directive No. 34, that is, a successful offensive and the destruction of Group Timoshenko.

Hitler

Directive No. 35

The Führer and Supreme Commander   Führer Headquarters
  of the Armed Forces   6 September 1941
OKW/WFSt./Abt.L (I)
Nr. 441492/41 g.Kdos
Top Secret

Directive No. 35

Initial operational successes against enemy forces between the Army Group South's and Centre's adjoining flanks and additional successes in encircling enemy forces in the Leningrad region, create prerequisites for conducting a decisive operation against Army Group Timoshenko, which is conducting unsuccessful offensive operations on Army Group Centre's front. It must be destroyed decisively before the onset of winter within the limited time indicated in existing orders.

To this end we must concentrate all of the efforts of ground and air forces earmarked for the operation, including those that can be freed up from the flanks and transferred in timely fashion.

On the basis of the OKH's report, I am issuing the following orders for the preparation and conduct of this operation:

1. *In the southern wing of the Eastern Front*, destroy the enemy located in the Kremenchug, Kiev and Konotop triangle with the forces of Army Group South, which have crossed the Dnepr to the north, in cooperation with the attacking forces of Army Group Centre's southern flank. As soon as the situation permits, the freed up Second and Sixth Armies' formations, and also the Second Panzer Group, should be regrouped to carry out new operations.

The mobile formations on Army Group South's front, reinforced with infantry and supported along the main axes by the Fourth Air Fleet, are to begin a surprise offensive northwestward from the bridgehead created by the Seventeenth Army through Lubna no later than 10 September, at the same time the Seventeenth Army is advancing along the Poltava and Khar'kov axis.

Continue the offensive along the lower course of the Dnepr toward the Crimea supported by the Fourth Air Fleet.

Movement of mobile forces southward from the lower course of the Dnepr to Melitopol' will considerably assist the Eleventh Army fulfill it missions.

2. *In the sector of Army Group Centre.* Prepare an operation against Army Group Timoshenko as quickly as possible so that we can go on offensive in the general direction of Viaz'ma and destroy the enemy located in the region east of Smolensk by a double envelopment by powerful panzer forces concentrated on the flanks.

To that end, form two shock groups:

The first – on the southern flank, presumably in the region southeast of Roslavl' with an attack axis to the northeast. The composition of the group [will include] forces subordinate to Army Group Centre and the 5th and 2nd Panzer Divisions, which will be freed up to fulfill that mission.

The second – in the Ninth Army's sector with its attack axis presumably through Belyi. In so far as possible, this group will consist of large Army Group Centre formations.

After destroying the main mass of Timoshenko's group of forces in this decisive encirclement and destruction operation, Army Group Centre is to begin pursuing enemy forces along the Moscow axis, while protecting its right flank to the Oka River and its left to the upper reaches of the Volga River. The Second Air Fleet, reinforced in timely fashion by transferred formations, especially from the northern sector of the front, will provide air support for the offensive. While doing so, it will concentrate its main forces on the flanks, while employing the principal bomber formations (Eighth Air Corps) for support of the mobile formations in both attacking flank groupings.

3. *In the northern sector of the Eastern Front.* Encircle enemy forces operating in the Leningrad region (and capture Shlissel'burg) in cooperation with an offensive by Finnish forces on the Karelian Isthmus so that a considerable portion of the mobile and First Air Fleet formations, in particular, the VIII Air Corps, can be transferred to Army Group Centre no later than 15 September. First and foremost, however, we must seek to encircle Leningrad completely, at least from the east, and, if weather conditions permit, conduct a large-scale air offensive on Leningrad. It is especially important to destroy the water supply stations.

As soon as possible, Army Group North's forces must begin an offensive northward in the Neva River sector to help the Finns overcome the fortifications along the old Soviet-Finnish border, and also to shorten the front lines and deprive the enemy of the use of air bases. In cooperation with the Finns, prevent enemy naval forces from exiting Kronshtadt into the Baltic Sea (Hanko and the Moonzund Islands) by using mine obstacles and artillery fire.

Also isolate the Leningrad area of combat operations in the sector along the lower course of the Volkhov as soon forces necessary to resolve this mission become available. Link-up with the Karelian Army on the Svir River only after enemy forces in the Leningrad region have been destroyed.

4. During the further conduct of operations, ensure that the southern flank of Army Group Centre's offensive along the Moscow axis is protected by an advance to the

northeast by a flank protection grouping in Army Group South's sector created from available mobile formations. [Also ensure] that Army Group North's forces be directed to protect Army Group Centre's northern flank and also the advance along both sides of Lake Il'men' to link-up with the Karelian Army.

5. Any curtailment of the period for preparing and acceleration of the operation's beginning will accompany the preparation and conduct of the entire operation.

Hitler

Addendum: In so far as the Fourth Air Fleet has not allocated forces to support the offensive from the Dnepropetrovsk bridgehead, the Führer considers it desirable that all of the motorized divisions participate in the First Panzer Group's offensive from the Kremenchug bridgehead.

The 198th Infantry Division and also Italian or Hungarian forces are holding on to the bridgehead.

The Chief of Staff of the OKW

Directive No. 39

The Führer and Supreme Commander   Führer Headquarters
  of the Armed Forces   8 December 1941
OKW/WFSt./Abt.L (I)
Nr. 442090/41 g.Kdos
Top Secret

Directive No. 39

The early arrival of cold winter on the Eastern Front and resupply difficulties associated with it are forcing us to halt immediately all large-scale offensive operations and go on the defense. The manner of this defense's conduct depends on the aims that it pursues, namely:

  a) Hold on to those regions that have important operational and military-economic importance for the enemy;

  b) Rest and replenish the forces;

  c) By doing so, create conditions necessary to resume large-scale offensive operations in 1942.

  Accordingly I order:

I. *The ground forces*

1. As soon as possible, the main forces of the Eastern Army will go over to the defense in sectors designated by the ground forces High Command and then begin to refit all formations while withdrawing, first and foremost, all panzer and motorized divisions from the front.

2. In those sectors of the front where the front lines will be shifted to the rear on our initiative, that is, where the enemy has not yet forced us to, it is necessary to prepare rear positions that provide better conditions for our units withdrawal and the organization of defenses than the previously occupied positions.

The abandonment to the enemy of important lateral communications in connection with the withdrawal of the front lines can create danger for other sectors of the front that have not been fortified. In these instances time, based on the overall situation, it is necessary to designate the time for the forces withdrawal to separate sectors of the front lines.

3. The configuration of the new front line must favor the forces with regard to their dispositions and the organization of the defense and provide the most favorable conditions for the provision of supplies, in particular during thaw conditions.

It is necessary to select cut-off and rear positions and, while exploiting the entire work force at your disposal, to construct them as rapidly as possible.

4. Within the framework of the main defensive mission, the forces must resolve the following specific missions:

a) Seize Sevastopol' (This decision is relative to the further employment of the Eleventh Army's main forces, with exception to those units necessary for coastal defense, which will be determined upon the completion of combat operations).

b) Despite all difficulties, in favorable weather conditions, in the course of the winter, Army Group South will prepare an offensive to reach the line of the lower Don and Donets Rivers; thanks to which prerequisites will be created for the successful conduct of a spring offensive against the Caucasus.

c) Army Group North will shorten the front of its eastern and southeastern defense line north of Lake Il'men'. However, it is to do so while denying the enemy the road and railroad from Tikhvin to Volkhovstoi and Kolchanovo that support restoring, reinforcing and improving his positions in the region south of Lake Ladoga. Only by doing so can we finally complete encircling Leningrad and establishing communications with the Finnish Karelian Army.

d) If we determine that the enemy has withdrawn his main forces from the coastal belt on the southern coast of the Gulf of Finland and does not intend to offer serious resistance there, we should occupy that sector of the coast to economize forces.

II. The Luftwaffe

1. The Luftwaffe's mission is to deprive the enemy of the capability of refitting and filling out its armed forces. To that end, it should destroy his military industrial and combat training Centres, first and foremost, those such as Leningrad, Moscow, Rybinsk, Gor'ki, Voronezh, Rostov, Stalingrad, Krasnodar and others. Attach special importance to the constant destruction of enemy communications, which, for the enemy, are the railways by whose use the enemy threatens a series of our front sectors.

In addition, together with the suppression of enemy aviation, the Luftwaffe must support the ground forces in repelling subsequent enemy attacks with all available forces.

2. I agree with the plan presented to me on the dispositions of the air forces within the limits of the army groups and the quantity of air force units located in the East. Upon completion of the ground forces' operations, if conditions permit, selected Luftwaffe formations can be withdrawn to the rear for combat training and refitting.

3. For the effective repelling of possible enemy winter attacks and considering our forces intended winter operations, we must maintain an airfield network sufficient to allow us to conduct rapid transfers of operating air force formations and their reinforcement at the expense of air force units refitting in the rear. Therefore, the refitting and combat training regions must be disposed as close to the front lines as possible.

4. It is especially important to conduct continuous and careful long-range aerial reconnaissance that can reveal and control all regroupings by enemy forces. The ground force and air forces must cooperate in that matter, both in the matter of allocating forces to fulfill that mission and on the matter of deploying their own forces.

5. Henceforth, I reserve for myself the approval of force withdrawals from the Moscow front and, in addition, those that envision their employment on Army Group South's combat region.

6. The air force must provide for the defense of force deployment regions, supply regions and also important rear communications objectives. In the event of enemy air attacks we must rapidly concentrate our fighter aviation units along the main axes of the enemy's air forces' operation...

OKW Order (excerpt)

OKW   Führer Headquarters
The Staff of the Operations Department   16 December 1941
Nr. 442182/41 g.Kdos
Top Secret

Order

I order:

1. *Army Group North* is permitted to withdraw the Sixteenth and Eighteenth Armies' internal flanks to the Volkhov River line and the railroad line running northwest from Volkhov Station. Establish continuous communications with the XXVIII Army Corps' right flank along that railroad line.

The army group's mission is to defend that line to the last soldier, do not withdraw a single step, and, at the same time, continue to blockade Leningrad.

I especially call your attention to reinforcing air defenses south and southeast of Leningrad.

2. *Army Group Centre*. Any sort of significant withdrawal is inadmissible since it will lead to the complete loss of heavy weaponry and equipment. By their personal example, army commanders, formation commanders and all officers must inspire the forces with fanatic persistence to defend their occupied positions without paying attention to enemy forces penetrating along and into our forces' flanks and rear. Only such methods of conducting combat operations will gain time necessary to bring forward from the Homeland and the West the reinforcements that I have already ordered forward.

We can think about a withdrawal to the rear cut-off positions only after reserves have arrived at these positions

3. *Army Group South* will hold on to its occupied positions.

You must seize Sevastopol' with all of your energy in order to free up reserves and transfer them from the Crimea to other sectors of the army group's front....

[signed] Adolf Hitler

APPENDIX II

Russian Planning Documents Associated with Operation Barbarossa

NKO Directive No. 1

NKO Directive No. 1 'Concerning the Deployment of Forces in Accordance
  with the plan for Covering Mobilization and Strategic Concentration'
To: The Military Councils of the Leningrad, Baltic, Western and Kiev Military Districts.
Copy to: The People's Commissar of the Navy.

1. A surprise attack by the Germans on the fronts of the Leningrad, Baltic, Western
Special, Kiev Special and Odessa Military Districts is possible during the course of
22-23 June 1941.
2. The mission of our forces is to avoid provocative actions of any kind, which might
produce major complications. At the same time, the Leningrad, Baltic, Western
Special, Kiev Special and Odessa Military Districts' forces are to be at full combat
readiness to meet a surprise blow by the Germans or their allies.
3. I order:

> (a) Secretly man the firing points of the fortified regions on the state
> borders during the night of 22 June 1941;
> (b) Disperse all aircraft, including military planes among field airfields
> and thoroughly camouflage them before dawn on 22 June 1941;
> (c) Bring all forces to a state of combat readiness without the
> additional call up of conscript personnel. Prepare all measures to
> black out cities and installations.

Take no other measures without special permission.

[signed] Timoshenko
Zhukov

Received by the Western Special Military District at 0045 hours 22 June 1941
Dispatched to subordinate forces at 0225-0235 hours 22 June 1941

NKO Directive No. 2

NKO Directive No. 2

0715 hours 22 June 1941

To: The Military Councils of the Leningrad, Baltic, Western and Kiev Military Districts.
Copy to: The People's Commissar of the Navy.

On 22 June 1941 at 0400 hours in the morning, without any cause whatsoever, German aircraft carried out flight to our airfields and cities along the western frontier and subjected them to bombing.

Simultaneously, in a number of places German forces opened fire with artillery and crossed our border.

In connection with the unprecedented attack by Germany on the Soviet Union, I ORDER:

1. Troops in full strength and with all the means at their disposal will attack the enemy and destroy him in those regions where he has violated the Soviet border. In the absence of special authorization, ground troops will not cross the frontier.

2. Reconnaissance and combat aircraft will determine the concentration areas of enemy aircraft and the deployment of his ground forces. Bomber and assault [ground-attack] aircraft will destroy the aircraft on enemy airfields by powerful strikes and will bomb concentrations of his ground forces. Mount aviation strikes on German territory to a depth of 100–150km (60–90 miles).

Bomb Königsberg and Memel'.

Do not conduct flights over Finland and Rumania without special authorization.

[signed] Timoshenko
Malenkov
Zhukov

NKO Directive No. 3

NKO Directive No. 3 to the Military Councils of the
    Northwestern, Western, Southwestern and Southern Fronts
Concerning Force Missions on 23–26 June
2115 hours 22 June 1941

1. Delivering main attacks from the Suvalki salient to Olita and from the Zamost'e region to the Vladimir-Volynskii and Radzekhov front and secondary attacks along the Til'sit, Shauliai and Sedlits, Volkovysk axes, during the course of 22 June the enemy has achieved considerable success while suffering great losses.

In the remaining sectors of the state border with Germany and on the entire state border with Rumania, the enemy attacks have been beaten off with heavy losses to him.

2. I assign the forces [the following] immediate missions for 23–24 June:

a) Encircle and destroy the enemy's Suvalki grouping by concentric, concentrated attacks by the Northwestern and Western Fronts and capture the Suvalki region by day's end on 24 June.

b) Encircle and destroy the enemy grouping attacking in the direction of Vladimir-Volynskii and Brody by powerful concentric attacks by mechanized corps, all southwestern Front aircraft and other forces of the 5th and 6th Armies. Capture the Lublin region by day's end on 24 June.

3. I ORDER:

a) The Northern Front's armies to continue to protect the state borders firmly.

The left boundary – as exists.

b) While firmly holding on to the coast of the Baltic Sea, the Northwestern Front's armies will deliver a powerful counterstroke from the Kaunas region against the flanks and rear of the enemy's Suvalki grouping, destroy it in cooperation with the Western Front and capture the Suvalki region by day's end on 24 June.

The left boundary – as exists.

c) While containing the enemy on the Warsaw axis, the Western Front's armies will deliver a powerful counterstroke with a force of no fewer than two mechanized corps and frontal aviation against the flank and rear of the enemy's Suvalki grouping, destroy it in cooperation with the Northwestern Front and capture the Suvalki region by day's end on 24 June.

The left boundary – as exists.

d) While holding firmly to the border with Hungary, the Southwestern Front's armies will encircle and destroy the enemy grouping advancing on the Vladimir-Volynskii, Krystypol' front with concentric attacks in the general direction of Lublin with the 5th and 6th Armies, no fewer than five mechanized corps and all of the *front*'s aviation, and capture the Lublin region by day's end on 24 June. Cover yourself reliably along the Krakov axis.

e) The Southern Front's armies will prevent an enemy invasion of our territory. In the event the enemy attacks along the Chernovtsy axis or forces the Prut and Danube Rivers, destroy him by powerful flank attacks by ground forces in cooperation with aviation; concentrate two mechanized corps in the Kishinev region and the forests northwest of Kishinev on the night of 23 June.

4. I authorize crossing of the borders along the front from the Baltic Sea to the state border with Hungary and operations without regard for the borders.

5. The Aviation of the High Command:

a) Support the Northwestern Front with one flight from the 1st Long-range Aviation Corps and the Western Front with one flight from the 3rd Long-range Aviation Corps while they are fulfilling their missions of destroying the enemy's Suvalki grouping;

b) Assign the 18th Long-range Aviation Corps to the Southwestern Front and support the Southwestern Front with one flight from the 2nd Long-range Aviation Corps while it is fulfilling its mission of destroying the enemy's Lublin grouping; and

c) Leave the 4th Long-range Aviation corps at my disposal in readiness to assist the Southwestern Front and, with part of its forces, the Black Sea Fleet.

The People's Commissar of Defense,   Member of the Main Military Council
Marshal of the Soviet Union Timoshenko   Malenkov
Chief of the Red Army General Staff
Army General Zhukov

Sent at 2115 hours 22 June 1941

APPENDIX III

Summary Orders of Battle, 22 June 1941

GERMANY

Army of Norway
(Col. Gen. Nikolaus von Falkenhorst)

Finnish Army
(Field Marshal Carl Mannerheim)
Karelian Army

Army Group North
(Field Marshal Wilhelm von Leeb)
Eighteenth Army
Fourth Panzer Group
Sixteenth Army

Army Group Centre
(Field Marshal Fedor von Bock)
Third Panzer Group
Ninth Army
Fourth Army
Second Panzer Group

THE SOVIET UNION

Northern Front, formed 24.06.41
(Col. Gen. M.M. Popov)
7th Army
14th Army
23rd Army
10th Mechanized Corps
1st Mechanized Corps

Northwestern Front
(Col. Gen. F.I. Kuznetsov)
8th Army
12th Mechanized Corps
11th Army
3rd Mechanized Corps
27th Army (400km east)
5th Airborne Corps

Western Front
(Army Gen. D.G. Pavlov)
3rd Army
11th Mechanized Corps
10th Army
6th Mechanized Corps
13th Mechanized Corps
4th Army
14th Mechanized Corps
13th Army headquarters
17th Mechanized Corps
20th Mechanized Corps
4th Airborne Corps

GERMANY

Army Group South
  (Field Marshal Gerd von Rundstedt)
      Sixth Army
      Eleventh Army
      Seventeenth Army

Third Rumanian Army

Fourth Rumanian Army

THE SOVIET UNION

Southwestern Front
  (Col. Gen.M.P. Kirponos)
      5th Army
          9th Mechanized Corps
          22nd Mechanized Corps
      6th Army
          4th Mechanized Corps
          15th Mechanized Corps
      12th Army
          16th Mechanized Corps
      26th Army
          8th Mechanized Corps
      19th Mechanized Corps
      24th Mechanized Corps
      1st Airborne Corps

Southern Front, formed 25.06.41
  (Gen. I.V. Tiulenov)
          9th Army (separate until 25.06.41)
          2nd Mechanized Corps
          18th Mechanized Corps
          3rd Airborne Corps (Odessa MD)

Stavka GK Reserve (still deploying)
      16th Army
          5th Mechanized Corps
      19th Army
          26th Mechanized Corps
      20th Army
          7th Mechanized Corps
      21st Army
          25th Mechanized Corps
      22nd Army
      24th Army
      21st Mechanized Corps

Orel Military District
      23rd Mechanized Corps
Khar'kov Military District
      18th Army headquarters
Odessa Military District
      3rd Airborne Corps
Transcaucasus Military District
      28th Mechanized Corps
Central Asian Military District
      27th Mechanized Corps

APPENDIX IV

Detailed Opposing Orders of Battle, 22 June 1941

GERMANY	THE SOVIET UNION
AXIS FORCES IN NORWAY AND FINLAND	NORTHERN FRONT

Army in Norway
Mountain Corps Norway
  2nd Mountain Division, 3rd Mountain
  Division
XXXVI Army Corps
  169th Infantry Division, SS Combat Group
  'Nord'
Finnish III Army Corps
  6th Division, 3rd Division
	14th Army
	42nd Rifle Corps
	  104th Rifle Division, 122nd Rifle Division
	14th Rifle Division
	52nd Rifle Division
	23rd Fortified Region (Murmansk)
	104th High Command Reserve Gun Artillery
	  Regiment
	1st Tank Division (1st Mechanized Corps)
	1st Mixed Aviation Division
	42nd Corrective-Aviation Squadron
	31st Separate Sapper Battalion

Finnish Army
14th Division
 	
Karelian Army
Group Oinonen
  Cavalry Brigade, 2nd Jager Brigade, 1st Jager
  Brigade
VI Corps
  5th Division, 11th Division
VII Corps
  7th, 19th Divisions, 1st Division (reserve)
II Corps
  2nd, 15th, 18th Divisions, 10th Division
  (reserve)
IV Corps
  12th, 4th, 8th Divisions, 17th Division
  (Hango)
	7th Army
	54th Rifle Division
	71st Rifle Division
	168th Rifle Division
	237th Rifle Division
	26th Fortified Region (Sortavalo)
	208th Separate Anti-aircraft Artillery Battalion
	55th Mixed Aviation Division
	184th Separate Sapper Battalion
	
	23rd Army
	19th Rifle Corps
	  115th Rifle Division, 122nd Rifle Division
	50th Rifle Corps
	  43rd Rifle Division, 70th Rifle Division,
	  123rd Rifle Division
	27th Fortified Region (Keksholm)

	28th Fortified Region (Vyborg)
	24th Corps Artillery Regiment
	28th Corps Artillery Regiment
	43rd Corps Artillery Regiment
	573rd Gun Artillery Regiment
	101st Howitzer Artillery Regiment
	108th High-power Howitzer Artillery
	  Regiment (RGK)
	519th High-power Howitzer Artillery
	  Regiment (RGK)
	20th Separate Mortar Battalion
	27th Separate Anti-aircraft Artillery Battalion
	241st Separate Anti-aircraft Artillery Battalion
	10th Mechanized Corps
	  21st Tank Division, 24th Tank Division,
	    198th Motorized Division, 7th Motorcycle
	    Regiment
	5th Mixed Aviation Division
	41st Bomber Aviation Division
	15th Corrective-Aviation Squadron
	19th Corrective Aviation Squadron
	109th Motorized Engineer Battalion
	153rd Separate Engineer Battalion

	Front Units
	177th Rifle Division
	191st Rifle Division
	8th Rifle Brigade
	21st Fortified Region
	22nd Fortified Region (Karelian)
	25th Fortified Region (Pskov)
	29th Fortified Region
	541st Howitzer Artillery Regiment (RGK)
	577th Howitzer Artillery Regiment (RGK)
	2nd Corps PVO
	  115th, 169th, 189th, 192nd, 194th and 351st
	    Anti-aircraft Artillery Regiments; Vyborg,
	    Murmansk, Pskov, Luga and Petrozavodsk
	    Brigade PVO Regions
	1st Mechanized Corps
	  3rd Tank Division, 163rd Motorized
	    Division, 5th Motorcycle Regiment
	2nd Mixed Aviation Division
	39th Fighter Aviation Division
	3rd Fighter Aviation Division PVO
	54th Fighter Aviation Division PVO
	311th Reconnaissance Aviation Regiment
	103rd Corrective-Aviation Squadron
	12th Engineer Regiment
	29th Engineer Regiment
	6th Pontoon-Bridge Regiment

GERMANY	**THE SOVIET UNION**
ARMY GROUP NORTH	NORTHWESTERN FRONT

Eighteenth Army	*8th Army*
XXVI Army Corps	10th Rifle Corps
291st, 61st Infantry Division and 217th	10th, 48th and 50th Rifle Divisions
Infantry Divisions	11th Rifle Corps
XXXVIII Army Corps	11th and 125th Rifle Divisions
58th Infantry Division	44th Fortified Region (Kaunas)
I Army Corps	48th Fortified Region (Alytus)
11th, 1st and 21st Infantry Divisions	9th Antitank Artillery Brigade
	47th Corps Artillery Regiment
Fourth Panzer Group	51st Corps Artillery Regiment
XXXXI Motorized Corps	73rd Corps Artillery Regiment
1st Panzer Division, 269th Infantry Division,	39th Separate Anti-aircraft Artillery Battalion
6th Panzer Division, 36th Motorized	242nd
Division	12th Mechanized Corps
LVI Motorized Corps	23rd Tank Division, 202nd Motorized
290th Infantry Division, 8th Panzer Division,	Division, 10th Motorcycle Regiment
3rd Motorized Division	25th Engineer Regiment
SS 'Totenkopf' Motorized Division	
	11th Army
Sixteenth Army	16th Rifle Corps
X Army Corps	5th, 33rd and 188th Rifle Divisions
30th and 126th Infantry Divisions	29th Rifle Corps
XXVIII Army Corps	179th and 184th Rifle Divisions
122nd and 123rd Infantry Divisions	23rd Rifle Division
II Army Corps	126th Rifle Division
121st, 12th and 32nd Infantry Divisions,	128th Rifle Division
253rd Infantry	42nd Fortified Region (Shauliai)
Division (reserve)	46th Fortified Region (Til'sit)
	45th Fortified Region
Army Group Reserve	10th Antitank Artillery Brigade
254th, 251st and 206th Infantry Division	270th Corps Artillery Regiment
	448th Corps Artillery Regiment
OKH Reserve (in Army Group North)	615th Corps Artillery Regiment
L Army Corps	110th High-power Howitzer Artillery
86th Infantry Division (in transport), SS	Regiment
'Police' Infantry Division (in transport)	429th Howitzer Artillery Regiment (RGK)
	19th Separate Anti-aircraft Artillery Battalion
Army Area 101 (Rear area security)	247th Separate Anti-aircraft Artillery Battalion
207th Security Division	3rd Mechanized Corps
285th Security Division	2nd and 5th Tank Divisions, 84th Motorized
281st Security Division	Division, 5th Motorcycle Regiment
	38th Separate Engineer Battalion

27th Army
22nd Rifle Corps
  180th and 182nd Rifle Divisions
24th Rifle Corps
  181st Rifle Division and 183rd Rifle
  Divisions
16th Rifle Division
67th Rifle Division
3rd Rifle Brigade
613th Corps Artillery Regiment
614th Corps, Artillery Regiment
103rd Separate Anti-aircraft Artillery
  Regiment
111th Separate Anti-aircraft Artillery
  Regiment

Front units
65th Rifle Corps (headquarters)
5th Airborne Corps
  9th, 10th and 214th Airborne Brigades
41st Fortified Region (Libau)
402nd High-power Howitzer Artillery
  Regiment
11th Separate Anti-aircraft Artillery Battalion
10th PVO Brigade
12th PVO Brigade
14th PVO Brigade
Riga Brigade PVO Region
Estonia Brigade PVO Region
Kaunas Brigade PVO Region
57th Fighter Aviation Division
4th Mixed Aviation Division
6th Mixed Aviation Division
7th Mixed Aviation Division
8th Mixed Aviation Division
21st Fighter Aviation Regiment PVO
312th Reconnaissance Aviation Regiment
4th Pontoon-Bridge Regiment
30th Pontoon-Bridge Regiment

GERMANY	THE SOVIET UNION
ARMY GROUP CENTRE	WESTERN FRONT

Third Panzer Group	*3rd Army*
VI Army Corps	4th Rifle Corps
26th and 6th Infantry Divisions	27th, 56th Rifle Division and 85th Rifle Divisions
XXXIX Motorized Corps	68th Fortified Region (Grodno)
14th and 20th Motorized Divisions, 20th	7th Antitank Artillery Brigade
and 7th Panzer Divisions	152nd and 444th Corps Artillery Regiments
V Army Corps	16th Separate Anti-aircraft Artillery Battalion
35th and 5th Infantry Divisions	11th Mechanized Corps
LVII Motorized Corps	29th and 33rd Tank Divisions, 204th Motorized
18th Motorized Division, 19th and 12th	Division, 16th Motorcycle Regiment
Panzer Divisions	
	4th Army
9th Army	28th Rifle Corps
VIII Army Corps	6th, 49th, 42nd and 75th Rifle Divisions
161st, 28th and 8th Infantry Divisions	62nd Fortified Region (Brest-Litovsk)
XX Army Corps	447th, 455th and 462nd Corps Artillery
256th and 162nd Infantry Divisions	Regiments
XXXXII Army Corps	120th High-power Howitzer Artillery Regiment
129th, 102nd and 87th Infantry Divisions	12th Separate Anti-aircraft Artillery Regiment
	14th Mechanized Corps
4th Army	22nd and 30th Tank Divisions, 205th Motorized
VII Army Corps	Division, 20th Motorcycle Regiment
258th, 23rd, 7th and 268th Infantry	
Divisions	*10th Army*
XIII Army Corps	1st Rifle Corps
17th and 78th Infantry Divisions	2nd and 8th Rifle Divisions
IX Army Corps	5th Rifle Corps
263rd, 137thand 292nd Infantry Divisions	13th, 85th and 113th Rifle Division
XXXXIII Army Corps	6th Cavalry Corps
252nd, 134th and 131st Infantry Divisions	6th and 36th Cavalry Divisions
	155th Rifle Division
Second Panzer Group	66th Fortified Region (Osovets)
XXXXVI Motorized Corps	6th Antitank Artillery Brigade
'Grossdeutschland' Infantry Regiment,	130th, 156th, 262nd and 315th Corps Artillery
10th Panzer Division, SS 'Das Reich'	Regiments
Motorized Division	311th Gun Artillery Regiment
XXXXVII Motorized Corps	124th and 375th Howitzer Artillery Regiment
29th Motorized Division, 167th Infantry	(RGK)
Division, 17th and 18th Panzer Divisions	38th and 71st Separate Anti-aircraft Artillery
XII Army Corps	Battalions
31st, 45th and 34th Infantry Divisions	6th Mechanized Corps
XXIV Motorized Corps	4th and 7th Tank Divisions, 29th Motorized
10th Motorized Division, 3rd and 4th	Division, 4th Motorcycle Regiment
Panzer Divisions, 267th Infantry Division	13th Mechanized Corps
255th Infantry Division (reserve)	25th and 31st Tank Divisions, 208th Motorized
	Division, 18th Motorcycle Regiment
Army Group Reserve	
LIII Army Corps	*13th Army* (headquarters only)
293rd Infantry Division	

OKH Reserve (in Army Group Centre)	*Front units*
XXXV Army Corps	2nd Rifle Corps
52nd, 197th, 15th and 112th Infantry	100th and 161st Rifle Divisions
Division (all in transport)	21st Rifle Corps
XXXXII Army Corps	17th, 24th and 37th Rifle Divisions
110th and 106th Infantry Divisions (both	44th Rifle Corps
in transport), 900th Motorized Lehr	64th and 108th Rifle Divisions
Brigade	47th Rifle Corps
	55th, 121st and 143rd Rifle Division
Army Area 102 (Rear area security)	50th Rifle Division
403rd Security Division	4th Airborne Corps
221st Security Division	7th, 8th and 214th Airborne Brigades
286th Security Division	58th Fortified Region (Sebezh)
	61st Fortified Region (Polotsk)
	63rd Fortified Region (Minsk-Slutsk)
	64th Fortified Region (Zambrov)
	65th Fortified Region (Mozyr')
	8th Antitank Artillery Brigade
	293rd and 611th Gun Artillery Regiments
	360th Howitzer Artillery Regiment
	5th, 318th and 612th High-power Howitzer
	Artillery Regiments (RGK)
	29th, 49th, 56th, 151st, 467th and 587th Corps
	Artillery Regiments
	32nd Separate Special-power Artillery Battalion
	(RGK)
	24th Separate Mortar Battalion
	86th Separate Anti-aircraft Artillery Battalion
	4th and 7th PVO Brigades
	Baranovichi, Kobrin, Gomel', Vitebsk and
	Smolensk PVO Brigade Regions
	17th Mechanized Corps
	27th and 36th Tank Divisions, 209th Motorized
	Division, 22nd Motorcycle Regiment
	20th Mechanized Corps
	26th and 38th Tank Divisions, 210th Motorized
	Division, 24th Motorcycle Regiment
	43rd Fighter Aviation Division
	12th Bomber Aviation Division
	13th Bomber Aviation Division
	9th Mixed Aviation Division
	10th Mixed Aviation Division
	11th Mixed Aviation Division
	184th Fighter Aviation Regiment PVO
	313th Reconnaissance Aviation Regiment
	314th Reconnaissance Aviation Regiment
	59th Fighter Aviation Division (forming)
	60th Fighter Aviation Division (forming)
	10th Engineer Regiment
	23rd Engineer Regiment
	33rd Engineer Regiment
	34th Pontoon–Bridge Regiment
	35th Pontoon–Bridge Regiment
	275th Separate Sapper Battalion

GERMANY	**THE SOVIET UNION**
ARMY GROUP SOUTH	SOUTHWESTERN FRONT

GERMANY	THE SOVIET UNION
First Panzer Group	*5th Army*
XIV Motorized Corps	15th Rifle Corps
SS 'Viking' Motorized Division, 16th and	45th and 62nd Rifle Divisions
9th Panzer Divisions	27th Rifle Corps
III Motorized Corps	87th, 124th and 135th Rifle Divisions
14th Panzer Division, 298th and 44th	2nd Fortified Region (Vladimir-Volynskii)
Infantry Divisions	1st Antitank Artillery Brigade
XXIX Army Corps	21st, 231st, 264th and 460th Corps Artillery
299th and 111th Infantry Divisions	Regiments
XXXXVIII Motorized Corps	23rd and 243rd Separate Anti-aircraft
11th Panzer Division, 75th and 57th Infantry	Artillery Battalions
Divisions	9th Mechanized Corps
16th Motorized Division (reserve)	20th and 35th Tank Divisions, 131st
25th Motorized Division (reserve)	Motorized Division, 32nd Motorcycle
13th Panzer Division (reserve)	Regiment
SS 'Adolf Hitler' Motorized Division (reserve)	22nd Mechanized Corps
	19th and 41st Tank Divisions, 215th
Sixth Army	Motorized Division, 23rd Motorcycle
XVII Army Corps	Regiment
56th and 62nd Infantry Divisions	5th Pontoon-Bridge Regiment
XXXXIV Army Corps	
297th and 9th Infantry Divisions	*6th Army*
LV Army Corps (reserve)	6th Rifle Corps
168th Infantry Division	41st, 97th and 159th Rifle Divisions
	37th Rifle Corps
Seventeenth Army	80th, 139th and 141st Rifle Divisions
IV Army Corps	5th Cavalry Corps
262nd, 24th, 295th, 296th and 71st Infantry	3rd and 14th Cavalry Divisions
Divisions	4th Fortified Region (Strumilov)
XXXXIX Mountain Corps	6th Fortified Region (Rava-Russkaia)
1st Mountain Division, 68th and 257th	3rd Antitank Artillery Brigade
Infantry Divisions	209th, 229th, 441st and 445th Corps Artillery
LII Army Corps	Regiments
101st Jager Division	135th Gun Artillery Regiment (RGK)
100th Jager Division (reserve)	17th and 307th Separate Anti-aircraft Artillery
97th Jager Division (reserve)	Battalions
	4th Mechanized Corps
Eleventh Army	8th and 32nd Tank Divisions, 81st Motorized
Rumanian Mountain Corps	Division, 3rd Motorcycle Regiment
4th, 1st and 2nd Rumanian Mountain	15th Mechanized Corps
Brigades, 8th Rumanian Cavalry Brigade,	10th and 37th Tank Divisions, 212th
7th Rumanian Infantry Division	Motorized Division
XI Army Corps	9th Pontoon-Bridge Regiment
239th and 76th Infantry Divisions, 6th	
and 8th Rumanian Infantry Divisions, 6th	*12th Army*
Rumanian Cavalry Brigade	13th Rifle Corps
XXX Army Corps	44th, 58th and 192nd Mountain Rifle
5th Rumanian Cavalry Brigade, 14th	Divisions
Rumanian Infantry Division, 198th Infantry	17th Rifle Corps
Division	60th and 96th Mountain Rifle Divisions,
LIV Army Corps	164th Rifle Division
170th and 50th Infantry Divisions	10th Fortified Region (Kamenets-Podol'sk)

Rumanian Cavalry Corps headquarters
 (reserve)
22nd Infantry Division (reserve)

Army Group Reserve
99th Jager Division

OKH Reserve (in Army Group South)
XXXIV Army Corps headquarter
4th Mountain Division
125th Infantry Division
113th Infantry Division (in transport)
132nd Infantry Division (in transport)
LI Army Corps (in transport)
 79th and 95th Infantry Divisions

Army Area 103 (Rear area security)
213th Security Division
444th Security Division
454th Security Division

11th Fortified Region
12th Fortified Region (Mogilev-Podol'sk)
4th Antitank Artillery Brigade
269th, 274th, 283rd and 468th Corps Artillery
 Regiment
20th and 30th Separate Anti-aircraft Artillery
 Battalions
16th Mechanized Corps
 15th and 39th Tank Divisions, 240th
 Motorized Division, 19th Motorcycle
 Regiment
37th Engineer Regiment
19th Pontoon-Bridge Regiment

26th Army
8th Rifle Corps
 99th and 173rd Rifle Divisions, 72nd
 Mountain Rifle Division
8th Fortified Region
2nd Antitank Artillery Brigade
233rd and 236th Corps Artillery Regiments
28th Separate Anti-aircraft Artillery Battalion
8th Mechanized Corps
 12th and 34th Tank Divisions, 7th Motorized
 Division, 2nd Motorcycle Regiment
17th Pontoon-Bridge Regiment

Front units
31st Rifle Corps
 193rd, 195th and 200th Rifle Divisions
36th Rifle Corps
 140th, 146th and 228th Rifle Divisions
49th Rifle Corps
 190th, 197th and 199th Rifle Divisions
55th Rifle Corps
 130th, 169th and 189th Rifle Divisions
1st Airborne Corps
 1st , 204th and 211th Airborne Brigades
1st Fortified Region (Kiev)
3rd Fortified Region (Letichev)
5th Fortified Region (Korosten')
7th Fortified Region (Novograd-Volynskii)
13th Fortified Region (Shepetovka)
15th Fortified Region (Ostropol')
17th Fortified Region (Iziaslav)
5th Antitank Artillery Brigade
205th, 207th, 368th, 437th, 458th, 507th,
 543rd and 646th Corps Artillery Regiments
305th and 555th Gun Artillery Regiments
 (RGK)
4th, 168th, 324th, 330thand 526th High-
 power Artillery Regiments
331st, 376th, 529th, 538th and 589th Howitzer
 Artillery Regiments (RGK)
34th, 245th, 315th and 316th Separate
 Special-power Artillery Battalions (RGK)

263rd Separate Anti-aircraft Artillery Battalion
3rd, 4th and 11th PVO Brigades
Stanislav, Rovno, Zhitomir, Tarnopol' and
  Vinnitsa PVO Brigade Regions
19th Mechanized Corps
  40th and 43rd Tank Divisions, 213th
  Motorized Division, 21st Motorcycle
  Regiment
24th Mechanized Corps
  45th and 49th Tank Divisions, 216th
  Motorized Division, 17th Motorcycle
  Regiment
44th and 64th Fighter Aviation Divisions
19th and 62nd Bomber Aviation Divisions
14th, 15th, 16th, 17th and 63rd Mixed
  Aviation Divisions
315th and 316th Reconnaissance Aviation
  Regiments
45th Engineer Regiment
1st Pontoon-Bridge Regiment

9th Separate Army
14th Rifle Corps
  25th and 51st Rifle Divisions
35th Rifle Corps
  95th and 176th Rifle Divisions
48th Rifle Corps
  30th Mountain Rifle Division, 74th and
  150th Rifle Divisions
2nd Cavalry Corps
  5th and 9th Cavalry Divisions
80th Fortified Region (Rybinsk)
81st Fortified Region (Danube)
82nd Fortified Region (Tiraspol')
84th Fortified Region (Upper-Prut)
86th Fortified Region (Lower-Prut)
320th Gun Artillery Regiment (RGK)
430th High-power Howitzer Artillery
  Regiment (RGK)
265th, 266th, 374th and 648th Corps Artillery
  Regiments
317th Separate Special-power Artillery
  Battalion (RGK)
26th and 268th Separate Anti-aircraft Artillery
  Battalions
Kishinev Brigade PVO Region
2nd Mechanized Corps
  11th and 16th Tank Divisions, 15th Motorized
  Division, 6th Motorcycle Regiment
18th Mechanized Corps
  44th and 47th Tank Divisions, 218th
  Motorized Division, 26th Motorcycle
  Regiment
20th, 21st and 45th Mixed Aviation Divisions
131st Fighter Aviation Division PVO
317th Reconnaissance Aviation Regiment

	65th Fighter Aviation Division (forming)
	66th Fighter Aviation Division (forming)
	8th and 16th Separate Engineer Battalions
	121st Motorized Engineer Battalion

GERMANY	THE SOVIET UNION
OKH RESERVE	STAVKA RESERVE

Second Army	*16th Army*
XXXX Motorized Corps (in transport)	32nd Rifle Corps
60th Motorized Division (in transport)	46th and 152nd Rifle Divisions
46th Infantry Division(in transport)	126th Corps Artillery Regiment
93rd Infantry Division(in transport)	112th Separate Anti-aircraft Artillery Battalion
96th Infantry Division(in transport)	5th Mechanized Corps
98th Infantry Division(in transport)	13th and 17th Tank Divisions, 109th
260th Infantry Division(in transport)	Motorized Division, 8th Motorcycle
94th Infantry Division(in transport)	Regiment
183rd Infantry Division(in transport)	
73rd Infantry Division(in transport)	*19th Army*
5th Panzer Division(in transport)	25th Rifle Corps
294th Infantry Division(in transport)	127th, 134th and 162nd Rifle Divisions
2nd Panzer Division(in transport)	34th Rifle Corps
707th Security Division (in Germany)	129th, 158th and 171st Rifle Division
713th Security Division (in Germany)	38th Rifle Division
Rumanian Third and Fourth Armies	442nd and 471st Corps Artillery Regiment
(4 corps, 9 divisions and 2 brigades)	26th Mechanized Corps
	52nd and 56th Tank Divisions, 103rd
	Motorized Division, 27th Motorcycle
	Regiment
	111th Motorized Engineer Battalion
	238th and 321st Separate Sapper Battalions
	20th Army
	61st Rifle Corps
	110th, 144th and 172nd Rifle Divisions
	69th Rifle Corps
	73rd, 229th and 233rd Rifle Divisions
	18th Rifle Division
	301st Howitzer Artillery Regiment
	537th High-power Howitzer Artillery
	Regiment (RGK)
	438th Corps Artillery Regiment
	7th Mechanized Corps
	14th and 18th Tank Divisions, 1st Motorized
	Division, 9th Motorcycle Regiment
	60th Pontoon-Bridge Battalion
	21st Army
	63rd Rifle Corps
	53rd, 148th and 167th Rifle Divisions
	66th Rifle Corps
	61st, 117th and 154th Rifle Divisions
	387th Howitzer Artillery Regiment (RGK)
	420th and 546th Corps Artillery Regiments
	25th Mechanized Corps
	50th and 55th Tank Divisions, 219th
	Motorized Division, 12th Motorcycle
	Regiment

22nd Army
51st Rifle Corps
  98th, 112th and 153rd Rifle Divisions
62nd Rifle Corps
  170th, 174th and 186th Rifle Divisions
  336th and 545th Corps Artillery Regiments

24th Army
52nd Rifle Corps
  91st, 119th and 166th Rifle Divisions
53rd Rifle Corps
  107th, 133rd and 178th Rifle Divisions
  524th Heavy Gun Artillery Regiment (RGK)
  392nd, 542nd and 685th Corps Artillery
    Regiments

Separate Formations
20th Rifle Corps
  137th and 160th Rifle Division
45th Rifle Corps
  187th, 227th and 232nd Rifle Division
67th Rifle Corps
  102nd, 132nd and 151st Rifle Division
267th Corps Artillery Regiment
390th Corps Artillery Regiment (Transbaikal)
21st Mechanized Corps
  42nd and 46th Tank Divisions, 185th
    Motorized Division, 11th Motorcycle
    Regiment

LIST OF
ILLUSTRATIONS

All illustrations are fron the author's collection

INDEX